HNC in Social Care

Elizabeth Bingham

Cathy Busby

Aileen Conner

Billy Grier

Sue Price

Helen Russell

Shona Sh

Heinemann is an imprint of Pearson Education Limited, a company incorporated in England and Wales, having its registered office at Edinburgh Gate, Harlow, Essex, CM20 2JE. Registered company number: 872828

www.pearsonschoolsandfecolleges.co.uk

Heinemann is a registered trademark of Pearson Education Limited

Text © Elizabeth Bingham, Cathy Busby, Aileen Conner, Billy Grier, Sue Price, Helen Russell, Shona Shaw 2009

First published 2009

14

10 9 8 7 6 5

British Library Cataloguing in Publication Data

A catalogue record for this book is available from the British Library.

ISBN 978 0 435 50110 5

Copyright notice

Typeset by Dickidot Limited

Original illustrations © Pearson Education Ltd, 2009

Illustrated by Artful Doodlers Limited

Cover photo/illustration © Pearson Education Ltd

Printed in the UK by CPI

CONTENTS

Introduction

Social Care in Scotland

'...*more than a job.... It's a career that makes a difference.*'

'Social Care' is the generic (umbrella) term used to cover a wide range of service provision and job roles in Scotland today.

You can apply to work in the statutory, voluntary or independent sectors of Scottish Social Care, where you will provide practical and emotional support to a number of service user groups. These include:

- *older adults*
- *people with physical, learning and/or mental health difficulties*
- *children and families*
- *adults and young people involved with the criminal justice system*
- *people who have experience of substance misuse*
- *people who are experiencing or who have experienced homelessness and/or are of refugee / asylum-seeker status*
- *people living with HIV/AIDS*

You may study and qualify to become a Support Worker in either Home, Day, Respite, Supported Living, Residential or Close/Secure Care. You may (with HNC and SVQ3) aim to become a Social Work Assistant and with further graduate-level study, a Social Worker.

Whatever your job title, wherever you work and whoever you work with, your role as a Social Care worker will be to empower individuals and groups, to support people from all backgrounds, of all ages and with varying levels of need and ability, to 'problem-solve' in their own lives and to make real and informed decisions and choices.

Encouraging and enabling people to become as far as is possible, the 'expert' on their own situation is so much more than 'just a job'.

Social Care is one of Scotland's most diverse and fastest-growing employment sectors. The Scottish Social Services Council aims by 2015 to have over 100,000 of Scotland's (139,000) social services workforce formally registered.

This means Scotland is aiming for a workforce which is trained, qualified and regulated – and a Social Care sector which is rigorously professional and forward-thinking. Regulation and registration are important ways in which our society is trying to ensure the 'right' people are in the 'right' jobs and are practising to recognised standards and providing real and consistent quality of care.

The HNC in Social Care is a challenging programme which focuses on generic and 'transferable' values, knowledge, understanding and skills; relevant to supporting any service user group, in any setting.

Students come to HNC Social Care with hugely varied life experiences, skills, qualities and confidence. Rather than 'what' you are it's *who* you are.

As an HNC student what matters is your energy for and commitment to learning, communicating and making relationships with others – and to 'making a difference'.

About the HNC in Social Care

The HNC in Social Care is a Scottish Qualifications Authority (SQA) award. Candidates must achieve 12 SCQF (Scottish Credit and Qualification Framework) credits, nine from mandatory units and three from options.

Each HNC credit is worth eight credit points. On completion of HNC Social Care therefore, a candidate (via his or her twelve credits) will have achieved **96 credit points at SCQF level 7** (this level is very important; a nationally-recognised 'marker' of achievement).

While the qualification of HNC in Social Care is standard across Scotland, teaching, learning and assessment approaches and processes do vary. Staff at the centre to which you are attached will keep you informed on options, choices and those all-important approaches to and regulations for, assessment.

Whether you study the HNC in Social Care on a part-time or full-time basis, the work experience element is key to your progress and development. Via placement (full-time) or your workplace (part-time), you will evidence your developing skills in matching theory with practice.

Via work experience also, you will work towards completing at least three Scottish Vocational Qualification (**SVQ**) units at level 3. These units enable you to collect evidence to show effective practice and how informed you are when supporting the needs of others.

SVQ units form a part of the HNC in Social Care. But post-HNC these will also take you almost halfway toward the full **Health and Social Care (SVQ) Level 3** award. SVQ units are an important response to employer and SSSC Registration requirements – and of course, very much enhance your own 'employability'.

About this book

This book is designed to support your progress through important units and themes of HNC in Social Care.

Each core unit has been allocated a chapter, for example *Social Care Theory for Practice, Sociology for Social Care Practice, Psychology for Social Care Practice*..... as has the SVQ via *Health and Social Care, level 3*.

Two additional themed chapters are included too; *Protection and Risk Assessment* and *Interpersonal Skills and Understanding*.

Your overall grade – and whether or not you pass the HNC in Social Care is determined by your graded unit result.

The graded unit will be your final assessment; a larger-scale piece which integrates across all mandatory units of the HNC and requires detailed evidence and analysis of your practice.

Chapter 5 has been especially designed to support you with the processes of planning, developing and evaluating your graded unit activity.

Each chapter in this book aims to provide explanation and discussion, to prompt–and ask–questions on important areas of theory and practice.

Key Terms, Consider this and Further research features are included throughout, to support, consolidate and encourage you to extend your learning and understanding.

Case studies highlight real issues from practice and provide opportunity for group debate and/or personal reflection.

Each chapter concludes with a Check Your Progress feature; a number of questions on key elements from that chapter. While Check Your Progress exercises don't precisely match or replicate unit outcomes and criteria, they do reflect key areas for assessment and will help you prepare for exams.

The legislation grid in the appendix shows clearly, the HNC units and themes covered in each chapter.

The writers of this book have extensive experience, as practitioners and teachers. All currently teach HNC in Social Care.

For and on behalf of the writing team, I wish you every success in your studies and work in the uniquely challenging and rewarding world of 21st century Social Care in Scotland.

Aileen Connor, June 2009.

Author details

Elizabeth Bingham gained MA (Hons) in Philosophy and Psychology at the University of Glasgow. She has been a Social Care practitioner for a number of years in the areas of mental health and learning disabilities. She taught extensively on the HNC Social Care programme at Ayr College where she now holds a development role in the area of Essential Skills Development.

Cathy Busby is a specialist in sociology and anthropology and an experienced practitioner, lecturer and course leader in Social Care. She has significant previous experience in a range of local authority and voluntary agency care services, specialising in mental health, learning disabilities and homeless services.

Aileen Connor is a specialist in Sociology and Anthropology and in experienced practitioner, lecturer and course leader in Social Care. She has key interests in the fields of sexuality and adolescent mental health. She has authored and co-worked on a number of research and practice initiatives, both academic and vocational. She is currently working on an ethnography of womens' sexuality in Scotland.

She would like to dedicate her work on this book to Christie.

Billy Grier is a lecturer in care and psychology at Motherwell College.

Sue Price is Curriculum Manager for Social Care, SVQs in Care an Social Sciences at James Watt College. She was initially involved in the planning and delivery of the HNC Social Care in the mid 1990's at Aberdeen College and subsequently developed the integration of SVQ units within the current HNC Social care framework for the HNC team at James Watt College. She has expertise in SVQ planning, assessing and internal verification gained over the last ten years of her active involvement in this area.

Helen Russell has worked in further education for 14 years and currently manages and leads the curriculum in Social Care, Counselling and all SVQ programmes in Health and Social Care at Motherwell College. A qualified teacher and social worker, having worked as a social worker/senior social worker for many years, she has recently completed a Masters degree in Education (tertiary education).

Shona Shaw is a full-time lecturer in Health and Social Care at Motherwell College, a post she has held for the past 17 years. Her background is in Social Work and until recently she was also a sessional social worker with a local authority Social Work Department.

Acknowledgements

The authors would like to thank all those who are motivated by and committed to a new depth, breadth and pursuit of excellent in Scottish Social Care.

The publishers would like to thank Toni Mcilwraith for a very thorough review of this book.

The publishers and authors would both like to thank Jo Baldwin for her invaluable work this title throughout the writing and editing process.

Aileen Connor would also like to thank Dorothy McCorkindale and Marion Corcoran.

Every effort has been made to contact copyright holders of material reproduced in this book. Any omissions will be rectified in subsequent printings if notice is given to the publishers.

Photographs

The authors and publisher would like to thank the following for their kind permission to reproduce photos:

Bob Thomas/Getty Images – page 50

Corbis – page 114

Digital Vision – page 118

iStockphoto/Paul Prescott – page 258

iStockphoto/Sean Locke – page 250

Lebrecht Music and Arts Photo Library/Alamy – page 47

Pearson Education Ltd/Gareth Boden – pages 9 [left], 58, 266

Pearson Education Ltd/Jules Selmes – pages 23 [houses], 23 [car], 179, 188

Pearson Education Ltd/Lord and Leverett – pages 29 [right], 100, 173, 197, 210

Pearson Education Ltd/Mind Studio – page 226

Pearson Education Ltd/Rob Judges – page 285

Pearson Education Ltd/Tudor Photography – page 23 [girl]

Photodisc – pages 1, 112

Richard Smith – page 29 [left]

Shutterstock/Corepics – page 93

Shutterstock/Mandy Godbehear – page 81

Shutterstock/Photomak – page 237

Shutterstock/Rob Marmion – page 79

Shutterstock/Monkey Business Images – pages 30, 71

Shutterstock/Yuri Arcurs – page 9 [right]

Trinity Mirror/Mirrorpix/Alamy – page 12

Websites

The websites used in this book were correct and up-to-date at the time of publication. It is essential for tutors to preview each website before use in class so as to ensure that the URL is still accurate, relevant and appropriate. We suggest that tutors bookmark useful websites and consider enabling students to access them through the school/college intranet.

Chapter 1
Social Care theory for practice

Introduction

Social Care Theory for Practice is a major component of your HNC in Social Care. You may note that it is worth two credits within the framework of your qualification, and it certainly underpins major concepts in Social Care. It covers important elements like values, anti-discriminatory practice, legislation, Care Planning and intervention methods, as well as teamwork, and is very much focused upon how theory relates to day-to-day work. You may also find that it lends itself to other areas of study, like psychology, social policy or sociology, and hopefully, as you gain experience in workplaces, you will benefit from understanding how theories and class work relate to actual real-life work. It will challenge your thoughts and experiences, help you to analyse your own understanding of the world around you, and hopefully encourage you to consider the nature of your own opinions. This is a challenging area of study; Social Care Theory should enhance your analytical skills and while it may not make you change your mind about some things, it should help you to understand your own views and the views of others.

This chapter aims to explain the main concepts relating to the central themes of the unit in a step-by-step way. However, in any work setting, you should be mindful of individual policies and procedures, team structures and mission statements which relate to some of the areas mentioned.

Certainly, as an area of study, Social Care Theory for Practice is aptly named:

it aims to help you to understand some of the broad themes in the huge field of Social Care and equip you with enough underpinning knowledge to practise safely, ethically and responsibly. It will also give you a degree of factual knowledge in relation to theories on teams, management styles and communication. It should also give you an insight into the sometimes daunting area of legislation, covering major Acts which impact upon a Social Care worker's role, responsibility and duty.

Social Care theory provides ample food for thought.

On completing this unit you should be able to explain how Social Care values and principles influence practice; understand the Care Planning process; be aware of a variety of Social Care intervention models; evaluate and describe types and models of teams and team working. While every study centre will have its own methods of assessment, as this is such a broad area, it is likely that you will be expected to produce evidence of a significant level of knowledge through essay, case study exercise and/or presentation.

Wherever and however you complete this complex unit, your tutor will keep you informed of assessment processes and detail.

Key terms

Intervention to get involved; to interfere with events or processes

Knowledge awareness and understanding of concepts and facts

Method a way of doing something, especially systematic

Principle a rule of conduct or expected practice

Process routine way of dealing with something

Skills capacity to do something – demonstrated ability to do something

Values the worth we place upon someone or something.

In this chapter you will learn:

Values and underpinning care principles:
this area challenges assumptions, helps you to analyse your own thoughts and understand how values underpin all elements of practice

The Care Planning process:
this part introduces some common models of Care Planning and considers the diversity, and evolution, of the Care Planning process as a tool of care delivery

Methods and models of Social Care practice:
this part explains a variety of interventions and introduces a broad range of skills considered to be central to successful practice in the care sector

Effective team working:
this section introduces some of the many theories and concepts around effective teamwork and encourages you to evaluate teams and consider some of the complexities involved in team working.

Values and underpinning care principles

Through general discussions and perhaps through prior learning, you may already have quite a fixed idea of what values may mean. We talk a lot about 'respect', 'individuality', 'equality' or 'diversity' in Social Care. This chapter aims to challenge and unearth a deeper comprehension of values and look at wider social issues which may influence our understanding of what is 'right' or 'wrong', 'good' or 'bad', in Social Care. Values are about ethics, moral dilemmas, challenges and cultural awareness; they reflect our own personal belief systems, backgrounds and socialisation and they can, and probably will, change! You not only have to consider your own value base, but also the values of those around you – team members, other professionals and people who use services for example. Our first area to consider is very simple – what exactly is a value?

Key term
Ethics moral principles or a recognition of right and wrong.

Different values

In our culture, widely speaking, we have many influences placed upon us – some are rather more obvious than others; some we feel we can control or ignore, and others are deep rooted and intrinsic. Generally, in wider society, you may recognise that we value money, possessions, family, friends, status, celebrity, popularity or beauty. The list goes on and on. Equally, in wider society, you may recognise that we do not value deceit, dishonesty, the unemployed, or people with disabilities. It is important to recognise that, at this point, we are considering society in its widest sense – try to put aside your already formed 'Social Care' values and consider how the media portrays certain societal groups, for example. You could pick up a 'popular' magazine and look at adverts or articles, counting the number of different social 'groups' portrayed. This may help you to grasp the very fluid meaning of values. In simple terms, a value is the worth we place upon something or someone.

Values, in society, may include a variety of areas like *cultural values* – respecting dress code, or specific rituals at certain times; *personal values* – recognising self-esteem and confidence; *social values* – manners, etiquette, choice of language; *ethical values* – moral boundaries and a sense of what is right and wrong; *spiritual values* – a sense of faith or belief. Later we will look at some examples of Social Care values and demonstrate that indeed, they are often linked together.

Of course, this is a very basic exercise, but it should illustrate that values are complex and often difficult to identify; sometimes we act or react in an instinctive way or do things because they 'feel right'. However, by studying values, you should come to understand their origins and limitations; there are many issues which bring our values into scrutiny.

You should be aware that a professional's role can often be a powerful one. While you may not consciously enter into a relationship with a person who uses services with power on your mind, you are potentially able to exercise a relatively high degree of control in a situation. French and Raven (1959) identified five types of power:

- Reward Power – based upon the perceived ability to guarantee positive consequences
- Coercive Power – based upon the perceived ability to ensure negative consequences
- Legitimate Power – based upon the perception that someone has the right to expect certain behaviours (sometimes called *position power*)
- Referent Power – based upon the desire of subordinates to be like leaders they believe have desirable characteristics
- Expert Power – based upon the perception that a leader has expert knowledge the subordinates don't have (sometimes called *information power*).

Personal values

As individuals we are laden with values and opinions, and sometimes also prejudices and stereotypes, as products of our lives, interaction and experiences. It is crucial that we consider how we might influence others and take stock of our own beliefs and by doing this we must consider our own personal viewpoints.

Our personal values also cover a range of areas and can even be contradictory. Within a social group, shared values (positive or negative) may bind people together. Pressure groups, like Greenpeace; or charitable organisations like Save the Children, for example, aim purposefully to capture a particular value base among society. Conversely, extreme movements like the Ku Klux Klan also 'tap' into a very different set of values.

In Social Care, as a sector, the Regulation of Care (Scotland) Act 2001, led to a clear set of standards being published, and expected of workers. Buying into these standards is non-negotiable, and if we are brutally honest, may pose challenges for some. However, aspiring to those standards, which we look at later, can only safeguard and enhance the care experience of many individuals.

Key terms

Prejudice beliefs held about individuals or groups based on an assumption and stereotype – pre-judging someone or a situation without personal insight or knowledge

Ku Klux Klan American organisation proposing white supremacy.

Consider this

Quietly consider some of your own values, past or present, and try to be honest. Working in a Social Care setting are there individuals you may find it more difficult to work with? Why? How might you overcome this potential barrier?

Case study

Considering your prejudice

Look at the following scenarios and, being as honest as you can be, explore your reactions to the situation. In the past would you have reacted differently? Do you feel you have developed a value base since childhood, or through specific life events? How do you react now to the information in the cases below?

Sammy

You are in primary school and have a strong group of friends you play with – both inside and outside your school time. Sammy is the new boy. He doesn't support the same football team as you and your friends. He has moved from England and has a different accent. He also lives in a rough part of town, and doesn't have the same sorts of clothes as you. Some of your friends have started to pick on him. They call him names as he walks past and one of your friends threw paper balls at him during maths class. You go along with your friends although haven't actually 'picked' on him to date.

After class, one of your mates dares you to go over to Sammy and tell him he smells. You feel uncomfortable about this, but your group of friends are all watching. You do as they say, going over to him and shouting at him 'You smell' and run away laughing. All your mates think this is brilliant and for a moment you feel strong and accepted. Later, at home, you think again…

Shopping

You are visiting your local shopping centre and have some money to spend on clothes for a night out. In a clothes shop, you are trying to look at some nice tops. The shop is busy, and your temper is beginning to fray. There are two women in front of you with buggies, they are chatting and blocking the aisle. From behind them, you have said 'Excuse me', but they just keep chatting. In the end, you get very frustrated and 'tut' loudly, barging past. One of the women throws you an unfriendly stare and the other mutters 'Sorry' in a sarcastic tone. Would you have done the same if the aisle was blocked by a wheelchair user?

The tenement

You live in the top flat of a tenement building. You get on well with all of your neighbours and the close is clean and well kept. There is no security entry on the door, but this has never been a problem. Until now! Over the past few nights gangs of Asian youths have been standing in the close smoking and hanging around. You feel intimidated and usually make sure your door is locked when you get home. One of the downstairs neighbours lives alone and is getting angry. This is particularly bad for him, as his front door is right next to the main entrance. A meeting is called between all residents to discuss what is seen to be a menace. In the end, you decide to get a security intercom fitted in the close, with all residents paying a share. During the meeting, when this was decided, one of your neighbours makes a racially inappropriate claim saying 'Who wants those kind hanging around anyway?' You feel uncomfortable with this comment, but are aware that you are sure one of the guys hanging around called you a 'piece of white trash' under his breath. You are also aware that there have been racially motivated attacks in the area on previous occasions.

Social division, on a broader scale, offers us a diversity of values and can often be influenced by class, gender, sexual orientation, religious affiliation, age or ability. However, if our personal value base is that we 'respect all others' or 'like different people', meeting not so like-minded individuals should not create tension or fragmentation, but be embraced as a positive opportunity. Contrary to this, values like 'I don't like gay people' or 'disabled people are stupid' clearly create negative images, thwarting open communication and contributing to negative stereotypes and damaging interpersonal relationships. Quite often, we sense incongruence and, as individuals, tend not to trust people who display it. If we fail to recognise our own values and some of the potential prejudices we may have, we may buy into discriminatory practice and indeed contribute to it (albeit in ignorance).

Key term

Affiliation to be alongside someone/something – or be in close agreement.

Activity

Consider the following examples of work situations.
How might a worker's lack of congruence show or be read by others?

The team leader

You work for a small group home, meeting the needs of six physically disabled youngsters. The team leader is expected, as part of their role, to contribute to the 'ground work' of the provision of care. While they are expected to complete leadership tasks, like making up rotas, completing supervision and appraisals, and covering absences, about one-third of time should be allocated to making up the core team. You know that the team leader, Carol, struggles with some aspects of personal care. She is generally reluctant to work with one of the youngsters, who can be very sick after meals. Indeed, in team meetings, Carol has referred to this young person as 'the spew boy', while sniggering. You notice that she rarely interacts with this client, and will address other clients before him. She also sighs when he is sick, even when other staff are cleaning him. However, if his parents visit, she is keen to stress her leadership role and report back that he is doing well and is a popular child. While this client has limited vocabulary, he has indicated to other staff that he does not feel respected by Carol.

Stu

Stu is a hostel assistant in a modern, comfortable hostel providing support to ten teenagers facing homelessness. His role includes some cleaning and housekeeping, but more centrally, working with two key clients to improve budgeting and household skills. Stu has worked within the hostel for a year, and was a student beforehand. He ultimately wants to gain employment with the Local Authority and sees this job as a stepping stone. Stu has openly expressed a dislike of drug users; particularly heroin users and has even used the term 'junkie' when talking to non-drug using residents. A recent change in occupancy has resulted in Stu working closely with Gary, a methadone user. Gary has been working hard to try to stabilise his lifestyle, and longs to secure a tenancy and reunite with his girlfriend and small daughter. Stu has already expressed doubts over his potential to other staff, saying things like, 'It won't be long until he is evicted.' One morning, you go to work on an early shift and indeed, overnight, Gary has been evicted for turning up at the hostel 'under the influence'. Stu was the nightshift worker responsible for the eviction. You are not sure if all of the facts are indeed accurate in the written account Stu prepares. You know he has acted defensively towards Gary in the past, and wished him failure, in many ways. You plan to discreetly address this matter with the Manager today. In the meantime, Gary has turned up at the hostel shouting and swearing at the locked door – he wants to 'have it out' with Stu, who he is calling a 'liar'.

HOW ARE YOU? WHAT HAVE YOU BEEN DOING?

NOT MUCH TO SAY I BET!

Prejudice leads to discriminatory practice.

So – a value is the worth we place upon something. It may be a monetary worth (for example a house is worth £150,000) but for Social Care, we focus on the intrinsic worth of individuals. Sometimes this can be known as unconditional positive regard. It is also important to realise that, in Social Care, ultimately our professional conduct is not negotiable: the National Care Standards clearly communicate ways in which we should behave and several pieces of legislation guide our actions towards others, and we will move on to consider some of these legal guidelines later.

Central to the concept of values is the issue of self-awareness, and it is important that we consider our own awareness of ourselves. Self-awareness includes recognition of our personality, our strengths and weaknesses, our likes and dislikes and how our lives have been shaped and influenced by our own experiences and the experiences of others. In order to check our own self-awareness, we need to reflect upon our own actions, thoughts and beliefs as well as seeking guidance and feedback from others.

Activity

It can often be challenging to consider our own prejudices or stereotypical views. Often, we may have our own ideas on how we can justify our thoughts and actions. It may be helpful to consider how others you know, such as close family or friends, express views you disagree with; you can then think about views which you have or present, which they may disagree with.

Jot down your thoughts and consider if there are any areas of your own belief system which you may need to be wary of in a Social Care context.

Some examples have been given in the table below to help you to start this process, but think carefully about any beliefs you have which may clash with the beliefs of others.

Person: e.g. my mum thinks...	but I think...	others may see me as...
that all abortions should be outlawed unless two doctors agree that continuing a pregnancy will result in the serious ill-health of the mother.	that sometimes an abortion is someone's only hope. If someone is young or has been raped, I think they may need help and counselling to sort out how they feel. Only under these circumstances, can an abortion be carried out – but only up to a point in pregnancy.	being overly cautious – it is a woman's individual human right to decide what happens to her body, and her future. Without justification, abortion should be granted, without counsel to women who seek it.
euthanasia should never be allowed – whether someone is old or ill, all human life is sacred.	euthanasia should be allowed, for anyone who considers it the only route out of a miserable physical exsistence.	being too quick to make such a statement – can parents abort disabled foetuses or disabled people be encouraged to take their life because they may feel they are 'useless'?

all people should be allowed to marry – whether they are heterosexual or not.	only Christian, or other religious people, should marry and then only one man to one woman – for life.	being too hard on same-sex couples who have the same relationships as different sex couples.
women should wear make-up and present themselves as attractive people – always looking after their appearance and clothing.	women should wear make-up too – it is important to be seen as someone beautiful and confident.	being too concerned with vanity – what about people who choose to look scruffy or who do not get the chance to buy and use make-up because of their life circumstances?

Examples of different beliefs and views.

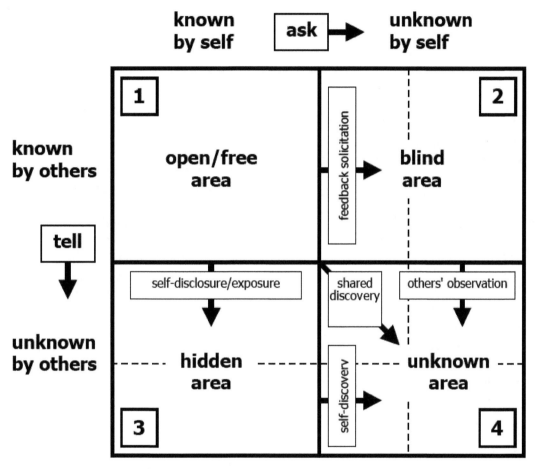

The Johari window model.

Johari window

A useful tool to enable us to consider the complexities of human interaction and how we can develop self-awareness is the Johari window. As the diagram above illustrates, this divides personal awareness into four different types: open, hidden, blind and unknown.

As you can see, there are clear elements which are 'unknown' areas as well as blind areas. While these may always exist, your aim is to minimise these in favour of the open/free elements, with the 'hidden' element becoming less well hidden through openness and self-awareness.

This model assumes that ongoing disclosure between two parties will lead to openness from both. In Social Care practice, in order to promote fulfilment and potential, it may be necessary to increase your self-awareness, but also to minimise the 'blanks' about others. It is not always service-appropriate or desirable to become overly familiar with people who use services; however, in different kinds of services the professional boundary should be drawn according to policies, ethos and level of engagement.

Anti-discriminatory practice

Ultimately, you should engage with people who use services in a professional manner, in a role appropriate to identified boundaries and in a way which promotes anti-discriminatory practice. It is central to your work that you should be seeking to reduce oppression, increase independence and be mindful about not perpetuating discrimination: indeed, challenging stereotypes, sexism, racism, disablism and other forms of discrimination are key areas which link directly to your value base, power base and your self-awareness.

Key term

Oppression to keep down or make suffer – to oppress is to exert power over others negatively.

While other subject areas like sociology and psychology detail significant related topics like discrimination, socialisation and oppression, it is important to remember that the effects of discrimination and oppression on groups and individuals are far reaching. Those who face discrimination tend to feel a sense of alienation and isolation, have lower self-esteem and negative self-image as well as lesser social expectations and life chances. Being aware of your value base and conforming to the standards published goes some way to enabling staff and teams to, at the very least, understand the role our values have in effecting positive change. Anti-discriminatory practice helps to protect people who use services from manipulation, abuse and other forms of harm and generally creates an environment where individuals feel respected, supported and safe.

Key term

Self-esteem feeling of pride or competence in yourself (or lack of) – how a person feels about themselves.

Codes of Practice

In relation to these care principles are rules, guidelines or conduct standards which demonstrate our values. The Scottish Social Services Council publishes guidelines relating to conduct expectations in their 'Codes of Practice' literature. These guidelines promote positive practice across the sector and also empower workers to ensure they are supported to carry out their duties with robust policies and procedures, training and development opportunities and organisational support to combat discrimination, dangerous or exploitative practice. The Codes are specific and clearly define acceptable standards of practice. The broad Codes include:

- protecting the rights and interests of people who use services and carers
- establishing and striving to maintain the trust and confidence of people who use services
- promoting the independence of people who use services and protecting them (as far as possible) from danger or harm
- respecting the rights of people who use services while seeking to ensure their behaviour does not harm themselves or others
- upholding public trust and confidence in social services
- being accountable for the quality of your work and maintaining and improving your knowledge and skills.

Consider this

These Codes may seem simple at a glance, but consider each in turn and identify how each might impact upon everyday practice.
What might some of these Codes mean to workers within the Social Care field?

Case study

Codes of Practice in action

Read the scenarios suggested below, then identify the Codes of Practice which you feel have been affected by the practice suggested in each.

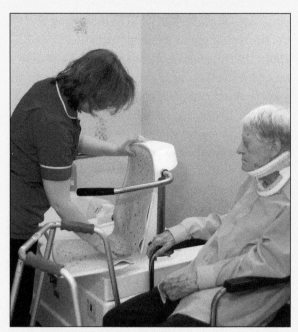

Some people need assistance with basic hygiene, such as taking a bath.

Depression can strike anyone.

Scenario 1: James is supported in his own home every morning for three hours. He is assisted to take a bath in the morning, prepare a breakfast and make sandwiches for lunch, to deal with any correspondence requiring attention and to attend to basic household duties. He has two staff who support him on a rota basis – Margaret (his Key Worker) and Saad (his Support Worker). Yesterday Margaret was running late, she arrived an hour later than usual and did not phone ahead. She brought with her, a pack of pre-packed sandwiches for James' lunch and said 'that'll save a bit of time'. Today she was due, as usual, to arrive at 8am, now it is almost 10am, and there is still no word from her. James has tried to phone Saad but he only gets through to an answering machine. James is becoming worried.

Scenario 2: Rohan has spent a good deal of time in institutional care for severe depression. However, he has now successfully moved from such care, to his own flat. Occasionally he becomes depressed, but his 24-hour staffing support package helps him through his 'darker' times and he has a good relationship with all of his staff. During times of depression, Rohan can become isolated and can display self-harming behaviour. He feels he requires stronger intervention from his staff team, but so far they just tell him it is 'his choice' and they will support him by leaving him alone to cut himself. Rohan feels ashamed of his actions and one member of staff has already told him he is 'just an attention seeker'.

Core values

Core values which underpin conduct include dignity, privacy, choice, safety, confidentiality, individuality and access to services based upon individual need. While these suggestions are by no means exhaustive, they are areas which broadly relate to the principles discussed, and it would be hard to imagine a positive care environment which neglects one or more of these values. We shall briefly discuss some of the values mentioned and consider them in a practical context.

All too often, these words (often familiar in everyday language) are not necessarily analysed in any way. We may claim to practise in a way which ensures an individual's dignity; but what do we mean by this? Practical explanations invariably include examples such as closing a toilet door when supporting someone with personal care or ensuring blinds are drawn in someone's bedroom at bedtime; but in a broader sense, dignity encompasses many features of the relationship between a carer and a person who uses services. Dignity implies a sense of worth being placed upon an individual, an awareness of power differentials and recognising the individuality of another person; in essence this is their distinctiveness as individuals. It implies the worthiness of another person, and can be demonstrated in so many ways – using a preferred name, for example, or respecting someone's privacy and working with their sensitivities.

Choice

Another area we may not always think deeply about is the area of choice. Is choice simply about giving people what they wish for? In reality, in every service, is there an unlimited availability of options and choices? Are choices somehow tempered by other important issues like safety, risk and health? In our lives, are choices limited by circumstances or other factors beyond our control and, in care services, how might we ensure meaningful choices and empowerment remain central to the work we do with people who use services? On the other hand, what might a lack of choice mean to someone? It is likely to cause some form of disengagement, even hopelessness if the lack of choice is persistent and the role of advocacy (self or otherwise) is central to combating lack of choices for individuals. It is also important that choice be explained to an individual receiving care – i.e. what is meant by that term in the context of their care and how empowerment will be central to the professional relationship; after all, choice without empowerment seems inconsistent and meaningless. Choices are about a whole range of issues and respect preferences and have individuality at their core.

Safety

Safety is also an important area to consider – indeed, it touches upon a sense of protection and a sense of risk. We should all have the right to feel safe, both in ourselves and in our environment, and we should feel safe expressing ourselves as individuals and in our hopes for the future. Safety in the workplace then, can be about the 'nuts and bolts' of environments like plugs and sockets being correctly wired, but can also be about our trust in others not to harm us physically or emotionally. It can be about people who use services feeling secure and recognised for their own qualities and may also be about staff ensuring people are not harmful to themselves (through support arrangements which may tackle difficult issues like addictions or abuse), or others.

Social justice

In addition to the values mentioned above, underpinning many of these is a sense of social justice. As a key theme in Social Care Theory, this relates to some of our earlier discussions in this chapter: a recognition that we inhabit, and indeed make up, a society, a structured collection of values and ethics, norms and values. Social justice is not so much about criminal justice (with which it should not be confused) but more about a sense of obligation in society to look after us all; it indicates that as a society we will look after each other – something you will encounter in your studies of sociology. In this context, social justice means ensuring a sense of fairness for individuals, getting a chance to reach our own potential and have our needs met, being included and valued in society; being responsible citizens who benefit from society and contribute to it in a way which is both accountable and responsible. It is essential that the theme of social justice is the very theme which underpins anti-discriminatory practice and which feeds into so many of the values and principles discussed.

Key term

Social justice the distribution of advantages and disadvantages in society.

Conclusion

It may seem that this section of the Social Care theory chapter has actually posed more questions than it has offered answers – and that can only be a good thing. In changing times, it is important that the ability to question and remain flexible is central to your practice as you change and grow as a person. It is important that this flexibility is not boundless however, and standards of conduct are fixed to a degree through Codes of Practice. It is hoped that you can now reflect upon your own values with more certainty and can show a degree of self-awareness that will enhance your practice and your own learning throughout your studies and beyond.

The Care Planning process

Having considered values and also identified the Standards of Care expected through legislation, we will now consider a major vehicle for the delivery of a service, namely the Care Plan.

The Care Plan

Care Plans can go by many names – such as Personal Files, Development Plans, Person-Centred Guides – and they come in many forms: in pictures and photos, in graphics and text, in binders, in discreet diaries, in mammoth texts or in electronic files. Do not worry. In essence the Care Plan, by whatever name, and in whatever format, is essentially a contract. It is some form of agreement as to the care or support being offered to a person who uses services by an individual/organisation; it identifies relevant needs, recognising how these needs may be addressed and it applies a timescale of validity before review. A Care Plan is never final or inflexible and it should consolidate a range of information which is relevant to current needs and service provision.

ISLAND COUNCIL
PRIVATE AND CONFIDENTIAL
MERRY VALE COURT

Name Sarah Lukeson	
D.O.B. 23/1/56	
Former address: 22 Rightworth Place, South Street, Isle South	
Next of Kin 1: Mary Barber **relationship:** Sister	
Contact details: 00990 22343	
Address: 22 Rightworth Place, South Street	
Next of Kin 2: James Rowe **relationship:** Friend	
Contact details: 00990 55642	
Doctor: Dr Brer, The Surgery, Greens Close Practice, High Street **Contact number:** 00998 228282 **Emergency number:** 04228671919	

An extract from a Care Plan.

Consider this

Care Plans have certainly changed over the years. Having briefly summarised what they are above, take a few moments to consider what they are not.
An example of what they are not might be – a diary of a person's every move…
Can you think of some other examples?

We have already considered (in the previous section of this chapter) some areas relating to values and self-awareness but to recap, values in practice can mean partnership arrangements where the client and the Social Carer/worker function together through problem-solving processes; the partnership is about increasing independence, self-determination and opportunities for choice. It is not about the worker reforming or changing people. Each person is unique with an inherent dignity that is to be respected; diversity and variety among individuals is to be welcomed and encouraged. This partnership is about establishing a link between individuals and their environment and not about moving an individual or the environment towards an ideal model.

Think about the house or flat you have just left today – is it clean? Is it tidy? Is it well decorated/organised/spotless? Are your clothes ironed and neatly stored? If you have one, is your garden immaculate with pretty flower borders and mowed grass?

The chances are it may not be – if you were to go home right now, to find someone filling out a Care Plan based on your accommodation, and what they find in it, what conclusions might they come to?

With these principles in mind, it is quite obvious that one of the main communication tools (i.e. the Care Plan) is an important and central method of carrying forward the actual momentum of support.

Care Plan information

While different organisations have very different types of paperwork and recording procedures, a general overview of the type of information contained within a Care Plan might include the following:

- medical conditions, allergies and factual information on contact numbers, next of kin and such
- areas of daily living which the individual can expect support with
- the duration and frequency of that support
- any communication issues which are relevant and current
- any team members involved in support and their role (i.e Key Worker)
- any other special needs relevant to the individual receiving care.

It is unlikely that any one organisation will deliver every aspect of care – so perhaps external agency information would be included in care plans; this might include the GP, pharmacist, community nurse and any informal support networks. Indeed, reviews of care plans can often involve a wide range of others – from relatives and friends, to professional advocates and specialist services.

Consider this

Years ago, institutions often catered for an individual's every need (whether to their benefit or detriment). For example, large institutions or asylums often had on-site laundries, kitchens, dentists, nurses, doctors, hairdressers and even power stations. What else can you find out about institutions in the past?

Institutions in the past provided very different types of care.

How might care provision have changed now? What 'mixed economy of care' exists to ensure appropriate services?

Formal care often differs from informal care, in its contractual nature. By this, we mean that formal care relates to an agreement or contract stipulating the responsibilities of agencies, individuals and others in a support 'package'. Informal care, although absolutely vital, is more likely to be non-contracted support carried out by partners, children and family members, or friends. Professional teams must be clear about exactly who is responsible for what and when. Contracts have to show accountability, cost and quality assurance and it is a very real fact that, as a service, the contractual element of providing care is very much a legal issue. Employers and their employees face very real consequences if their care is seen to be less than what has been agreed, either in terms of time or quality. While Care Plans serve a communicative function, you should be aware that they can be viewed as legal documents which are central to investigations or complaints, should the situation arise. Care Plans mean lots of things to different people, but whatever form the actual Plan takes, the general model of Care Planning is given below

The planning cycle

Rational planning is central to the Care Plan – so eliminating emotive language, discriminatory language or leading information is vital. A successful Care Plan needs to be structured, clear, organised and often methodical. Of course, feelings, intuition or opinion should not be excluded; but a good Care Plan should identify what is factual, what is conjecture and what is belief. It is often beneficial to seek information from a variety of sources, not least from the person who uses services themselves, in terms of content, style, colour or format and while an individual may be responsible for collating and presenting information, it is highly unlikely that only one individual's opinion or perception should make up the bulk of the Plan's content. In terms of the formality of Care Planning as a process, there are recognisable, identifiable stages to Care Planning.

Assessment

This involves gathering information about the person who uses services and assessing their needs in relation to that information; the assessment of needs should also be mindful of the organisation's role in meeting those needs.

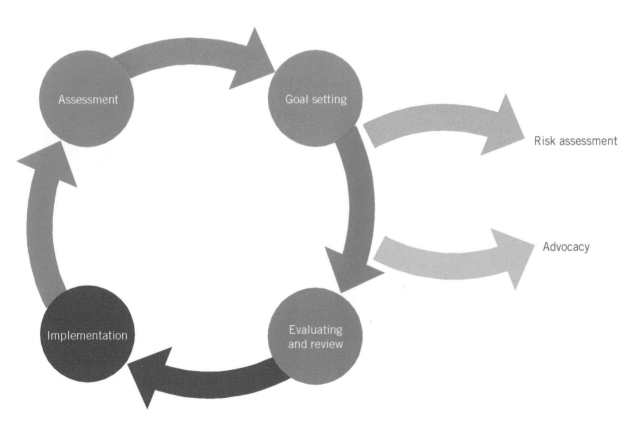

The Care Planning cycle.

Case study

Andy

At 23 years of age, Andy has been discharged from a year's stay in a psychiatric ward. He has suffered from a debilitating eating disorder since his mid-teens and, at one point, was so weak, he was advised that he would die. His recovery has been slow and painful, but he has maintained his target weight for about four months, and as he is keen to go to college and move on with his life, his psychiatrist feels it is a positive step forward for him to get community support in his own tenancy. As part of his discharge plan, he is moving into a town centre bedsit; it is close to shops and nightlife, in an area where many of his friends stay. He will be supported by a community psychiatric nurse on a weekly basis, and the local GP's practice will monitor his weight weekly. He will also be visited by a youth befriender one evening a week, to socialise in planned activities. Once his social life has been established, it is anticipated this support will stop. Because of his dietary needs, and complex attitude towards food and exercise, he will also be supported every day of the week, for three hours, by a local voluntary agency. This agency will specifically support him with household maintenance, food shopping and food preparation.

1. In such a situation, who may take a lead role in co-ordinating the Care package on offer?

2. What might Andy's Care Plan look like?

Consider this

Another way of thinking about the complexities of Care Planning is to consider these examples:

- an individual with a 24-hour support package may identify the need for daytime occupation – a college course for example – the Care organisation may not directly provide a college course, but may be able to facilitate and support the individual to access one
- another individual may receive two hours support a day to cover mealtimes – their identified needs reflect only the fact that they require some basic food hygiene support. However, a service providing that support may not identify or meet another need, such as specialist mental health monitoring.

Activity

Needs can be broadly grouped into the SPECC range:
- S stands for Social
- P stands for Physical
- E stands for Emotional
- C stands for Cognitive and the final
- C stands for Cultural.

Think of the needs (under each of the SPECC headings) after reading the case study below (please be aware there are other groupings of needs available to use).

Case study

Janet

Janet is a 40-year-old single mother of three children. She moved to Scotland from England three years ago, to escape an abusive relationship. Her three children are all at secondary school and there has been concern expressed from the school about their personal hygiene and general well-being. Janet is devoted to her children, but after a particularly violent incident with her past partner, she suffers mild memory loss. While her children support her as much as they can, Janet sometimes struggles to budget well, and can become confused by routine tasks; she has missed appointments and meetings with the school on two occasions. She has also come close to causing a fire in the home while cooking.

She lives in a small estate and has a three-bedroomed house. The neighbourhood is quiet, but Janet doesn't know the neighbours very well and has no relatives nearby.

Janet is a heavy smoker, but doesn't suffer from any physical illnesses she is aware of. Janet is very frail, and obviously prioritises her children when it comes to spending money! She doesn't have many clothes, and she is underweight, and doesn't seem to have a balanced diet. She drinks lots of fizzy juice and relies upon quick microwave food for herself.

Janet hasn't been in another relationship since she left her last partner, and has low self-esteem and seems to lack confidence. Although there has been no contact from her ex-partner, she is anxious that he will find the family and also feels guilty that her children have had 'so much to endure'.

Janet is not in employment and always wanted to learn more about beauty and alternative therapy. Her children are old enough to allow her some time to study at night classes but Janet feels unsure about how to proceed with her aspirations.

Social needs	
Physical needs	
Emotional needs	
Cognitive needs	
Cultural needs	

Try to fill in Janet's needs in this table of needs.

Understanding assessment

In the past, assessment has been more closely linked with a medical model of care and can seem to start from the premise that there is something 'wrong' which needs to be fixed. This is not necessarily the case; assessment can be far more than the traditional medical stance might imply – it is not about being judgemental about someone's needs but about assessing a situation. People assess things differently, and have different perceptions, so it is always vital to enter into partnership with the client throughout the process; assessment is not about finding solutions or right answers. More mundanely, it might be about filling in forms and discussing the content of these forms or chasing basic information – it is always about communication and interaction and sometimes it can be surprising and revealing!

Consider this

Needs can often be confused with wants. We may not all be in agreement about what a need is. For example, a balanced diet may be a physical need, but should that be of a pleasant and varied nature? If we say it should, is it acceptable that we include champagne and truffles in our menu? Should we be providing or making provision for diets which offer someone the opportunity to eat fine cuisine in restaurants every night, or to buy basic produce at a local supermarket?

Bradshaw identified a way of looking at needs in his 'Taxonomy' – he identified the following kinds of needs:

- normative need
- felt need
- expressed need
- comparative need.

Normative need relates to the 'norm' of usual expectations in society at large – needs can be defined as those which relate to general standards. For example, a house which is damp, unheated and has an outside toilet may not be seen as adequate by 'normal' standards.

Felt need relates to an individual's personal sense of need. If people feel they need something, that might be one way of defining the need. 'I need to make some new friends' may be a valid identification of social needs.

Expressed need: people can often feel a need, which they don't openly express. People may feel very vulnerable and lonely, but don't admit to this. Equally, people may express that they need something but which is not the actual solution to the underlying need. An example of this would be 'I need a cigarette to calm me down' – actually having this need expressed does not address the underlying need to feel calmer.

Comparative need relates to needs being identified in the context of comparing situations – using the earlier example of acceptable housing standards, would poor housing in Britain be the same as housing standards in poverty stricken regions of India or Africa?

In reality, Social Care works within a framework which relates to budgets and generally agreed standards of living – often linked to social structures such as benefits payments, public housing standards or educational opportunities and attainment.

It is likely that, at some point in your studies, you will be expected to show your understanding and awareness of how needs relate to practice through the tool of assessment and planning of care.

Goal setting

This may involve a process of identifying minor steps in a bigger plan, or it may be deciding on broad targets for care and prioritising those targets. For many people who use services, support is not seen as a static intervention. Many organisations ultimately hope their services are reduced or redundant, as an individual's independence grows. With this in mind, there may be small steps taken at the goal-setting stage to identify and promote the independence and autonomy of the person who uses services or simply enhancing their circle of social opportunities or broadening their experiences.

Planning, the process by which agreed actions are written down, is central to the 'working' of the Care Plan itself. Goals should, therefore, be SMART (Specific, Measurable, Achievable, Relalistic, Time-bound – see below); the goals should be realistic, and discussed with the person who uses services and all the relevant professionals involved in a package of care.

Implementing care

Linked to the previous goals, the implementation stage identifies the nuts and bolts of support. This part of the process instructs and records how goals may be met and who/how delivery of support is achieved. In implementing care and in readiness for the next phase of evaluation and review SMART can be applied. SMART goals are those which are:

- Specific
- Measurable
- Achievable
- Realistic
- Time-bound.

Evaluation and review

As a point of reflection, this may be a chance to consider what has been achieved through the current Plan. At this review stage, the opinions of others may be sought in terms of changes to be made to the assessment of need at a given point in time – this then leads to a re-evaluation of the status quo and, typically, amendments to the Care Plan, as the cycle continues.

Negotiation is a central part of the planning process and views and opinions should always be sought – relatives, partners and people who use services may all hold a stake in this process.

Consider this

Earlier in the chapter we considered values. How might values influence the Care Plan process? Whose values may be relevant and why?

Person-centred Planning

In addition to the more general cycle of Care Planning already discussed, other specific planning tools have emerged in recent years; for example Person-centred Planning or Essential Lifestyle Planning. Innovative in its approach, certain methods used in Person-centred Planning have become embedded in general planning work; however, as a tool, there are several useful concepts which are worthy of particular recognition.

Key themes often associated with Person-centred Planning include the following.

Circles of support

Developed in Canada, the UK first started to become aware of this in the mid-1980s. Simply put, a circle of support is a group of people who help another person achieve their desired outcomes or goals. This is not about being a paid member of staff or team, but about valuing an individual enough to 'freely' offer support. Such a relationship negates issues of power or authority and all parties can experience a great deal of satisfaction and achievement from being part of the circle.

Paths

Paths often focus upon an individual's ultimate goal and work back from there – unlike more traditional methods of Care Planning, this allows the achievement to be the focus, so working back through potential barriers rather than moving from the 'here' to the 'future' and anticipating difficulties along the way.

Essential Lifestyle Plan

This is simply a version or tool of Person-centred Planning. Like more traditional Care Planning there are various stages of progression but a typical recording of an Essential Lifestyle Plan may include the following sections or processes:

- the administration section
- who owns the plan, when was it done, who added to the plan
- the person's section.

This is an introduction to the person upon whom the plan is based, including 'good things about me' and positive things others see. This part usually identifies what is important to the person in terms of order i.e. most important, second in importance and third in importance to produce distinct listed information.

Person-centred Planning has features which move away from more 'traditional' medical models of care, as summarised below (adapted from Miller and Gibb (2007) *Person-centred care Planning*).

Clinical labelling of people	Seeing the whole person
Professionals being in charge	Sharing power
Professionals inviting people in	Person choosing who attends meetings
Meeting in offices at times to suit service	Meeting in venues chosen by person who uses services
Meetings being 'chaired' by professionals	Facilitators co-ordinating meeting
Not asking what the person wants	Encouraging the person to dream
Writing notes of meeting	Drawing/graphics to illustrate points
Filing plans away	Giving the plan to the person
Professionals putting the plan into action	All team members having some responsibility for the plan and its implementation

Person-centred Planning has moved away from the medical model of care.

Activity

Consider your own life – can you map out the things and people that are important to you? Can you order them, to help you to identify your own 'essential life plan'?

The support section

This details what others need to know in order to provide the focus individual with a healthy and safe experience, to work out what they want and what is important to them. Various sections can be added here, such as communication information or important medical details. Where there is a conflict between the focus individual and the planner, health and safety must prevail and details should be sensitively included in the plan, acknowledging the focus individual's reticence or discomfort.

The action section

Issues to work out are included here – perhaps a list of questions might be included which still have to be answered. Also in this section, it is noted who is doing what to maintain the individual's health, safety and chosen lifestyle. What needs to change is noted, as well as what does not need to change.

The main focus of this Person-centred approach is to consider someone's needs in terms of their perspective and not from a service or specialist perspective alone.

Systems approach

Another form of Care Planning is known as the Systems Approach – this has come from work conducted by Pincus and Minahan in 1973. As a model for social work, this approach is useful to examine in a wider context and as an approach to identifying a range of needs and services designed to build up a package of care. It recognises that people in society depend upon systems generally and that social work must therefore, recognise and evaluate these systems in the context of meeting needs.

Pincus and Minahan argue that there are three kinds of systems which may help people:

- informal or natural systems such as friends, family, neighbours, peers
- formal systems such as community groups or trade unions, clubs or community services/centres
- societal systems such as schools, hospitals, benefit agencies and so on.

It is also important to recognise that such systems can sometimes hinder people's development and realisation of potential. Pro-actively, as care workers, being aware of the impact of such systems on an individual's need helps the planning of care to be recognised as complex and not only about the individual in the 'here and now'.

The work of Pincus and Minahan therefore progresses to recognise that individuals experiencing problems may not be able to utilise help through these systems for a range of reasons:

- perhaps the system does not exist for them
- the system may not have sufficient resources
- the system may be inappropriate
- individuals may not know about or wish to use a system
- different systems may conflict with each other/the individual.

Case study

Sharon

Sharon is an 18-year-old lone parent. She lives in a council house which is very damp, with her two sons aged three months and 2 years. Her mother is an intravenous drug user and has led a chaotic lifestyle for several years. Sharon herself has experienced social work intervention as she grew up, spending extended spells of her childhood in various foster homes. Sharon keeps in regular contact with her mother, who lives a few streets away, but is reluctant to allow her children access to their grandmother. Sharon's father has never been a part of her life and she does not know much about him.

The estate where Sharon lives has a 'bad' reputation – there is a high volume of lone parents living in the area and crime is increasingly a problem in the neighbourhood.

Sharon is not in employment and has no contact with the father of her children; nor does she desire contact at this point. Her youngest child has been in and out of hospital with chest infections and she is receiving support from her local community centre, which welcomes her and her children to the crèche held twice a week. Sharon is keen to consider her future and would like to take up a college place next year when her youngest child is older – she hopes to become a hairdresser at some point. Sharon has recently been diagnosed with depression and is keen to 'take stock' of her life.

1. Consider this case study and try to identify the systems contained within the scenario.

2. Which are beneficial to the individual?

3. Which systems may hinder the individual?

The Systems Approach is keen to fully assess an individual, family or group in the context of their environment and community. It recognises that systemic influences are direct and indirect – for example, someone's location, age, gender and background can and does influence where they are now and where they see themselves. The current systems may be functioning in harmony or at odds, or simply not functioning at all; and in order to assess an individual we should consider issues such as their self-image, attitudes, values and beliefs about themselves and their current position. We should then consider looking at the family – is there a system here and, if so, is it contributing well or not so well? What social networks are around at present and how do these influence the individual and what environmental systems are available or apparent?

The work is complex and can be time-consuming, but it certainly encourages a holistic approach to Care Planning. Four further systems are then identified to explain the working relationships around delivery of solutions to meet need(s):

- change agent – professionals (for example a social worker) who can help a client bring about change
- client system – individuals, groups or families and communities who seek support
- target system – people who the change agent is trying to target in order to meet aims (client and target systems may or may not be the same)
- action system – people with whom the change agent may work to achieve its aim (again, the client, target and action systems may or may not be the same).

As stated in *Social Work Practice – an Introduction* by Victoria Coulshed and Joan Orme (1994) 'Assessment is an ongoing process, in which the client participates, the purpose of which is to understand people in relation to their environment…'

Consider this

All of the language used here, about systems and agents and so on, may seem confusing. Identify the systems/agent in the scenario below to illustrate the theory.

David is six years old and is on the Child Protection Register. He has been referred to Social Services by both his GP and his school. His father is known to Probation and Addiction Services locally and Social Workers are keen that the family take up parenting classes and a respite 'babysitting' service.

David's attendance at school has recently become erratic; he has been to the local Accident and Emergency Department on four separate occasions in the last six months – presenting with a variety of cuts and on two occasions broken bones. He is generally pale and quite withdrawn and, developmentally, his language skills seem to be below the expectations for a child of his age. Use the grid below to guide you.

Change agent	
Client system	
Target system	
Action system	

The Systems approach may use four further systems as shown.

Anti-discriminatory practice

Positive Care Planning, following a variety of methods or models, should reflect the principles of choice, empowerment and risk taking. The design and development of a Care Plan should also promote anti-discriminatory practice and promote fulfilment and potential.

How might anti-discriminatory practice evidence itself in a Care Plan?

As a record of work, to a degree, a Care Plan is a powerful document. It contains important and private information and builds a picture of someone's needs and support. It reflects practice and agreements of work. By picking up such a document, an Inspector or Commissioner is able to glean a 'flavour' of a service.

Activity

Imagine you are a member of the Care Commission and you are asked to visit a local Care Home to report upon standards of service. What kind of things might you look out for in a Care Plan? What types of language do you expect to see?

Consider the following list of words and phrases – circle those which you think suggest positive practice and then consider those which may give you cause for concern.

Need	Bored	Same as usual
Opportunity	Empowered	Made an enquiry
Given choices	Considered	Conflict
Disagreed	Did not allow	Attention seeking
Hoped	Gave out money	I listened to him
Phoned	Will ask	Told
Same everyday	Going out	Ate all food
As usual	Invited friends	Shouted
Happy	Complained	Listened
Referred	Ended	Reviewed

Identify the positive and negative language.

A discriminatory workforce, or individual, is likely to use (however inadvertently) discriminatory language. If a Care Plan is written in a way which suggests poor practice, concerns over *actual* practice may be raised.

As we have touched upon earlier, values are implicit in Care Plans – some of those values include:

- empowerment
- right to self-determination
- promoting independence
- protection from harm and abuse
- social justice.

People who use services can be vulnerable for a variety of reasons, and the very fact that they receive care may indicate that vulnerability, however temporary. Promoting positive Care Planning ultimately promotes anti-discriminatory practice. It is essential, throughout any Care Plan, that the focus remains with the person who uses services.

Miller and Gibb (2007) identify ten points of good practice in assessment and Care Planning. These are:

1. a firm value base underpins respect and dignity of every individual and promotion of choice, rights, empowerment and protection
2. the person who uses services should be at the centre of the process – the plan is with, and not of, the person who uses services. The plan should be an agreement and highlight areas of disagreement sensitively
3. good communication is needed, including listening
4. the plan should be ongoing and never be regarded as finished and complete
5. it is important to be needs led and not service led: 'needs led' means focusing upon the 'whole' examination of need and how they relate; 'service led' means the service leading the identified needs. An example of this would be someone who is depressed requiring counselling, but a service led agreement may not prioritise the counselling because resources are few and far between

6. accurate, up-to-date information is needed; if something is opinion, it should be identified as such
7. labelling, stereotyping or scapegoating a person is not acceptable – if an individual's behaviour is described as 'attention seeking' it can lead to a negative image of that behaviour
8. the Care Plan should be specific about responsibilities (who does what) and outline rights
9. it should have built-in evaluation processes and time frames
10. it is important to emphasise that there is no one 'right' Care Plan; there are no absolutes and Care Planning can be as individual as the person upon whom it focuses.

Relevant legislation and policy

While individual employers will have their own particular policies and procedures, there are several items of legislation that are relevant to the Care Planning process and which play a role in promoting positive care.

This legislation includes the following:
- Regulation of Care (Scotland) Act 2001
- Data Protection Act 1998
- NHS and Community Care Act 1990
- Mental Health Care and Treatment (Scotland) Act 2003
- Adults with Incapacity Act (Scotland) 2000
- Community Care and Health (Scotland) Act 2002.

While Social Policy as a subject covers many of these Acts in more detail, some will be mentioned here in the context of anti-discriminatory and positive practice. Not all have been given in detail in this chapter.

Regulation of Care (Scotland) Act 2001

This piece of legislation is responsible for some major changes in Scotland's care provision. The Act set up two important bodies: the Care Commission (The Scottish Commission for the Regulation of Care) and the Scottish Social Services Council.

The Commission, broadly, is responsible for the inspection and registration of care services and identifies those services which then adhere to the National Care Standards – if a service fails to meet, or fails to comply with standards, they can lose their registration or face penalties under this Law. The Care Commission also has the power and duty to inspect and regulate services and Inspectors have the power to insist on changes to a service if standards are not met. Ultimately, should a service fail to comply with recommendations, or if the quality of that service is found to be substandard, the service can be closed down. Care standards are based upon six principles (as discussed earlier in the chapter) and these are:
- dignity
- privacy
- choice
- safety
- realising potential
- equality and diversity.

It is vital that Care Plans relate to and echo these fundamental standards and principles.

Data Protection Act 1998

This Act relates to the lawful collection of personal information. Care Plans often contain information of a highly personal and confidential nature. Personal data includes factual information like date of birth, telephone number and bank details and this Act relates to information stored electronically and manually. All data held on a person has to be up to date and accurate, and it must be kept safely to prevent loss, damage or unauthorised access or use of the information. A copy of information can be requested via Subject Access Request, but Care Plans, usually, should hold information the person who uses services is aware of. Individuals, under the Act, have the right to:
- know if you, or someone else, is processing information about them
- know what that information is and why it is being processed and who has access to the information
- receive a copy of personal information about them
- know about the sources of the information.

NHS and Community Care Act 1990

This Act had an impact upon provision of care for people in community settings. Care could be tailored to meet the needs of people in their own home, or in residential care as necessary. This Act gave local authorities the responsibility of assessing need and providing care from a range of sectors (as required). Community Care Plans must be produced by local authorities every three years; considering budgeting, development of new services if required, service demand and the closure of services no longer needed.

If a person needs a service, there is an obligation to provide the service and this should be provided from the client's perspective; this was an important move away from people with support needs having to fit into services available in communities. It is worth mentioning, however, that there have been some amendments by subsequent reforms.

Conclusion

This section of the chapter has introduced a few concepts – some general discussion on what a Care Plan may be and how it may be used. We have looked at some of the areas a Care Plan should cover and the ways in which it may be recorded or processed. More specific examples of Care Planning have been suggested, but be aware that there are more theories and Care Plan tools in use; your tutor will direct you to the most relevant subject areas. We have also considered the interplay between values, anti-discriminatory practice and the Care Planning process and finally we have looked at the influences on the process from some of the legislation.

Care Plans are an inevitable and important part of a carer's role and you will almost certainly be using and contributing to plans during your career.

Methods and models of Social Care practice

In this section, we will consider some of the methods of intervention available to Social Care workers. We will also discover some of the skills required for working with others and consider some interventions or useful skills available in challenging situations. The theory of intervention can seem to be very separate, and they are seen as distinct theories academically; however, in practice, you are likely to soon recognise that several interventions can be used; although perhaps not in their entirety.

Methods of intervention

On pages 17 and 18, we touched upon Person-centred Planning and Systems theory – these are not only useful concepts linked to Care Planning, but can be viewed as models which workers can adopt when supporting a person who uses services. There is a framework of an approach, a way of looking at a situation, contained within these theories. In addition to models of working with others, there are also methods which can be adopted. For example, a basic model of Care Planning may be to Assess, Intervene and Review – this being a very simple framework upon which to build complex arrangements for agreeing support.

Just as this is an example of a framework for Care Planning, other theoretical frameworks exist which attempt to structure and identify specific areas of practice. While these models do not claim to represent social work solutions in a 'parcel', they help us to consider and understand some methods of dealing with others/situations. Equally true, is the fact that no one theory, method or model, is likely to contain a solution to an individual's support needs – but they allow us to be aware of a range of possible interventions and practice which may be useful. No one intervention is likely to be a perfect fit for supporting others, but bits of some may be useful and, at least, help us to consider solutions more broadly. While the different approaches may be called something distinct, elements of each are often used in practice.

In considering potential assessments in your HNC, it is likely that you will be expected to identify and describe a theoretical framework, and apply that framework to practice with an evaluation. Some of the approaches to social work we will consider include:

- psychodynamics
- psychosocial casework
- behavioural social work.

These are not specifically models of intervention in themselves, but rather large backdrops/theoretical influences on approaching social work/care practice. Much has been written on such theories, and here we will just briefly outline the main points of each.

Psychodynamics

You may come across this approach as you study psychology as part of your HNC. Broadly speaking, psychodynamics is a school of thought attributed, most commonly, to Sigmund Freud. Just as Freud's personality model reflects the conflict between the Id and the Superego, with the regulatory Ego caught in the middle, so society and the individual are seen as conflicting extremes. The individual in crisis is at the centre.

This approach recognises that an individual's Id drive may result in anti social behaviour. Society (and the Superego's urge to conform to societal expectations) presents constraints, rules and obligations often at odds with the Id's unruly nature. Psychodynamics can be broadly seen as the workings of the mind and this approach focuses very much upon how our mind-set and personality can put us in harmony or conflict with others' views. Quite often, Social Care intervention is kick-started when a person's attitudes or behaviour seem to be at odds with the normal and expected patterns of society.

| Society | Person in crisis | Consequences |

The person in crisis is at the centre of the conflict.

Activity

In the table below are some examples of conflicts which may precipitate Social Care or social work involvement – how might social workers/carers intervene?

Situation	Suggested intervention
A young child is not encouraged to attend school so therefore misses most classes.	
A father expresses sexual interest in his children, by using inappropriate language around and about them – this may not involve direct action at this point, but does suggest unusual boundaries in relationships.	
A husband feels he is entitled to beat his wife for disobeying him.	
An elderly man, suffering from dementia, wanders the streets in his pyjamas late at night.	
A 13-year-old girl is addicted to alcohol and is sexually active – already she has a sexually transmitted infection and has had a miscarriage.	
After an accident, a 20-year-old man is unable to control his body below his neck – he cannot move or eat independently and his 'old' life seems unattainable.	
A young, single father struggles to care for his two children. He loves them dearly, but the house is a mess; bills don't get paid and he cannot cope with all of the demands placed upon him.	

What interventions might be necessary in these examples of conflict?

Case study

An example of conflict

Aidan is seven years old and has been diagnosed with ADHD. He sometimes becomes very agitated in social situations and has been displaying inappropriate behaviour towards other children – hitting out at them or shouting at them. He finds sleeping difficult, so is often tired and grumpy. At other times, he is full of energy and finds it hard to concentrate on school work in class situations. He can display socially inappropriate behaviour, by snatching food at snack times, eating very quickly and then trying to take other's food. Aidan is quite a big boy, so he is physically intimidating other students by using threatening gestures at times. To date he has been included in mainstream school classes, but his social worker has been asked to attend a school meeting to address his needs and identify additional support required, to ensure minimal disruption to the school, classmates and to encourage his success at school.

1. What behaviour may Aidan display that will contradict the 'normal' rules of school?

2. How might the school be able to offer a more appropriate environment?

3. How might Aidan's social worker work with him to encourage more useful behaviour and to develop a stronger sense of self?

Intervention is seen in terms of strengthening the Ego in such circumstances to enable the individual to deal with their social and personal situation in a healthy way. When we consider Ego strengths, we do not do so in a fixed manner – if someone's Ego can deal with reality, their ability to present as a mature, rational and balanced individual is clear. Conversely, if defence mechanisms are used and the Ego is weakened, an individual may be seen to be confused, in denial, needy or impulsive. This approach helps the individual to react to their situation in a positive way or a more useful way. Often, a Social Carer cannot make an environmental problem just disappear – the individual receiving care has to accept their situation and deal with it differently or think about it differently. If this is achieved then the stress and difficulties faced by the individual might make their health, life and interactions easier and more appropriate.

Psychosocial casework

A step beyond psychodynamics, this approach is linked to the work and writing of Erikson. As the title suggests, *psycho* (of the mind) meets *social* (environment) in this approach. It recognises that the individual's psychology may have to alter but goes a little further – recognising the importance of the social structures around in setting the scene for behaviour. Social work practice need not only look at an individual's Id and personality, but also at the wider social scene. Altering the social and family situations around a person who uses services may have just as much impact as making mental adjustments. Also of importance in this approach are theories of psychosexual development. Psychosocial casework often aims to identify at what stage a person who uses services may be 'caught in', which can help to explain current behaviours, attitudes or difficulties. In this context, an individual's current presentation and difficulties may be linked to Freud or Erikson's stages of development.

Case study

A psychosocial approach to Jim

Jim is in his early 40s and is a single dad to Cath, aged nine. He was happily married and employed two years ago, living in a beautiful village near the coast. He was happy and content, and looking forward to watching his child grow up. One day, he returned from work to find his wife had left him for another man. He lost his job and his house, as the family home had to be sold, and he was left 'homeless'. His daughter begged to stay with him, and this was agreed. However, the divorce arrangements are still not finalised and this is a source of great stress. Jim also has been forced to move into a Glasgow city-centre, high-rise scheme. He is on floor 34 of a block of flats and his neighbours seem to be mainly younger mums. The flat is well kept by Jim and Cath, but the communal areas smell and often rubbish is scattered around. Loose dogs also roam the corridors, leaving their mess behind them. Whereas his daughter used to attend a small rural school, she now walks to the nearby primary through dirty streets, where she has already been asked if she wants any drugs. Jim is unable to work as he has to look after his daughter and his wife is using this as evidence that he is incapable of supporting her. Jim has no savings and is receiving basic benefits. He gave all of his belongings, household goods and savings to his wife when they separated. He still loves his wife and is very hurt by her actions and by her growing animosity towards him, and more recently, his daughter (who visits her mother during school holidays).

Jim's mental health is faltering; he has panic attacks and recently visited his GP where he was immediately given some anti-depressants and told to get a repeat prescription. Jim has no friends or family nearby, and devotes all of his energy to his child.

1. What psychological factors may be affecting Jim at this time? Think about the losses he has faced and changes he has encountered – how may his self-esteem be affected?

2. What social factors are affecting him at present? Think about his environment and his concerns over his daughter and try to consider what may be sources of stress and demotivation for him.

3. What could a worker bring to the situation using the psychodynamic approach?

Behavioural social work

Behavioural practice recognises, in the context of Social Care, that thoughts, attitudes and feelings are a result of a range of past and present influences; in practical terms, the use of behavioural social work may not be entirely neat when compared to Skinner's initial behaviourist theories, but this approach does allow us to contextualise an individual's present condition or situation.

Behavioural social work, very loosely, recognises that we respond and behave in certain ways because of a range of factors. These factors include: trial-and-error, instinctual responses, learned responses and thinking about how to respond as individuals (*cognitive learning*). Usefully, this approach can be directed towards assisting a person who uses services with a specific problem or particular issue. For example, this type of approach gives rise to some commonly used Social Care practices like reward schemes or the ABC approach. The ABC approach recognises that we may actually encourage or invite certain behaviours without realising it and it forces us to look at a situation in a more analytical way.

By considering the broad approach you may take towards a person who uses services, or a particular situation, you can focus your support in different ways. It is also worth considering that not all clients or people who use services can express complex communication or language, which can mean that accessing details of their psychological state or history may be very difficult or impossible.

Case study

Using ABC

Every Tuesday morning Marie encourages John, a service user, to have a bath. The rest of the week, he chooses to shower, but his Care Plan has been amended to include a bath to allow him to receive treatment for his dry skin condition. John requires some physical support to get in and out of the bath. No hoist is used, but Marie gently supports him as he steps in and out.

Other staff members have also supported John to have a bath, and there have been no problems. However, when Marie does it, John tries to lash out at her and grabs at her. This is potentially a problem given the confines of the bathroom, the health and safety implications in terms of slip and trip hazards, and is also leading Marie to lose self-confidence in her ability to work with John. Usually they get on with no problems whatsoever, and John speaks highly of Marie as a worker.

The sequence of events leading to this unusual display of behaviour is examined.

A = Antecedent	B = Behaviour	C = Consequences
What went on leading up to the incident?	What type of behaviours were displayed?	What did the behaviour result in for the person who uses services?
John enjoying bath = left in privacy while support staff tidy kitchen. Marie washed worktops and then comes through to bathroom. Speaks to John to say bath time finished, asks to assist out of bath. Clothes piled on toilet and towels on heated rack next to sink.	John turns his head down and shouts 'No... no... no...' as Marie reaches over to support him. Hits out at Marie's arms and hands as she moves towards bath – moves from sitting to standing position. Sits down again and points at towels.	Person who uses services asked to calm down, but no clear discussion/ communication enabled. Left in bath for a few minutes before Marie re-enters the room and tries again. Person who uses services seems uncomfortable in bath and as the water cools, can become quite unhappy looking.

After a team meeting to discuss John's support, and with discussion among all staff, it becomes clear that Marie does not do quite the same thing as other staff. Marie does not offer John a towel before she helps him from the bath. Repeating the ABC study has allowed staff to identify a simple support step, which has now been remedied and specified in his Care Plans.

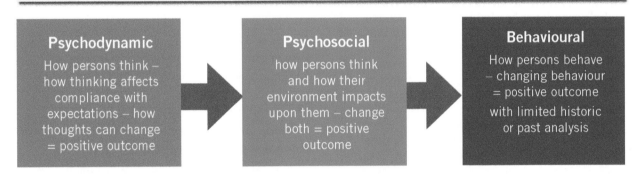

Psychodynamic
How persons think – how thinking affects compliance with expectations – how thoughts can change = positive outcome

Psychosocial
how persons think and how their environment impacts upon them – change both = positive outcome

Behavioural
How persons behave – changing behaviour = positive outcome with limited historic or past analysis

Crisis intervention

Another social work approach is crisis intervention. Crisis intervention recognises, within it, the usefulness of some types of interaction – like life-space work or gentle teaching, and these are explained further in this section. While these are not only useful for crisis intervention they are a way of assisting individuals through a period of upset or change.

While we have considered broad approaches to tackling someone's needs, some situations (rather than some people) lend themselves to specific types of work. Crisis intervention should not be confused with dealing with an emergency; an emergency situation may well be life-threatening and short-lived. A crisis is something a bit different. Gerald Caplan defined crisis as an upset in a 'steady state' or loss of equilibrium. He recognised a crisis as a response to a serious stressful event.

There are different kinds of crisis, which we may all face at different points in our life. These types of crisis include:

- developmental – where transitions between different stages of life create stress. Dying might be an example here. Another might be moving from childhood to adulthood
- situational or accidental – specific life events or situations create a crisis for an individual like job loss or loss through divorce
- complex – these examples are less likely to be seen as the normal 'everyday experiences' and might include becoming a victim of assault or other crime, severe mental illness, or physical illness, or post-traumatic stress syndrome.

Crises can be seen as a perceived threat, a loss or a challenge. It is important to recognise that the crises refer not only to actual threats, but to imagined ones too – the threat can be physical or psychological; loss might be about losing health, a limb or others but can also be about losing direction or feeling isolated and empty.

Looked at positively, this approach recognises that a crisis is a new opportunity to learn and progress; it can be a time to try new methods of solving problems or to discover new strengths.

Case study

Siraq

Siraq was a healthy young man, who enjoyed an active social life. He was looking forward to university when he was involved in a motorbike accident. He was hospitalised immediately after the crash, was in a coma for some time, and awoke to discover he had lost his right leg below the knee. His rehabilitation was a slow and painful one, and while his family were supportive, he began to lose touch with friends and his girlfriend during his time in hospital. He missed his final exams for university, and the whole experience had left him feeling isolated, depressed and hopeless. He also suffered some scarring to his face and body, which he was assured, would fade in time. He was allowed to go home after several weeks of therapy, agreeing to continue physiotherapy for the coming months. However, Siraq now feels anxious a lot of the time and his confidence is low; he becomes aggressive towards his family at times and feels he may as well have died in the crash.

1. How might the crisis intervention method help you to understand Siraq's position?

2. How might Siraq be offered support?

Intervening using crisis intervention is not about drawing out a year's worth of support, but is about focus and communication between a person who uses services and staff. It is about allowing the person who uses services to explore their situation and feelings under the circumstances, and introduces optimism by allowing the worker to guide the individual through conversations, but also to introduce some practical ways to support them.

Life-space work

Life-space work is specifically about using a crisis to gain new opportunities. By supporting someone in a crisis, the worker recognises (and helps the person who uses services to recognise) that growth, insight and change are all positive elements of their situation.

Interviews or meetings can be set up to explore the situation, reflecting on what happened and acknowledging the individual's emotional pain or confusion. By discussing feelings early on in the process, it is hoped that there is more clarity of thought in later discussion, where some solutions can be found. Midway through the process, there can be more discussion on what the real areas of change need to be; the worker can encourage the individual to identify the most urgent problems which seem to block progress in the 'here and now'. If there is missing information about past events, it is fine to revisit them here, but hopefully the intervention is not about total reflection or counselling, but about ultimately moving forward and progressing while acknowledging, without dwelling upon, emotional issues. By working together, the social worker acts as a kind of role model in attempting to solve problems; encouraging change in thinking, feeling and action.

Gentle teaching

Gentle teaching may also be used to encourage someone in crisis. This approach is often used where an individual is unable to use complex language to express themselves as they might, or where there are poor opportunities to reward the individual with praise or insight. It may be necessary to use several tools of intervention, in a planned and agreed way. Over a short period of time, we may use ignoring/interrupting, redirecting and rewarding as tools of communication and assistance. Indeed, when we are faced with behaviour we find difficult or challenging to manage, some of these techniques are useful.

Some examples of crisis intervention and the associated practice of gentle teaching or life-space work may be found in the case studies which follow.

Case study
Katy

Katy is a worker in a busy day centre for adults with learning disabilities; she works two days a week, between 9.30 and 5pm. She greets people who use services at the door of the service before organising the groups and activities for the day. Usually, Katy will work with people who use services in the kitchen area, baking and encouraging food hygiene skills.

Ben is a person who uses services with limited communication skills; he is very fond of Katy and calls her 'sister'. However, as soon as Katy works with one of the other people who use services in the presence of Ben, he sits and screams loudly. After discussions with staff and Bens relatives, the team have agreed to tackle this issue through planned ignoring and redirection. If Ben becomes vocal, and there is no danger or risk to her, Katy will ignore him and carry on working with others. If the behaviour continues, Katy will redirect Ben, another staff member will offer him an activity to complete and remove him from the group he is with/task he is completing. When the situation is calmed, both Katy and another worker will gently explain to Ben the reasons for his removal from the group and why Katy cannot only work with him.

1. Although Ben resists 'losing' Katy to others in her group, what crisis does he seem to experience?

2. How might such an intervention present an opportunity for Ben to learn and grow?

3. What might be the positive outcomes for Katy and Ben during this difficult period?

Case study
Daniel

Daniel works in a nursing home for elderly residents. For an hour each afternoon, the residents are encouraged to use the common sitting room to get together, chat, play games or watch television. During this time, Daniel often organises a quiz to stimulate the residents. Two particular residents, Charles and May, do not seem to get along very well. During quiz times, Daniel has noticed that May shouts out answers if Charles has been asked to answer. Charles finds this very frustrating and has responded by shouting and swearing at May. Recently, he has even refused to take part because of 'that woman!' The care team have thought about ways to help this situation and another staff member has agreed to sit alongside May to assist with her quiz answers. When it becomes apparent that she is about to interrupt Charles, the worker intervenes and gently reminds May to 'keep her answers to herself' until the results are put in. By redirecting May from shouting out, May has been persuaded not to give out her answers, and has even been rewarded by coming first in the quiz on two occasions. Charles feels he has an opportunity to respond and interact independently, and the tension seems to have passed, for now.

1. How is gentle teaching being used here?

2. What may be the experience of crisis for the people in this scenario?

Case study

Jock

Jock lives in his own tenancy and is visited by his support team three times a day to get support with cooking and household chores. Jock is a lively character who has spent most of his life in hospital, but he now enjoys an active social life and is well known in the community. He has a great sense of humour, has an 'eye for the ladies' and goes fishing with a neighbour once a month. He also goes to the bookies every Saturday for a one pound bet.

He can neglect to keep his flat tidy, and has little experience of living on his own. Before being placed in hospital, Jock lived with his mother who did all of the housework and cooking. While in hospital, little was done to encourage his independent living skills and this is now a major area of support for him. At teatime, staff support Jock to assist with food preparation and to do any dishes from the day. Jock really does not appreciate having to do the dishes, and not only hides dirty cups and plates in the cupboard under the sink, but can become quite outspoken when prompted to either wash the dishes or dry them and put them away. After tea, staff have agreed that he will share the responsibility of cleaning up plates and utensils – one party will wash, the other will dry.

More recently, when one of his support staff asked him what he preferred to do, he stormed out of the house, saying he was 'off to the pub'. At his evening visit, the staff member agreed that they would share the washing up; if Jock did ten minutes of supervised cleaning, the staff would finish it off, leaving him only the washing machine to switch on after the dishes. The Care Plan reflects this new approach with a view to reducing the staff intervention time, on dishes, by two minutes every month. Staff have also agreed that the racing results be put on the radio at this time, to redirect attention from the chores alone. If this is not available on any given day, then Jock's favourite music will be played while doing the dishes. So far, Jock seems happier with this arrangement.

Task-centred work

Another model of intervention is Task-centred work. This model realises that open-ended work may be less effective than specific, small-step approaches to tackling issues for a person who uses services. In 1969, research conducted by Reid and Shyne set up two systems of intervention in a voluntary child welfare agency in America. Two contrasting care options were offered; one being the more traditional open-ended approach lasting around 18 months, the other being a series of eight interviews in Planned Short-Term Treatment. Upon evaluating the services offered, it was found that those on the short, structured route improved more than those on the more traditional route! Analysis of the results gave several potential reasons for these findings – including a lack of confidence in clients who had enduring intervention, perhaps a degree of learned helplessness becoming apparent, or evolving dependency upon services. Researchers in the UK began to look into Task-centred work during the 1970s and 1980s which gave rise to the implementation and development of Task-centred work in the UK.

Task-centred work deals with eight main areas which are:

- interpersonal conflict
- dissatisfaction with social relations
- difficulties in role performance
- problems with formal organisations
- problems of social transition
- behavioural problems
- reactive emotional distress
- inadequate resources.

Consider this

Consider the headings above, can you identify an example for each?

For example, problems with formal organisations may mean children or parents who are in conflict with schools.

Furthermore, there are distinct phases and steps to use when helping people who use services to achieve their goals:

- problem exploration
- agreement
- formulation of an objective
- achieving the Task(s)
- termination.

The emphasis of this model is to allow the client to choose the areas or tasks most appropriate to their situation. Solving these concerns focuses on their input and achieving, over agreed timelines, what small steps are necessary. The worker and the client jointly visit the priorities identified by the individual, ongoing assessment recognises the completion of these small-scale tasks until the 'whole' has been resolved.

Task-centred work builds up gradually, like completing a jigsaw.

An example of a Task-centred agreement might look a bit like this.

Case Worker Notes

– discussion and plan with Susan 23/02/09

Problem area/task

Susan needs to become more confident in social settings – she has been aware of this for some time and feels she would benefit from an action plan to result in more social confidence and the building of relationships.

Step one – to discuss past relationships and how they felt for Susan

Step two – to meet with Susan once a week in public place e.g. Tazzo café

Step Three – to meet with Susan once a week at night class (Tuesday for six weeks) 7pm–9pm pottery class

Step Four – liaise with befriending team about removing employee key worker for befriender at night class (weeks 4–7)

Step Five – review this programme once weekly to week 6/7

Step Six – continue weekly café meeting for further three weeks pending review (to week 10)

Signed – Susan McBreen

Signed (Key worker) – Saad Mehann

Date – 23-02-09

A Task-centred agreement.

Termination of the plan is open and agreed; both parties are aware of the termination period and, at this point, it can be very obvious and clear to identify the achievements of the person who uses services and the worker. By agreeing with the individual what parts of the process will be completed by the worker, it enables the person who uses services to feel empowered and in control of the whole process. The pressure of time limitation can be a great motivator in focusing on tasks at hand. Unlike crisis intervention work, where the client finds themselves in a state of turmoil at intervention, this approach holds the client's perception of a problem as key. Hopefully, this enables crises to be avoided.

Counselling

Another important approach to supporting individuals, families or groups is counselling. While more depth will be given to the topic of counselling in the Interpersonal Skills chapter (page 234) it is worth mentioning here as a type of support.

The term counselling is frequently used today and has many different meanings and connotations. In different settings, counselling means different things; for example in education, it is often linked to guidance or helping someone to find a course or a job. In medical settings, or in the military, to be 'counselled' may mean you have been told what to do. Debt counselling is a term often used to describe advice services which help people to manage their finances and budget accordingly. Counselling in some services might be about advice or information. Overall, counselling usually links itself to some form of helpful activity or discussion. The British Association for Counselling (1991) considers *'...the task of counselling is to give the client an opportunity to explore, discover and clarify ways of living more resourcefully and towards greater well-being.'*

Counselling skills

The task of counselling can help another person to explore thoughts and feelings to reach a clearer understanding or make appropriate decisions and take appropriate action. Whatever the outcome of counselling, it is important to recognise the role of counselling – as a set of skills enabling practice. An effective helper will demonstrate a set of values and skills which are beneficial to communication, which might include:

- active listening
- patience
- positive regard
- confidentiality
- congruence
- acceptance.

While counselling in its purest form goes beyond advice giving, guidance and befriending, it is important that boundaries are recognised when it is undertaken. Counselling requires that the person who uses services should feel empowered, should have a sense of self-awareness and understanding and also that the process should be about gains which are recognisable and enduring.

Carl Rogers is an important figure in the approach and use of counselling. Rogers devised a Person-centred approach model which recognises that individuals are responsible for themselves and will grow and develop as they work through obstacles – as they are the true experts on themselves.

Rogers identified four main qualities which are needed by workers in the counselling process. These are:

- empathy – ensuring the client feels secure, understood and accepted by understanding the client's viewpoint
- genuineness – being open and trustworthy, not playing a role in counselling
- non-judgemental acceptance – suspending criticisms and reactions to views expressed which may conflict with a worker's own views and beliefs
- warmth – non-threatening and welcoming experience where an atmosphere of trust can develop.

In addition to work by Rogers, Gerard Egan also contributed to the understanding of counselling through his three-stage model of counselling. The three stages are represented below.

Stage One – building the helping relationship and exploration

Stage Two – new understanding and explore new coping strategies offering different perspectives

Stage Three – action - help the client to develop and use new strategies – worker helps client to see what resources and strengths could be used

Egan's three-stage model of counselling.

Whatever different models you may use, it is important that the counselling skills are identified through reflection on practice and self-evaluation.

Activity

Think about counselling and some of the skills we have mentioned.

Try to identify any of your own strengths and weaknesses using the following list of questions as a prompt.

Are you able to:

- control your own emotions in difficult situations?
- relax – control a tremor in your voice or have awareness of breathing patterns?
- listen to what someone is saying without appearing bored or pre-occupied?
- reflect back to someone what they have just said without feeling uncomfortable?
- listen to someone else's problems without wanting to share your own?
- let someone finish what they are saying without interrupting or fidgeting?
- contemplate a conversation and analyse its content?
- organise goal setting and time keeping?
- accept people's desire to talk about a topic you are bored with or have little interest in?
- accept people at face value without making judgements?

Simply considering this brief activity may already alert you to some of the skills required in counselling situations – it isn't just about talking!

Advocacy

Closely linked to counselling, and enforced more and more through legislation, is the use of advocacy. Whereas counselling requires the person who uses services to undertake a series of complex communications with a worker, advocacy is about standing up for and talking on behalf of another. Advocacy enables an individual, for a variety of reasons, to be represented in meetings, Care Plan reviews or when dealing with agencies. An advocate is someone who communicates with a person who uses services and/or their families and friends to represent that individual or ensure their rights are upheld. This may require a degree of interpretation, depending upon the skills and abilities of the person who uses services, and may indeed bring the worker into conflict with others; but it is increasingly recognised as important in safeguarding individual rights.

Conclusion

We have considered a range of interventions useful to the Social Care context, and there are many additional sources of information available to you. Hopefully you have gained a basic insight into some of the forms of intervention, which will allow you to pursue specific models and methods appropriate to your client group and course demands. You may also, through work placements, be given the opportunity to take part in contemporary training in marketed and recognised intervention strategies. Examples of these may include CALM, TCI and SCIPrUK training. These opportunities will allow you further insight into the theories covered here and, in some instances, practical interventions used in specialised settings. Further details on individual psychological theories can be found in the Psychology chapter of this book; and there are more details concerning counselling and interpersonal skills in the Interpersonal Skills chapter. Remember, it is likely that you will be expected to demonstrate a theoretical knowledge of interventions and methods, as well as applying them in your placement, as part of your HNC assessment programme.

Effective team working

The final area of study for Social Care Theory is that of teamwork. In context, this unit has covered important areas like values, Codes of Practice, Care Planning and Methods of Intervention. It is, therefore, important that the final area of learning is in relation to teams.

What is a team?

Teams are certainly talked about a lot in class work and in practice – but what do you think being a team is about? Often in Social Care, people may not work in an obvious team setting; workers may work one-to-one with a client for the majority of their time, or carry quite a distinct and seemingly individual caseload. Even if you don't work in a traditional team; that is, in a group situation working with others at the same time, the relevance of teams cannot be disputed.

On one level there is the team created by an organisation's identity and structure, but there is also the team element in working alongside, and with, other agencies, as well as more obvious team work side-to-side with people in similar posts to you. We will look more closely at all of these factors throughout this section and also consider some of the many theories relevant to analysing and understanding teams.

Consider this

Bearing in mind some of the brief examples above, identify what teams might look like in Social Care and try to identify any common themes.
You may have considered a range of possible answers.
Now can you think about why we might work in teams?

Some of the issues raised about why we work in teams may be about all sorts of things. For example:

- maybe there is too much work to do for one person to cope
- maybe the hours of work are not traditional and so extra staff are needed
- perhaps a range of people and skills best suits the needs of clients.

Also the organisation employing workers might be a large one, covering a lot of services in a variety of places. You can see that there are likely to be a range of factors influencing any team and contributing to that team's identity and role.

To generalise, a team can be seen as a group of individuals sharing a common goal or purpose.

Teams are usually characterised by:

- individuals sharing goals
- a requirement for working, not independently, but interdependently (relying on one another to an extent)
- a shared commitment to working on group activities
- accountability to each other and/or management.

Teams, therefore, rely upon the group process to problem solve, communicate and deliver services; but does that mean they are always effective?

Consider this

Think about teams you may have been part of; this may include work teams or other kinds of teams like clubs, or sports teams.
Does working together always prove to be effective?
Is working as a group quite simple and easy?
What can go wrong in a team situation?

You have probably thought about all sorts of examples for this exercise. Certainly, teams are useful at achieving a great deal, but they can go through various periods of greater or lesser effectiveness. Woodcock (1979) identified some characteristics of effective teams, some of which are given below:

- appropriate leadership
- clear roles
- commitment to the team
- well-organised team procedures
- positive relationships
- time spent on developing individuals.

From the brief list above, consider how each of the effective team characteristics could be achieved, and how they may be difficult to achieve. You can use the grid below to start you off, but try to add some more examples of your own.

Woodcock's characteristic	Working well	Working not so well
Appropriate leadership	Clear roles within team and clear leadership roles. Procedures for supervision and appraisal of staff.	Frequent changes of leadership team. Lack of recognition of roles. Lack of pro-active action from leadership members.
Clear roles	Realistic and reviewed job descriptions. Procedure for identifying roles and communication between team members on expectations.	Some team members do some tasks, some do all tasks and some do very little with no clear recognition of poor or strong practice. Weak leadership and lack of flexibility among team members.
Positive relationships	Open and professional manner. Clear boundaries around roles and relationships. Inclusive staff attitude. Sense of enthusiasm in workplace with opportunity for peer mentoring if needed. Supportive team members who take responsibility for team spirit.	Individuals losing professionalism and concentrating upon personal relationships. Divisions within team based on various factors like roles, friendships or even gender/age.
Time spent on developing individuals	Recognition and sharing of positive practice and group's responsibility not only for success but also recognising weaknesses. Planned and timed training and development opportunities equally available to all staff. Procedures available for individual appraisal and accountability.	Poor training opportunities or opportunities being given to some, but not all staff. Lack of feedback on progress in post and little interest in personal development. Little or no supervision. Weak debriefing in stressful situations. Little time given for team meetings or peer mentoring.

Some characteristics of effective teams (after Woodcock, 1979).

Team development

Teams are not simply born overnight, and they will go through various stages of development throughout their existence. They also have to respond to various forces – sick leave, changes in staffing or leadership, expansion, reduction, role changes. There are many factors which prohibit or maximise an effective team at any given time. While any individual cannot fix a team alone, it is important to be aware of some of these factors in order to clarify expectations of teams. One of the better known theories relating to team development and change is that devised by Tuckman (1977). Tuckman's Stages of Group Development was not written with Social Care in mind, but is relevant to teams in most circumstances or industries. Tuckman identified five stages that groups go through to develop. These are:

- forming
- storming
- norming
- performing
- ending (or adjourning).

Each of these stages represents a sequence of development for the team and, indeed, Tuckman recognised that in many ways, the five stages are cyclical. Any given team will progress through each stage at its own pace and each stage may last for a different period of time. Members must be prepared to move onto the following stage, or move from the existing stage, before development can occur. It is also recognised that outside factors, or the 'forces' mentioned above, may also shift a group from one stage to another (either positively or negatively!).

Forming

As the title suggests, this first stage is about the formation of the group. At this stage people are keen to know a bit more about each other and to understand the roles and expectations placed upon them; bonds may appear between members of the team which may later become cliques. Members are keen to move towards their goals and each other with the expectation and need for clear guidance from leaders/managers. The group relies upon safe, predictable and comfortable behaviour to an extent.

Storming

This stage is characterised by conflict and competition. This may be evident not only in ability or focus to achieve goals, but in personal relationships between team members. Some individuals may dominate at the expense of others. Cliques may now form and there is a sense of vying for position within the group. Some individuals may have to be more flexible in their personal opinions and behaviours to meet the needs of the group. There also tends to be a fear of making mistakes and personal accountability becomes important, rather than group thinking or group problem solving. Listening and negotiating are positive ways out of the Storming stage.

Norming

With the storm of the second stage passing, team members are more comfortable within the team and seem more able to acknowledge each other other's contributions. Problem solving becomes easier, and members are willing to question each other and negotiate or change preconceived ideas rather than blaming each other. Creativity is at a high level and there seems to be an increased sense of belonging. Cliques are dissolved and shared ideas free flow. While all this positive behaviour is good, one downside is that members may become over-protective of the harmony and resist change or overt challenge. Members may become fearful of further turmoil or a lack of harmony and become overly complacent.

Performing

Not all groups reach this stage – some may be yo-yoing between earlier stages. At this point, there is a balance struck between clarity of roles and inclusive team membership and questioning preconceptions and challenging each other. True interdependence occurs among professional roles and there is a sense of loyalty and identity within the team. The emphasis is on achievement and creativity; challenge is not feared and experimental problem solving is attempted. Team members can confidently work alone, alongside each other, as subgroups or as a whole.

Ending or adjourning

Disengagement from relationships may occur. Individuals, after a time, may feel they need to move on to develop and tasks may no longer require completion to the same extent. This can create apprehension among members and anxieties may increase. Some theorists even call this stage mourning and deforming!

Activity

Think about the description of the team below and try to apply various examples from Tuckman's stages to it.

'My name is Alison and I have just started a new job as a manager of a 24-hour residential home for six men with learning disabilities. These men have lived here for over ten years and share a large house on the main street of a small Scottish town. I came to this management post from another leadership post in a similar organisation. My last post was in mental health services so I am looking forward to the new challenges ahead.

I only just met some of the team last week, on a brief induction visit. They didn't seem very friendly to me – they know I don't come from the same small town as them and I think a couple of them had applied for the promoted post but didn't get it. They are all older than me and have worked here for years – I think they must see me as a young do-gooder from the city.

One lady was really nice though and I think her name was Max. She introduced me to one of the people who use services there and he was really bubbly and friendly. He even gave me a big hug to say hello, but one of the staff shouted him over as I tried to chat. She told him he must sit back down for lunch as he had a chiropodist appointment coming up and they mustn't be late.

Anyway, Max says she is an acting team leader and is very happy to have some 'new blood' in the place. It wasn't until I went back to Head Office to sign my contract, that someone says she is married to my boss! I hope I didn't say anything out of turn. Not only that, it turns out her sister works there as well!

Anyway, I'll just have to see how it goes. I have very clear ideas of changes I want to make and if the staff don't like it… well, I'm not afraid to just tell them what I want! I didn't like the way the office was laid out and the Care Plans I saw were rubbish – I think they are in for a shock and I feel ready for the challenge!'

Belbin's team roles

Another theorist who has contributed to our understanding of teams is Dr Meredith Belbin. Belbin did not look so much at the transitional phases a team may go through, but at the individual team members. Belbin identified team roles and, in doing so, recognised that a team requires a group of characteristics to be present in members. Belbin defined a team role as 'a tendency to behave, contribute and interrelate with others in a particular way'. Belbin explains individual behaviour in terms of how the right combination can influence the team's success.

Belbin presents nine broad Team Roles covering the type of behaviour each plays in a team setting. These roles include, among others:

- the **Plant** – someone who is creative, perhaps a bit quirky and who creatively problem-solves
- the **Teamworker** – co-operative and diplomatic, this role involves supporting the team and fostering a team spirit; however the individual can seem indecisive if isolated
- the **Shaper** – this role involves being challenging and potentially directive in driving the team towards outcomes and activities
- the **Specialist** – a strength of the Specialist is that they are single-minded, seek out knowledge and can be technical and informative. In some instances, however, this role can lead to quite narrow contributions.

There are many articles and websites which further explain Belbin's work and while there is limited capacity to go into detail here, Belbin's work is generally useful and highly regarded. Considering only the roles mentioned above, you may already begin to form an idea of the consequences of teams missing some of these roles. Generally, teams require a balance of roles and Belbin is not the only theorist to consider this.

Benne and Sheets' classification of group behaviour

Benne and Sheets classify typical group behaviours into three broad headings:

Task-orientated behaviour	Individualistic behaviour	Team maintenance
Seeking information	Attacking	Encouraging behaviour
Co-ordinating	Blocking	Harmonising
Recording	Defending own position	Expressing group feelings
Evaluating	Seeking individual recognition	Setting standards

These types of behaviours are not roles taken on board by group members, but are types of behaviours which can be displayed by any team member at any time. It is clear that task and team maintenance behaviours are more desirable than individualistic behaviours.

Consider this

Can you think of any circumstances where either you, or colleagues around you, have displayed some of the behaviours mentioned above?

Teams and leadership

While much of what we have considered so far focuses on team members, it has to be recognised that teams require a degree of leadership and management. The nature of leadership is seen as crucial in ensuring that goals and tasks are completed. Leadership includes motivating others, ensuring individuals feel supported and ensuring clarity exists in terms of roles and outcomes. Leadership as a term can mean many things and most commonly, we may suppose leadership comes from management. While this may not necessarily be the case in all circumstances, leadership implies a sense of authority and accountability. Leadership may be seen as a role specific to a job, role modelling and achieving effective performance from others.

Consider this

What would you expect from a leader of a team?
What would you expect from a manager of a team?
Are there differences and similarities?

Leadership styles

A leader may be formally appointed, imposed on a team, chosen informally or simply emerge naturally. Leaders should be aware, not only of their own role, but of the impact their own role has on others. There are three classic types of leadership styles:

- autocratic
- laissez-faire
- democratic.

The *autocratic leader* dominates team members; things are done under pressure and there is a clear hierarchy of leadership. While this may be seen an outdated, uncomfortable approach to achieving goals, there may be times when it is entirely appropriate. Urgent action may be called for, or a team may need to get to grips with poor performance. A team may be in a state of dysfunction, so a short, sharp autocratic response may jolt things along nicely!

The *laissez-faire leader* prefers to allow the team to sort things out for themselves; shying away from out-and-out authority. This does not necessarily mean that the leader is neglecting to lead, but rather the leader allows teams to own and potentially sort out any issues for themselves. The downside to this is that teams may flounder without very clear leadership. A laissez-faire leader may be seen as ineffective as they do not openly use authority in a way that people may expect. Again, there are some situations where this approach can be appropriate and effective. Highly motivated, skilled and enthusiastic workers who are confident and capable may welcome the opportunity to self-direct. A team may feel empowered if they are given space and time to tackle issues for themselves, without being 'told what to do'.

The *democratic* approach involves a leader consulting and including others in decisions and tasks. Such a leader encourages participation, but does not become too distanced from the team. Democratic leaders can be seen as being unsure of their roles and afraid of using authority. If issues are important and need to be resolved quickly, individuals might find consultation and group decision making frustratingly slow and laborious.

Motivation theories

When considering teams and leaders and managers, the motivation of all involved in service delivery is a huge factor. This is one area which is also well researched and documented in team analysis. A motivational theory is simply a framework of understanding why people do the things they do. In relation to team motivation, such theories consider what motivates workers. In a lifetime of employment, it is important that motivation is not ignored – if someone is not motivated to do a job, the chances are they won't, or that they may well do it badly.

What motivates you?

Consider this
What motivates you towards studying for Social Care?
What motivates you to get up in the morning?

Scientific management

F. W. Taylor (1856–1915) looked at what motivates men and women to work – given the conditions of the 19th century; he concluded that the main motivator for any worker was money! His ideas became known as 'Scientific Management'. Taylor's theorising concluded that people do not like work, and that money was the most important factor inducing people to work hard. While this may seem like quite a drastic interpretation of motivation in the workplace, think about the type of industries which offer cash incentives to productive workers, or bonus payments for achieving targets. In Social Care, it is a fair assumption that getting rich is not a major motivator. Therefore, there must be something else at play.

Herzberg's motivators and hygiene factors

Fredrick Herzberg carried out a survey in the 1950s to try to establish, among a group of engineers and accountants, what aspects of their work they found highly satisfying and which they found dissatisfying. Herzberg referred to these as two factors: 'motivators' and 'hygiene factors'. The motivators were positives which people identified as being positive factors, the hygiene factors being those people were not satisfied with. (He used the term *hygiene* to mean those factors which are required to maintain the organisation but which are not in themselves satisfiers.)

Examples of Herzberg's 'hygiene' needs (or maintenance factors) in the workplace are:

- policy
- relationship with supervisor
- work conditions
- salary
- company car
- status
- security
- relationship with subordinates
- personal life.

Herzberg's research identified that true motivators were other completely different factors, such as:

- achievement
- recognition
- work itself
- responsibility
- advancement.

This may seem quite obvious to some, but Herzberg's work was important – it showed that people's sense of satisfaction and dissatisfaction within a workplace were not just opposites; that those things which motivated people and created enthusiasm and 'settled' staff were not the opposite of those which depressed and demotivated staff.

Activity

The grid below illustrates some of the factors which are seen to motivate workers – can you identify ways in which a Social Care career may meet some of these positive factors? There are some suggestions already made to help you start.

Factor	Example
Achievement	making a difference to someone's life
Recognition	being told by a person who uses services they enjoyed your company
Work itself	enjoying the company of a person who uses services
Responsibility	arranging a review for a person who uses services
Advancement	moving from a sessional worker's post to a full-time worker

Factors which motivate Social Care workers.

Theory X/Theory Y

Another motivation theory is McGregor's Theory X/Theory Y proposal. This model focuses not only on what motivates individuals, but also on what motivates approaches to managing people. The work of McGregor rests on two contrasting assumptions. Theory X states that an individual needs to be coerced, and almost threatened with punishment, to be motivated towards achieving goals. According to Theory X, the average worker is lazy, avoids work if they can, and doesn't want to do any more than needed. Employees have no motivation for themselves, have no ambition and require close supervision and control.

Theory Y, on the other hand, recognises that an organisation's view of people is altogether different. Theory Y recognises that people are productive, are self-motivated and are naturally ambitious. Rewards for achievement generate activity and commitment from employees and, if given freedom, individuals will increase their productivity.

The acceptance of one of these theories leads to a particular management strategy. Theory Y is seen as encouraging teams and organisations to reduce conflict and differentiation, which in turn raises morale and productivity/success/service. Leaders should adopt a supportive, rather than directional, approach. Ultimately, by providing a positive work environment and ethos, an organisation can encourage each individual to feel that the organisational goals are his or her own goals – in Social Care, when considering values, it makes sense that these are shared, positive and believed values, rather than imposed and directed ones.

Goals

Finally, we will consider goals and their importance in forming cohesive teams. Organisations should have clear goals identified – this helps to define activities and roles and gives a clear identity to a group. Goals can be identified as formal and individual or informal. Ideally, as mentioned before in this section, an organisation and the people working within it should hold very similar views. First we will consider formal goals.

Formal goals

Formal goals:

- focus the attention of members on appropriate and productive behaviour providing motivation and reward
- give an indication of what the organisation is like (for example a mission statement)
- form a basis of action plans/strategic plans/team development
- are a basis for procedures and organisational objectives.

Individual/informal goals

Individual or informal goals:

- different people will experience different motivation
- individual goals may differ from person to person
- individual goals may differ from organisational goals.

If individual and organisational goals are

very different, conflict may result. In a conflict situation, performance is likely to be affected and individuals may become disillusioned.

Activity

Consider goals for a moment. Read the scenario below and try to identify some of the factors which relate to goals, influencing the team.

Sadiq has joined a small, private organisation which provides home support to people with learning difficulties. The mission statement of the organisation states that the company 'promotes inclusion, empowerment, involvement and choice for clients – ensuring needs are met and opportunities taken'. Sadiq currently has involvement with one person who uses services, to whom he provides 12 hours of support. He is part of a team of three full-time, three part-time and two sessional staff. Sadiq mainly works alone, as per the Care Plan and Review arrangements. However the person who uses services, Madge, has recently been diagnosed with epilepsy. As her condition is poorly controlled at this point, her staffing ratio has been increased to allow two support staff to support her at any one time. For the first time since joining the organisation, Sadiq is working very closely with a number of colleagues.

Most of his peers seem to be positive and share a strong value base. However, one staff member, Colin, seems less friendly. Colin is a football fan and uses his time in Madge's house to catch up on major football games. Colin eats Madge's bread, uses her teabags and milk, and never seems to bring in any replacements. He says he will soon be leaving his current employment to travel, and wishes he got more wages so he could save more for his planned trip. Sadiq thinks Colin is an abrupt type of person who doesn't really seem to care about people who use services or their needs and wishes. However, more infuriating still for Sadiq is the change in behaviour displayed if Madge's Social Worker or family visits. At these times, Colin appears busy and interested in Madge and cannot do enough for anyone – until the visitors leave. Sadiq plucked up the courage to say something to Colin after a recent visit from Madge's mother. When confronted, Colin just told Sadiq not to be such a 'yes man' and to enjoy his freedom at work as it's a 'cushy number'.

Where personal and organisational goals are compatible, organisations are more effective. Overall, an organisation requires informal and formal goals to be similar or, at least, compatible so that individuals can satisfy their own needs as well as meeting the needs of the service.

Conclusion

Teams and their success are often central to the success of organisations. The success of an organisation often reflects the success of people who use services, and in Social Care that is of the utmost importance. Teamwork, collaboration and joint working are all key aspects of a Social Carer's professional role, and it is useful to be aware of some of the concepts and theories relating to teamwork to equip and enable you to progress your career. By considering, however briefly, some of the better known theories, you are more able to understand some of the dynamics of a team and some of the motivational factors which influence the performance of groups at any point. By being aware of roles and expectations, there is an increased likelihood that any future team issues will be understood from a more objective point of view. Working with others is not always easy, but understanding some of the reasons for conflicts or changes may just ease the process a little!

1. Think about the culture you identify with – it may be linked to your nationality, where you live, your upbringing or your religion. What are the key themes of your culture and how might these differ from other cultures?

2. Draw yourself a Johari Window, and ask someone you know (someone who is quite close to you would be best) to help you with identifying different areas of that window for yourself. If you feel comfortable, attempt a Johari Window on another person and ask them to swap ideas with you.

3. What is meant by the term 'social justice' and what examples of discrimination or injustice in society, can you identify?

4. Identify the main stages of the Care Planning process.

5. What is 'assessment' in Care Planning work and why do we undertake it?

6. How does the Regulation of Care (Scotland) Act 2001 aim to safeguard the rights and protection of care service users?

7. Identify the main themes of the psychodynamic approach to interventions – what are the limitations of this approach?

8. Consider Behavioural Social Work and identify triggers which may precipitate negative behaviour from you (or someone you know) – draw yourself an ABC chart.

9. What are the benefits or strengths of task-centred work?

10. Identify and explain Egan's three-stage model of counselling.

11. Identify and give examples of Belbin's team roles.

12. What are some of the differences between formal and informal goals within an organisation? Identify examples of each.

References: Social care theory for practice

Banks, S. (1995) *Ethics and Values in Social Work (Practical Social Work Series)*, BASW Macmillan Press Ltd: Hampshire.

Caplan, G. (1961) *On becoming a person*, Mifflin: Boston

Coulshed, V. (1994), *Work Practice: An Introduction (Practical Social Work Series)*, MacMillan Press Ltd: Hampshire.

French Jnr., J. P. R., and Raven, B. (1960) 'The bases of social power' in Cartwright, D. and Zander, A. (eds.), *Group dynamics* (pp. 607–623), Harper and Rowe: New York.

Gross, R. (2005) *Psychology: The science of mind and behaviour*, Hodder and Stoughton: Oxford.

Kantel, J. (1994) 'Evaluation of task-centred social work practice', *Clinical Social Work Journal*, Spring: Netherlands.

Miller, J. (2005) *Care Practice for S/NVQ*, Hodder and Arnold: Oxford.

Mulins J, (1994) *Management and Organisational Behaviour*, Pitman Publishing: London.

Winslow, F. (1911) *The principles of scientific management*, Taylor Harpers and Brothers Publishers: New York.

Recommended further reading

Coulshed, V. (1994) *Social Work Practice*, Macmillan: Hampshire.

Howe, D. (2000) *An introduction to Social Work Theory*, Ashgate: Hampshire.

Mulins J, (1994) *Management and Organisational Behaviour*, Pitman Publishing: London.

Thomson, N. (2003) *Promoting Equality*, Palgrave: Basingstoke.

Thomson, N (1994) *Anti-Discriminatory practice*, Macmillan: Hampshire.

Recommended websites

www.mindtools.com/
www.belbin.com
www.bacp.co.uk/

Chapter 2

Social policy and its application to social services provision

Introduction

Social policy is a central area of study for the HNC qualification. It is worth one credit of the overall framework and covers three main outcomes. As ever, your tutor will guide you through the main themes to concentrate upon, and the expected assessment tools appropriate to your Centre's assessment criteria.

At first glance, social policy may seem a strange area to cover. It covers a wealth of legislation, requires you to decipher legalities in relation to workplace policies and practice and also encourages you to form a broad understanding of historical and contemporary issues. To some, it may seem more like a social science or a political topic. However, in the context of Social Care Practice, it is fundamental that you have a basic, working knowledge of legislation and understand how that legislation is made, the factors influencing regulations and laws, and the influences in the making of those laws. There is likely to be room for debate, in your classes, and you will touch upon themes relevant to other areas like Social Care Theory, Sociology and Protection from Abuse. You may also use your understanding of legislation and European and national laws in relation to SVQ elements of your course. This may be the closest topic to politics you come across in your vocational studies; so enjoy the topic and integrate your knowledge with other areas of study; this area of study has real vocational relevance.

The three broad outcomes for this unit are designed to allow students to gain an understanding of current legislation and policy, and apply both local and government policy/legislation in day-to-day practice. In meeting these outcomes, you will:

- consider what shapes and influences social policy
- examine relevant legislation
- identify how legislation makes a difference to actual work practice and how the rights and responsibilities of all individuals are promoted and protected
- consider the role of local policies and procedures in promoting positive care.

You are likely to be assessed, at some point in your course, on how legislation actually impacts upon service delivery; but your individual learning centre will advise you of this. The Social Policy and Social Services Provision topic covers a range of areas, all potentially assessment topics.

In this chapter you will learn:

What is social policy?
We will consider what is meant by the term social policy, linking it to other relevant areas. We will look at the development of social policy and some of the consequences of legislation.

Legislation and how it affects practice:
here we will consider some of the most significant pieces of legislation which play a role in shaping current Social Care work. We will visit Codes of Practice and National Standards and how these impact upon the work of carers. There will also be a brief overview of the Scottish Parliament in this section.

In the workplace – quality of service:
here we will recognise the role of legislation, but also the role of policies and procedures in making a positive difference to standards of care and worker's roles.

What is social policy?

The term 'social policy' may be new to you. It might make you think about rules, laws or regulations and you may also think about social problems. Social policy broadly, is an attempt to tackle social issues: by policy we mean standard rules, and by social we mean society. In contemporary Britain, an item of social policy is essentially a piece of legislation which aims to tackle an issue or issues. In short, an item of social policy can be a law designed to promote or control certain behaviour or situations.

Alcock et al (1998) state that social policy can be described as 'actions aimed at promoting social well-being'.

Government legislation certainly touches on a wide area of all of our lives. It advises us when we can marry, when we can drink alcohol, what wages we can earn and what tax we should pay. It sets rules for what should happen if we become unwell, what benefits we are entitled to if we cannot work and what protocols should be developed when we die! In many ways, it would often seem that the government actually influences most of our lives!

Social policy in the past

The influence of social policy (or law) has not always been as sophisticated as it is today. Two or three hundred years ago, life was very different and the government had a lot less influence on our day-to-day lives. In many ways, people were left to fend for themselves and people in need had to rely upon the church or other forms of charity to survive. People encountered **private problems** which remained private; that is, they were left to deal with difficulties without much intervention.

Case study

An example of a private problem – Mary

Imagine that it is two hundred years ago in Scotland and you are living in a small croft on the outskirts of a village. Your name is Mary, you are 20 years old and have three children. Your children do not go to school, but help with the farm work. Your youngest child is 4 months old, and you carry him around with you as you work on the land. Your other children play nearby, or carry out duties as you instruct them. You grow most of your own food and receive accommodation in a small single-room croft house for your work. You may receive a few pence every month or two in additional payment. You rarely leave the village, and work long hours every day of the week. For entertainment, you socialise with other crofters at important times of the year; you may gather together and play music and sing songs, but you do not travel far. Your second child seems to be unwell – she has a fever and seems to be very weak. She also has a rash starting on her back. You cannot take a lot of time away from your duties – either on the farm or in the home – and your husband cannot support you in any way as he has so much work to do. You grow increasingly concerned about your sick child, and worry that your other family members will pick up this illness too.

1. What options might be open to Mary and her family then?

2. What would be different today for a working family? (Think about free access to medical advice, parental leave from work to look after a sick child and so on.)

Hopefully you have identified that people today have many more rights to access help and services compared to years ago. However, it would be a mistake to think that such laws only came into existence very recently and we will consider the history of the welfare state, in particular, later in the chapter.

What should be clear when you think about Mary's situation in the past is that private problems were clearly difficult for individuals to solve for themselves, given their circumstances. Private problems grow to become **public issues** when people experiencing the issues are highlighted in a wider sense. In modern-day society there are certain issues which we can identify as being those which have more recently moved from the private forum to the public forum.

Private problems encountered by individuals throughout their lifetimes are great and varied; some examples might be ill health, divorce, having to care for others, being unable to register for a dentist, having to wait too long for a medical operation or living without enough money to buy essentials. If these private problems become significant for enough individuals, and if politicians or those in power recognise the impact of these issues, there is a greater likelihood that the private problem will become a public issue. Once in the public domain, it is easier to tackle the problem and seek help through legislation. This is how social policy often comes to bear.

Activity
Can you identify any issues which were once private but which are now areas of social policy?

An example of a change in social policy is domestic violence against women, which was quite often ignored and considered a family issue – it was 'swept under the carpet'. Police and courts often failed to act in domestic violence situations, but now there are increased rights for married people and more services available to protect women from violence.

Culturally this has led to a change in general opinion, so that domestic violence is now seen as something unwanted and illegal; or at least something to be spoken about and debated. In today's society, do you think there are equal rights for men who are victims of domestic violence? Do you think that male victims would be viewed in the same way as female victims?

Another example of a change in attitudes is smoking cigarettes. Smoking was once considered fashionable and even encouraged as a sophisticated pastime. It wasn't uncommon for children to smoke and certainly was not seen as unhealthy but something that everyone did.

Smoking was once considered fashionable and glamorous.

Now attitudes have changed and legislation is tightening the ways in which smoking is allowed and portrayed. Legislation has moved this private issue into the public domain through restricting who can smoke and where, who can buy cigarettes and how much they cost. In addition, anti-smoking campaigns tackle the culture of the positive image of smoking by controlling advertising and using media campaigns to make people aware of the negative consequences of smoking. All of these methods are seen to reinforce the legislation brought about to limit smoking in public places.

There are significant influences on social policy; these include the opinions of people as to whether something is actually a problem or not. Depending upon your own experiences, upbringing and attitudes, what is a problem to one person may not be a problem to another. An example of this may be the foxhunting debate. Recent legislative attempts to ban foxhunting, for some, may not represent an answer to a social problem. It may seem irrelevant or not so important. But how these issues are brought to the public forum can ultimately influence people's reactions to them.

Influences on social policy come from a range of directions. Some examples include:

- party politics
- demographics
- public opinion
- perceived threats to society
- media campaigns
- economics.

Party politics

There is a range of political parties in Scotland and the UK and each party can believe in certain principles above others. For example, the Green Party may prioritise environmental issues over other issues. The Scottish National Party may prioritise issues around independence above others. It is important not to forget that the political machine which passes legislation (the government in power) is a complex one. Governments may push for legislation to be passed which is potentially unpopular, but considered necessary; the example of the smoking restrictions mentioned earlier is potentially unpopular in the short term, but does protect the health of a country's citizens.

Demographics

This is the population make-up of an area at any given time. For example, the current rise in the elderly population in the UK will have a direct impact upon care provision in the future. More demand and greater expectations may be placed upon future governments to provide affordable care for this social group – and care of the highest standards which is accessible and affordable. In addition, the rising retirement population may place a financial burden upon the pension funds available to the country; there may be more reliance upon private, rather than state, funding of income. A knock-on effect of this issue may be flexibility around the retirement age, in order to boost taxation and ensure inclusion of the older population.

Public opinion

The concerns and opinions of the general public have an influence on legislation in certain ways. Politically, in order to win votes and remain in power, a government needs to address issues that are important to the public. Public opinion can be swayed by certain factors like the media, new issues or perceptions of general well-being. For example, in a recession, people who lose their jobs and who have mortgage payments to keep up may ultimately lose their homes. It may become such an issue that politicians attempt to legislate to help people to stay in their homes through periods of unemployment or 'economic downturn' or will concentrate on providing affordable, pleasant housing in the public sector.

Perceived threats to society

In a threatening situation, governments are often expected to act quickly to protect the nation. Examples of perceived threats can be varied but could include issues like 'swine flu'. This could lead to strict international quarantine rules and media coverage of how the threat is handled. Other perceived threats may be about national security and terrorism; this could result in increased security checks at borders, airports and docks and more stringent rules in relation to passport control or applications to travel to certain parts of the world.

Media campaigns

The power of the mass media cannot be ignored in today's society. We are often bombarded with images and information on mobile phones, Internet sites, television, radio and in newspapers and magazines. One of the most reported issues, such as crime, for example, can often influence our perception of the criminal justice system and how safe we feel. We may be led to believe, for example, that sexual offenders are roaming our neighbourhoods unchecked, or that terrorists lurk within our communities, by the way in which certain stories are reported. We may also be appalled to be shown the extent of 'fat cat' salaries or 'pay offs', which leave us asking questions about fairness and the economy. Quite often, the media will highlight a very individual case, but then that single private issue becomes a very public one.

Economics

Providing services to the general population clearly has a financial cost. But a government has to consider all the different financial implications when introducing any new services. It may not be simple to 'balance the economy', and different political parties have different ways of raising and distributing income to fund services and widen provision of public services. An example of this was the introduction of prescription charges (a concept first debated in the 1950s when drug availability and sophistication began to grow). The revenue raised from prescription charges (many tens of millions of pounds) is seen to benefit the many people who still qualify for free prescriptions. However, given the 'universality' and 'free' nature of the NHS, politically these charges were viewed often with suspicion. It is now the case that the Scottish Government is looking to reduce, fix and ultimately scrap the charge; this is a very popular political move, but the cost in loss of revenue is yet to be fully explored.

A brief history of British social policy

British social policy goes back a long way. More recently, it may seem that legislation exists in a multitude of areas, but historically legislation has aimed to tackle some of society's problems.

Helping 'sturdy beggars'

As long ago as the 1500s an Elizabethan Act made provision for the punishment of 'sturdy beggars' and the 'relief of the impotent poor'. We can translate this early piece of legislation to being a real contemporary issue; namely that

begging and giving to the undeserved should be discouraged, yet relief (or help) must be given to those genuinely in need. Today we may have local authorities or councils, which are fairly complex administrative machines, catering for a wealth of local needs.

Activity

Briefly consider the range of services your council provides and make a list of them. You should discover that local councils provide many different local services.
Here are a few examples to start you off:
- recycling and rubbish disposal
- libraries
- schools
- cemeteries and graveyards.

Before local authorities or councils were established, the basic unit of administration was the parish, the size and role of which differed considerably from area to area. Remember too, that local churches also had an influence in caring for the sick and poor.

Workhouses

Workhouses were developed under the Old Poor Laws of the 1600s (a set of Laws later updated in the 1800s to look at welfare). These workhouses were places where those in need could be 'set to work' to earn their keep. The poor may have been poor for a variety of reasons, and with no National Health Service or benefits system such as we have today, the workhouse was a very real alternative to complete destitution for many disabled, elderly, young, orphaned or sick people. For those deemed unfit for work due to old age, illness or disability, 'outdoor relief' was an option, and accommodation granted in 'almshouses'.

In 1697 Scotland had 'houses of correction' and in 1740, Edinburgh opened its first workhouse. The Gilbert's Act of 1788 changed workhouses to poorhouses; that is, offering relief for those unfit for work. For those who were deemed fit for work, the workhouse was often a place to stay, offering basic meals and shelter in return for long hours of work. Men and women could be segregated and the types of work offered were laborious and monotonous. Relief was not solely confined to being offered to people staying in workhouses however; 'out-relief' was sometimes available where cash and benefits could be paid to people outside the workhouse. However, some notoriety was gained in terms of the use of out-relief in the late 1700s, as it allowed employers to pay extremely low wages while workers were forced to top-up their meagre income with relief donations. Parish Officers levied a local parish 'poor rate' where a local tax was paid by every householder within a parish to fund these benefits.

Industrialisation had a massive impact on how people lived and worked.

Life in the workhouse was hard and was always seen as a last resort.

Industrialisation and reform

Times were changing and the Industrial Revolution led to the development of towns, rapid population growth and unemployment. Families and individuals who had lived in rural settings often travelled to the emerging cities to work in the new heavy industries of textile making, coal mining, manufacturing steam power, ship building or iron founding. During the 1800s this rapid industrialisation changed the face of the economy and social policy. In response, the Poor Law of 1834 reformed much of the previous legislation in place. (In Scotland, the Scottish Poor Law was introduced a little later, in 1845.)

Three main principles proposed by those involved in these early laws shaped these reforms.

- Malthus believed that the rise in population was not helped by the 'care' provided by Poor Laws. He believed that such 'care' increased illegitimacy and therefore encouraged a boom in birth rates. He further believed that such a boom would eventually end in mass starvation and the population increasing beyond the country's ability to sustain it.

- Ricardo's 'iron law of wages' proposed that the Poor Laws were undermining the wages of basic workers: 'paupers' were hired out to local employers at a cheaper rate than workers. This led to the fear that those in receipt of Poor Relief would choose to remain on Poor Relief rather than become the lowest paid worker.

- Bentham argued that people should be encouraged not to claim relief at all, and hoped to stigmatise Relief, making it an 'object of wholesome terror'.

The Poor Law Commission between 1832 and 1834 emphasised that there was to be no relief outside the workhouse. In order to test whether people really needed help or not, the work was to be of the most unpleasant kind – men and women would be segregated, food would be adequate but unappealing and strict discipline would abound.

Twentieth-century reforms

The face of industrial Britain had changed and was very different from when it had been a rural economy. The rise in population, and the change in employment habits, meant that now unemployment became a real social issue. In addition to this, ensuring that workers were adequately cared for – and fit to do their work – also impacted upon social responsibilities of the time. Poorly built accommodation for workers led to slums being built up around industrial cities – poor sanitation, overcrowding and disease were prevalent. Unemployment cycles allowed employers to reduce their wages, often leaving families in poverty.

In the early twentieth century, the Liberal government took steps towards a welfare system which stood firmly outside the Poor Law. In order to ensure an efficient infrastructure, the foundations of a social welfare system were established to provide:

- labour exchanges (rather like job centres) for unemployed workers (1905–1909)
- free school meals under the 1906 Education Act
- unemployment and health care provision for citizens under the National Insurance Act of 1911.

The Beveridge report

Basic services and laws continued to be introduced between the First and Second World Wars, but arguably one of the most influential changes to social policy came via the Beveridge Report of 1942. This report was implemented after World War Two by the newly elected Labour government and aimed to provide security 'from the cradle to the grave'.

Beveridge identified 'five giants' to be tackled in post-war Britain:

- want
- disease
- ignorance
- squalor
- idleness.

Activity

Consider Beveridge's 'five giants' – what might we identify under each of his headings? For example; *want* may mean needing something, like food. Look at the table below and give as many examples as you can for each column.

Want	Disease	Ignorance	Squalor	Idleness
e.g. needing food or shelter	e.g. poor living conditions mean infections are rife			

Beveridge's 'five giants'.

In many ways, Beveridge identified an array of social problems which are still considered central to today's society. More importantly, in response to the recognition of these 'giants', some essential legislation came to be established. It is generally agreed that the report formed the welfare state of the time and led to the welfare state we know today.

When we look at the history of social policy, we can identify that it is not necessarily something new and it has taken several forms throughout the last few hundred years. The Beveridge Report tackled some of the major social problems of Britain after the Second World War and it is something we may recognise today in the National Health Service or benefits system, for example. In addition, social policy broadly tackles social problems and issues, but has many influences in its making and is also influenced by a variety of external factors. We cannot always reach agreement on what may or may not be a priority at any point in time, but having a sophisticated welfare and legal system today encourages debate and discussion on crucial issues in our society.

Legislation and how it affects practice

At the core of essential services we must always consider legislation and how it guides our actions and provides limitations. It may not always be obvious that legislation is working 'in the background' as we are not employed as lawyers in Social Care. However, legal awareness has to be demonstrated as part of your studies – showing how that backdrop of legislation influences quality and provision of service. In essence, as a social worker you have to work within the law; this affects health and safety, recording and storing of information, the rights and responsibilities of others and the type of services which can be delivered and how.

Specific legislation

The diagram below suggests some of the more important areas of legislation which you may learn about during your studies. There is a wealth of information on these pieces of legislation on the Internet, and you are likely to receive guidance on areas most appropriate to your course, chosen client group or placement as appropriate. There will be other pieces of legislation too – this is a suggested 'starter guide'.

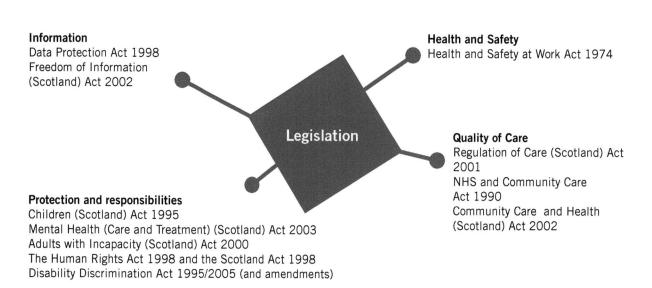

Information
Data Protection Act 1998
Freedom of Information (Scotland) Act 2002

Health and Safety
Health and Safety at Work Act 1974

Legislation

Quality of Care
Regulation of Care (Scotland) Act 2001
NHS and Community Care Act 1990
Community Care and Health (Scotland) Act 2002

Protection and responsibilities
Children (Scotland) Act 1995
Mental Health (Care and Treatment) (Scotland) Act 2003
Adults with Incapacity (Scotland) Act 2000
The Human Rights Act 1998 and the Scotland Act 1998
Disability Discrimination Act 1995/2005 (and amendments)

Some of the essential legislation which informs Social Care practice.

Data Protection Act 1998

This Act was established throughout England, Scotland and Wales in 1998. It applies to anyone who deals with personal information on individuals. It seeks to prompt people who hold information to analyse:

- why they hold it
- whether there is permission to hold it
- who can access it.

The Data Protection Act allows the subject of the information to access that information.

Eight general principles underpin the Act including whether personal information is:

- secure
- adequate and relevant
- kept for no longer than needed.

The Act led to the setting up of an independent public body, the Information Commissioner's Office (ICO), which oversees the use of the Data Protection Act as well as the Freedom of Information Act and others.

Freedom of Information (Scotland) Act 2002

This Act, which came into force on 1 January 2005, recognises that anyone in the world has the right to see information held by Scottish public bodies. These public bodies might include colleges, police boards and local authorities, among others. It includes information on paper, microfiche, video and computer. The type of information which can be seen includes meeting minutes, budgets and services that may be provided or cut. However, personal information is exempt from freedom – as are certain types of information relating to national security. If, however, you want to know why a particular service has been cut or threatened, then under this Act, a local authority should respond to your request.

The Children (Scotland) Act 1995

This Act was a major piece of Scottish legislation, which is borne from the ratification of the United Nations Convention on the Rights of the Child. The Act aims to protect and promote the rights of children in all circumstances and focuses on major themes such as:

- the welfare of the child is paramount and
- any intervention to protect children must be more favourable than no intervention. (This is often referred to as the 'no order' principle.)

In addition the Act recognises and promotes children being given a 'voice' and having their say when decisions are made about their care or welfare.

The four main parts of the Act can be broadly broken down as follows:

Part 1 concerns children, parents and guardians; their roles and responsibilities.

Part 2 deals with local authority and Children's Hearing's promotion of child welfare.

Part 3 covers adoption.

Part 4 deals with general provisions under the Act.

Some key provisions of the Act are summarised below:

- that children who are cared for by the local authority should now be referred to as children who are 'looked after' rather than children 'in care'
- parents have responsibility for children and must exercise these responsibilities even if they no longer live alongside the child. An 'absent' parent should maintain contact with their child
- courts must take into account a child's wishes when dealing with a case and they should take into account the age and maturity of the child. A child aged 12 years is considered to be mature and capable of forming views and contributing to decisions
- children with, or affected by, disabilities are catered for in the Act. Local authorities have specific responsibilities to provide services for children in these circumstances, which minimise the impact of disability
- child protection needs are identified and legal duties and powers described. Interventions in protection cases can be carried out under Child Protection Orders, Child Assessment Orders and/or Exclusion Orders.

Mental Health (Care and Treatment) (Scotland) Act 2003

This important Act replaces much of the 1984 Act and has essential principles at its core; these include:

- non-discrimination
- equality
- informal care (caring for someone without use of compulsory powers)
- respect for carers.

The Act also defines mental disorders as any illness, personality disorder or learning disability, however caused or showing itself. Not only does it define mental disorders, it clearly states what a mental disorder is *not*. A person is not mentally disordered because of only the following:

- they express behaviour which is likely to or does, cause alarm, distress or harassment, or by acting in a way no person would prudently act
- their sexual orientation, transsexualism, sexual deviancy or transvestitism
- a dependence on, or use of, alcohol or drugs.

The Act details how Compulsory Treatment Orders (CTO) can be applied for and used with strict criteria enforced to ensure the best practice in such incidents.

The Act very clearly specifies the rights of the individual to have access to independent advocates as needed. Local authorities and health boards must jointly ensure the availability of advocacy services in their area. Local authorities also have a duty to provide or secure care and support for people who have, or have had, a 'mental disorder' and are not in hospital. Local Authorities must also assess the needs of the individual to stipulated time frames.

The Act also set up a new, independent body called the Mental Health Tribunal for Scotland which makes decisions about applications made under the Act. The tribunal consists of a president and around 300 members; legal members, medical members and general members.

The Act also recognises the Mental Welfare Commission, an independent organisation which monitors the carrying out of the Act. Any general points of interest or concerns are investigated by the commission which can then bring such matters to the attention of various parties; from Scottish ministers in parliament to the Care Commission.

Case study

Tanesha

Tanesha lives in a small flat and receives 24-hour care from a voluntary agency to help her manage her severe mental illness. She has been unwell since her mid-teens and is now in her mid-thirties.

While she manages her home well enough, her social life is very limited and she can often act on impulse which others may interpret as being moody. When Tanesha feels well, she hides her medication and doesn't tell anyone. This has happened before, and as a consequence, for a while, her medication was administered intravenously. As part of her progressive support, after a Review, it was decided that she should be given oral medication again; this has worked well, until recently. The situation came to a head when Tanesha had to be taken to hospital by the police, who found her wandering the local town centre in her night dress. Her feet were cut where she had trodden on debris on the ground, and her handbag was empty – the police feared she had been mugged by someone. When Tanesha couldn't tell them her name or where she lived, and became extremely emotional, they contacted the local hospital which was able to identify her. An ambulance was sent to collect her to be an in-patient, pending a full review the following day.

Consider the mental health legislation outlined above and how it might relate to Tanesha's situation.

Adults with Incapacity (Scotland) Act 2000

This is one of the earliest items of social policy passed by the Scottish Parliament and is in place to protect vulnerable adults who are unable to make financial or welfare decisions alone.

While the general assumption is that adults are capable of making informed choices and their own decisions, this Act recognises that some individuals, perhaps because of dementia, significant communication difficulties or enduring learning difficulties, are more vulnerable. This Act uses courts to grant various interventions in people's affairs and welfare decision, through the Office of the Public Guardian (Scotland). This office administrates and considers each application and concludes on the appropriate level of intervention appropriate to any case.

Anyone authorised to make decisions on behalf of another must apply the following principles:

- benefit to the person – is the impaired individual in need of assistance?
- least restrictive option
- taking account of the individual's wishes
- consulting with relevant others – is the whole family aware of an intervention, for example?
- encouraging the individual to use existing skills and develop new ones.

There are various interventions which can be granted to allow a third party to take on financial, decision making and welfare responsibilities for another. Some examples of this include the following.

- Power of Attorney – this can be granted to someone to act on another's behalf in relation to financial matters or about welfare decisions. This essentially allows someone to act on another's behalf in relation to day-to-day maintenance of living standards.
- If someone is given the power to access finances, for example, there may be limitation on what types of financial affairs are accessible. General accounts and benefits issues may be accessed, but not, for example, investments or more complex financial portfolios.
- A guardianship order can be used to cover property, personal welfare, health or financial matters and is more likely to be granted where an individual has long-term needs or has never had the 'capacity' to govern such matters themselves.
- In some circumstances, where practical, care homes and hospitals may be permitted to manage limited funds and property of residents who are unable to do so themselves. The Mental Welfare Commission has a role in protecting users of this Act – from carrying out visits to guardians to providing advice and information on application issues.

Consider this

Read and think about the following two scenarios about Corrance and Jack.
How might the Adults with Incapacity Act be applied to each?

Case study

Corrance

Corrance is 32 years of age and has a moderate learning difficulty. The youngest of five children, Corrance lives with her mother who is in her 70s. Her dad died a few years ago, and her brothers and sisters often pop over to see her and her mum. Her mum does everything she can for Corrance and they get on very well. They manage the bungalow they live in well, and take it in turns to cook and clean. However, Corrance's mum is unwell with a bad cold and she is feeling she has too much to do. Corrance's sister Dianne has asked if she can help, even by collecting benefits from the local post office for both Corrance and her mum. She doesn't want to do any more than is needed but feels, as the winter draws in, that this might be really helpful for the two of them. She also wants her mum to get direct debit payments sorted for the bills, as their local post office is closing soon and the nearest one will be too far away.

Case study

Jack

Jack is 79 years of age and has moderate to severe dementia. His wife felt she could not cope with his illness and the family agreed that Jack should move to a care home on a full-time basis a year ago. Jack is the owner of the marital home, and now his wife, Edie, wants to sell up and move to a smaller bungalow near her daughter. Edie also wants to cash in some bonds they both opened when they were married. Jack is hardly able to recognise his family at all and the family are worried about how to proceed.

The Human Rights Act 1998

The Human Rights Act of 1998 applies to all public authorities – making it unlawful for organisations like the police, local councils or government departments to violate the rights of people, as contained in the European Convention on Human Rights. The Scotland Act of 1998 simply underpins Scottish Parliament's commitment to the Human Rights Act of 1998. This means that any laws or pieces of legislation must be compatible with the wider sense of human rights and cannot go against this. Examples of rights enshrined in the Human Rights Act include:

- right to life
- prohibition of torture
- prohibition of slavery and forced labour
- right to a fair trial.

Many of the rights (or articles) contained in the Act may seem obvious, but there may be situations where individuals can go to court to have their human rights examined. In certain circumstances, individuals may even proceed to the European Court of Human Rights based in Strasbourg.

Looking at the first example of 'right to life', there are cases examining abortion of foetuses and euthanasia which have challenged this article. In Care, abusive practice towards vulnerable people on an institutional or personal level may be interpreted as 'torture'. This Act is very important in underpinning rights across a wide spectrum of circumstances, and is particularly relevant to vulnerable people in less advantaged situations.

Disability Discrimination Act 1995/2005 (and amendments)

This Act of 1995 (reflecting strengthened powers and amendments in 2005) aims to end discrimination for disabled people in everyday life. It specifically relates to goods, services, employment and education; functions of public bodies and the renting or buying of land and property.

The Disability Discrimination Act considers someone disabled if they have a physical or mental impairment that has a substantial and long-term adverse effect on their ability to carry out normal day-to-day activities. The previous Disability Rights Commission has been taken over by the Equality and Human Rights Commission in 2007; this oversees the Act and offers individual advice and assistance in matters

relating to disability, and other issues.

Areas to which the Disability Discrimination Act can be applied include all employment situations (except for the armed forces) and it aims to promote inclusion by expecting an employer to make 'reasonable adjustments' to include disabled people. This may mean changing interviewing and recruitment procedures, altering buildings to ensure fair access for all, or ensuring awareness training is offered to staff.

A recently published Equality Bill (you will read more about Bills later in the chapter) may look at bringing together various equality legislations (including the Disability Discrimination Act) under a new legislative framework in 2011.

Regulation of Care (Scotland) Act 2001

This Act has had a major influence on the delivery and quality of care and covers a range of services, including:

- care homes for adults
- nursing agencies
- housing support services
- schools
- accommodation for offenders
- adoption and fostering services
- children's early education.

This Act supports the welfare of people who use services, and staff, through the regulation of services being offered, the standardisation of practice and the inspection of services. Two bodies set up under the Act are the *Scottish Social Services Council* and the *Scottish Commission for the Regulation of Care* (or Care Commission).

Scottish Social Services Council

The SSSC is responsible for registering Social Care Workers in Scotland and regulating their training and education. The SSSC also publishes Codes of Practice for Scottish Social Care workers and employers and, overall, is responsible for raising standards across the sector in terms of staff competency and public confidence; and it has the responsibility to register service staff (in the way that nurses and teachers may be expected to register with their appropriate bodies).

Scottish Commission for the Regulation of Care

The Commission is the independent regulatory body, set up under the Regulation of Care (Scotland) Act, and it inspects, registers and deals with complaints about services, as well as promoting National Care Standards and their application. The National Care Standards are written by Scottish ministers and are available via the Care Commission. In terms of providing useful boundaries for the sector, the six Standards are clear and succinct, underpinning all care services provided:

- dignity
- privacy
- choice
- safety
- realising potential
- equality and diversity.

No matter what service you are using, in whatever part of the country, these standards must underpin all decisions and actions. It is against these six standards that the commission will report and respond to any inspection issues raised during an Inspection of a service. In conjunction with the work of the SSSC, this commission aims to raise the standard of services for all, including employers and employees.

NHS and Community Care Act 1990

Although it is an older Act, coming into full force during 1993, this Act is very important in terms of establishing community care as a political and social concept. It was brought in by Margaret Thatcher's Conservative government, and led to the closure of many traditional institutions and the birth of the idea of needs-led, community-based services. As the name suggests, it brought about much joint working between medical services (such as psychiatry) and community services.

Local authorities were charged with assessing the needs of individuals as required and then providing care either directly or indirectly to meet that person's needs. The emergence of different sectors of care led to a mixed economy, where several services could work to provide holistic support to an individual in the community setting (group homes, small-scale housing complexes or, indeed, in an individual's own home).

The mixed sectors of care included:

- **statutory** services (those required directly by law, like doctors, dentists, social workers and so on)
- the **voluntary** sector (which included charities and not for profit organisations)
- the **private** sector (for profit organisations like some nursing homes).

This dramatically reduced the numbers of people who were cared for in large hospitals or institutions, often being socially isolated and receiving general rather than individualised care.

This Act also set up provision for complaints to be made about services; inspections to be carried out and for Local Authorities to publish Care Plans for their area highlighting service provision and anticipated provision.

Community Care and Health (Scotland) Act 2002

The Community Care and Health (Scotland) Act came into effect in late 2002 and allowed further support and assessment to be carried out for carers. It strengthened the rights of people (including children) who care for others regularly, or substantially, to be assessed in their own right.

This Act then put conditions upon local authorities to assess carers specifically, and take account of the demands placed upon a carer in such a situation. Ultimately support could then be offered to the significant numbers of unpaid carers in Scotland. Furthermore, local authorities were encouraged to reinforce direct payment measures which are otherwise less firmly enforced in law.

The introduction of this Act also brought financial implications for those who financed their own care. It introduced the concept of free personal care and/or health care (with certain provisions attached) further enhancing the quality of care received by individuals.

Health and Safety at Work Act 1974

The Health and Safety at Work Act (HASAW) was a major contribution to modern safety standards in all workplaces, in all sectors. For the first time, a major responsibility was put upon not only an employer, but upon all staff in ensuring their working environment is safe and effective. While Social Care workers may not face the same potential hazards as other industries (such as mining, heavy industry or construction), the relevance of this Act is no less important.

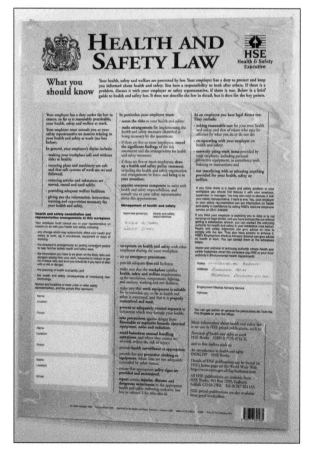

Signs like this must be displayed in all buildings used by employers and employeer.

This law basically rules that employers must ensure 'as is reasonably practicable' the health, safety and welfare of not only their employees, but sub contractors and the general public too.

Some of the areas covered by this, and subsequent legislation, includes reporting of accidents and incidents; the notification of certain diseases or illnesses; the proper hygienic preparation and management of food hygiene; and risk assessment specific to job function and tasks.

Under the broad umbrella of health and safety, it is also important to be aware of any Personal Protective Equipment required in a workplace – aprons or gloves, for example. In addition, regulations also exist to maintain the safe storage and use of chemicals and this may include household items like paint, bleach or other cleaning materials.

In some instances of care, a service may be provided in an individual's own home, but compliance with health and safety legislation is still required. In addition, risk assessments must be completed for any potentially hazardous activities or events which require risk analysis. Many workplaces use standard forms to enable staff teams to consider the risks to themselves and their clients in the performing of duties.

There are other laws and regulations which are also relevant to Social Care and, depending upon your chosen sector or workplace, some may be mentioned in this chapter. To help you to understand the context of different legislation, and how the laws can interplay, consider the next exercise – using the suggested scenarios.

Activity

Read the scenarios below and try to think about which laws and Acts considered above may apply to each. There may be more than one.

Case study

June

June is a 70-year-old woman who currently lives in her own bungalow but she recently fell at home and broke her hip. Since her accident, she has been in hospital and her rehabilitation has been slow. Her family live close by, but feel she is unable to return to her own home without a package of professional help. Her two daughters try to do some things for their mother but as they both work full time, and have their own families, they believe additional help is needed. The hospital staff are not happy to let June go home without further support, as they feel she will be unable to care for herself.

Case study

Ashan

Ashan is 7 years of age and has been missing a lot of school recently. This has become such a concern, that his school has tried to ask his parents to attend a joint meeting. They are having trouble contacting anyone, and letters have been returned unopened to the school. One of Ashan's friends told his teacher that Ashan has been looking after his grandmother recently – she lives in a nearby town and the family have moved.

Case study

Brian

Brian works as a carer in a privately run nursing home. He has been happy in his work for almost five years and enjoys the company of the people who use services. However, Brian recently had to take time off work due to a bad back problem which he feels is made worse by all the lifting he does at work. He knows the home is understaffed at the moment, as there are several unfilled vacancies for care assistants, and he has done as much overtime as he can. Brian now thinks he will have to go to the doctor to be signed off work as the pain is getting so bad. He feels very bad about this, knowing that it will only make the staffing problem worse. He is also worried about the quality of care which the residents are receiving as all of the staff are under so much pressure.

The Scottish Parliament

In 1999 the Scottish Parliament was brought to Edinburgh, after a Labour referendum in the run-up to the 1997 elections. A devolved parliament is not the same as a full or independent parliament. Scottish Parliament, made up of 129 members, has certain powers of legislation – these are devolved powers. However, Westminster still has overall power in Scotland on certain matters. Devolved powers include areas such as education, prisons and health and can be decided by the Scottish Parliament; reserved powers, or powers maintained by Westminster, are mainly about UK-wide matters or international matters, for example going to war. Scottish legislation can be identified by the use of Scotland in the title, and the date for such legislation is likely to be after 1999 (when the devolved parliament was set up).

European Parliament

It is not just the Westminster or Edinburgh parliaments which can influence our practice in Social Care, but also the European Parliament. There are 785 members of the European Parliament, representing 27 member states of the European Union. The European Parliament produces guidance or legislation which is relevant to standardising issues across the varying countries of the European Union. Examples of such areas include environmental legislation, consumer rights, equal opportunities and the free movement of workers. One area of European legislation pertinent to Social Care is the Working Time Directive of 1993 where the UK had chosen an 'opt out' clause for a maximum working week of 48 hours (allowing workers to agree to work over the optimum weekly hours). The European Parliament will review this clause as discussions continue.

How is legislation made?

The Scottish Parliament designs and delivers legislation tackling Scottish issues; this includes care services, health services and other welfare areas. The process which leads to legislation being passed is important to understand.

Often, legislation is preceded by reports or 'papers' which look at particular areas of concern; working groups can be set up by the Parliament to consider issues and may include members of the public, academics, politicians and other interested parties. An example of this is the Griffiths Report which commented upon NHS services and management in the 1980s. A now well-known quote from this relatively short report stated:

'In short if Florence Nightingale were carrying her lamp through the corridors of the NHS today she would almost certainly be searching for the people in charge.'

Griffiths' findings directly impacted upon the release of the NHS and Community Care Act 1990, which was also influenced by responses to the Griffiths Report in the form of a White Paper called 'Caring for People'. This is just one example of the ways various mechanisms can influence the eventual release of legislation.

The legislative process

Before legislation can come into effect, there are various 'stages' of progression. In some cases not all stages are used, in others, it may take considerable time for a piece of legislation to be finalised.

In general, the process can be described as shown in the diagram below.

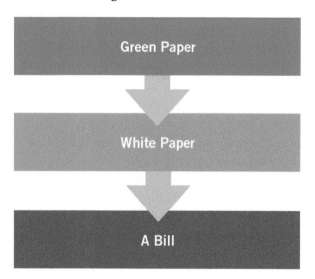

The legislative process follows different stages.

The earliest stage of producing a Green Paper (a stage not always completed, depending upon the circumstances under which a piece of legislation is being considered) involves the government providing consultation documents on a proposed area. The document will generally outline broad options and ideas being considered and others will be invited to comment and consult on these early proposals.

The White Paper is the next stage, which is a tidied, amended and more in-depth consideration of the Green Paper's content. White Papers may also represent the first intention of a government to release new legislation if the Green Paper stage has been missed for some reason.

Again, there is usually a consultation period for White Papers, where interested parties are invited to comment upon proposals and it is unlikely that there are significant variations between a Green and White Paper.

A Bill is the next stage of the legislative process. After the closure of a consultation period, when considerations have been made, a Bill is a legally drafted paper with a variety of clauses and provisions contained within. Again, on some occasions a Bill may be the first stage of a piece of legislation.

Stages of a Bill

Not all Bills follow the same parliamentary process but generally Bills are considered through three stages, as shown below. At any stage a Bill can 'fall' and fail to be progressed further.

Stage One	The Bill's principles are considered and are agreed to. Various committees may be involved in this to consider how new proposals may affect existing laws. At this stage, significant revision and re-consideration may be given as to how the Bill will be constructed.
Stage Two	Parliamentary Committee considers the details for the Bill. Each part of the Bill may be considered in detail and separately.

Stage Three	Final consideration is given to the Bill and the Parliament decides whether it should be passed or rejected. At least a quarter of MSPs must be involved in a vote on the matter; for, against or abstain. Up to half of the Stage Two material can be referred for further amendment, but if passed the Bill must go to the Presiding Officer, to the Queen, for 'Royal Assent'. Upon receiving Royal Assent, the Bill becomes an Act of the Scottish Parliament.

The three stages of a Bill.

There are also three types of Bill:

- an Executive Bill
- a Members' Bill
- a Committee Bill.

An Executive Bill is one which is introduced directly from the government. An example of this is the Regulation of Care Act 2001.

A Members' Bill is introduced by a member, or members of parliament. An example of this is Tommy Sheridan's introduction of the Bill for the Abolition of Warrant Sales.

A Committee Bill is one introduced by one of the Parliamentary Committees, for example, the Equal Opportunities Committee introduced a Bill on Domestic Violence.

In Westminster, Committees cannot introduce legislation; however, in Scotland they can, which reflects the Scottish Parliament's commitment to encourage maximum participation in legislative processes.

Activity

You are a member of a new mini-parliament and have a brand new country to run. Identify, based on your current views of society, a law that you would like to pass. You may, in doing so, consider things which annoy or worry you now. What would you change?

Now consider the following:

What is the law enforcing?

Who is it aimed at?

How might it be used/misused by others?

Are there other laws you might need to pass, to allow this new one to be enforced?

Is the law you have considered unfair towards any particular people or groups who may not understand why it is in place?

Now think about the legislative process discussed and draw up an outline of your law and what it should achieve. Are you going to include any penalties if the law is broken? If so, who manages this and how will penalties be applied? Is it fair and equal across the whole of your society?

Map out a chart of how you must address each stage of the process of introduction and what objections, at each stage, you might anticipate and from whom.

In the workplace – quality of service

One of the major influences on the types of service delivered to potential users was the NHS and Community Care Act 1990. The significance of this legislation led to a 'mixed economy of care', where a variety of services from the different sectors could be brought together to meet the needs of an individual. These sectors are broadly identified as:

- statutory
- voluntary
- private.

The Community Care White Paper identified four key components for services which aim to meet the needs of individuals:

- services should be flexible and responsive to individuals and their carers
- a range of options and choices should be available to an individual
- services should intervene no more than is necessary
- services should concentrate upon those with the greatest identified need(s).

Six service objectives were then identified:

- to promote the development of domiciliary day and respite services to enable people to stay in their own homes
- to ensure that service providers make practical support for carers a high priority

- proper assessment of need and
- good case management are recognised as the cornerstone of high-quality care
- agencies must be clear about responsibilities and accountable for performance
- to ensure better value for taxpayers' money by introducing new funding mechanisms.

The thrust of the Act was to ensure a new dynamic in service delivery, joined-up working, accountability, needs-led and flexible, responsive services and better value for money.

Activity

Consider the following case study scenario and identify how the introduction of these principles could change the type of care received and how it is delivered, and through what types of services.

Case study

Donnie

Donnie is a single man, aged 47 years. He has progressive ME and had to give up his house as he was unable to manage the stairs. He walks with the aid of a walking frame but, on bad days, he may be forced to use a wheelchair for even the shortest of journeys. He has trouble preparing meals, finds it hard to eat and drink properly and struggles to use a bath or use the toilet comfortably. He knows he will eventually need a lot of care, but hopes to maintain his links with his community.

To address his care needs, Donnie's sister has encouraged him to sell his house (left to him by his parents who died some time ago) and go into a private nursing home. The charge for this is around £490 a month. He has savings and the money from his house, but is worried about how much the service is costing.

Donnie's daily routine is to be assisted to get up and washed, and he then takes breakfast in his room. He has a room with a nice en suite toilet and shower and can mostly manage to take care of himself when toileting; although sometimes he has had to pull the buzzer for help. He will generally stay in his room most of the day as he doesn't feel he gets much conversation with the elderly residents, if he goes to the lounge. Because all of the other residents are very elderly and frail, he doesn't want to burden the very busy staff with his problems. About once a week his sister will visit, and depending on the weather, they may go for a short walk around the park. His sister brings Donnie any new clothes he needs, but he thinks she dresses him up as an older man! He tries to take lunch in the communal dining hall, where he sees how poorly some of the other residents are. While he likes to try and manage his eating without help, sometimes the staff assist him – but they hardly have any time and he doesn't get a chance to chat. One day, he spilled his soup and no one got him another bowl; the staff just took him to the toilet to change his trousers and wheeled him back to his room. As a result, his sister brings him boxes of biscuits which he nibbles on, when peckish. She also brings him cartons of juice, which he can manage to open and drink by himself. The rest of the time he remains in his room, watching TV or listening to the radio, and he takes his main dinner in his room. But as he is at the end of a corridor, the food is often a bit cold by the time the trolley reaches him.

Each day seems to run into the next and he dreams of doing the things he used to do – riding his motorcycle, reading books on science fiction and playing in a jazz band or even having a good curry. Donnie doesn't want to feel sorry for himself but cannot imagine spending the rest of his life like this – he also knows that the money in the bank won't go on forever.

In brief, you should have identified that Donnie's needs were not being met on an individualised basis here: emotionally he is isolated, mentally he is not stimulated and the cost of the service to him is a personal financial burden outweighing the benefits he seems to gain. It would be much more realistic to maintain Donnie's independence through a mixed economy of care, sustaining his place in the community and encouraging his physical well-being.

Funding care

Care is an expensive business, in terms of finances. In caring for someone, economically there is no end item produced and sold; and often needs will increase for us all, as we age and become more inclined to suffer ill health. At certain points in our lives we may receive higher levels of intervention, and we have to rely upon different services to see us through the particular stages of our life cycle. An example of this might be reliance upon the NHS and midwifery services if we start a family, or support from the government financially if we become unemployed.

Birth	Midwifery and specialist medical services
	Monitoring for development by professionals
Childhood	Education services
	Protection services
Adolescence	Education services
	Sexual health services
Adulthood	GP and doctors
	Additional support from social work staff
Middle age	Employment services
	Benefit services
Older adulthood	Adaptations to home
	Benefits services

We need different services at different stages of our lives.

Even people without additional needs will require services at certain points in their lives, as circumstances change either temporarily or more permanently. The expectation is that we will have high-quality and responsive services for ourselves and our loved ones. But it is impossible to ignore the question of how those services will be funded.

Statutory services

Statutory services are those required by law to be provided by local authorities or other government bodies. An obvious example is the National Health Service, or social work departments in each locality. (Can you identify any others?)

Such services are funded by the government where a national budget is set via the Scottish Executive. Each area, whether local authority area or health board area, is required to manage its budget accordingly; allowing some autonomy in providing appropriate services to meet local demand. This central funding may be topped up from specific grants to respond to changes in legislation (for example, mental health specific projects) but the funds are largely fixed within a financial period. This encourages local authorities to manage their own budgets responsibly; but in times of economic hardship, decisions may be made which essentially cut back on peripheral services which may have been offered.

More recent changes by the SNP government have lessened the amount of power the Scottish Executive has over what local authorities spend their money on. Previously, money from government could be ring-fenced to be spent only in certain areas. While this guaranteed that priorities were set, it did not always allow local areas to respond to local needs. Now, for example, a local authority (providing, to government, an annual report on efficiency and financial status) may move money from tackling urban poverty to dementia services, for example. This may reflect an already successful tackling of one issue, which now requires less funding, to be replaced by a more pressing issue. While this is not a flawless system, this change has been largely welcomed.

Voluntary services

Voluntary services are a major section of the care economy in Scotland. The SCVO (Scottish Council for Voluntary Organisations) is an umbrella organisation which aims to advance Scotland's voluntary sector. A voluntary agency is one which does not operate for profit and while many organisations can hold significant budgets, there is not an 'owner' of the company to make decisions and profit financially. (What voluntary organisations are you aware of?)

Local authorities have funded much of the work of the main voluntary organisations: either through the benefit of local authorities making grants available to this sector, or through the payment of contracts for work agreed. An example of this may be that the local authority pays for a voluntary organisation to provide 18 hours a week of specialist support to an individual with autism. The voluntary organisation would bid for this work at a cost, and the local authority would choose the supplier of the service based on agreed criteria – quality, cost, reputation and so on.

Voluntary organisations may also be eligible to apply for Lottery Funds, or from grant-making trusts (which themselves may be charitable organisations). Voluntary organisations will often undertake fundraising events in order to supplement any existing income, or just so that they can continue to operate. These may be sports events, charity shops or sales or even sponsorship deals. (Have you encountered any of these? Think about charity shops you have seen or raffle tickets you have been asked to buy.)

Private sector services

The private or independent sector largely consists of organisations which are run for profit. Private sector businesses provide services which people pay for; unlike voluntary services, profits must be made for the individual or companies which are owners of such services. One example of this may be private nurseries offering care for babies and children aged under three.

Unpaid carers

Not all care is carried out by recognised services: it is also the case that unpaid carers provide invaluable support, not only to those for whom they care but for the services already available. With the rise of the elderly population, the Scottish Executive considers unpaid caring as being an area of increase in the future and has pledged to increase support available to those who are in this position. This includes additional funding to allow respite for carers and a focus on Carers' Allowance being maximised by individuals.

In 2005, the Scottish Executive published a report, 'The future of unpaid carers in Scotland – headline report and recommendations' which identified principles of:

- greater respect and recognition of unpaid carers
- the development of a rights-based policy framework to support unpaid carers.

The report considered the position of unpaid carers in the context of human rights and recognised the need for various changes in current practice to include: flexible working/employment options for carers; providing better and more frequent respite breaks; offering carers cash payments rather than only services so that they can identify what care should be brought in themselves; a greater degree of emotional support.

Case study

Jean

Jean is a 40-year-old woman who is married with two children under the age of ten years. Her husband works shifts in a local factory. Three years ago she was involved in a serious road accident and she suffered a neck and spine injury. At one point, her expected chances of survival were very slim. Jean also sustained a head injury which has left her a bit forgetful; her speech can be slurred and she cannot concentrate for long. Because of the accident, Jean uses a wheelchair and has no sensation below her waist. She could no longer carry on with her part-time job in a supermarket. However, she is still active and takes her role as a mother very seriously. She has a catheter fitted and is visited by a catheter nurse on a regular basis.

Upon Jean's release from hospital, an assessment team considered her needs – involving local medical services and the social work department. As Jean's husband has a history of mental health problems, it was decided that she, and her family, would require support after her rehabilitation.

Jean's children have been affected by the trauma of the episode; they thought they might lose their mum altogether and their dad became distant and at times, hostile, while their mum was in hospital.

They missed school, were seen to be unkempt by their teachers, and began to disrupt classes. As a result, they are now subject to voluntary involvement with a youth service run by a local charity.

Housework can be an issue for Jean, who has employed a local woman to assist with cleaning her house for three hours a day twice a week. She also has the children's clothes ironed by a local company which collects and delivers the clothes.

Jean's husband has slightly reduced his work hours under a flexible agreement with his employer and he now attends a day centre, on a Saturday, run by other people who suffer with mental health problems. He enjoys these events; he follows football with his friends and has already made some suggestions about what else the group could offer. His confidence has soared and he enjoys this leisure time immensely.

Jean has received confirmation that she will be eligible to attend a head injury rehabilitation service run by the local authority as a day centre user. This fits in with her children's school times and will allow her to learn ways to overcome the limitations she feels she faces. In the first instance, this will be for two days a week.

An ongoing insurance claim, relating to her accident and which has taken months to process, is about to be paid. This will secure the family's immediate financial status, and allow them to consider converting their garage to a downstairs bedroom for Jean and her husband.

1. Which elements of the services provided may be statutory?

2. Which services may be private?

3. Which of the services provided may be voluntary?

Local policies and procedures

With so much legislation in place to protect users of services, staff and employers, it is important to recognise the role of local protocols and policies. Often, these are an organisation's attempt to guide practice within the existing legal framework. If, for example, a new law is in place, many workplaces will offer training and update policies accordingly.

Every workplace will differ in the type, quantity and style of policy and procedure documents. Some workplaces may hold thick binders of policies; others may cover some policies in inductions or have a database available online. In most workplaces, it would be anticipated that staff are familiar with different policies and how to apply them. If policies are *not* working, it is often the case that an organisation will offer some form of feedback device, to allow suggestions to be made by those on the 'shop floor'. It is also important to recognise that even employment contracts can contain important procedures and policies.

Activity
Take a few minutes to think about a place where you have worked – it need not be a care environment – what type of policies, guidelines or procedures were you aware of?

Some examples might include:
- weekly hours of contracted work
- fire evacuation procedures
- reporting sickness or time off work
- supervision or training procedures.

Many workplaces have similar guidelines; in care environments some guidelines may be specific to individual projects or services. To sum up, legislation, policies and procedures all help to set boundaries of work, to clarify who is responsible for what and what is expected of different people.

Campaigns and charters

In conjunction with legislation and policies, there are valuable campaigns or charters which enable certain issues to be highlighted in society. One such example is the 'see me' campaign in Scotland. This campaign is focused on tackling stigma and inequality in the area of mental health. This influences people's reactions and actions towards people experiencing mental ill health and impacts upon our perception of individual rights. This campaign includes media information, websites and fact sheets among other things; the aim is to promote better rights and clearer responsibilities towards those with mental illness.

It is not just the area of mental health which has such influences. Another example of an additional mechanism used to enforce rights and responsibilities is Scotland's Children's Charter called 'Protecting Children and Young People: The Charter'. This charter was initially launched by First Minister, Jack McConnell, on 22 March 2004. The Charter proposes thirteen statements which will enable all those involved with children and young people to experience better relationships, understand situations more fully, and tackle discrimination and prejudice. The Charter is aimed at everyone; including police, education workers, neighbours, communities and families. Examples of some of the statements (derived from consultation with young people by Save the Children) include:

- **'get to know us'** - being aware of building positive relationships with individuals based on trust, respect and being genuine

- **'speak with us'** – don't make assumptions about 'normal' family life and recognise the diversity of young people

- **'take us seriously'** – this represented some children's views that they had to work harder than adults to be believed

- **'think about our lives as a whole'** – be aware that an action taken in one area will have an impact in another area.

The Charter includes highly relevant information which guides us all on better interactions with each other and reinforces many of the more technical and legal measures covered in official legislation, like the Children (Scotland) Act 1995. Other Children's Charters also exist, such as the 'Who Cares? Scotland Charter of Rights' aimed at young people who are looked after.

In 2002, Rehab Scotland (now named Momentum) launched their *'Client's Charter of Rights and Responsibilities'* aimed at ensuring disabled people in Scotland have an equal voice. This charter was launched by Malcolm Chisholm, Minister for Health and Community Care, and represented feedback from Rehab Scotland's users of services.

Again, the use of charters allows political influence to come from very real experiences – with charters being a valuable, holistic guide to good practice and topical issues, often not available through legislation alone.

Together with local policies and procedures and legislation, the use of charters can further strengthen the compliance of organisations and individuals to innovative expectations. However, enforceable standards come from the Care Commission's Inspection of registered services and the powers which can be imposed on organisations are very real.

Services must comply with National Care Standards or face the consequences.

Inspection

The Care Commission (set up by the Regulation of Care (Scotland) Act 2001) inspects registered services and has statutory responsibility to ensure care providers are fit to provide a service, comply with regulations, and take account of the National Care Standards. Although the Commission seeks to promote continuing improvement of services, punitive action can also be taken against services failing to improve, or comply, with standards. Inspections are usually undertaken annually, and need not always be announced.

The Commission also has a duty to investigate complaints against a service and Enforcement Notices may be issued which specify actions to be taken within an agreed time frame. Ultimately, in extreme circumstances, failure to comply with agreed standards can lead to the cancellation of a service's registration. Most organisations, however, have internal procedures which prevent situations from being so serious that such actions are needed.

Case study

Inspection of Rose Home – Day Centre for Adults with Learning Difficulties

I entered the main foyer which looked neat and tidy. The reception staff asked me to sign in the visitor's book and the area was free from hazards. All staff wore name badges.

I progressed to the kitchen area. I am told that people who use services enjoy a cooking group every morning here – the group rotates on a daily basis so the kitchen is not overcrowded. While the area was clean, I noted there were no hand washes available, or hand drying facilities. The group was meant to start at 10 am; at the time of my visiting, at 11 am, the group still hadn't started. I asked a member of staff about this and they said they were short staffed today. I then moved to the day room.

This room was very neat and tidy with a television available, a piano and various craft materials were on show. About six people who use services were in the room at this time and I chatted to a few of them. Some respondents told me they were bored today as they had hoped to have a trip to the local bowling alley.

They didn't seem to be aware of any reason as to why this trip was not happening.

As I left the day room, I noticed that one of the day centre clients was sitting in his wheelchair, rather than in a soft chair. I asked a passing member of staff if he was going out; she replied that he had just arrived a short while ago, and she couldn't move him alone and was waiting for a relief worker to appear for shift.

I then checked the toilets in the corridor – none had locks on the door, or lights indicating their occupancy. One had a bin overflowing with papers and there was what I can only assume to be a used pad, lying behind the toilet. While the area appeared to be generally tidy, the bin did smell a little.

Next I checked the documents held in the office. Three Care Plans I found lying on a desk – the office was not locked and no staff were in the office at the time. I had been informed by another member of staff that the Manager was off sick today. I looked at the staff noticeboard for a rota but all I could see was a payment list for a staff night out at a local club. I checked the policy folders and found gaps in the contents – no supervision policy could be seen and the complaints policy was hard to read and outdated. I checked with a client, who was passing, if they had held any meetings about the activities on offer – she said they didn't get a choice in what they did.

Finally, I noticed upon leaving the service that a staff member was using his mobile phone in the day room – he seemed to be laughing about one of the clients in the room and spoke about 'getting off shift as soon as he could' because it was a nice day. He certainly didn't seem to be interacting with any of the clients.

Imagine that you have carried out this inspection of the Rose Home service.

1. What recommendations or notes of interest do you think you might make?

2. What would alert you to make these notes?

Conclusion

Social Policy, as a topic in your HNC, covers a wide range of areas. While the task of understanding legislation may seem daunting, you should grasp, from the elements of this chapter, an understanding of how legislation, policies, charters and campaigns lead to a culture of understanding the rights of people who use services. Significant legislation has been mentioned here, although individual workplaces will have their own interpretations of legislation and good practice within their own policies and procedures. Charters and campaigns influence legislation, or add to it, to build a holistic approach to a better future for all. By being more aware of some of these influences, and understanding the intentions behind them, day-to-day practice should be influenced and reflected upon in order to better everyone's experiences.

We have also considered the rise of social policy and some of the pivotal historical changes which influenced our current Scottish Parliament – a unique legislative situation in the UK. We have also briefly considered some of the consequences of failing to meet standards; least of all there is a personal consequence as a professional in failing to carry out duties to the best standards possible. With government and cultural support to better the future of care services, enhancing your understanding can only strengthen your position within the care field and lead to increased welfare for all concerned.

1. How might private problems become public issues? Identify some examples of areas of life where this has happened.
2. What were Beveridge's five giants?
3. What is meant by the term 'devolved parliament'?
4. What is meant by the 'mixed economy' of care, and what sectors make up this mix?
5. How might different sectors of care be funded?
6. What are the main stages of a Bill's conception?
7. What are the main themes of the Adults with Incapacity (Scotland) Act 2000?
8. How might The Human Rights Act (1998) influence working practices in a care environment?
9. What is the role of the Scottish Social Services Council?
10. What policies and procedures may be in place to enhance practice in a care environment?

References: Social policy and its application to social services provision

Blakemore, K. (1998) *Social Policy an Introduction*, Open University Press: Buckingham.

Lovell, T and Cordeaux, C. (1999) *Social Policy for Health and Social Care*, Hodder and Stoughton: London.

Moore, S. (2002) *Social Welfare Alive*, Nelson Thornes Ltd: Cheltenham.

Recommended websites

www.opsi.gov.uk
www.scottish.parliament.uk/
www.victorianweb.org/
www.workhouses.org.uk/
http://www2.rgu.ac.uk/publicpolicy

Chapter 3

Psychology for Social Care practice

Introduction

Psychology provides the Social Care worker with a wider frame of reference in their challenge to understand more fully the individuals they work with. The principle that theory should inform practice is central to Social Care. Theory can facilitate the design and implementation of the most appropriate strategies of help and support.

This chapter is designed to help you explore and understand key perspectives, theories and concepts from psychology. It will develop your ability to apply psychological theories and concepts in understanding and explaining development and needs throughout the life cycle. It will support you in analysing influences on development of identity and personality from a range of psychological perspectives. It will develop your knowledge of a range of life experiences which can affect development and behaviour.

How you will be assessed:

You may be studying *Psychology for Social Care Practice* as a single unit or as part of an HNC in Social Care.

- Single unit assessment is likely to be via a case study and written assignment.
- Where this unit forms part of an HNC programme, assessment may be as above or may follow an integrated format. Integrated assessment is where key elements of several HNC units (for example, Sociology for Social Care Practice, Social Care Theory and Practice, Psychology for Social Care Practice) are combined in one assessment exercise.

Wherever and however you study Psychology for Care Practice, your tutor will keep you informed of assessment processes and detail.

In this chapter you will learn about:

Human development and needs
Psychological perspectives and theory on development and needs
Identity and personality
Life events and life experiences

Human development and needs

The claim that human development is a complex business will come as no surprise! We consider ourselves unique but we are also aware of our similarities with others, particularly those of a similar age. This section will provide you with an understanding of, and greater insight into, the complexities of human development. This new awareness should support your understanding of individuals who need and/or receive Social Care services.

The lifespan perspective

This unit requires you to adopt a lifespan perspective in understanding human development. The lifespan perspective asserts that development is a *process* involving changes throughout the life cycle. The generally accepted stages include: *infancy, childhood, adolescence, adulthood* and *older adulthood*. Earlier perspectives on development focused mainly on changes in infancy, childhood and adolescence; adulthood and older adulthood were thought of as relatively stable periods of development and therefore not worthy of significant attention (some instability in the few years preceding death was acknowledged!). Recent thinking has challenged this view.

Consider this

Why *now* might developmental psychologists be drawn to study adulthood and older adulthood? (You could think about such issues as increased life expectancy, divorce rates, changes in family structures, career changes and changes in attitudes and beliefs.)

Lifespan development is a psychological perspective but over recent years has become 'interdisciplinary'. Other disciplines including anthropology and sociology have made significant contributions to our understanding of development. Anthropology provides insight into

The lifespan perspective sees development as a process involving changes throughout the life cycle.

developmental expectations and experiences of other cultures, while sociology highlights the influence on development of societal features such as race, socio-economic status and gender.

Understanding human development

A distinction between *norms* and *maturation* can be made here. Norms are developmental milestones. Milestones are behaviours and/or abilities which are expected and/or acquired at a particular age. These norms or milestones are to a large degree influenced by culture. *Maturation* can be thought of as the gradual unfolding of a biologically programmed sequence of events. Health professionals and child care practitioners often use the term 'milestone' to describe a maturation event. *Development* includes both maturation events and norms.

Activity

Referring to the list below, which events would you consider to be maturation events and which events would you consider to be culturally influenced developmental milestones (*norms*)? Think also about the extent to which maturation events are facilitated or inhibited by the environment. In other words, what is *needed* for a maturation event to be successfully realised?

- marriage
- able to balance on one leg
- walking unsupported
- talking in complete sentences
- rebellious behaviour at the adolescent stage of development
- onset of puberty
- grey hair and wrinkles
- retirement
- having children.

Off-time/On-time experiences

A further important concept in development is that of *timing*. Neugarten (1979) in Boyd and Bee (2006) proposed the concept of *off-time* and *on-time* experiences. This is the idea that events can be expected or unexpected at specific stages of development. The death of parents or becoming widowed could be considered

anticipated adult experiences. In contrast, a child experiencing the death of a parent, or a wife experiencing the death of her husband in early adulthood would be considered *unanticipated*. In studying adults, Neugarten found that *unanticipated* experiences were more likely to result in serious life disruption and pathology, such as depression. Significantly fewer difficulties resulted from *anticipated* experiences.

Consider this

In what ways might an unplanned pregnancy impact on the development of a 14-year-old girl? To what extent would this differ if she experienced the unplanned pregnancy at 30 years old?

Atypical development

So far the focus has been largely on 'normal' development. It is important however, to recognise that many individuals follow an *atypical process of development*. Atypical development can be thought of as development which is in some way inhibitory or damaging to the individual. Atypical development can arise, for example, from poverty, disability or emotional deprivation. To suggest disability is 'damaging' to the individual may be thought controversial and this will be explored later in the chapter. Factors influencing development will be the continued focus of this chapter.

> Normal development includes a wide range of individual differences. Some influences on individual differences are inborn. Others come from experience. Family characteristics, the effects of gender, social class, race and ethnicity, and the presence or absence of physical, mental or emotional disability all affect the way a person develops.
>
> (Papalia et al, 2001)

The nature/nurture debate

This debate, concerned with the influence of 'nature' and 'nurture' on development and behaviour, is perhaps one of the most controversial debates in psychology – and certainly one of the longest running! The nature side of the argument claims that change results from forces within a person, with biological processes such as genetics, maturational blueprints, neurochemical and hormonal influences and brain activity being responsible for development and behaviour. The nurture argument asserts, in contrast, that development and behaviour result from our environment, as consequences of experience and learning.

Developmental psychologists have moved away from an 'either/or' position to accepting that both nature and nurture contribute to an individual's development. The debate is now much more about which plays the bigger part. The nature/nurture debate will be a recurrent theme in this chapter.

Quantitative or qualitative change?

A further issue is whether development involves *quantitative* or *qualitative* changes. Put simply, do we change in 'amounts' or does change relate to our developing new strategies, new qualities and/or new skills? If development involves a change in amount (i.e. if at two years we can walk two miles before exhaustion, and at 20 years we can walk 40 miles before exhaustion), then the notion of *stages of development* is not useful. This suggests development consists largely of 'additions' to what is already present. However, if development involves a *qualitative* change associated with age, then the idea of stages of development becomes much more useful. A key difference between theorists in psychology is whether they consider development to be a *stage-free continuous process,* or a process involving qualitative changes linked to age-stages. This will be explored in more detail further in the chapter. For now however, it is important to know that development theories *do* largely agree on the following: there are three main categories of change!

Universal changes	Universal changes are those experienced by every individual. These are closely related to age. Usually maturation events (i.e. *biologically programmed*), universal changes are linked to the physical body, e.g. the hair of older adults changes to grey, infants follow crawling with walking.
Group-specific changes	Group-specific changes are those which occur within individuals who are members of a particular group. It could be argued that the most important group to which we belong is our culture. Sharing a culture means sharing experiences and expectations. The persuasiveness of culture means changes within a particular culture are likely to be *considered* 'universal'; i.e. expected times to start school, marry, bear children and retire.
	A further variation is historical influences. Within a culture there will be generations and within these generations there will be specific experiences and expectations associated with development.
Individual differences	Individual differences arise from a number of events which are unique and unshared. In your role as a Social Care practitioner you will become aware of the impact of a number of unique and unshared events experienced by the individuals you work with.
	Individuals can be characterised by a number of *variations* i.e. personality, intelligence, atypical behaviour etc. In conception, there is a unique combination of genes and thus each individual is conceived and born 'unique'.
	Atypical development is another example of individual difference.

Categories of change.

1. Can you think of further examples of *universal changes* and what conditions/resources might be needed to facilitate these changes?

   Research in the area of 'feral children' could provide insight into what a child might 'need' to fulfil these most basic biologically programmed changes.

2. Consider 'age norms' within UK culture. How might these lead to prejudice, stereotyping and discrimination?

   How might the behavioural expectations of 17-year-olds differ from those of 80-year olds?

3. A class group debate on the question, 'Am I unique?' would provide an exciting exploration of the idea of individual differences. Alternatively, you could investigate the varying responses to a typically 'shared' event such as, retirement, childbirth etc. Why do some individuals cope better with retirement than others? Why do some individuals develop post-natal depression while others do not?

Strands of human development

Aspects of development can be grouped into what is often described as strands or domains of development. This unit requires that you are familiar with five main strands or domains: *cultural processes, physical, emotional, social and cognitive development.*

Social development	Refers to changes associated with the relationship an individual has with others i.e. interacting with others, adopting social roles, developing knowledge, qualities, skills and attitudes which facilitate effective social relationships and learning social norms.
Emotional development	Refers to changes in feelings, self-esteem, the development of our self-concept, our ability to control, express and cope with emotions, attachment.
Cognitive development	Refers to changes in our thought processes in relation to memory, language, thinking, problem solving and decision making.
Physical development	Refers to physical changes in growth i.e. height and weight and changes in physical abilities i.e. development in gross and fine motor skills, development of wrinkles and grey hair.
Cultural development	Refers to the development of beliefs, values, behaviours – and qualities of citizenship – specific to groups and institutions within a particular culture.

Strands of development.

It is useful to define and explain the strands separately, however these are in real terms, inseparable – and development should be thought of as a *holistic* process.

Case study
Rene

Rene is 72 years old, widowed and lives alone in a sheltered housing complex. She has dementia and her cognitive functioning is significantly impaired. She finds it difficult to concentrate and has significant difficulties with her memory. She finds it difficult to remember promises to visit her family, when her favourite television programmes are on and can often forget to eat.

While dementia can be viewed as impacting largely on *cognitive* functioning, in what ways are other strands of development involved?

Stages of development

Ages and stages of development

The process of development can be divided into five main stages, as shown in the table below.

Stage	Approximate age
Infancy	Birth–2 years
Childhood	2–12 years
Adolescence	12–21 years
Adulthood	21–65 years
Older adulthood	65 years onwards

Five stages of development.

The stages as set out above suggest fixed timescales and abrupt transition from each to the next. This is not the case! Lifespan development should be considered as a gradual unfolding of developmental events. The age range shown above is an approximation; you need only ask your colleagues at what age they first started to walk or talk and responses are guaranteed to vary. However, it *is* highly likely that a majority of your colleagues will have been walking, and making (at least) two-word sentences before they were two years old. What is perhaps most predictable about these stages, and the expected developments within each, is the sequence in which they occur. It would be considered 'abnormal' after all, if a 40-year-old woman threw herself on the floor of a shop, kicking her legs and waving her arms in a tantrum when the shop did not stock a dress in her size! Infants generally crawl before they walk and generally use single words before joining two together to create a sentence. Grey hair is a typical aspect of the older adult stage of development. Rarely do we spend our childhood with grey hair and as we age see it change to brown, black or blonde.

In terms of individual differences, some individuals will fail to achieve milestones and/or norms and this can impact on later stages of development. This can have particular relevance to individuals who receive and/or need Social Care services. There are often strategies which can be adopted to address these gaps in development. You will cover this idea in more depth as you explore psychological perspectives and theory, and life experiences and events further on in this chapter. However, some psychologists claim that for many aspects of development there are *critical* or *sensitive* periods for development. This means that if an individual does not acquire a particular skill, knowledge or quality within a given time frame they will never acquire it – at least not in a fully functional way. Key areas of development *claimed* to be subject to a 'critical' or 'sensitive' period include language development, moral development and aspects of visual perception.

Case study

John

John is 45 years old and lives in supported accommodation with three friends. His parents never taught John how to solve problems or discuss issues calmly. His parents were quite aggressive and confrontational in dealing with even the most minor issues. They did not like to be challenged on anything they said or did. They would interpret even the most sensitive challenge as a confrontation. John shows this same pattern of response to disagreements and challenge as his parents. This leads to countless confrontations with the friends he lives with.

1. Do you think John can change his behaviour?

2. Do you think it is possible for him to learn new ways of interacting with others?

3. To what extent do you think this delay in normal development can be rectified at this stage in John's life?

The following table will highlight some of the main aspects of development for each stage. These will include both maturation events and norms. The aspects of development identified for each stage will be grouped in the five main strands of development.

Physical	• Rolling over (4 months) to sitting with support (6 months), sitting without support and crawling (8 months) • Fine motor skills ('building' with one or two bricks) develop rapidly from 10 months • By 12 months – pulling herself up, walking 'holding-on', beginning to walk independently • By 24 months – jump, run, and walk 'baby-style' upstairs
Emotional	• Baby responds to attention and stimulation from earliest age • By 6 months – signs she sees herself as someone separate. She 'asks' for (or demands!) attention, love and care. Is learning to trust crucial for a developing sense of 'self'?

Social	• Baby relates to others through smiles and cries. By 6 months begins to show 'attachment behaviour' • By 12 months plays in parallel (beside but not together) with other children • By 24 months – more established social confidence (to play away from her main caregiver)
Cognitive	• Crying at birth to 'babbling' (6 months) to understanding simple words (receptive language – 9 months), baby's first words (expressive language) usually 12 months • By 2 years, rapid growth of vocabulary (the 'naming explosion'), increasing confidence in using words to describe objects and colours
Cultural	• Routine, activities and events (e.g. whether baby is cared for at home, at Gran's, or in nursery) begin to shape understanding of what is 'normal' • Culturally-specific 'codes' and habits important, e.g. local dialect games and songs

Aspects of development: infancy (0–2 years).

Physical	• Early childhood body becomes taller and stronger, skills in running, balancing etc. develop. Co-ordination and fine motor control improve. Learns full bladder and bowel control • Fine-motor control (can ties shoelaces) highly developed by later childhood. May show early signs of puberty
Emotional	• She sees herself clearly as a 'girl' – and a person in her own right • Growing independence, self-awareness and capacity to establish and maintain relationships
Social	• Moving from parallel to co-operative play. A greater emphasis on friendships and her 'group' • Shows awareness of social and peer pressure and tends to prefer to 'conform'
Cognitive	• Language, understanding and expression become increasingly developed and complex. • Shows great curiosity and capacity for learning new skills

Cultural	• Sense of cultural 'belonging' reinforced in school and via outside interests • Similarities and differences of other cultures are introduced via education, media and travel

Aspects of development: childhood (2–12 years).

Physical	• Puberty: significant all-body changes, including development of reproductive system (internal) and secondary sex characteristics
Emotional	• Greater introspection and self-awareness (development of 'new' identity, via transition from childhood to adulthood) • First sexual relationship
Social	• Preferred (peer) group assumes importance over parents/carers • Changing roles and new experiences (i.e. leaving school, employment)
Cognitive	• For many, a time of intense learning (school, university); for others, new learning is practical and work-related. • More capable of informed argument via personal and social interests
Cultural	• Cultural and subcultural affiliation likely to be evident via personal presentation, activities of choice, etc.

Aspects of development: adolescence (12–21 years).

Physical	• Physical peak in young adulthood. After this, development depends on heredity, nutrition, levels of activity, etc. • Becoming a parent likely, with increased physical demands • By 65, many adults retain relative physical fitness, others experience decline in function and energy • Body shape tends to become more 'solid', signs of ageing apparent – reduced skin elasticity, loss of muscle tone, etc.
Emotional	• Sense of 'self' and esteem relate predominantly to role(s) and relationships – as parent, partner, worker and friend • Likely to be transition from 'first job' to established career or work pattern • Likely to be time of reflection on the effectiveness (or not) of one's 'contribution'

Social	• Considered 'social' in terms of her role(s) and/or 'status', tend to mix with 'like-types' • For many, social world reduces and is dominated by family roles and responsibilities
Cognitive	• Accrued knowledge and skills (learned in previous life-stages) are applied (i.e. in employment) • For many, cognitive development via re-training/further training
Cultural	• Typically responsible for transmitting cultural knowledge and understanding to the next generation

Aspects of development: adulthood (21–65 years).

Physical	• Relative physical fitness and health for some • For most older adults a gradual decline in physical strength and capacities, with pronounced signs of ageing
Emotional	• Social isolation likely to increase, new perceptions of 'self', one's role and status • Role of grandparent can significantly boost identity and esteem
Social	• Often a return to smaller social networks (i.e. family-based) following experiences of loss • For some, a renewed independence and freedom following retirement
Cognitive	• Likely to consider knowledge base and skills-set as 'established'; the wisdom of life-experience • Cognitive capacity and development link to physical health. Gradual and comparative 'slowness' can occur, but should not be regarded as typical
Cultural	• A sense of culture is firmly established. Perceptions of the self as a valid and valued member of one's culture can depend on own culture's attitudes to 'being old' • May be opportunity now to develop interests

Aspects of development: older adulthood (65 years onwards).

Needs

It is important also to understand that associated with each aspect of development there are *needs*. This term refers to what is *needed* for a particular milestone or norm to be achieved or acquired. Often when working with individuals you will play an important part in identifying unmet needs which underpin the successful acquisition of skills, qualities and/or knowledge. In a similar way to the strands of development, 'needs' can be divided into five main categories: emotional, social, cognitive, physical and cultural. They similarly continue in terms of the relationship the categories have with each other. They do not function independently but maintain a complex and inseparable relationship to each other. While human needs are considered to be universal, different needs and the ways in which they are met can be individualistic, culturally specific and vary according to age and stage of development.

Further research
You are asked to choose one stage of development and provide a *detailed* account of milestones and norms for each strand of development.

Activity
Identify a range of needs from each category (emotional, social, cognitive, physical and cultural) in relation to that stage of development. Consider the implications for future development if these needs go unmet.

A whole-group activity could involve subgroups completing the above for a different stage and presenting their findings to the rest of the class.

It is important to acknowledge that unmet needs can be created by the lack of Social Care services, inadequate and poor quality of services and by a failure of services to identify the needs of individuals who need and/or receive Social Care services.

Consider this
Reflect on your experience and/or observations of the unmet needs of people who use services being a consequence of the action and/or inaction of Social Care service providers.

Psychological perspectives and theories on development and needs

Psychology can be described as the *scientific* study of the mind and behaviour of individuals. Psychology should be based on research using the same methodology and criteria as the natural sciences such as physics and chemistry.

This section will provide you with an understanding of development and needs from three psychological perspectives. A *perspective* is a way of interpreting and explaining a phenomenon, situation or issue. In simple terms, it is a point of view and as Social Care practitioners you will be familiar with the idea of looking at an issue from another's point of view! A *theory* is consistent with the underpinning principles of the perspective to which it belongs but will have its own distinct differences and focus; however, these will not conflict with the basic principles of the relevant perspective. In this section you will explore four theories from three perspectives – psychodynamic, humanistic and behaviourist perspectives.

Psychodynamic perspective

Sigmund Freud (1856–1939) pioneered the work which was to provide the basis of the psychodynamic perspective. The underpinning principles of this perspective are as follows.

- Behaviour is motivated largely by unconscious forces. This means the individual has no salience about why they behave, feel and think in the ways they do.
- Biological forces play a significant part in development. Individuals are born with drives and instincts.
- Past experience – in particular, early childhood experiences – influence future behaviour.
- Individuals experience unconscious conflicts which require positive resolution for healthy development.

Freud postulated that in the years from 0 to 7 children had all but completed their qualitative development and that this development relied on the resolution of conflicts with a sexual basis. Erikson's psychosocial theory of development rejects the claim of unconscious sexual motives in development and as an alternative presents a *psychosocial* explanation. Erikson was able to include a wider range of influences on development, such as peers and work groups, by proposing a lifespan account of development. Bowlby's theory of attachment will be the second theory from the psychodynamic perspective to be explained. Bowlby emphasised the significance of infant attachment and suggested this is a blueprint for future relationships and development. Not without controversy, he cites the mother as responsible for a positive outcome in attachment.

Erikson's psychosocial theory of development

'Hope is both the earliest and the most indispensable virtue inherent in the state of being alive. If life is to be sustained hope must remain, even where confidence is wounded, trust impaired.'

(Erikson, 1950)

Erikson (1950, 1963) believed that the individual develops through eight genetically programmed sequences of *stages*. He considered these stage changes to be *universal*, which means that *every* individual goes through these stages and in the same order. Each stage involves an opportunity to resolve a specific *crisis*. The outcome can be positive or negative for the individual. Positive resolution results in the individual developing a 'virtue' such as, hope and wisdom. Further strengths can derive from positive resolution and Erikson calls these 'second strengths'. The accumulation of positive outcomes results in 'ego strength'. In short, the individual becomes competent in all areas of life.

Erikson emphasised the significance of the social relationships with others. At each stage, specific social and cultural influences will be the focus of the interaction the individual has with their environment. The crisis outcome depends on this interaction being positive. It depends on the individual's *needs* being met by the relevant social focus for that stage.

For example, in the first year of life the infant will attempt to resolve the conflict 'trust versus mistrust'. Individual stages generate specific needs that must be met before healthy development can occur. A positive outcome for the child is that she develops *hope* – she has developed sufficient amounts of trust *in* and *from* her environment. The focus at this stage is the mother or mother figure. Important events at this stage could be feeding and the speed at which the mother responds to the infant's crying. An important idea to grasp here is that moving through the stages is a biological event – like time, you can't stop it! If someone does not resolve the crisis in a positive way they will resolve it in a negative way. They will be disadvantaged as they attempt to resolve the subsequent stage. Later psychological difficulties are the result of a negative outcome to earlier stages of development. The quote above emphasises Erikson's claim that hope is the fundamental virtue for an individual to develop. Implicit in this is the claim that early experiences play a crucial role in healthy development.

The psychosocial perspective claims that early experiences are very important for long-term healthy emotional development.

Stage number and age	Name of stage *Crisis*	Virtue and second named strength	Significant aspects of the environment	Needs for a positive outcome
1. 0–1 yr	Basic trust vs. mistrust	**Hope** and drive	Mother or mother figure	Care, affection, responsive parents, reliability, feel safe and secure.
2. 1–3 yrs	Autonomy vs. shame and doubt	**Willpower** and self-control	Parents	Sensitive discipline, able to exert independence and make choices.
3. 3–6 yrs	Initiative vs. guilt	**Purpose** and direction	Wider family	Able to explore, demonstrate power over environment, support to cope with new demands and new experiences.
4. 6–12 yrs	Industry vs. inferiority	**Competence** and method	School	Experience success at school. Acknowledgement of success by others. Acquisition of skills and knowledge.
5. 12–18yrs	Identity vs. role confusion	**Fidelity** and devotion	Social groups: peer groups, non-peer groups, models of leadership	Opportunity to develop a sense of self, try new roles, success at trying roles.
6. 20's	Intimacy vs. isolation	**Love** and affiliation	Partners in friendship, sex, competition and co-operation	Intimate relationship with other, warm and secure bond with other.
7. Late 20's–50's	Generativity vs. stagnation	**Care** and production	Work and parenthood	Opportunities to produce, nurture and outlast things. Opportunities to be productive at work/career. Opportunities to contribute to the lives of others.
8. 50's +	Ego integrity vs despair	**Wisdom** and renunciation	Humankind and my kind/ reflect on life	Able to look back with a sense of fulfilment. Able to come to terms with mistakes and avoid regrets.

Erikson's theory of psychosocial development.

Trust vs. mistrust	Sensory overload/develops insecurity, fear and suspicion
Autonomy vs. shame and doubt	Impulsive/compulsive/doubt ability to cope
Initiative vs. guilt	Ruthlessness/inhibition/develop feelings of guilt and fear of punishment
Industry vs. inferiority	Narrow range of interests/inertia/develop feelings of inadequacy and inferiority
Identity vs. role confusion	Fanaticism/reject authority/no real sense of identity/confusion of self-concept
Intimacy vs. isolation	Promiscuity/exclusivity/ability to develop only superficial relationships
Generativity vs. stagnation	Over extension/rejectivity/boredom/preoccupation with self
Integrity vs. despair	Presumption/disdain/regret/fear of death.

Potential negative outcomes.

Adolescence marks the transition from child to adult and is a time to establish an identity.

Erikson claims the stage of adolescence marks the transition from child to adult. The onset of puberty propels the child into the challenge of establishing their adult identity during a 'moratorium' – a socially constructed delay. Western cultures facilitate freedom from responsibilities so adolescents can experiment with different attitudes, beliefs and roles. The aim is to make this transition easier. There are no 'rites of passage', ceremony or clearly defined way to become an adult. If the adolescent chooses an identity too soon they may experience role confusion which can manifest in delinquency and no real sense of self.

Activity

The following statement could be used to form the basis for a group debate. (Alternatively, reflect on the statement and discuss your thoughts with your colleagues.)

'Adolescence is *not* a biological time of storm and stress because of raging hormones. It is merely a stereotype – culturally created.'

Consider this

Erikson claims that the outcome of the crisis in one stage influences the way in which the individual addresses and resolves the subsequent crisis. The outcome is taken forward as the basis for the next stage. For an adolescent who settled too early on a specific identity, what might be the impact on development over the next two stages?

Think about the positive outcome in adolescence. What conditions are necessary for a positive outcome and how does this equip the adolescent for the next stage in development?

Can you link these stages to maturation milestones and norms?

Evaluation of Erikson's psychosocial theory of development

Adopting a lifespan approach to development and acknowledging the interdependence of biological and environmental factors in development are key strengths in Erikson's theory. However, Marcia (1980) argued that adolescence involves too many aspects of identity to be resolved in the time span suggested by Erikson. He argues further that variation in the adolescent experience has been found in relation to culture and gender, so questioning the universal nature of stages. Given that the stages are biologically programmed, '*returning*' to an earlier stage to seek a more positive outcome could prove extremely difficult. The accumulative impact of negative outcomes could make remediation a long and difficult task.

Bowlby's theory of attachment

Bowlby (1907–1990) pioneered attachment research. Commissioned by the World Health Organization to research the impact of being raised in an institution, he produced his report, 'Maternal Care and Mental Health' (Bowlby, 1951). The report focused on the idea of *maternal deprivation*. Today, we think of this term to mean absence of a mother and/or family. However, Bowlby has much more to say on the subject than the term implies.

Attachment is an enduring, strong and close emotional bond between two people. Periods of prolonged separation will cause distress in the attached person. In terms of the mother and child relationship, the mother has a *bond* with the child whereas the baby is *attached* to the mother. *Attachment* and *bond* are distinct concepts. Attachment has a whole set of complexities distinct from those of an emotional bond and it is these complexities which will be explored here.

Pre-attachment: 0–2 months

In this stage the infant responds to all objects – people and things – in a similar way and can be comforted by a stranger as well as the mother. Towards the end of this phase infants begin to show a preference for familiar faces and voices. They begin to prefer people to objects.

Indiscriminate attachment phase: 3–7 months

In this phase the infant becomes more sociable and enjoys the company of other people. They recognise familiar people and prefer those individuals when in need of comfort. They do not get anxious when with strangers.

Discriminate attachment phase: 7–9 months

Attachment is beginning to develop and the infant experiences distress on separation from the primary care giver. This is termed 'separation protest'. The infant shows pleasure on being reunited with the primary care giver and displays anxiety if handled or approached by a stranger. The infant has now developed a 'specific' attachment.

Multiple attachment phase: 9 months +

Infants become increasingly independent and form additional bonds and attachment. It is very much a matter for debate whether these bonds/attachments are as strong as the initial attachment with the primary caregiver.

Four stages of attachment.

Bowlby argues that attachment between infant and mother is genetically programmed. The infant is biologically programmed to seek out an attachment figure – a female. While the mother is biologically programmed to respond to the infant's '*social releasers*' i.e. cries, smiles, grunts. He claims this is *adaptive* behaviour, equipping the infant with a better chance of survival. This kind of programming is often referred to as a '*genetic imprint*' for behaviour and can be observed across countless species.

A significant claim by Bowlby is that the attachment the infant has with the mother or mother figure is the *prototype* for future relationships. The child uses this as a model for future relationships. The implication here is that a negative attachment experience and outcome is likely to lead to later psychological and relationship difficulties. For Bowlby, this effect cannot be reversed as there is a *sensitive* period in development for attachment, i.e. the first two and half years of life. However, he says it is likely to be the first few months that are the most significant. Beyond 30 months there is **no** hope of reversing the effects of a negative attachment experience and outcome.

Consider this

To what extent do you agree with Bowlby's claim that the effects of a negative attachment experience and outcome cannot be reversed?

Bowlby's maternal deprivation hypothesis

Bowlby (1951) argued that if infants were deprived of their mother during this critical period of development, then a host of serious and permanent consequences could follow. These might include: impoverished IQ and physical condition, delinquency and affectionless psychopathology.

Deprivation and privation

Deprivation refers to the temporary, prolonged and permanent separation of a child from its attachment figure. Privation is where no attachments have been formed. Bowlby identified a number of possible short- and long-term effects of maternal deprivation and these are detailed in the table below.

Short-term effects	Long-term effects
Protest – the infant demonstrates fear, anger, frustration etc. **Despair** – the infant shows behavioural signs of depression, avoidance and apathy. **Detachment** – infant appears to carry on as though nothing is wrong. This does not reflect the emotions the child really experiences. Re-attachment is resistant and the infant does not show a preference between other people. **Delay** – there can be a temporary delay in cognitive development.	Separation Anxiety: • increase in aggression, clingy behaviour, refusal to comply, detachment. Psychosomatic disorders such as skin rashes, aching stomach • increased risk of depression and other psychological disorders as an adult where the separation is permanent i.e. death of a parent.

Possible short-term and long-term effects of maternal deprivation according to Bowlby.

Bowlby's (1944) study '44 Juvenile Thieves' compared two groups of 44 boys. All 88 had been referred to the Child Guidance Centre in London. One group had been referred for their involvement in criminal behaviour while the other 44 had expressed emotional difficulties but not criminal or antisocial behaviour. He found 14 boys of the 'criminal' group to be 'affectionless psychopaths' – they showed no guilt or remorse for their crimes. He found that 86 per cent of the affectionless psychopaths had experienced separation from their mother at an early age. No 'affectionless psychopaths' were found in the non-criminal group and no one from this group experienced maternal separation. Bowlby thus claimed that separation from the attachment figure at a sensitive stage in development may cause later psychological and emotional problems. This study suggests a strong link between unmet needs in infancy and future development.

Bowlby's study was criticised by Rutter (1981) who claimed there may be alternative explanations for the onset of affectionless psychopathology, such as, pre-existing family and social issues. It was not the separation which caused the difficulties but the reasons why the separation occurred in the first place determined a negative outcome for the individuals.

Further research

Research the life events and experiences listed below and their relevance to attachment – its formation, privation and deprivation (separations). In what ways does privation and deprivation impact on an individual's development? (This could be a class group exercise with different groups researching distinct areas and presenting their findings to the rest of the class group.) Consider the ways they impact on the individual's earlier, current and later development.

- Parenting styles
- Divorce of parents
- Death of parents
- Hospitalisation of child or parent
- Child being taken into care
- Under twos using regular day care

Limitations of Bowlby's theory of attachment and maternal deprivation hypothesis

Rutter questions the idea that development is influenced largely by one main attachment. He rejects the notion that the first attachment creates a prototype for future relationships. He claims that multiple attachments can be formed. Bowlby may well have underestimated the impact of good-quality care in the absence of the primary caregiver and the value of relationships beyond the mother.

Behaviourist perspective

J B Watson (1878–1958) pioneered the behaviourist perspective by arguing that the study of behaviour should be scientific. This means that only behaviour which can be *directly observed* should be the subject matter of psychology – this *excludes* internal mental processes such as thinking and reasoning. This is in contrast to the psychodynamic approach where the focus is unconscious processes. Behaviourism is a perspective about learning, not why we learn but how we learn.

Behaviour is learned through *conditioning.* Conditioning is the mechanism by which we learn and this is what is explained as we explore behaviourist theory. There are two types of conditioning – Classical and Operant Conditioning. We will explore Operant Conditioning in this chapter.

Basic assumptions of the behaviourist perspective include the following:

- learning occurs by *association*
- the environment determines behaviour (nurture)
- interested only in behaviour that can be directly observed and measured
- it claims change within the individual is *quantitative*. There are no stages in development. Change is an accumulation of learned associations
- there is no qualitative difference between humans and animals. They vary in amount only – humans have more neurons than animals
- all behaviour is learned – with the exception of biological reflexes.

Operant conditioning

B.F. Skinner (1904–1990) and J.B. Watson (1878–1958) are key theorists of operant conditioning. Skinner will largely be the focus of this section.

With operant conditioning the *association* the individual makes is between the behaviour and the consequence of that behaviour. The consequence can be either negative or positive. The consequence of the behaviour determines whether that behaviour will reoccur. For example, if you eat a cake and enjoy it the theory predicts you will eat that sort of cake again. However, if you don't enjoy it the theory predicts you will not eat such a cake again. The best indicator of future behaviour is past behaviour. We learn through the consequences of behaviour. There are potentially four outcomes/consequences of behaviour and these are the mechanisms for learning – this is *how* we learn!

Mechanism	Consequence	Impact on future behaviour
Positive reinforcement	Pleasant consequence	Behaviour increases in frequency and/or intensity
Negative reinforcement	Pleasure/relief experienced by avoiding a painful or uncomfortable stimuli	Avoidance behaviour increases in frequency and/or intensity

Punishment	Unpleasant experience i.e. pain	Behaviour decreases in frequency and/or intensity
No reinforcement	No pleasure or pain is experienced	Behaviour decreases in frequency and/or intensity. Likely to lead to extinction of behaviour

Operant conditioning and the possible consequences of behaviour.

Behaviour is neither 'good' nor 'bad' as this suggests an innate moral awareness. Behaviourism claims *all* behaviour is learned using the above mechanisms, so desirable and undesirable behaviour can be reinforced. Consider the parent and child in the supermarket – the child sees sweets and cries, the parent gives the child sweets to keep them quiet as they shop. The parent is reinforcing an undesirable behaviour.

In terms of challenging behaviour, often the task of the Social Care practitioner is to acknowledge this behaviour is being reinforced and to identify what is reinforcing the behaviour.

The mechanisms above are rules for behaviour. *Any* behaviour that is maintained or increases is being reinforced and is reinforcing to the individual – even behaviours we cannot fully understand, such as a woman returning to an abusive relationship again and again. Further, it is not possible to predict what will be reinforcing to a particular individual e.g. praise can be punishing or reinforcing to a specific individual. The only way to predict this is to know how the individual responded to that reinforcer in the past.

Schedules of reinforcement

This describes the pattern the reinforcing event takes; for example, *continuous reinforcement* is when the behaviour is reinforced on every occasion. *Variable reinforcement* is when reinforcement occurs at indeterminate times. Behaviour which is learned through variable reinforcement is the most difficult to extinguish. Variable reinforcement is when you know something is coming but you just don't know when; for example, the child who keeps asking for a lolly from the ice-cream van and whose parents refuse a number of times but occasionally give in. *Extinction* means the individual no longer displays that particular behaviour. Although it should be noted that behaviour cannot be unlearned – it is merely replaced.

Learned helplessness

Learned helplessness is a state where an individual cannot escape a punishing and painful consequence. The individual does not know what it is they are doing wrong, when the punishment is coming and cannot afford any control over their environment. The individual essentially gives up. Examples of this could include people being overcome with the worry of financial difficulties, serious illness or depression. Learned helplessness has also been applied to people living in institutions who have little or no control over their environment.

Phobias

Behaviourism claims that phobias result from *negative reinforcement*. The pleasure and relief of avoiding painful stimuli reinforces the avoidance behaviour – therefore avoidance behaviour increases. This is further compounded when the individual generalises their fear i.e. they not only avoid the dog that bit them but they avoid all dogs. *Generalisation* involves associating consequences with a range of similar stimuli. Continuing this example, being afraid of dogs but not cats is an example of *discrimination.*

Shaping behaviour

This is a technique used to evoke a desired behaviour in stages. The first stage is reinforced until it is achieved while other behaviours are ignored. Once this has been successfully learned, the next stage becomes the focus. Successive approximation is also used. This technique involves reinforcing behaviour which is *similar to* or *a part* of the desired behaviour and thus gently guiding the learning of a specific behaviour. These techniques are used in training animals and are highly successful. (Parents may also use them with their children!)

Evaluation of the behaviourist perspective

The behaviourist perspective does not acknowledge qualitative, biologically programmed stages of development. This means that it is possible to address maladaptive behaviour by learning adaptive and desirable behaviour. Behaviourist techniques can be the most successful in dealing with phobias. The majority of phobias can be resolved quickly and easily using behaviourist techniques. They acknowledge basic survival needs similar to those of like species; however this does not fully address the complexities of human needs. Suggesting that humans and animals differ on a quantitative basis only is controversial. Rejecting the existence of internal mental processes such as thinking and reasoning is considered a major flaw of this perspective. The cognitive/behaviourist approach developed to address this. This approach brings together learning and thinking.

Case study

Delton

Delton is 20 years old. He has been convicted of petty theft on a number of occasions. His parents have always supported Delton and hoped he was just going through a *phase*. Delton did not enjoy school. He was verbally bullied by peers and never seemed to receive any praise from teachers, no matter how hard he worked. Then he met Wayne, who had had a similar experience at school, and who introduced Delton to shoplifting. Delton is now facing going to court for aggravated burglary and his parents have no idea what they did wrong. Delton's father says he doesn't care what happens.

1. Using operant conditioning theory, provide an explanation for Delton's behaviour.

2. How would you explain his parent's attitude and behaviour?

Humanistic perspective

'A musician must make music, an artist must paint, a poet must write, if he is to be ultimately at peace with himself. What a man can be, he must be'.

(Maslow, 1968)

The humanistic perspective rejects the deterministic and pessimistic views of behaviourism and psychodynamic theory. Humanistic psychology alternatively focuses on an individual's *potential for growth*, their conscious experience and aims in life. A fundamental belief is that people are innately good. Individuals who experience psychological difficulties do so because of the conditions imposed on them by their environment which make it difficult for them to accept and be their true self. Key theories from this perspective include: Maslow (1908–1970) and Rogers (1902–1987). We will explore Maslow's theory of the *hierarchy of human needs* in this section and Rogers' work in the area of self-concept in the next.

Key assumptions of the humanistic perspective include the following:

- individuals have free will
- human beings are *qualitatively* different from animals
- there are qualities which are uniquely human i.e. love, hope, creativity
- the importance of the individual's interaction with their environment *as the individual perceives it* is emphasised
- falls on the nurture side of the nature/nurture debate but not as radical as behaviourism
- individuals have a biological drive to fulfil their potential – *self-actualisation*.

Maslow's hierarchy of needs

Maslow's theory is about motivation. Without motivation we do very little! According to Maslow we are motivated to meet our *human needs*. He emphasised the importance of self-actualisation, which can be a tricky concept to grasp. Think about a sunflower: the seed is programmed to develop and grow into a sunflower; it cannot grow into a thistle or nettle! Similarly, a human being is programmed and driven to develop and grow into a self-actualised person. This *self-actualising tendency* drives us to become all we are capable of becoming. Going back to the sunflower – how tall, strong and healthy it becomes will depend on the environment and what that environment provides. Similarly, the

Transcendence.
Helping others fulfil their potential.
Self-actualisation.
Realising one's full potential.
Becoming what one is capable of becoming.
Aesthetic needs.
Beauty – in nature and art. Appreciation of symmetry, order, form and balance.
Cognitive needs.
Knowledge and understanding. Meaning and predictability.
Esteem needs.
Respect and admiration from others, self-respect, self-esteem. Self-confidence and self-efficacy.
Love and belongingness.
Affection, trust, acceptance, being part of groups i.e. family, friends, work. Loving and being loved.
Psychological and physical safety.
Protection from potentially dangerous objects, situations and circumstances i.e. fear of the unknown. Familiarity and routine are important.
Physiological needs.
Food, oxygen, water, temperature regulation, rest, activity, safety needs.

Maslow's hierarchy of needs.

environment can frustrate and prevent *our* growth and development. The self-actualised person perceives themselves, others and the world realistically and is not egocentric. Such an individual is motivated by responsibility and ethics; enjoys relationships with others but is happy being alone; conforms to rules but is open and honest when he or she does not agree with them. The self-actualised person appreciates, is inspired and transformed by experience. 'This person' is who we all are driven to become as the sunflower is driven to become a sunflower.

Types of needs

Maslow's hierarchy of needs can be represented in the form of a pyramid divided into eight levels. The first four levels are considered *deficiency* needs. These include: physiological, security, emotional, social, and esteem needs. These needs are considered as basic for adequate functioning in life. Where these needs are not met the individual is considered to be lacking or deficient. The additional higher four levels encompass *growth* needs. These are not about deficiency but rather individuals are motivated to meet those needs because they *add* to their lives and experiences – they promote *qualitative* growth towards self-actualisation.

Maslow asserts that needs lower down the hierarchy have to be sufficiently met before higher level needs can be fully attended to. Reflect on how you felt when you first started college or entered a new situation. You may have lacked confidence and/or felt as though you did not belong in that environment. However, as you became familiar with how to find your way around, got to know your colleagues and what was expected of you, your sense of confidence and belonging also increased. As you met your lower level needs, you placed yourself in a better position to meet your higher level needs of esteem and efficacy. Developing familiarity with your environment meant you were able to sufficiently meet your psychological safety needs and move on. A frequent cause of psychological difficulties and problems is that people try to meet needs higher up on the hierarchy before they have adequately met needs lower down. Needs are not an 'all or nothing' thing. We can survive and function well enough without *all* of our needs being met at each level but the notion of needs being sufficiently met is an important one.

Maslow and human development

The hierarchy not only plots our understanding of situations – it reflects development. The higher up the hierarchy we go the more the needs become linked to life experiences and the less biological they become. In addition, higher levels take longer to fulfil. The levels reflect approximate levels of development; for example the infant operates at levels one, two and three as it progresses through the early years. Adolescence can be reflected in level four – identity and esteem needs. It is not that we no longer have the needs lower down, it means they are not the prime motivating needs at that stage. The adolescent still has physiological, safety and love and belongingness needs; however, esteem needs will be the prime motivators.

The hierarchy continues to plot development through adulthood/older adulthood. The notion of stages in development implies it is not possible for a child to self-actualise. However, in response to an unanticipated life event, such as redundancy, disability or bereavement, we may well operate at a level below our chronological age/level. Given that these needs have been met earlier in development, the individual can return more quickly to the stage they were at before the event. The role of the environment is significant. There will be features in the environment which facilitate or inhibit development. It is the individual's *perception* of these features which determines whether they are inhibitory or facilitating.

Case study

Lucy

Lucy is 17 years old. She lives with her parents who are both alcohol-dependent. They have always been aggressive and sometimes violent towards her. Her father is emotionally and physically abusive to her mother. Lucy rarely attended school when she was younger and would often be responsible for keeping the house clean and doing the shopping. Lucy is now pregnant and wants to live with her boyfriend, who can also be physically and emotionally abusive towards her. But she says she loves him and is looking forward to them being a real family when the baby comes along and the local authority finds them somewhere to live.

1. What stage of development is most relevant to Lucy's *age*?

2. What stage of development is most relevant to Lucy's *situation*? Which needs are being adequately met? What needs are not being adequately met?

3. Lucy is trying to meet needs. What needs are these?

4. According to Maslow, is Lucy trying to meet the needs she *should* be? If not, what needs should Lucy be trying to meet?

5. In what ways are environmental factors frustrating Lucy's attempts to meet her needs?

Transcendence: facilitating earlier stages of development

While it is considered to be the latest stage of development, transcendence can be a useful tool for an individual to adopt in earlier stages to facilitate their own development. It could be argued that people who are dealing with issues such as low self-esteem and depression can improve their feelings about themselves and their mood by helping others. This is often seen in schools where disaffected learners support the learning of others; this in turn improves their own self-esteem and sense of belonging to a learning environment.

Evaluation of Maslow's hierarchy of needs

Maslow emphasises the role of the individual in controlling and determining their own lives. It recognises that the environment can thwart an individual's attempt to be in control of their own life. These ideas are consistent with basic Social Care values. The idea of human needs being categorised and ordered is useful in care assessments and Care Planning. You may recognise some of Maslow's categories in Care Plans from your workplace. Subjective matter is difficult to objectively study and measure i.e. how can we tell if someone is self-actualised? It is only by the individual's own account and in scientific terms this is unreliable.

The claim that there is a hierarchy of human needs is controversial. Examples of this controversy include not only transcendence needs facilitating an individual's own earlier development but also, for instance, the artist who would rather paint than eat, the parent who neglects herself to provide for her children, and demonstrate that a hierarchy may not be applicable in every eventuality.

Identity and personality

In this section you will examine the influences on the development of identity and personality. Genetic/biological and environmental factors both *interact* to impact and contribute to the development of identity and personality. Some of these factors will be explored more fully, i.e. disability, cultural expectations, sexual orientations, socio-economic influences. You will cover two theories – one which lays greater emphasis on biological influences (Eysenck) and one which emphasises the role of the environment (Rogers). However, it should be noted that behaviourist and psychodynamic theories could be used to explain the development of identity and personality and, similarly, theories covered here could be applied to development and needs.

Defining identity and personality

Personality can be thought of as the characteristic patterns of feelings, thoughts and behaviours which make up an individual and which ultimately makes each of us unique. Personality remains fairly consistent throughout a person's life. Personality also causes the individual to act in certain ways and can be seen in our thoughts, feelings, choices, relationships and interactions with others. Identity – an essential component of personality – can be thought of as the fairly consistent views and feelings we have about ourselves, how we perceive ourselves and what we think we can do and cannot do – our self-concept. Our perception of ourselves in relation to the rest of the world plays an important role in our choices, behaviours, and beliefs. While our self-esteem and behaviour can fluctuate to some extent across situations, identity and personality comprise those enduring characteristics and behaviours.

Components of the self-concept

The self-concept is usually thought to contain three main components; *self-image, self-esteem* and *ideal self*.

Self-image refers to how we perceive and describe ourselves in terms of our traits, physical characteristics and social roles we adopt, for example 'I am tall, friendly and a good brother to my little sisters.' The self-image is largely descriptive.

Self-esteem refers to how much we like and approve or ourselves. It is a measure of our perceived self-worth. Certain abilities and characteristics have a perceived value and worth in particular societies, cultures and social groups and therefore there will be variation in terms of what it is about us that is considered likeable and worthy.

Ideal self is the kind of person we would like to be or think we should be. Influences from the environment can impact on who we would like to be or think we should be. The ideal self can be thought of as an *idealised* self-image. Generally, the greater the gap between our self-image and ideal self, the lower our self-esteem will be.

Rogers' self theory

Humanistic psychologist, Carl Rogers' (1902–1987) self theory is built around the actualising tendency – this life force which drives us towards self-actualisation. The emphasis is on the individual and how *they* perceive themselves, their behaviour and the environment. Rogers is without doubt a prominent theorist in the areas of education, Social Care and counselling.

The healthy person

A *fully functioning* person (Rogers, 1961) is healthy and well balanced and will demonstrate equilibrium between the three components of the self-concept. There will be consistency or *congruence* between their self-concept and the individual's internal experiences and behaviour. This means that someone experiences their true feelings and does not deny or distort them.

Openness to experience	• accurate perception of one's experience in the world • not defensive • able to accept reality and own feelings • openness to self and actualisation
Existential living	• living in the here and now • recognise memories and dreams for what they are
Organismic trusting	• trust your real self • do what feels right and natural
Experiential freedom	• feel free to make choices which are available to us • acknowledge the relationship between responsibility and freedom

The fully functioning individual demonstrates equilibrium according to Rogers.

An individual must receive unconditional positive regard in order to develop a healthy personality. *Unconditional positive regard* is the acceptance and love from others without imposing conditions for this love and acceptance. This is termed, '*Conditions of worth*'; for example, 'I love you because you do well in exams.' The idea is that love and acceptance should not depend on meeting conditions. Rogers argues that it is essential to the healthy development of self for a child to grow up with parents who demonstrate unconditional positive regard and for people to experience this throughout their lives. Similarly, it is essential that individuals demonstrate positive self-regard which includes self-esteem, self-worth and having a positive self-image. A healthy self-concept should be flexible and allow a person to enjoy new experiences and ideas without feeling threatened.

The unhealthy person

Low self-esteem can result from an imbalance between the self-image and ideal self. The individual may have difficulty distinguishing real feelings from anxieties brought on by external expectations and conditions. The person may alter their behaviour to meet their need for positive regard and, over time, this *conditioning* can lead to *conditional positive self-regard* – we like ourselves only if we meet the standards imposed by others. This involves an individual repressing their true feelings and needs, which eventually results in alienation from themselves, distortion of their true feelings and limiting their potential to feel fulfilled and self-actualise.

Case study

Mike

Mike is 46 years old. He is married and lives with his wife and three children (who are 15, 12 and 10 years old). He has recently been made redundant and his wife has taken on extra hours at the local supermarket where she works. Mike is becoming short tempered and spends most of his time in his garden shed. He did start looking for another job but he has not managed to get so far as an interview yet. He thinks it is because of his age and feels he is on the scrap heap. Mike's work was tiring but he enjoyed it and he was so much happier. His wife has told him that the redundancy is a family problem and everyone should pull together to get through it. She tries to tell him that money being tight and not getting another job is not his fault but he doesn't seem to see it that way. Mike seems to be withdrawing from his wife and children more and more. He used to take a lot of pride in his appearance but now he seems not to care.

1. How might Rogers' self theory explain Mike's behaviour?

2. Is Mike a fully functioning individual?

With regard to the case study above, think about the components of the self-concept and the impact of environmental factors – events and expectations of self and others. Consider concepts such as incongruence/congruence, positive self-regard, conditions of worth and unconditional and conditional positive regard.

Evaluation of Rogers' self theory

Rogers' theory and concepts have contributed significantly to Social Care, counselling and education. They are wholly consistent with Social Care values and you are likely to come across his work many times. As a humanistic theory it has the similar weaknesses to Maslow's hierarchy of needs – the problem of subjective experience being the subject matter. Humanistic therapies are often used to *complement* medication and behavioural techniques in addressing serious mental health issues such as schizophrenia and severe depression.

Eysenck's theory of personality

Eysenck (1916–1997) and his theory of personality (Eysenck, 1967) is firmly on the nature side of the nature/nurture debate. He claimed that there are three *genetically programmed universal* traits. Traits can be seen as predispositions to behave and respond in particular ways.

1. **Introversion/Extroversion:**
   Introversion involves directing attention on inner experiences, while extroversion involves directing attention to the environment. So an introverted person might be quiet and reserved, while an extrovert might be sociable and outgoing.

2. **Neuroticism/Emotional stability:**
   This relates to moodiness versus even-temperedness. Neuroticism refers to an individual's tendency to become upset or emotional, while stability refers to the tendency to remain emotionally in control.

3. **Psychoticism:**
   Individuals who demonstrate characteristics from this dimension tend to have difficulty dealing with reality and may be anti-social, hostile, non-empathetic and manipulative.

Each person exhibits traits from the three dimensions – the particular combination of characteristics you have from each of the three dimensions will determine your personality.

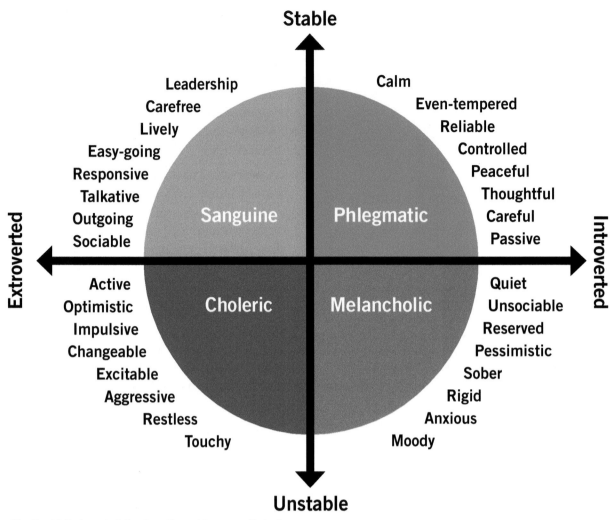

We all exhibit characteristics from Eysenck's personality traits.

Neuroticism (stable/unstable)

This ranges from normal, fairly calm and collected to nervous. The dimension of neuroticism ranges from *stable* (not neurotic) to *unstable* (neurotic). Individuals who are high on neuroticism are more likely to experience neuroses. Eysenck cites the cause of this to be differences in the sympathetic nervous system of neurotics from non-neurotics.

Stable (not neurotic)	Even-tempered, calm, carefree, reliable, controlled, peaceful etc.
Unstable (neurotic)	Restless, aggressive, changeable, pessimistic, anxious, moody, rigid etc.

Characteristics of neurotics.

Extroversion–introversion

Introverts focus on the inner world of ideas and impressions – they are influenced more by their own thoughts and understanding of things; while extroverts focus more on the outer world of people and things. Extroverts are influenced more by the environment, which adds further complexity to the relative influence of biological and environmental factors in the development of identity and personality – the nature of the interaction itself can be individualistic. The specific characteristics of extroversion and introversion will depend on the individual's levels of neuroticism.

Extroverts are generally considered to be more sociable and outgoing.

Extroverts
Active, optimistic, impulsive, sociable, outgoing, talkative, responsive, easy-going, changeable, excitable, aggressive, restless, touchy, lively, carefree and/or have good leadership skills.
Extroverts are more active sexually, in terms of frequency and sexual partners and are much more suggestible. Extroverts prefer jobs that involve interaction with other people whereas introverts prefer more solitary vocations. Extroverts have a need for diversion from routine while introverts have less need for novelty.

Introverts
They *could* be: moody, anxious, rigid, sober, pessimistic, reserved, unsociable, quiet, passive, careful, thoughtful, peaceful, controlled, reliable, even-tempered and/or calm.
Introverts tend to be more sensitive to pain, become fatigued more easily and excitement interferes with their performance whereas it improves the performance of the extrovert. Introverts do better in school however they are more likely to withdraw from college for psychiatric reasons!

Characteristics of introverts and extroverts.

Traits and neurological functioning

Eysenck claimed that extroversion–introversion is a matter of the balance between *inhibition* and *excitation* in the brain itself: inhibition is the brain calming itself down, perhaps in response to some stimuli it finds overwhelmingly stimulating, while excitation is the brain waking itself up, getting into a state of alertness.

The extrovert will have *strong inhibition* i.e. when confronted with a traumatic situation the brain inhibits or numbs itself. They do not feel the full mental impact of a traumatic/stressful episode and therefore do not avoid similar situations. The introvert can be said to have *weak inhibition*. When faced with a traumatic situation their brains do not protect themselves quickly enough – the brain does not numb itself; instead they remain alert and remember everything that happened.

So, how does this lead to shyness or a love of parties?

The introvert would remember any embarrassing moments/situations and would not want to repeat them while the extrovert would not remember the embarrassment of dancing on the table at a party – hence they are likely to be busy organising another party straightaway! Eysenck claimed that violent criminals tended to be non-neuroticistic (stable) extroverts and this makes sense because it is difficult to imagine a person who is painfully shy, learns from experience and who has panic attacks committing an armed robbery!

Psychoticism

People who score high on this dimension tend to be solitary, insensitive, uncaring about others and opposed to accepted social custom – that is, they are antisocial. People who score low on this dimension are caring, friendly, sensitive and conforming.

Genetics, neuroses and criminality

Eysenck claims that neurotic symptoms develop because of the action of the biological system and experiences that contribute to the learning of strong emotional reactions to fear producing stimuli. Neurotic patients tend to have high neuroticism and low extroversion scores. In contrast, criminals and antisocial individuals tend to have high levels of neuroticism, extroversion and psychoticism. These individuals tend to show weak learning of societal norms. The extrovert requires stimulation and excitement which could lead them to be impulsive and thrill seeking, potentially leading to criminal behaviour.

In spite of personality largely being a result of genetic and biological factors, Eysenck firmly believed that behaviour modification techniques can help people acquire positive codes of social conduct and positive responses to certain situations.

Evaluation of Eysenck's Theory of Personality

The relationship between biology and personality is recognised fully within Eysenck's theory and this is often ignored within other perspectives. This relationship produces a number of interesting hypotheses in terms of such things as criminality, psychological difficulties and intelligence. A notion of a trait is controversial – it describes behaviour; however, does it adequately attend to concepts such as self-concept, identity and the influence of the unconscious? These could be considered significant in an explanation of personality and identity.

Biological and socially constructed factors

Disability

In defining and exploring the medical and social model of disability you will develop an awareness of the extent to which disability can be considered to be socially constructed.

The medical model

The medical model is a traditional perspective on disability which has a *deficit* focus – meaning a focus on what the individual *cannot* do (by sheer fact of their disability). According to this model, an individual's condition merits treatment – and management – by experts in the field. The further assumption is that the disabled person should be supported, as far as is possible, to fit with 'normal' society. Where the disability is too 'bad' or severe, then specially-tailored and typically separate, education and care should be provided. A separation of 'special needs' from 'mainstream' education might be considered evidence of this.

The social model

The social model of disability asserts that the disabled individual is as *completely* 'human' as anyone else and must be accorded *ordinary* rights and the means to engage with and be part of, their community and society. The social model rejects all forms of separation between disabled and non-disabled people. This model is expressly political, identifying the many complex ways in which disabled people are *oppressed* by the society in which they live. Social, political and economic *barriers* are constructed which limit and/or devalue the individual's perception of self and development. These can include a lack of ordinary and real education, a greater-than-average chance of experiencing poverty and unemployment and a cultural life where attitudes, beliefs and media reinforce inferiority and exclusion. This model recognises an individual's impairment as a loss or limit of function but impairment is an aspect of the person, not 'who' the person is.

Disability does not refer to the individual's impairment but to the limits *placed* upon that individual. Disability by this model, is a complex, whole-society, form of discrimination; it is one which is sanctioned by economics, power and politics – and reinforced by prejudicial attitudes.

Beyond the social model

By emphasising the structures and forces in society which *create disability*, critics have charged the social model with the same crime as the medical model: describing and defining people *in terms* of disability! Dr Tom Shakespeare, one of the UK's foremost writers on disability experience and 'disability politics', argues that our 21st century perspective on disability should look *beyond* the social model. He encourages us to *widen* our perspective, by acknowledging that we are all, at given times in our lives, affected by illness and/or impairment and by this globalised perspective, no one is 'non-disabled'!

Sexual orientation

'Being gay' – is it biological destiny or lifestyle choice? An individual's sexual orientation and related perceptions and experiences are important aspects of identity and personality.

Notoriously in 1993, USA geneticist Hamer announced 'the gay gene'. He claimed to have discovered 'genetic markers' on part of the 'X' chromosome of gay men. So *the* gene to confirm the biological origins of homosexuality was heralded by world media. However, subsequent research failed to replicate Hamer's findings and the controversy continues, in spite of a long history of research into the biological origins of homosexuality.

The nature argument claims that sexual orientation is biologically determined. Biological influences include genetics, pre-natal hormones and differences in neurological structure. Bailley and Pillard (1990) found that identical twins were more likely to share sexual orientation than non-identical twins. Identical twins not only share their genes; they share the conditions in the womb.

Bem (1996) argued that while biological factors do not 'create' homosexuality they do influence the temperament of the developing child, which in turn influences the child's preferences for doing 'boy' or 'girl' things, and for tuning into and seeking out 'sex-atypical' friends and activities. Children feel 'different' from same-sex friends, to consider *them* as 'different', 'unfamiliar' and 'exotic'. Ultimately, this sense of difference, this curiosity and perception of same-sex others as 'exotic', leads to a physiological arousal which later, via puberty, is likely to transform into a sexualised arousal and responsiveness; the 'exotic' has become 'erotic'.

The individual with minority identity, who lives and works within a heterosexual 'mainstream', is vulnerable to perceptions and experiences of 'difference' and is likely to have to make adaptations in terms of how they present and share their identity. For some homosexual individuals, 'straight-acting' provides protection and a level of social ease, but this is at a cost. On the other hand, where the individual identifies and affiliates with a very 'out' and deliberately separatist gay lifestyle and subculture, s/he experiences limitations on mainstream social engagement.

Interdisciplinary contribution

Sociology can contribute greatly to understanding the influence of socio-economic factors in the development of identity and personality. The unit 'Sociology for Care Practice' explores a number of key issues such as income related to age, relative deprivation, family roles and family structures, which impact on how a person perceives themselves – particularly in relation to others and the wider culture. Batmanghelidjh's work covered in the Sociology for Care Practice chapter (under 'Family Sociology', see page 124) is of particular interest in terms of exploring both internal and external influences on the development of the self concept and personality.

Life events and life experiences

This section explores the impact that anticipated and unanticipated life events and life experiences may have on individuals at various stages of development. You will be introduced to theories of transition and loss and will explore a range of life events.

Life events

Holmes and Rahe's (1967) *Social Readjustment Rating Scale* (SAR) identifies 43 'life-change events' such as, 'death of a spouse', 'divorce', 'personal illness or injury', 'change in financial circumstances' and 'change in living circumstances'. The scale prioritises these events in terms of the stress they induce in the individual. The model has been criticised in terms of its simplicity; however, it provides an insight into the kinds of events a person might experience.

Life events and life experiences can be anticipated or unanticipated. Earlier in the section you investigated *anticipated* events – events consistent with age and stage developmental milestones and norms. Possible *unanticipated* events are described in the table below.

Stage of development	Unanticipated life experiences/ events
Infancy	Loss of parent, developmental disability, neglect, failure to thrive
Childhood	Change in school, expulsion from school, domestic violence
Adolescence	Homelessness, being taken into care, pregnancy/becoming a parent
Adult	Redundancy, acquiring disability, requiring residential care, separation/divorce, change in social network and activities, deaths among peer group
Older adult	Loss of child, marriage, maintained or increased levels of energy and function

Unanticipated life events and experiences.

It is not possible to list or discuss *all* of life's potential events and changes – anticipated or otherwise! You will explore a selection and these will include stress, learning disability, family life, unexpected ill health, retirement, bereavement and grief. It should be noted that *attachment* is a significant life event and this has been covered earlier.

Stress

In biological terms, stress is the body's response to something we perceive to be threatening (a stressor). Stress is not always undesirable. It can motivate us to put in that extra effort and improve performance just when it is needed – to submit an essay on time, to study for exams, to tidy the house when you expect visitors. Stress becomes undesirable when it is severe or prolonged. One way to look at stress is through the analogy of an elastic band: the band has quite a bit of stretch, however if it stretches too much, it will break.

It is important to recognise that stress is also likely to be a feature of other life events and life experiences. *Short-* and *long-term effects* of stress will create **unmet needs** and impact on the development of the individual.

Short-term effects	Long-term effects
Disturbed sleep, appetite and energy levels, disrupted memory and concentration, headaches, stomach and bowel upset, raised blood pressure and heart-rate, feelings of low self-esteem… **and more**	Chronically low levels of energy and esteem, relationship-vulnerability, lasting feeling of depression, hopelessness and/or anger, skin and other psychosomatic disorders develop, 'sociability' is relegated, unhealthy lifestyle changes, sexual malfunction/loss of libido, development of serious and irreversible health issues, including cardiovascular disease… **and more**

Potential short- and long-term effects of stress.

Activity

Potentially, what needs are created for the individual who experiences prolonged stress? You should make reference to all the categories of needs.

What is the potential impact on development of prolonged stress for someone at the adolescent stage of development? Make references to all the strands of development.

Self-esteem changes during transition

Adams et al (1976) suggests that our *self-esteem* fluctuates as we go through and manage transition, following a significant life experience/event. Theirs is a framework designed to show *generally-identifiable* patterns and expectations for behaviour and esteem in periods of transition. The illustration shows a visual representation of the model, which highlights the vulnerability of the individual who is undergoing transition; it can be a useful tool for the Social Care practitioner in understanding behaviour.

Career crises and transistions

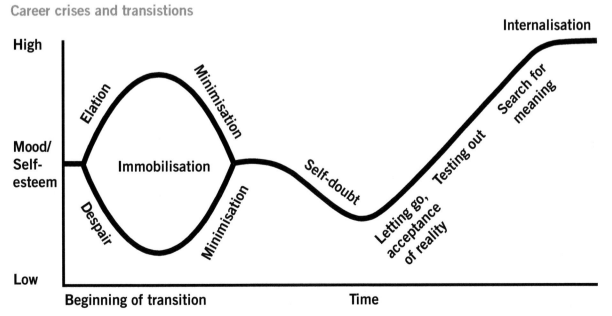

Adams et al (1976) have established this model of transition and self-esteem.

1. **Immobilisation**	Immediate response to experience or event? The individual experiences shock and disbelief	Initial fall in self-esteem followed by a brief recovery
2. **Minimisation**	A first-line coping strategy – the individual attempts some kind of denial or reduction ('it can't be *that* bad')	Fall in self-esteem
3. **Depression**	The individual begins to feel real pain and is typically angry – and fearful	Fall in self-esteem
4. **Acceptance of reality**	A realisation that things have changed and he will need to make his own changes in response	Fall in self-esteem
5. **Testing**	Begins to try alternatives to how it was before (the event/experience); esteem often rises, a developing sense of 'taking control'	Rise in self-esteem
6. **Search for meaning**	The individual begins to rationalise, justify and see themselves in their new way of life	Rise in self-esteem
7. **Internalisation**	The individual has worked through and adapted to changes and has a new vision of 'self' and how to live	Transition complete.

Seven stages of transition – Adams et al (1976).

Personal agency and resilience in periods of transition

Personal agency

Rotter (1966) in Gross (2005) asserted that when an individual has an '*external locus of control*', that is s/he assumes they have little or no control over their lives they are more likely to experience prolonged difficulties and/or stress in response to life events and perceived stressors. On the other hand, where the individual has a confirmed sense of *personal*

agency – belief in their rights to and capability for, self-determination – they are more likely to have more effective coping strategies and consequently experience lower levels of 'lasting difficulty' and/or stress.

Gilligan (1997) identified the importance, in Social Care practice, of enabling and supporting vulnerable young people to develop a package of self-awareness and life-skills which promote 'resilience'. Resilience is about being able to overcome setbacks and a willingness to try again following disappointment.

Life experiences

Dyslexia

A lifelong neuro-developmental condition, dyslexia is likely to become apparent (although not necessarily recognised) in childhood. Dyslexia is commonly misconceived as 'trouble with spelling' or about 'writing letters backwards'. More accurately, dyslexia is a learning difficulty where, among other things, the child's short-term and working memories are affected, together with capacity to organise and sequence information. Often physical co-ordination is affected too. Dyslexia does *not* reflect an individual's cognitive abilities but *does*, without early diagnosis and intervention, impact on the whole person's development.

Consider this

In a series of books titled *Hank Zipper the World's Best Underachiever,* American actor Henry Winkler writes semi-autobiographically of a childhood shaped by dyslexia. Of his own time at school he says:

'The information slid off the blackboard of my brain. That was my life. I was called stupid, lazy. I was told I was not living up to my potential. My self-image was down around my ankles.

'The one thing I had going for me was my sense of humour. I was funny. The class clown. When the teacher read us a story, I would act it out. That sure didn't get me any A's. It got me a trip downstairs to the Principal's office. And that wasn't funny at all.'

http://www.ldonline.org/article/The_World%27s_Greatest_Underachiever (7/7/09)

Marriage and parenting

'Woman's discontent increases in exact proportion to her development.'

(Elizabeth Cady Stanton, American suffragist and abolitionist (1815–1902))

What would we consider *developmental norms* in adulthood? For a majority, these include marriage and/or parenting. However, do these norms equate with personal expectation and 'preparedness' for these norms?

Consider the following statements:

- Married people are, in the long term, happier and healthier than unmarried people. Marriage and parenthood inevitably mean changes in the individuals' lifestyle, their attitudes and their priorities. These changes are in line with developmental norms.

- Married men are physically and mentally healthier than unmarried men.

- Married women report as less physically and emotionally healthy than unmarried women *and* married men.

- Married women record less satisfaction with their marriage than married men.

- Married women do more housework than married men (although both usually have jobs outside the home).

- When a parent stays at home to prioritise child-care, it is more likely to be a married woman whose career dreams are compromised.

- Women often report a greater decrease in quality of life and 'life-satisfaction' during parenthood than men.

- Mothers most satisfied with parenthood were those with partners who were 'more than average' involved and supportive.

- Following divorce, women are likely to suffer most financially and to experience greatest reduction in esteem and changes to personal identity.

- Divorce for men and women generally leads to a decline in health and to changes in their network of friends.

Post-natal depression

Pregnancy and birth are anticipated life events for the majority of women. Does the fact that women have this 'reproductive capacity' equip and prepare them to be mothers?

Small and Luster et al (1994) reported that up to 20 per cent of mothers are depressed in their first year of motherhood due to three main factors: a 'lack of social and emotional support', 'illness and exhaustion' and 'lack of time to themselves'.

Early-onset dementia

Where certain developmental/acquired conditions are *already* present (including Down's Syndrome and multiple sclerosis), an increased incidence of early-onset dementia can be expected. Dementia is *not* however, an anticipated life-event for most adults under 65.

A diagnosis of dementia for an individual at the age of 50 is likely to have very different developmental meaning and impact than the same diagnosis at the age of 75. In terms of lifespan development, we can anticipate the 'average' 50-year-old to be 'actively' parenting, to be in full-time employment and to have current concern with typically 'adult' priorities such as keeping their job and paying their mortgage.

Consider this

With early-onset dementia occurring in relatively small numbers, specialist 'age appropriate' services and care are virtually non-existent. What needs might there be for appropriate service provision for the individual who has early-onset dementia?

How relevant and/or applicable is the Adams, Hayes and Hopson's model of 'self-esteem during transition' when the transition concerned is one of cognitive impairment?

Retirement

Retirement can be considered a developmental norm for the older adult. However anticipated retirement may be, it is still a transition and, as such, is likely to encompass forms of loss and stress. Atchley's model, *'Five Periods of Adjustment'* suggests a staged process from the period immediately following retirement to a new but stable lifestyle.

Honeymoon	Immediately following retirement – feeling free and invigorated, activity levels increase
Rest and relaxation	Acclimatising to the new lifestyle, less fast-paced, taking stock
Disenchantment	Experiencing some disappointment if retirement does not match up to all the individual had hoped for
Reorientation	A time for readjustment, when expectations about retirement are more realistic
Routine	When a stable and satisfying lifestyle is achieved

Atchley's 'Five Periods of Adjustment' model (1982, 1985).

It is not assumed that retirement is a linear process. A range of factors are likely to impact on the experience and 'event' of retirement.

- Whether or not retirement is a voluntary transition: enforced retirement is, for Atchley, less anticipated and therefore more of a disruption to an individual's lifestyle, identity, esteem and behaviour.
- Pre-retirement education: time and resources to support the individual to prepare for this transition, perhaps financial planning, make the transition easier.
- Interests outside employment: where the individual's identity and interests are highly work-related they can find retirement more difficult.
- Good health and financial security enable retirement plans to be fulfilled.

John successfully launched into active retirement after a long career as a colliery manager.

Chapter 3 Psychology for Social Care practice

Case study

John

John retired at the age of 64, having worked for the Scottish Coal Board for 42 years. By the time he retired, John had had many years experience of colliery management, with direct authority over a 2000-strong workforce. These working years were hard – and not without cost – for John developed severe cardiovascular disease, had several heart attacks and a leg amputation. At 64, John had no choice but to retire on grounds of disability. He walked from the pit-yard on his last day and never looked back. Immediately he signed up as full-time childminder for his 3-year-old granddaughter. Christie and her 'Papa' had great fun together; they spent their days reading stories, dressing up and working in the garden. With Papa's help, Christie was soon reading words, writing her name and tying her laces. John appeared to respond to this transition by leapfrogging straight to (Atchley's) phase 5: *routine*. Those who knew him best saw no signs of altered self-esteem or identity, no change in his levels of energy and activity.

1. What does this suggest to you about the degree to which John had established *resilience*?

2. What does this suggest to you about John's *esteem levels* in relation to the work–retirement transition?

Disengagement theory – the older adult

Here we will look at the disengagement theory of Cumming and Henry (1961). For Cumming and Henry, adjusting to older adulthood usually involves a *withdrawal from society* by the older adult and a *withdrawal from the older adult*, by society:

- the older adult voluntarily retreats to a smaller world and limited social network
- society expects and assumes less of the older adult and removes status and responsibility from them (for example via retirement).

Is this a matter of culture?

It is important to consider the impact of negative and limiting stereotypes which assume older adults to be physically and/or cognitively incapable (and therefore dependent), attitudinally stubborn and intolerant (especially of young people!) – and of limited 'practical value'. Stereotyping can have self-fulfilling consequences: if expectations of an older adult assume he or she 'can't', then limited opportunity is likely to be made available for him or her to show – to others and themselves – that as a matter of fact, she or he '*can*'!

Activity

This activity deals with cultural variations. You should identify via research, a culture where to be older is equated with being 'wiser' and of greater social status. Consider the developmental and behavioural effects for the older adult, of *positive* assumptions and social prestige.

You may for example, consider China, with its cultural traditions of revering the older adult. (Note, however, that contemporary research is suggesting that the more 'Westernised' in terms of post-industrial lifestyles China becomes, the more the older population are experiencing 'Western-style' isolation and reduction in social prestige.)

Bereavement and grief

Most people will experience bereavement in their lives. However the *ways* in which individuals respond to bereavement will be varied. Many taboos and mysteries persist in our culture about how death and bereavement *should be* experienced and managed. You need only consider for example, the multitude of 'dos' and 'don'ts' associated with 'funeral behaviour'.

Worden and Murray Parkes are key theorists in bereavement and grief. Kübler-Ross provides a theoretical framework for the individual at varying stages of terminal illness. Summaries of their theories are provided below. You may already have or intend to study the HNC (Social Care) Option unit, 'Understanding Loss and the Process of Grief'. If so, you will find clear crossover of content.

Theorist	Summary
Kubler-Ross (1969)	Kübler-Ross's work was based on work with individuals in varying stages of terminal illness. She identifies a 'stepped' model; a series of five stages, each self-explanatory by name: **Denial** – the individual's reactions are of disbelief at terminal diagnosis ('Are you sure? Did you check?') **Anger** – at realisation of what loss of life would mean; anger at others and at self. **Bargaining** – the individual pursues every route they can, to change the process ('What can you do to give me longer?'). Kübler-Ross is often cited in this respect for her 'doing a deal with God'. **Depression** – the individual is immersed in sadness and acknowledges the realities they face. **Acceptance** – in this, the final stage of the grieving process, the individual can understand, accept and find peace before dying.

Theorist	Summary
Worden, J. (1991)	Worden describes four 'tasks of mourning'; by use of the term 'task' he does imply the individual has 'grief work' to do. Rather than stages to be followed, these are features of cognitive, emotional and social adjustment and may be experienced in alternative order – or only partly. Incomplete mourning for Worden, however, is an indicator of future limitations on emotional growth. The tasks of mourning are: **Acceptance** – often delayed by denial and searching, to 'complete' this task the individual accepts the reality of death. **Working through the pain** – the task of acknowledging and expressing feelings of loss and pain; a time of sadness and depression. This task may be inhibited by repression when 'recovery' is perceived and expressed but is not yet real or masked by lifestyle behaviours – uncharacteristically heavy drinking for example. Such repression is likely to have a longer-term impact on the individual. **Adjusting to a changed environment** – the task here is for the individual to adjust via new learning and thinking – and typically new experiences, to live without the person they have lost. Having always been a 'daughter', for example, then to lose the parent who made you a daughter, requires a new perception of self, new kinds of thinking. **Emotional relocation** – in 21st century-speak this task might be referred to as 'moving on'; becoming equipped and ready to function, participate, contribute and enjoy again. The person who has died is not 'lost', in that s/he can remain 'key' but via influential memories. The person who has worked through their tasks of mourning is able to live again.

Theorist	Summary
Murray Parkes (1996)	For Murray Parkes, grieving is a process of no fixed time, but generally characterised by four identifiable phases. These are not distinctly 'boundaried' in psychological or behavioural terms and are likely to overlap as each individual experiences the grief process in their unique ways. The phases: **Numbness** – a temporary phase characterised by inability to feel the true extent of loss. **Searching and pining** – where the individual is distracted and distressed to have lost, often characterised by 'searching' for the person. **Depression** – the individual is immersed in grief and despair, often with feelings of hopelessness. **Recovery** – the individual has worked through and is 'released' from the attachment they have lost and able to make plans and begin to form new attachments. Murray Parkes has particular interest in why some people appear more vulnerable to grief and find reaching the phase of recovery more problematic. He put forward a number of determinants of grief as factors which might affect the extent and depth of an individual's experience of the grief process. Experiences of grief are influenced significantly also, by past experiences of *attachment* – as well as the specific nature of attachment with the person who has died. **Determinants of grief** include: The way the person died (prolonged or suddenly? via accident, suicide, murder?) Relationship to individual – your unborn baby, a partner no one else knew about, your partner in a relationship you thought had a long future? State of relationship prior to death (argument/ambivalent/troubled). Personality factors – has the person been prone to depression before this bereavement? Do they have a history of psychological vulnerability? Social factors – does the person have a strongly developed support network or are they isolated? Are they 'allowed' to express their grief in their preferred ways?

Key theories of bereavement and grief.

Case study

Sally (1)

Sally is 73. She and Geordie were married for 41 years; they had no children. They bickered constantly but were inseparable. Geordie died six months ago, following a sudden stroke. Everyone is amazed by how well Sally has coped, how positive and active she is – babysitting, social outings and as house-proud as ever.

1. Apply Worden's model to Sally's current situation. Consider the *work* Sally has done – or is yet to do, having lost Geordie six months ago.

2. Apply Murray Parkes' model, making reference to *determinants of grief* and *phase* of grief.

Case study

Sally (2)

There has been a mistake! Sally is in fact, 37 years old! She and Geordie were together for 14 years! Now complete the same tasks as above.

1. Comparing the two scenarios, are there likely to be any significant differences in Sally's experience?

2. How might Erikson interpret the differences?

Conclusion

In this chapter you have explored the complexities of development, needs and their interrelationship. You have covered a number of psychological theories from a range of perspectives in relation to development needs, identity and personality. Throughout the chapter, you have been considering features of the nature and nurture debate. The impact of anticipated and unanticipated life events and experiences has been highlighted and explored. This chapter will have given you a wider frame of reference in understanding individuals who need and/or receive Social Care services.

1. What is development?
2. Why is the nature/nurture debate significant in developmental psychology?
3. How would you differentiate between universal, group-specific and individual changes?
4. Considering the Psychodynamic Perspective – in what ways do key themes from Bowlby and Erikson compare and contrast?
5. According to the Behaviourist Perspective, 'behaviour is neither good nor bad'. What does this mean?
6. Maslow asserts 'What a man must be a man must be.' In what ways does this statement echo key themes and concepts from the Humanistic Perspective?
7. In what ways are biological and environmental factors important in the development of *identity* and *personality*?
8. In terms of lifespan development what makes a life event or life experience *anticipated* or *unanticipated*?
9. Is the experience of bereavement active or passive?
10. In what ways might your Social Care practice be influenced by what you have learned in Psychology for social care practice?

References: Psychology for social care practice

Adams, J., Hayes, J. and Hopson, B. (1976) *Transition: Understanding and Managing Personal Change*, Martin Robertson: London.

Atchley, R. C. (1982) 'Retirement: Leaving the World of Work', *Annals of the American Academy of Political and Social Science*, No. 464, pp. 120–131.

Atchley, R. C. (1985) *Social Forces and Ageing: an Introduction to Social Gerontology*, Wadsworth Publications: California.

Bailley and Pillard (1990) cited in http://www.stonewall.org.uk/at_home/sexual_orientation_faqs/2701.asp (accessed 01/07/09).

Bem (1996) cited in http://www.flyfishingdevon.co.uk/salmon/year3/psy364-gender-nature-nurture/psy364gender-nature-nurture.htm

Bowlby, J. (1944) '44 Juvenile Thieves', *International Journal of Psychoanalysis*, 25, pp. 19–52.

Bowlby, J. (1951) 'Maternal Care and Mental Health', World Health Organization: Geneva.

Bowler, E. (2009) cited in http://www.guardian.co.uk/beyondboundarieslive/willing-and-able

Cumming, E. and Henry, W. E. (1961) *Growing Old*, Basic Books: New York.

Erikson, E. H. (1950) *Childhood and Society*, Norton Publications: New York.

Erikson, E. H. (1963) *Childhood and Society*. 2nd edition. Norton Publications: New York.

Eysenck, H. J. (1967) *The Biological Basis of Personality*, Charles C Thomas: Springfield.

Gilligan, R. (1997) 'Beyond permanence? The importance of resilience in child placement practice and planning', *Adoption and Fostering*, Vol. 20 No. 1, pp. 12–20.

Holmes, T. H. and Rahe, R. H. (1967) cited in Gross, R. (2005) *The Science of Mind and Behaviour*. 4th edition, page 172. Hodder and Stoughton Educational: London.

Kübler-Ross, E. (1969) *On Death and Dying*, Macmillan Publishing: New York.

Marcia (1980) in Adelson, J. (ed.) *Handbook of Adolescent Psychiatry*, Wiley: New York.

Neugarten (1979) in Boyd, D. and Bee, H. (2006) *Lifespan Development*. 4th edition, International edition. Pearson Education Inc.: USA.

Papalia, D., Wendokos, S. and Feldman, R. D. (2001) *Human Development*. 8th edition. McGraw Hill: New York.

Parkes, C. Murray (1996) *Bereavement: Studies of Grief in Adult Life*. 3rd edition. Routledge: London.

Rogers, C. R. (1961) *On Becoming a Person*, Houghton Mifflin: Boston.

Rotter, J. (1966) in Gross, R. (2005) *The Science of Mind and Behaviour*. 4th edition. Hodder and Stoughton Educational: London.

Rutter, M. (1981) *Maternal Deprivation Reassessed*. 2nd edition. Penguin: Harmondsworth.

Small, S. A., Luster, T. et al (1994) 'Adolescent Sexual Activity – an Ecological, Risk-Factor Approach', *Journal of Marriage and the Family*, No. 56, pp. 181–192.

Watson, J. B. (1928) *Psychological Care of Infant and Child*, Norton Publications: New York.

Worden, J. W. (1991) *Grief Counselling and Grief Therapy: A Handbook for the Mental Health Practitioner*. 2nd edition. Routledge: London.

Recommended further reading

You will find *generic* psychology, human development and child development textbooks helpful and relevant. These give description, explanation and commentary on the perspectives, theories and concepts covered in this chapter. Given that *human development* is multidisciplinary in nature, a number of texts and resources in the areas of sociology, anthropology and biology may prove useful. The popularity of psychology means numerous exciting and useful websites exist.

The following are recommendations only. Some are generic (in terms of theory and or development); others are specific to a life-stage and/or area of interest.

Bowlby, J. (1981) 'Sadness and Depression', *Attachment and Loss*, Vol. 3, Penguin: Harmondsworth.

Boyd, D. and Bee, H. (2006) *Lifespan Development*. 4th edition, International edition. Pearson Education Inc.: USA.

Coleman, J. C. (1974) *Relationships in Adolescence*, Routledge: London.

Coleman, J. C. (1980) *The Nature of Adolescence*, Methuen Publications: London.

Dickenson, D., Johnson, M. and Katz, J. (eds.) (2002) *Death, Dying and Bereavement*. 2nd edition. Sage Publications: London.

Gross, R. (2005) *Psychology: The Science of Mind and Behaviour*. 4th edition. Hodder and Stoughton Educational: London.

Maslow, A. H. (1943) 'A Theory of Human Motivation', *Psychological Review*, 50, pp. 370–96.

Maslow, A. (1968) *Toward a Psychology of Being*. 2nd edition. Van Nostrand Reinhold: New York.

Maslow, A. (1970) *Motivation and Personality*. 2nd edition. Harper & Row: New York.

Recommended websites

www.about.com

www.psychologistworld.com/

www.allpsych.com

Chapter 4
Sociology for care practice

Introduction

This chapter is designed to help you explore and understand key theories, themes and ideas from Sociology. It will encourage you to 'think sociologically' about features of society which affect the experiences, behaviour and life chances of those who need and/or receive Social Care services.

In particular, this chapter will focus on ways in which **Sociological theory**, **concepts** and **current social research** can develop our understanding of:

- the influence '**family**' has, on the behaviour, experiences and life chances of individuals,
- the causes, nature and effects on groups in society, of **poverty**, **inequality** and **discrimination.**

How you will be assessed:

You may be studying *Sociology for Social Care Practice* as a single unit or as part of an HNC in Social Care.

- Single unit assessment is likely to be via a case study, an essay and/or a presentation.
- Where this unit forms part of an HNC programme, assessment may be as above or may follow an integrated format. Integrated assessment is where key elements of several HNC units (for example, Sociology for Care Practice, Social Care Theory for Practice, Psychology for *Care Practice)* are combined in one assessment exercise.

Wherever and however you study Sociology for Care Practice, your tutor will keep you informed of assessment processes and detail.

In this chapter you will learn:

Thinking sociologically here you will be introduced to what sociology is and what sociologists do. The relevance of sociology to the world and work of Social Care will be highlighted.

The sociological toolkit as with all academic disciplines, sociology has a 'language' and concepts (ideas) of its own. This section introduces you to and explains important examples of these, relevant to 'Sociology for Social Care Practice'.

Sociological theory the work of sociologists (as is the case with all social sciences: psychology, politics, economics and so on) is based around several key theories. Each theory represents a particular way of explaining and understanding 'society'. This section will introduce and explain the main themes from sociological theory and introduce you to some original and current theorists in sociology. Key ideas from writers such as Durkheim, Parsons, Marx, Engels, Becker, Goffman and others will soon become familiar!

Sociology of 'Family' this section will focus on how sociologists define 'family' and debates about the influence of family on the development, behaviour and life chances of its members. The theories introduced in section 3 will be applied here, to help us evaluate the role and importance of 'family'.

Sociology of 'Poverty, Inequality and Discrimination' Sociological explanations for and evidence of poverty, inequality and discrimination in Scotland will be considered, with particular reference to groups who use Social Care services. Again, those theories introduced in section 3 will be applied.

Thinking sociologically

For students new to the subject, it can be surprisingly difficult to find a clear and universal definition of 'sociology'.

For this reason, our chapter begins by *describing* (rather than *defining*) what sociology *is* and what sociologists *do*.

Sociology studies the ways society is organised and the behaviour of society's members, most specifically:

Sociology studies the structures, systems, processes and relationships which make up a society and how these might influence the lives of society's members.

For example, sociology helps us to examine and understand the importance and impact of being born into a particular 'social class', being born or becoming 'male' or 'female', being 'black' or 'white', experiencing impairment or disability.

Sociology studies social issues and 'social problems'

Sociologists have and continue to study any and all aspects of life important to society, e.g. power and politics, poverty and welfare, health, illness and disease, media and communication, sex, sexuality and gender, family, deviance, crime and law, religion.

Sociology is based on research and aims to be 'factual' and fair by using science-like methods in this research

Sociologists have a particular repertoire of research skills; these are methods used to try to ensure that the 'finding out' (about social issues) they do, is as free from opinion and bias as possible.

Sociological argument is based on a number of theories. Each theory offers us a particular way of understanding human society and the behaviours of its members

In the way that the umbrella term 'Christianity' divides into several differing forms of faith (Catholicism, Protestantism and so on), sociology divides into several key 'camps'; each camp is a theory with unique views on and understanding of, society.

Sociology urges us to question 'common-sense opinion' and 'received wisdom'

In studying sociology you are guaranteed to question aspects of what you have been 'raised' to believe and will almost certainly ask questions you haven't asked – or perhaps even considered – before!

> 'It can be said that the first wisdom of sociology is this – things are not always what they seem.'
>
> (Berger, P. 1963, page 34)

More than common sense

Sociologists reject 'common-sense' explanations for human behaviour.

By 'common sense' they mean those everyday ideas, opinions and judgements we hear, see and tend to make about how people *are*, what they *do*, or how they *should be*. Often these assumptions are based on information which is limited, untrue and unfair.

Common-sense assumptions are often expressed in our society in relation to disabled people, children and young people in care, people living with mental illness – in fact any and all groups whose needs and rights are of interest to us as Social Carers.

In the activity above, where you researched current social issues and reflected critically about the evidence that research produces, you made a start on 'thinking sociologically'!

Sociological thinking, i.e. the capacity to see past the myths and limitations of 'common sense', is of particular value to workers in Social Care, as the following ideas from C. Wright Mills and Helen Prejean demonstrate.

Developing a sociological imagination

For American sociologist C. Wright Mills (1959), we need to develop a certain kind of mindset, an approach to understanding human lifestyle and behaviour which he calls the *'Sociological Imagination'*.

For Mills, people tend to live 'close-up' and private, each of us preoccupied with our own 'small world' (*our* family, *our* health, *our* work, *our* relationships, *our* bank balance).

We lack awareness of the bigger picture; generally failing to see and understand the ways in which our experiences, behaviour and life chances are influenced, sometimes created, by aspects of the society in which we live. Mills argues:

'....consider unemployment. When in a city of 100,000 only one man is unemployed, that is his personal trouble and for its relief we properly look to the character of the man, his skills and his immediate opportunities. But when in a nation of 50 million employees, 15 million men are unemployed, that is an issue...The very structure of opportunities has collapsed.'
(Mills, 1959, page 9)

Sociological imagination and disability

While the experience of having an impairment or of 'being disabled' is, of course, specific to and different for each person, a sociological imagination urges us to look beyond the individual, to examine ways in which society around them has *constructed* and responds to, their disability. We might ask why, for example, in 21st-century Scotland, a disabled person is likely to experience barriers and limits which go beyond any associated with their disability? Why are disabled people in Scotland among those *less likely* to succeed (in line with their potential) in education and employment and *more likely* to experience inequality, poverty and discrimination?

By applying a sociological imagination, we work to develop our awareness of how over time, social forces (for example public attitudes, together with systems of law, politics and economics and all resulting policy) have separated 'disability', creating a '*less valued*' and '*less equal*' reality for disabled people. As such, disability should be considered more an (important) 'public issue' than simply a 'private trouble'.

But I'm not a sociologist!

That's fine. You can develop your awareness of ways in which big, broad and deep social forces around us can and do impact on apparently 'private' or 'personal troubles' and can apply this awareness to your practice in Social Care without being an academic sociologist!

In her book *Dead Man Walking* (1983), Helen Prejean, a Catholic nun, describes her experiences of working in St Thomas, a poor black 'ghetto' in New Orleans, in the 1970s.

In her early years in St Thomas, Prejean felt 'separate' from the population there, unable to make sense of behaviours and lifestyles and personally appalled by the extent to which 'life on welfare', drug addiction, gang violence, high incidences of teen and lone parenting and repeated/long-term prison sentences were considered 'normal'. Individuals and families seemed to Prejean, senselessly 'antisocial'.

Over time, however, her perspective changed. Prejean became aware of the real impact on the population of St Thomas of grinding poverty, under-resourced and substandard systems of schooling and healthcare, virtually zero adult employment and extremely limited opportunities for 'pro-social' leisure.

These realities she saw were not, in any meaningful way, relieved by the ill-equipped and unresponsive social services which had been put in place to 'help'. According to Prejean's new way of seeing, therefore, 'personal troubles' ('antisocial' behaviours and lifestyles) were often a direct consequence of specific economic, political and social systems and the policies and practices these produced.

Prejean had in effect, developed her own sociological imagination. For in the words of Mills:

'both the correct statement of the problem and the range of possible solutions require us to consider the economic and political institutions of the society and not merely the personal situation and character of a scatter of individuals.'
(Mills, 1959, page 9)

Prejean became much more 'in tune' with the realties of life in St Thomas and, by her own description, she became more insightful, empathic, challenging (in that she became 'political' and 'took on' the authorities) and effective, as a Social Care worker. She was able to reject limiting and prejudicial 'common-sense' assumptions about the population of St Thomas, and instead began to understand the behaviours and lifestyles within their larger, social and political contexts. Remember that Prejean is not by any stretch of the imagination, a sociologist!

The sociological toolkit

In exploring social issues and social problems, we know sociology has its own imagination. It also has a language of its own – essential terms and concepts which contribute to the 'Sociology-speak' with which you should become familiar. A number of these are identified, explained and/or exemplified in the table below. Prompts and/or questions for thinking and discussion are also provided to help you become competent and confident in their use.

Term	Definition	Thinking/discussion points
Culture	Patterns of thinking and behaving; essentially the 'lifestyle' accepted and practised by, a group or society. A 'culture' is made up of many features, including shared language, beliefs, customs and traditions. All cultures vary.	Why do you think awareness of the role and impact of 'culture' is vital for Social Care workers?
Subculture	Groups which are considered separate from mainstream. Economic migrants may constitute subcultures in today's Scotland, in terms of how they see themselves and are seen by others.	In what ways might individuals and groups who receive social services be considered a 'subculture'?
Ethnocentrism	Interpreting the lives of other groups and societies from our own 'world-view'; in terms of what we believe, how we live, what we have and consider to be 'normal'.	In what ways might a Social Care worker be 'ethnocentric' in his/her practice and what might be the consequences of this?
Socialisation	The lifelong process of becoming social, i.e. learning the language, beliefs, attitudes, customs and traditions which characterise one's culture.	What might sociologists mean when they say 'not all socialisation is conscious'?
Primary socialisation	The initial phase of socialisation, mainly 'family'-based, when we learn our culture's language, values, expectations for 'socially-accepted' behaviours, etc. Arguably, this is the phase of socialisation when we are capable of learning the most – and most quickly!	What for you, would be the features (and effects) of 'ideal' primary socialisation?
Secondary socialisation	'Second stage socialisation', mainly via influences and aspects of society outside and beyond family (for example our peers, systems and institutions of education, work, media, religion, etc.).	Identify ways in which aspects of 'primary' and 'secondary' socialisation may contrast – or 'collide' – and the possible effects of this on an individual's behaviour?
Social institution	A part of society which contributes to its overall structure. Social institutions each have their own role in society, e.g. the economy, media, political system, the family, education, church and work. Social institutions are major influences in our socialisation, they work separately and together to encourage a broadly 'common' socialisation.	How might social institutions work together to promote for society's members, the 'normality' of heterosexual marriage?

Term	Definition	Thinking/discussion points
Values	Beliefs about what is considered 'good' and 'right'. Values inform our thinking and our behaviour.	Why is 'unconditional positive regard' a core value for Social Care?
Norms	Rules which govern behaviour, norms may be formal (i.e. laws) or 'unwritten' and informal. Norms reflect the values of a culture – and 'sanctions' are applied when these are breeched!	For Afar tribeswomen of Ethiopia patterns of (deliberate) facial scarring to enhance natural beauty. Without such scarring (administered by the elder tribeswomen), young women would be considered unattractive, even 'ugly'. By what means do 'we' define and evidence beauty? Which culture has it right and why do you think this is so?
Roles	Patterns of behaviour associated with and expected from particular social 'placing', or occupation (e.g. 'minister', 'mum', 'MSP').	What kinds of 'role behaviours' are typically associated with being a 'person who uses services' and a 'care worker' in our society? What can and does happen when individuals are considered to act outside their 'assigned' (given) role?

Essential sociological terms and concepts.

Further research

Refer to the '*What is Sociology?*' or '*Introducing Sociology*' section in any recommended/ HNC-appropriate textbook. This will help you consolidate your understanding of what sociology is and the kind of 'topics' sociologists study, together with those key terms which make up your sociological toolkit.

Sociological theory – an introduction

By getting to grips in the previous pages with key ideas and terms, you have begun to *think sociologically.* Now it is time to develop an awareness of the main perspectives and theories on which sociology is based.

Sociological perspectives

Broadly speaking, sociology is split into two main perspectives ('perspective' being a generalised view and explanation for human behaviour); these are 'Structural' and 'Action' (or 'Interpretive').

The 'structural–action split'

A **structural** perspective has a 'macro' (large) focus and emphasises the ways in which society's systems and institutions influence and determine the lives of its members.

An **action** (or Interpretive) perspective has a 'micro' (small) focus, emphasising the ways in which small-scale interactions between individuals and groups in turn influence and 'create' their society.

Each perspective contains several **theories** ('theory' is a *specific* set of views about human behaviour). Often, an image or picture helps us understand ideas. Theories relevant to sociology for care practice are shown in the following illustration.

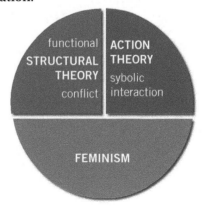

Sociological perspectives and theories relevant to Social Care practice.

The value of discourse

Sociological theories help us to understand and explain social issues and social problems. Theories and theorists often disagree – sometimes radically! This does not mean that sociologists 'can't make up their minds', or 'don't know the answer'; rather that sociology recognises the value of **discourse** – a kind of 'conversation (or argument!) between theories'.

The role of Social Carer is a challenging one, responding to complex situations, experiences and emotions, with 'answers' not always readily apparent, available or appropriate. Knowledge of sociological discourse supports the carer to develop greater depth and breadth of information, new understanding and more 'thinking' resources. In turn, the carer's practice is likely to be more 'open', aware, creative, challenging – and effective.

Note: the following provides an overview of and introduction to sociological theory; further reading is also required. You are advised to look up and take notes on each theory/area, using any HNC-appropriate/recommended textbooks. We will start with structural theories – looking at functionalism and conflict theories.

Functionalism

For Functionalist theorists, society's structure and shape is comprised of interrelated systems.

Social stability

For **Emile Durkheim** (1858–1917), as with all early Functionalist writers, society can be understood as a *system* made up of separate but interconnected parts. This can be illustrated by a biological analogy, where society is compared to a living body.

While each 'part' (organs, systems) of the body performs a unique and specialised function (the lungs oxygenate the blood), all the organs work together too, to ensure the body as a whole, 'functions' and survives.

Society as a system is similar. The 'organs' or 'parts' of a society are its **social institutions** (key institutions include family, education, the economic and political systems). Each institution has a special and particular function to fulfil (or job to do, in terms of society's 'needs') and all institutions co-operate and work interdependently to ensure society stays 'healthy', by remaining **stable**. The family, for example, socialises children in preparation for school, school socialises and 'prepares' children and young people for the world of work and so on.

Other features of society which contribute to social stability are **socialisation**, **social control** and '**managed' social change**.

Socialisation

A society is stable when sufficient of its members have been socialised into accepting and conforming to that society's **value consensus**: a broadly shared agreement about how society should operate and its members live (*heterosexuality*, *marriage* and *monogamy* can be considered features of 'our' value consensus).

Social institutions in the course of fulfilling their 'specialised' functions (e.g. the education system preparing the young population to enter the world of work) are, at the same time, society's main instruments for **socialisation** – where those social norms, values and roles expected of us are transmitted and are for Talcott Parsons (1952) 'internalised' by society's members.

Social control

Where social rules are breached, there are powerful individuals, groups and social institutions which have the responsibility and right to apply **social sanctions** (punishment). Sanctions can be minor and informal (for example, a warning look from a parent to child at the sweets counter!) or significant and formal – ranging from 're-education' to separation from society via imprisonment.

When 'rule-breakers' are made an example of, and receive social punishment, it confirms for the majority just how *different* (from the rule-breakers) they are and how 'right' they (the 'moral majority') are – and so the value consensus is further reinforced!

Social inequality

Society for Functionalists is recognised as hierarchical: economic, political and social inequalities and 'layers' of power, control, prestige and reward *do* exist and are seen as inevitable, 'natural' *and* desirable.

Inequality fulfils a **functional requisite** for society – ensuring, for example, that *all* the jobs get done – from the cleaner in your work setting, to the unit or area manager. Inequality is 'aspirational' too: those who lack social and economic means and status can see others achieving – and so are encouraged to 'work harder' and 'aim higher' as a result.

Social change

By Functionalist analysis, changes in society are inevitable and acceptable, providing that these occur gradually, in limited ways, and can be accommodated without threat to social order and stability – adaptation rather than revolution!

Functionalist theory is accused of being:

- over-deterministic : Functionalism implies humans are largely controlled and constrained by social structures – and exercise little free will
- over-emphatic on social stability and cohesion: is society *really* more stable than unstable? Do the majority *really* conform?

Conflict theory

For Conflict theorists, society has a pyramidal structure and shape, with concentration of ownership, wealth and power in the hands of a privileged few at the 'top' of the pyramid.

Society is unstable and unequal

Karl Marx (1818–1883) is renowned for his critique of **capitalism**, the economic system which had spawned industrialisation throughout Europe. Capitalism created and maintained powerful divisions between groups or 'social classes', with a relatively small ruling class (*bourgeoisie*) occupying the top of society's 'pyramid', owning most of society's wealth and resources. Via this ownership, the bourgeoisie become sufficiently powerful to assume power and control over the majority of the working class (*proletariat*).

A capitalist economy was seen by Marx as unstable and unsettled, with the social classes in constant competition and conflict. For, while the ruling elite seek continually to expand their ratio of ownership, wealth, power and control, the subject population struggles to improve on their economic and social experiences of inequality and powerlessness. For one group to have more, the other must necessarily, have less!

For today's Conflict theorists, economic and social inequalities between social groups remain critical – and can be seen in divides of social class, sex, ethnic group, disability; i.e. in all spheres of life where inequalities in wealth, power and participation are evident.

Capitalism in the 19th century of course evolved, with 'ownership' and 'wealth' occurring in new and more varied forms. As described by Kirby et al (2000, page 630):

'the property owned by the modern upper class is no longer the land, factories and industrial plants of yesteryear but the assets, pension funds and insurance funds flickering on computer screens in global money markets'.

Socialisation

For Conflict theory, the **dominant ideology** (a set of beliefs representing the interests of elite groups) is transmitted via the **social institutions** of capitalism throughout our experiences of socialisation. This ideology creates for society's members the *illusion* that society is 'fair' and social divisions are 'natural'.

In today's Scotland for example, law, policy and politicians (!) inform us that all citizens have equal right to free and 'needs-appropriate' education. We might assume from this level playing-field, that those who 'succeed' in the education system are Scotland's most academically capable students.

Conflict theorists would argue, however, that many forms of education exist in Scotland, with some more 'needs-appropriate', good quality, fair (and expensive!) than others. In effect, equality in Scottish education is a *myth* sold to us via the dominant ideology.

Social control

While society's members may assume their behaviour, experiences and life chances result largely from their own actions and choices and via *free will*, for Conflict theorists, lives are primarily shaped and determined by economic, political and social forces.

Control begins as **economic** (how much people can earn, what they can buy, where they can live), but extends to become political, social, personal – even spiritual.

In short, *all* areas of life experienced by subject class members have been shaped (or 'created') by the system(s) into which they have been born, are educated, work and/or raise their families.

Social change

The conflict theory position argues for radical change throughout and across society, achievable by a new economic system based on real redistribution (sharing out) of ownership, wealth, power and control. Where society and all its institutions are organised in such a way, then society's least powerful citizens *can* achieve economic, political and social equality.

Conflict theorists argue *against* limited and gradual social change, in the belief that 'tinkering' with a system allows that system, and those who control it, to continually regroup and hold tight to their ownership, power and control.

Conflict theory is accused of being:

- overly-deterministic: guilty of assuming society's members have little, if any, free will
- over-emphatic in focusing on 'conflict', tensions and divisions, thus failing to recognise forms of agreement and co-operation which do exist within and across society.

Conflict theory: key themes

- Society is based on an economic system which is unequal and exploitative (all forms of exploitation, financial and social, arise from that system)
- Society's social institutions work (alone and together) to falsely justify and reinforce economic and social inequality
- A majority (of the population) experience control and constraint via these systems, therefore are denied free will
- Redistribution of society's resources is vital, if society is to become more economically, politically and socially equal – and ethical.

Comparing consensus and conflict theories

The big difference:

- **Consensus** theory identifies society as a system of relative *harmony* and *stability*
- **Conflict** theory views (and criticises) society as a system of *conflict* and *instability*.

Social institutions:

- **Consensus** theorists see the function of social institutions as essentially positive and beneficial for the greater good in that they operate to ensure maximum social cohesion, conformity and stability.
- **Conflict** theorists are critical of the role social institutions play in manipulating society's members to accept and live within a system which is organised solely to meet the needs of a relatively small number of social elites.

The essential similarity is that both theories assert that **social structures** are more influential (than free will) in determining the behaviour, experiences and life chances of society's members.

Feminist theory

GO TO WORK
GET SHOPPING
MAKE THE TEA
TAKE JUNIOR TO YOUTH CLUB
WALK THE DOG
CLEAN THE BATHROOM
DO THE IRONING
PHONE COUNCIL ABOUT
HOLE IN PAVEMENT
HALT GLOBAL WARMING
END INTERNATIONAL
DRUG TRAFFICKING
SORT OUT
'WAR ON TERROR'....

A woman's work is never done.

Feminism is the umbrella term for a large body of theory, writing and political action which has at its core, attempts to identify, challenge and redress inequality and discrimination which is sex-based.

For feminist sociologists, if we are to study, interpret and respond to issues *about* 'social structures' and human experience, we must begin by considering the most fundamentally divisive social structures of all, those based on **sex** and **gender**.

Social construction of gender roles

Did Miss Muffet *learn* to scream when she saw a spider?

Gender roles are the patterns of thinking, attitude and behaviour that each culture associates with 'being *masculine*' and 'being *feminine*'. For feminist writers gender roles are socially constructed and assigned (given). We acquire these via our experiences of **socialisation**.

Gender-based differences are reinforced by society's social institutions, sometimes subtly, sometimes openly and with emphasis. According to Robert Connell (yes there are male 'Feminists'!) women in modern 'Western' societies are socialised towards the ideal of 'emphasised femininity'*:*

'The display of sociability rather than technical competence, fragility in mating scenes, compliance with men's desire for titillation and ego-stroking in office relationships, acceptance of marriage and childcare...'
(Connell, R.W. (1987), page 187, in Fulcher and Scott (2007).

> **Consider this**
>
> Research confirms that the same baby is spoken to, played with and spoken about, in very different ways by adults – depending on whether that baby is dressed in pink or blue!
>
> What might these 'differences' be, where might they come from – and why, for sociologists, are these differences important?

Power and patriarchy

For many feminist sociologists sexual inequality, disadvantage and exploitation are deeply rooted in society's *power structures* – most specifically within an **economic system** which expects women (as part of their 'natural' being and role) to carry out a disproportionate amount of unpaid domestic and 'caring' work.

By this model, women become effectively, a subject class *within* 'the' subject class: at greater economic, political and social disadvantage than men.

Patriarchy ('father-led'/male dominance of all economic, political and social systems) is a means by which male dominance and control is ensured.

Different schools of feminism

Feminism is not a single theory, in fact many 'schools' of Feminism exist.

Key ideas from **Liberal**, **Radical** and **Socialist/Marxist feminism** are summarised in the following table.

School of feminism	Key ideas (to explain sex-based inequality)	What is to be done?
Liberal	Disadvantage, inequality and discrimination are pervasive experiences for women, arising from social and cultural attitudes and are evidenced even when law exists to 'ensure' sexual equality!	**Change the system from within** – introduce or extend policy and law to frame and ensure equality (e.g. childcare provision, equal pay, prevention of sexual harassment). Note: The UK's 'Equality Package' means sex-based discrimination has been outlawed for over 30 years!
Socialist/Marxist e.g. Michele Barrett dual theory e.g. Sylvia Walby	Women are uniquely oppressed (via economic and ideological inequality): unpaid, lower paid and under-recognised labour market positions; with economic exploitation goes patriarchal domination.	**Change the system to a new system,** where economic and social equality between the sexes can exist.
Radical	Disadvantage, inequality and exploitation are the consequences of 'patriarchal hegemony' (where the ideology of patriarchy is embedded in all social institutions, beginning with 'family'). Natural differences between the sexes are socially manipulated and presented as justification for social, economic and political difference (i.e. women give birth and have 'maternal instinct' and are therefore, society's 'natural' carers).	**Sexual separatism:** change the system to a new system, where women disengage from patriarchal institutions and recreate alternative social systems.

Some of the key ideas from different schools of feminism.

Why are there so many 'Feminisms'?

- **Feminism** emerged as a response to 'malestream (male-dominated) thinking'.
- **Radical feminism** emerged as a politically and sexually-militant response to what were considered the limitations of original feminism.
- **Black' and 'lesbian' feminism** emerged to extend 'white' and 'straight' feminist analysis.
- **Postmodern feminism** is a development and expansion of 'structural feminism' and so on.

Feminist theory: key themes

- History and culture have been, and in respects remain, 'malestreamed' – characterised by sex/gender inequality.
- Gender roles are socially constructed – and have limiting implications for both sexes.
- Class- and sex-based power, authority and control, define and exploit aspects of girls' and women's experiences.

Activity

For most of her adult life, Libby was a renowned academic and political figure. Prior to retirement she held a senior Scottish Executive post. Having always lived independently, over the past three years Libby became increasingly frail and vulnerable via osteoarthritis, peripheral vascular disease and early-onset dementia.

No longer able to manage alone at home, Libby moved into a local residential home.

This time has been unhappy for her – and she is fast developing a reputation as a 'difficult' resident. The setting receives a newspaper every day, the *Daily Record*. On several occasions Libby has torn up this newspaper, describing it as 'unreadable'. When the activities co-ordinator arrived today and, producing a soft ball, arranged the residents in a circle to play 'catch', Libby caught then threw the ball deliberately, and with force, at the co-ordinator's head, shouting 'I'm not a baby, babies play ball.' Libby's response to suggestions that she may like to 'knit a scarf' instead, are unprintable. Staff are at a loss.

1. With reference to each of the **key themes** from **Feminist theories** outlined above, comment on this scenario.

For Action theorists, society's structures and shapes are mostly determined by the actions and interventions of its members.

Social reality (how society is organised and how we live) is for the action theorist primarily built *by* people in the course of what they do – and by how they do it.

Immediately you will have recognised that this contrasts directly with core ideas from Functionalism and Conflict theory!

Symbolic Interactionism

George Herbert Mead (1863–1931) is considered the 'founding father' of Symbolic Interactionism. His work combined themes and ideas from philosophy, psychology and sociology to explain the processes by which our **self-concept** is influenced and develops, via social interaction.

Importantly, Mead differentiated between what he described as our senses of **'me'** and **'I'**. 'Me' relates to the *social* versions of 'self' which we choose to present to the world around us, i.e. those versions based on what we know is most likely to be expected and accepted. 'I' for Mead, is the uniquely private, *individual* sense of self we have – and don't often share with others (this often contrasts hugely with the more socially-acceptable 'me'!).

Our senses of self derive from the 'feedback' we receive from interaction with others.

During social interaction, society's members exchange **symbols**. For Mead, *all* human interaction is based on and around this exchange of symbols. These will include the language and gestures we use, the dress codes we adopt, and so on. To make sense of other people, we must be able to make sense of the symbols they present and share and the meaning of those symbols to them (adapted from Miller, D.L. (1973)).

Verbal and non-verbal language is a key symbol in any society, a tool by which we act, react and interact with others and develop a picture of 'self'; to '*see ourselves as others see us*'..

Consider this

What might be the potential impact on a child's sense of self, of interactions at (a Scottish) school when the child's capacity to understand and express in English, is limited?

Mead's founding work on human interaction was taken forward by Erving Goffman (born 1928) in his *Presentation of Self in Everyday Life* (1969).

In this work, Goffman presents us with a form of **dramaturgical analogy**, meaning he used metaphors of 'theatre', 'stage', 'performance' and 'roles' to explain the processes, meanings and significance for society, of how humans interact.

For Goffman, we are effectively 'actors' playing a variety of roles, to a variety of audiences. We are always performing and present a particular version of 'self' to each audience – usually a version which we consider will bring positive feedback from that audience.

For Goffman, this process is termed **impression management** and, importantly it is not always done consciously. As with any performance and any audience, the feedback or response we (as actors) receive, is important for how we see ourselves; for our **self-concept.**

Consider this

How differently do you 'perform' when you play your roles of 'student', 'partner', 'parent', 'friend' and 'colleague' – and why is this?

Why are Goffman's ideas of **unconscious impression management** important for Social Care workers?

Social reaction theory: labelling

Howard Becker in *Outsiders: Studies in the Sociology of Deviance* (1963) formalised work on **labelling**. For Becker, while labels are universally used and can be abbreviated and 'handy' symbols and ways of summing up 'who' or 'what' a person is, we must consider the meaning and impact for an individual or group, of having a label applied. Labels can be affirming ('fabulous student!') and motivating.

However, labels can be negative too, creating and reinforcing prejudice and separation between individuals or groups. Labels also reflect wider inequalities in power. It is 'easy' for example, for teacher to label Mikey in class ('naughty'), but not quite so straightforward for Mikey to (publicly) label his teacher!

Where an individual or group has been labelled and, as a result, experiences an altered **self-concept** they can begin to identify *with* and retreat into the label and may ultimately evidence an increase in the 'difference' on which the label was based in the first place : a 'self-fulfilling prophecy'.

Consider this

From your own memories (and/or experiences!) of infant school, try to develop the next instalment of Mikey's story...

How, for example, might his relationships, behaviour and progress in school change over time, if the label which his teacher has applied, 'sticks' to him?

Much work has been done in sociology to examine the impact of 'mentally ill' as a label. Link and Phelan (1995) see labelling as a result of prejudicial attitudes and behaviour but also resulting from broader cultural expectations of what 'mental illness' *is* and *means*. Where, via socialisation, we learn to associate mental illness with social rejection, loss of credibility and suspicion from others, then the person who is diagnosed 'mentally ill' (who has been subject to this same socialisation) is likely to expect these reactions from others and likely as a result, to 'hide' or attempt to disguise their labelled status.

In turn, a *self-fulfilling prophecy* can occur, when the 'diagnosed person' keeps social distance from others and the ('not-diagnosed') others reinforce this distance.

In this way, those who are 'diagnosed' experience the suspicion, loss of credibility and social rejection their culture has led them to expect. (Adapted and abridged from Link and Phelan (1995) in Rogers, A., and Pilgrim, D. (2005)).

- 'Social reality' derives from the actions and interactions of society's members.
- Our self-concept is influenced by our interactions with others.
- We have, and present, various senses of 'self'.
- When labelling and modified labelling occur, these are important social actions – and can have 'self-fulfilling' impact on those who are labelled.

Activity

Christie has just recently started work in a respite unit for adults with complex needs. Following initial training and induction, she has been shadowing Mrs Brennan (a senior worker), in order to benefit from her experience and 'really' learn the job.

Mrs Brennan tells Christie she must always be 'strict', otherwise residents will 'manipulate' situations and 'take advantage' of her good nature. She warns her to look out in particular for Derek, described by Mrs Brennan as 'immature', 'aggressive', 'attention-seeking' and 'difficult to manage'.

Christie finds herself relating differently to the residents when Mrs Brennan is around – adopting an uncharacteristically 'stern' tone (especially with Derek!) and being less relaxed, open and friendly.

For Christie this role does not feel natural or comfortable and she regularly checks the rota for Mrs Brennan's off-duty. On those days she feels she can 'be herself'; with her confidence unaffected by Mrs Brennan's 'old school' authoritarian ways.

What **key themes** from **symbolic interactionism** can you see evidenced in this scenario – and in what ways?

Consider this

How might **labelling** and **modified labelling** relate to *other* groups who use services – and where might we look to find evidence of this?

Sociology of 'family'

Family has a huge influence on all of our lives.

Much 'family' sociology explores the *influences* of our experience of family, on our **behaviour**, **experiences** and **life chances**.

Key terms

Behaviour put simply, what people *do*!

Experiences what people see, learn, are taught and so on. What happens!

Life chances literally, chances in life – opportunities and resources people can – or cannot – access. A complex array of factors combine to determine for example, how long we will live, how 'educated', 'qualified' and 'employable' (etc.) we will become.

However, 'family' – as a concept and reality – can be surprisingly difficult to define. Family occurs in many forms.

Family structures (or 'types') include those outlined in the table below.

nuclear	a unit of man and woman, married or cohabiting, plus their biological children
extended	a 'network' of family members living together or close by and sharing the experience of family (for example a 'nuclear' family plus grandparents)
lone parent	one parent (usually mother) with children
same sex	two adults of the same sex, with children
reconstituted	(a 'stepfamily'), where adults establish a new relationship which includes their child(ren) from previous relationship(s)

Different family types or structures.

What other types of 'family' can you identify from your own culture – and beyond?

'Family' is a complicated creature, with enormous variation in understanding and experience. Consider the following social facts about 'family':

Families based on marriage are statistically subject to break-up and change.

- Children can be 'created' via artificial insemination and surrogacy.
- Some marriages and families are formed by choice, others are 'arranged'.
- Members in reconstituted families find themselves in new roles and relationships, with new 'family' members.
- Some children who live with two parents in a traditional nuclear family spend most 'awake time' with paid carers.
- For some people 'family' means being 'looked after' in a residential setting, by a team of carers.
- One in nine children in Scotland run away or are forced to leave home before the age of 16 due (mainly) to family conflict and instability, violence, emotional abuse and neglect.*
- Family types are 'culturally-specific', for example the established Scottish practice of grandparent 'childminders'.

- Some families are networked into society, with the adult(s) motivated to and capable of, effective and safe parenting.
- For others, parenting and being parented is an isolated, unsafe and developmentally harmful experience.

*http://www.york.ac.uk/inst/swrdu/
Publications/missingouttext.pdf

Consider this

What for you makes family life happy, or sad, 'healthy' or 'unhealthy'?

Family roles

In Scottish society, a long tradition exists of **roles** within family segregated on the basis of gender and supported by the institution of marriage. For women, roles of 'wife' and 'mother' were based in and around the home, with primary responsibility for domestic labour and child care. Men, with their roles as 'husband' and 'father', were expected to maintain roles of financial provider; their main locus (base) being outside the home, where they worked and socialised. The male provider role traditionally, was associated with authority *over* the family ('Wait until your father gets home!').

In 21st-century Scotland however, the picture is more complex. We assume greater equality and interdependence exists between parents (and the sexes) and many of us have 'alternative' views on and experiences of, relationships, 'marriage' and parenting.

Traditional segregation of sex roles within families does not fit with the realities of lone parenthood, gay or lesbian parenting, or with men and women who value the nuclear model of family but who reject sex-based segregation within it.

For most of us too, our experiences and understanding of 'family' varies throughout our lives, with new family structures and new roles accompanying each form of 'family'.

For many Sociologists however, we have not

moved as far as we think we have, for we still tend to *assume* 'nuclear' and 'marriage' when we think 'family'!

Equipped for life

Whatever and however we experience 'family', it *is* our primary link from our first small world as children, to understanding and engaging with wider society, as adults.

For Donaldson, 'healthy' family experiences and socialisation provide a framework (or a springboard) from which positive *self-esteem* and genuine feelings of *'belonging'* can and should develop. From this start in life, young people can become 'equipped' and 'resourced' adults, able to form and maintain relationships with others, cope with decision making, accept new challenges with enthusiasm and cope with complex interpersonal situations by using appropriately-developed skills and qualities. (Adapted and abridged: Donaldson (1986) in Moonie, N. (2005).)

… and less equipped

'Conditions of worth' (our internal sense of how much and in what ways we 'matter', 'belong' and 'can do') are established via the internal relationships and dynamic of family. Conditions of worth may be negatively and *conditionally* reinforced, where a child's primary socialisation is dominated by feelings of being loved 'but only if…' (for example, *if* you work hard at school, *if* you keep good company, *if* you always do as I/we say, *then* …).

Case study

Calum

Calum is 20 years old and lives at home with his dad and sister Jo. He has a moderate learning disability with associated mobility issues. Calum requires support to structure his day and some prompting and assistance with almost all aspects of daily living.

Jo has always been 'Mum' to Calum; highly protective of her brother, she forgoes a social life of her own to spend evenings and weekends with him. Together, Dad and Jo have provided a secure, stable and loving home life for Calum. He has a strong sense of being a vital family member and healthy levels of esteem and social confidence.

For his 'age and stage' however, and according to his teachers and support workers, Calum tends to lack practical and coping skills, living as he does with a family who do almost everything for him.

Since leaving school, Calum has completed several Foundation units at his local college and is keen to progress. He has gained work experience too, via a college placement. Working in the community library, Calum has developed real skills for work and has fast become a valued team member.

Recently, Dad and Jo have been very worried to hear Calum say he intends to get a flat and a job, of his own. When he signed up for a student exchange scheme to involve a supported visit to Prague, Dad and Jo immediately phoned the college to cancel it, arguing that Calum was 'too vulnerable' and 'wouldn't cope' away from home.

Calum finds it hard to accept his family's views. Relationships at home have become unsettled, with frequent arguments. Calum is angry, arguing his family are 'treating him like a baby'.

1. In what ways do you think 'family' has impacted on Calum's experiences, behaviour and life chances?

2. How can they move forward?

In *My Vision for the 21st Century*, Camilla Batmanghelidjh (founder of the innovative London-based service 'Kids Company' which supports the capital's 'hardest-to-reach' children and young people) argues that the 'trouble' in these young peoples' lives, and with which they are associated, originates primarily from their experiences of 'family'. It is then exacerbated by inadequate and ill-informed responses from the state, for example via the systems of education and/or social services.

Activity

From the adapted extract opposite from Batmanghelidjh's 'My Vision', identify features of a child/young person's primary and secondary socialisation which are likely to have destructive impact on his/her **behaviour**, **lifestyle** and **life chances.**

For Batmanghelidjh, family structure and the symmetry (evenness) or otherwise, of parental roles, is less important than the relationships and experiences of childhood and the presence of parents (whoever they are and whether or not they live together) who are themselves emotionally and socially developed and equipped to take responsibility for their child(ren); to parent. For her, *'The essence of childhood is the presence of loving parents who protect and nurture the child.'*

Further research

1. What do you think sociologists mean when they argue that modern society 'demonises' young people? Do some research in the current Scottish press for features on 'feral' or 'criminal youths'. What explanations do media and/or politicians give for instances of antisocial behaviour among young people? In other words, where do they say the 'blame' lies?

2. Carry out some research to uncover the philosophy, services and practice of 'Kids Company, London.

'Childhood in major parts of Britain is in crisis, because grownups on individual and institutional levels are failing to honour it. Grownups, who themselves have unfulfilled childhoods, refuse the task of parenting as they compete with their children to be cared for.'

'Often roles are reversed and children abandon their childhood to act as responsible carers for dysfunctional parents. This is a landscape of emotional depletion and distortion... (where) ... fathers abandon... and lone mothers reject, too psychologically and emotionally depleted to withstand the agitation of adolescence.'

'Origins of street violence often have their beginnings in experiences of early childhood... a very young child is living in conditions of extreme stress and fear; adults around the child are often terrifyingly violent. These young children initially protest, they cry, plead, cling, scream and when they see they have affected no change they feel desperate then emotionally exhausted they cease to react... unconsciously they kill off their capacities to feel. These children cannot feel for themselves and therefore they cannot feel for others. They are moving but emotionally vacant; their whole moral and emotional thermostat is damaged.'

'Many of these households do not have books, children are never read to. There is no genuine interest in any topic other than immediate survival and the acquisition of material goods. Music and video games are often criticised as negative influences on these children's lives.

These outlets do not create crisis, they simply reflect a state of mind and a way of living.'

'There are also environmental factors which draw these young people into crime... disaffected individuals see the State as having abandoned them. They in turn cease to be passive in their poverty and take on the meeting of their needs through the gains of crime. Drug dealing, theft, street robberies become an accepted norm amongst a group whose moral baselines are pushed below decency. Local authorities, often due to a lack of resources, fail to meet these children's educational and social needs. Many cannot read and write, their hyper-agitated mental state makes them difficult to manage in classrooms. The primary preoccupation of these youngsters is survival.'

'When these young people are advised about the benefits of gaining qualifications or the possibility of accessing jobs, they react with self-ridicule and disbelief. Tutors and bosses often despair at the young people's inability to obey rules, complete tasks and work systematically towards a goal. The young people in turn cannot calm down sufficiently to believe in long-term gains as they live in a temperature of immediate survival or extinction.'

(Adapted, abridged and reproduced with kind permission of Kids Company, London, 2008).

'In Place of Family'

In the last decade, numbers of children and young people who are looked after and accommodated by the state have risen by 20 per cent.

In publicising the 2008 'Couldn't Care Less' report from the Centre for Social Justice, former UK Conservative Leader, Iain Duncan Smith is cited as saying:

'Ironically, the plight of children in care is so dreadful that if they were living with their natural parents, the state would insist on taking them into care.'

(Duncan Smith, I. in Cassidy, S. *Independent*, 6 September 2008)

What research evidence can you find to support *and* refute this assertion?

A range of relevant reports and websites will help. Your sources might include:

- NCH Factfiles
- The Centre for Social Justice
- Joseph Rowntree Foundation.

What conclusions do you reach about the experiences and life chances of children and young people leaving care? What does this suggest to you about 'family'?

Theory of family

Theories emerge from ideology ('ideology' being a set of beliefs). Ideologies can be broken down (or 'unpacked'), helping us understand the core ideas upon which they are based. In a speech deploring the rise of 'illegitimacy' (children born/raised outside marriage) in Britain, former Prime Minister Margaret Thatcher said:

'It is far better to put these children in the hands of a good religious organisation, and the mother as well, so that they will be brought up with family values.'

Some fairly tricky arithmetic aside (Scotland has 162,000 lone parent families, with 280,000 children – according to the organisation One Parent Families Scotland – how many religious institutions would be required?!), *core beliefs* about what family structure, roles and 'values'

are and should be, are contained within and attached to, Thatcher's statement.

Consider this

What are these core beliefs about family? Why do you think Thatcher identifies 'religious organisations' in particular, as a solution to the 'problem' of lone parent families?

For every argument (in this case to support particular views on 'family values' and parenting), a counter-argument exists.

In his work 'Moral Politics' for example, George Lakoff argues that families who have fundamentalist Christian beliefs are those most likely to be unrealistic and excessive in their demands (of children), with expectations of parents being 'obeyed without question' and who are those most likely to resort to 'physical violence to teach children 'correct' behaviour'.

As you read through extracts from Sociological theory on family, you should attempt to 'unpack' these too, looking to identify and compare main ideas from theory, of how family structure and roles are considered to influence behaviour, experiences and life chances.

Functionalism

George Peter Murdock (1897–1985) considered the nuclear family a foundation of all 250 societies he studied. This family type, for Murdock, operates as a contained economic, emotional and social unit where members provide for each other and create and nurture the next generation – preparing them for societal 'fit'. More recently, for **Talcott Parsons** (1923–1979) the nuclear family fulfils two crucial functions for its members and for society:

- *the primary socialisation of children* by which children are encouraged to internalise the norms, values and behaviours of their culture – where 'personality' is nurtured and established
- *stabilisation of adult personalities*–where for two adults in a committed, socially sanctioned and heterosexual relationship, emotional security and safety are provided, together with a 'natural' division of labour for men and women (From: Parsons and Bales (1956) in Giddens (2001), page 175).

This is a picture of a family characterised by love, care, sharing, emotional balance and safety and 'socially accepted' sex. Via its close fit with 'society', the institution of family is where culture is 'learned' and reinforced; where transmission of social values is assured and, for Parsons, it is also the uniquely private place where we may truly be who we *really* are.

Conflict theory

For Conflict theorists, the nuclear model of family dominates analysis and is characterised by economic control and sexual division. Rather than a 'natural' social arrangement, nuclear family is, according to **Friedrich Engels** in *The Origin of the Family, Private Property and the State* (1894), a small-scale, privatised institution where men have legal and economic supremacy. The institution of family arose in response to a need for the capitalist class to maintain their ownership, wealth and social control by keeping it in the family – passing on wealth and ownership via male heredity. Adopted originally as a bourgeois model of family, the nuclear model became aspirational for the proletariat and was absorbed by them.

For Conflict theorists, women within modern marriage can be considered subject to men in the same ways that subject class(es) are to ruling elites; that is economically, socially and personally controlled.

What appears to be a contract of 'free will' ultimately signs each partner up to expect and accept different and unequal roles. Via the nuclear family, a continuing supply of labour is guaranteed, with the 'main' labourer (male) cared for by the 'secondary' labourer (female/wife/mother). Roles within the family for Conflict theorists are traditionally segregated, with male decision-making and authority linked to superior earning power, and relative female powerlessness linked to economic weakness. **Eli Zaretsky** in *Capitalism, the Family and Personal Life* (1976), described the nuclear family as a social system which props up and promotes capitalism. For men experiencing alienation (a sense of meaninglessness about the work they do and the role they play, working for the profit of others)

within a capitalist economy, home is where this dissatisfaction is played out, via male power and control over women.

Feminism

Feminist writers have been major contributors to our sociological understanding of family, providing new explanations for what 'family' means and how it affects its members. Feminist analysis informs us that family dynamics, relationships and experiences are dictated and controlled by economic and patriarchal structures.

In this way, family reflects inequalities found in wider society – and has particularly limiting effects on the behaviour, experiences and life chances of girls and women.

Radical feminist **Kate Millet** in *Sexual Politics* (1970) argues that 'consent' for a patriarchal control of women comes via socialisation, with gender roles and 'personality types' of men and women culturally made up, or 'determined'. In this way, 'family' is the lynchpin ensuring economic, social and sexual disadvantage for women, their relegation to a 'sub' working class. Evidence of women's status as an inferior social group includes what Millet describes as 'burgeoning' cultures of porn and 'anti-women satire' (comedy). The private nature of modern-day families further disempowers women, with high (and higher than reported) incidences of male-female domestic violence *and* by the misuse of 'biological difference' to 'explain' and justify relative powerlessness and the 'domestication' of women.

Marxist feminist **Michele Barrett** in *Women's Oppression Today* (1980), describes a capitalist ideology of segregated heterosexual 'husband' and 'wife' roles which exist to divide and separate the working class. The power of this dominant ideology which roots women in the domestic world has implications for them, and limits in real terms, their participation in economic, social and political aspects of society.

Action theory

Edmund Leach and **R.D. Laing** offer us broadly 'interactionist' analyses of 'family', both asserting that (mainly nuclear) family can be the deepest and darkest of environments.

For Leach, the nuclear family is likely to be overloaded with unrealistic expectations, pressures and stress. Modern family life tends to be private and separate from society, a place of secrets – a form of 'emotional prison'.

Almost all forms of antisocial behaviour and social problems can be traced back to experiences and relationships within the family. Leach for example, refers to family roles which are unhealthy and relationships of 'ever-decreasing emotional intensity'.

For R.D. Laing, in his highly controversial work with fellow psychiatrist **Esterson** *Sanity, Madness and the Family* (1964), the nuclear family is unhealthily private and controlling. Ideas for each of us about being 'socially separate' begin within 'family' and, for these writers, provide a rich breeding ground for all forms of prejudice and discrimination, including overt race-based hatred.

For Laing and Esterson, family life operates on a complex basis of emotional 'games' where individuals compete with, exploit and scapegoat others in their family.

Family life is characterised too, by roles and interactions which are contradictory (e.g. 'you're too young to do that' but, 'you're old enough to know better!').

According to this argument, forms of mental illness, including schizophrenia, arise from 'disturbed' family relationships. In an emotional environment where children face unrealistic expectations, the development of schizophrenia (where the individual is 'separate from reality') is for Laing and Esterson, ultimately a valid and understandable response.

Criticising theory

Functionalism is accused of recognising the nuclear model only, of promoting highly differentiated (and socially unequal) gender roles and of assuming family to be 'a good thing'.

Feminism is accused of 'malestreaming' the nuclear model and assuming women's role is largely determined; that women are more 'passive' than 'active' as individuals and family members.

Conflict theory is accused of the assumption that family and its members are effectively powerless in shaping their own lives; all elements of family life – including relationships – are tied down to elite models of socialisation and gender division.

Action theory is accused of 'extremism', with Laing for instance cited as generalising his research about schizophrenia and Leach criticised for ignoring the genuinely positive and reinforcing experiences of family many of us have.

Assessment

To evidence this outcome you are likely to be required to write a scenario which explains the impact of family on one individual whose needs you support. Alternatively, you may be presented with a pre-devised scenario with questions attached.

Whatever assessment approach your centre uses (including evidence-sampling), you must be able to show you know and understand:

- the current **diversity of family structures and roles** and are able to challenge ideas of 'normal' family type
- ways in which **theories** in sociology would explain the influence over time, on an individual, of family structures and roles (influences on **behaviour**, **experiences** and **life chances** must be specified)
- the potential **weaknesses** and **strengths** of **one** sociological theory in helping us understand the impact of family on the individual central to the scenario.

Activity

Apply key ideas from **Functionalism**, **Conflict theory**, **Feminism** and **Symbolic Interactionism** to this chapter's adapted extract from Batmanghelidjh's 'My Vision for the 21st Century'. The following should help you do this.

According to **Functionalist** analysis, a great deal of the moral and emotional harm these young people have experienced, originates from their *non-nuclear* family and unhealthy, antisocial experiences of socialisation.

For **Conflict** theorists, the Batmanghelidjh extract evidences the social and emotional consequences, for young people, of living in unsupported families and experiencing economic oppression.

For **Feminism**, patriarchal domination results in fathers who feel free to abandon and mothers who are unsupported and insufficiently resourced to respond to their children's needs.

For **Action** theorists, the 'insular' nature of family exacerbates the likelihood of private suffering and emotional torment and results in individuals experiencing and ultimately re-creating, family patterns of abuse and hatred.

Also with reference to Batmanghelidjh's 'Vision' (above):

1. Which Sociological theory, for you, *best* explains the influence of 'family' on the behaviour, experiences and life chances of its members? Why is this?

2. Which theory do you consider is most **limited** in explaining the influence of family structure and roles? Why is this?

Further research
Same-Sex Parenting:

Consult Sociological Research Online, Volume 8, no.4 (http://www.socresonline.orguk/8/4/hicks.html) or search '**Stephen Hicks**' to read his paper ('*the Christian Right and Homophobic Discourse: a Response to 'Evidence' that Lesbian and Gay Parenting Damages Children*'). Hicks' work is not as complicated as the title would suggest; rather it is a clear and well-evidenced analysis – and challenge – to writers he considers homophobic in their analysis of same-sex parenting.

Poverty, inequality and discrimination

Key terms

absolute poverty defined by a fixed idea of 'basic needs'

relative poverty defined in terms of a society's 'normal' lifestyle and standards

social inequality experiences of being more or less equal (to others)

deprivation having 'less than', a lack of (usually refers to society's resources)

social exclusion where access to 'normal' society's resources, opportunities and participation is restricted.

'A walk in Glasgow East'

'It takes about fifteen minutes to walk from Glasgow's Merchant City where you can buy £90 thongs from Agent Provocateur and £1000 suits from Emporio Armani, to the outskirts of Glasgow East; from the avenues built on the bounty of Victorian entrepreneurialism to what looks like a shanty town.'

'Once upon a time the Gallowgate was throbbing with life. But on a drizzly July morning it looks like it's been kicked in the teeth and left for dead...'

'... (poverty) here is endemic. This is at the root of most, if not all, of Glasgow East's problems, which range from the early deaths of males to high rates of unemployment and sickness, alcohol abuse, drug addiction and the gamut of antisocial behaviour.'

'Here, even if children leave school literate and numerate, they have much less chance of going on to higher education than their peers virtually anywhere else in the country. They are victims by virtue of where they've been born and brought up.'

(Alan Taylor in *Sunday Herald* 20/07/08)

What do *you* conclude from Alan Taylor's statement?

Problems of definition

'Common sense' tells us *real* poverty has been consigned to the past, together with Grandpa's tales of sixpence and a small wooden toy for Christmas; or that *real* poverty lies elsewhere in the world, where population groups are dispossessed, their survival under threat. Maybe Scotland isn't poor, simply *unequal*?

For sociologists, concepts of **poverty** and **inequality** can be complex in that each tends to be understood *subjectively*; that is, we all have our own ideas, beliefs and experiences of what poverty and inequality are and aren't.

How poverty is measured

In the late 19th and early 20th centuries, Britain's first attempts to measure poverty were carried out by **Charles Booth** (1840–1916) in London and **Seebohm Rowntree** (1871–1954) in York.

Both calculated a *minimum income* (in terms of shelter, food and fuel) necessary for survival. This sum came to be described as the subsistence line (or the poverty line), income below which signified *absolute poverty*.

A 'poverty line' gives us a clear-cut and definite statistic of who is and is not poor. Or does it?

Critics of this absolute view of poverty argue that it is packed with assumptions and value-judgements *about* the poor, by those who are not: what *are* 'minimum essentials' and who decides these? What does 'survival' mean and is 'survival' any way to live?

With the launch of Britain's welfare state in 1948, an eradication of 'want, idleness, ignorance, squalor and disease' was predicted and poverty, for a time, was edged off the political agenda.

In the late 1960s and throughout the 1970s, economic crises swept the developed world. For the majority of people in the 1970s, life in the UK was characterised by high inflation and rising prices, a decline in heavy industries and long-term industrial disputes (with the infamous 'three day week') affecting all major public sector workers. The Conservative government responded from 1979 with a raft of policies designed to cut public spending on one hand, while simultaneously promoting and rewarding new ventures in business.

This approach increased wealth and income in Britain – *for some*. But a 'rich–poor divide' became increasingly and dramatically apparent, to the extent that a European Commission report in the mid 1980s asserted that a quarter of Europe's 'poor' were families in Scotland. In response, left-wing commentators demanded new information on *who* was becoming poor in Britain and on the *differences* (in lifestyle and life chances) *between* social groups.

Peter Townsend, studying poverty in the UK (1979), set the bar for defining and understanding poverty in more qualitative ways; as a *relative* concept.

By Townsend's definition, *poverty of income* does not stand alone but is attached to a network of lost resources, activities and opportunities; the experience of being *less equal*.

Poverty and deprivation in Scotland

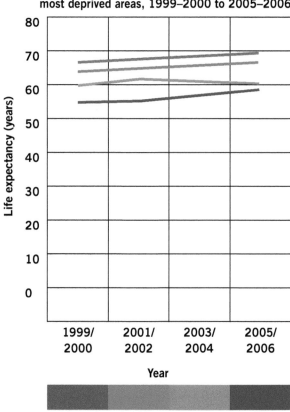

Healthy life expectancy at birth in SIMD 15% most deprived areas, 1999–2000 to 2005–2006

Source: www.scotland.gov.uk/Topics/Statistics (July 08).

Healthy life expectancy at birth.

Why do these figures differ in the ways they do? For many sociologists, the key lies with **multiple deprivation**, where experiences of *having* and *doing less* 'weaves' across and throughout people's lives. For **Neil Moonie** (2005, pages 183-198), a multiple deprived lifestyle may include combinations of:

- smaller homes in less developed and more polluted areas; homes that are more likely to be damp and cold
- 'food poverty', higher-fat and over-processed diets, resulting in diet-specific issues and conditions
- relatively low levels of educational achievement in less resourced, less 'successful' schools
- greater incidences of part-time and insecure work, with greater risk of unemployment
- relatively poorly networked and supported communities with higher crime figures
- proportionately more expensive services and consumer goods
- reduced options for leisure.

In June 2004, the **Scottish Executive** presented its first *Scottish Index of Multiple Deprivation* (SIMD). Updated in 2006 and due to be reworked in 2009, this is a vast analytical tool used to scrutinise small-scale 'data zones' (areas) where a high concentration of multiple deprivation exists.

The 2006 SIMD uncovers 48 per cent of the Glasgow City area (as being in the 15 per cent most deprived), with Inverclyde at 38 per cent Dundee City at 30 per cent West Dunbartonshire at 28 per cent Clackmannanshire at 23 per cent and North Lanarkshire 20 per cent

(For more information on the SIMD, go to this website: http://www.scotland.gov.uk/Topics/Statistics/SIMD)

Scotland's children

Scotland's **Child Poverty Action Group** tells us that in 2008:

'One in four children in Scotland are officially recognised as poor. Thousands of our children continue to miss out on the basics; adequate housing, clothes and shoes, healthy food, educational opportunities and the social activities that bind children to their families, friends and communities. Poverty continues to grind down the quality of children's lives and stunt their life chances.'

In July 2007, **Barnardo's Scotland** published the first 'Index of Well-being for Children in Scotland' (IWCS). This report compared the economic, social, physical and emotional well-being of Scottish children and young people with their peers from twenty-three OECD (Organization for Economic Co-operation and Development) countries:

Overall index rating

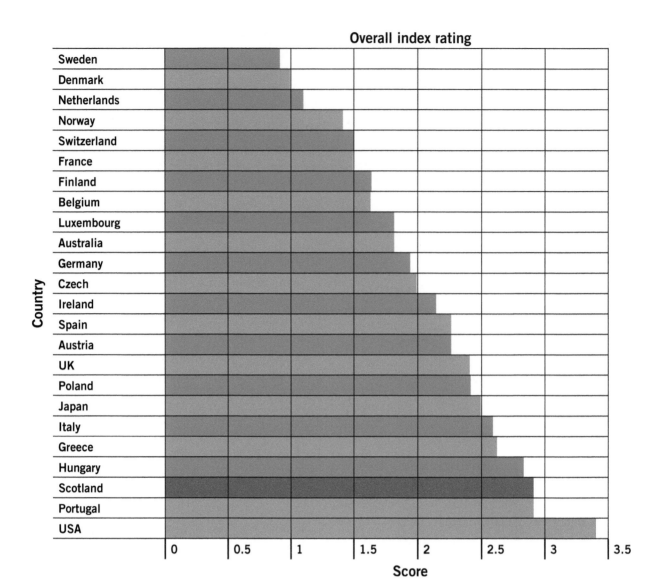

The position of Scotland's children in relation to other OECD countries.

This graph illustrates the *nexus* between poverty and inequality, where material poverty (poverty of income and resources) equates with impoverished and 'unequal' experiences and life chances. The groups most likely to experience this nexus include lone-parent families, disabled people, the unemployed, 'the sick', unskilled couples and, in relative terms, women.

Sex-based inequality, gathering evidence

In full-time work, women in Scotland earn on average 15 per cent less than men, while in part-time work, the differential is 34% (http://www.closethegap.org.uk/project.asp?h=Aims). Women's income on retirement in Scotland averages 53 per cent of that of men (www.engender.org.uk).

Current research informs us that economic inequalities experienced by Scottish women extend to affect and limit their experiences and life chances in terms of social and political participation and power.

Close the Gap, a Scottish lobby group, explains the 'pay gap' in terms of women's disproportionate employment in lower paid *'female' occupations* (e.g. catering, caring and administration). Women constitute the majority of *part-time* workers too, with relatively lower levels of pay, conditions and security. A high proportion of women who work part-time do so in relation to *additional caring responsibilities* (a child or family member who is sick, disabled or 'vulnerable') (http://www.engender.org.uk/projects/36/Poverty.html). In 2004, 66 per cent of Scotland's *unpaid carers* were women (http://www.engender.org.uk/UserFiles?File/Gender%20Audit/Care%20%20Caring(1).pdf).

Unpaid caring consistently means the carer's mental and physical health is compromised with high incidences of depression and stress. Financial and employment worries are commonly experienced, particularly in situations where the carer struggles to combine caring with working. Increased social isolation and loss of 'external focus' are widely reported (Scottish Exec. 06).

As formal carers, women currently make up 84 per cent of Scotland's Social Services workforce (http://www.engender.org.uk/UserFiles/File/Gender%20Audit/Care%20&%20Caring(1).pdf).

Pay, conditions and 'status' in these posts are low when compared with senior public service positions, for here, gender trends are reversed:

76 female	Secondary Head Teachers	286 male
6 female	Council Leaders	26 male
5 female	Senior Police Officers	38 male

(adapted from http://www.closethegap.org.uk/project.asp?h=Aims)

The **EHRC** 'Sex and Power' survey of 2008 shows evidence of a decline in women's representation in top business positions, in politics and in the public sector. A clear trend shows gender equality in the UK has either 'hit the buffers' or is 'in reverse'.

This slowed rate of change, according to the EHRC, indicates women's labour force parity (equality) with men is now 37 years away – eight years more than predicted in the Commission's last survey.

Activity

1. Examine the NS-SEC (National Statistics Socio-economic Classification) system for measuring social class in Britain (found in most Sociology textbooks since 2002 and specifically in Sweeney et al, 2003):
   a) which groups make up the 'lowest' social classes?
   b) in what ways are 'gender', 'race', 'disability' factored into this system?
   c) which groups within society are 'invisible' when social class is officially measured?

2. Government 'tracking' of Scotland's poor is based largely on *Households Below Average Income* data (collated annually by the Department of Work and Pensions). Find out which population groups are *not* included in this – and consider the impact of their absence from Scotland's official 'picture of poverty'.

3. Critics have argued that concepts of *'multiple deprivation'* and *'social exclusion'* effectively separate society's poor and most disadvantaged, portraying them as a distinct and 'homogenised' social group and that this separation promotes inequalities. What are your views on this?

Changing Face of Inequality

'New' inequalities are identified and prioritised as Scotland's demography, labour market (or government) change. In *'Older People in Scotland'* (2005), **Age Concern** tells us that 63 per cent of households experiencing fuel poverty are older adults with income limited to the state pension. This group is most vulnerable to 'excess winter mortality', i.e. unnecessary death from hypothermia.

According to the league table from consumer watchdog **Energy Watch**, 'The poor pay more' in September 2008, those least able to pay in Scotland are charged 'discriminatory tariffs' at higher costs. By this measure, therefore, the poorer you are, it costs significantly more, in real terms, to be warm – and this difference is increasing!

Scotland's response

'Poverty is when a person's household income is equivalised (adjusted for the size and composition of the household) and is less than 60 per cent of UK average income' (the Scottish Executive).

Attached to the Scottish Parliament's broadly 'relative' view of poverty are ideological and policy agendas identifying **social exclusion** as the 'scourge' of modern Scotland. Social exclusion can be described as the combined effects for an individual, household or community, of *'not having'* coupled with *'not doing'* (what others have and do).

For current policy makers (EU, Westminster and Scottish Parliaments), the solution to social exclusion lies with creating and developing resources and opportunities in education, employment and social life where none or few exist: **social inclusion**.

For further reading on the Scottish Executive's Social Inclusion Strategy, go to www.scotland.gov.uk/Publications/2012/01/17495, or simply key in 'Scottish Executive – Social Inclusion'.

Causes of poverty and inequality

The causes of poverty are much disputed by sociologists. The following is an introduction to some key theoretical positions. Our focus will be on two broad schools of thought on poverty and inequality: *'Cultural'* and *'Structural'*. Anthony Giddens (Giddens, (2001), page 316) refers to the main schism between these approaches as *'blame the victim'* (cultural) versus *'blame the system'* (structural).

Cultural

Some cultural theorists adopt a 'social pathology' model. If we consider in lay terms, 'pathology' refers to disease-causing agents; this is a powerful and controversial metaphor to apply to people.

First formalised as 'theory' in the 19th century, all who subscribe to a 'cultural' view, consider the causes of poverty and inequality to lie primarily with the poor themselves. Sections of society have established and remain locked into 'poor' ways of living, antisocial and unproductive, socialising each new generation to expect and accept the same.

Oscar Lewis, a social anthropologist studying poor South American townships in the 1960s, evidenced a 'culture of poverty', characterised by sixty-two defining traits including fatalism, helplessness and domestic violence (Kirby et al, (2000), page 772). In such a culture, life was lived for-the-moment, with neither investment in nor expectations about, the future. In contemporary Britain, **David Marsland**, a New Right theorist writing in 1996 cited a *'dependency culture'* as directly created by an overly generous welfare state. Those resourced in this way lack incentive – and responsibility:

'It (the welfare state) has made of its primary clients – perfectly normal, capable men and women before the state got to work on them – a festering underclass of welfare dependents.' (Marsland (1996), page 20)

American right-wing social commentator, **Charles Murray**, extended this conception of a new and rising British 'underclass'. Writing in the 1980s and 1990s, Murray gave fiery vent to his perception of 'ghetto lifestyles' characterised by immorality and crime and maintained by overly high state benefits. Society's most 'undeserving' include young female lone parents (and absentee fathers), raising their children to be undisciplined, work-shy and disengaged from mainstream society.

In 'the Advantages of Social Apartheid' (*Sunday Times*, April 2005), Murray argued that neither poverty nor social exclusion is the problem and providing additional resources no solution. Ultimately for Murray, we must be prepared to 'write off a portion of the population as unfit for civil society'.

A clear distinction is made here between the 'deserving' and 'undeserving' poor. While disabled people would be considered 'deserving', disability exists on a spectrum and, within 'the disabled', some are considered 'more' or 'less deserving' than others.

Structural

In sharp relief from 'blame the victim' theories, cultural theorists consider society's economic and social structures and institutions as the main cause of poverty, social division and inequality.

For **Peter Townsend** (1979) the main 'constraint' determining the lifestyles of society's poor are the ways they are excluded from or disadvantaged in, the labour market. When individuals and groups are not sufficiently skilled or educated, when they are considered 'too old', or 'too disabled', when they are female or black (or combinations of these defining criteria), then disadvantage in the labour market and beyond is guaranteed.

Lydia Morris (1993) challenges the idea of a distinct underclass culture. Rather than individuals and groups who are apathetic, fatalistic and irresponsible, her research concluded they remain motivated to work and to 'make good', but are systematically denied adequate opportunity to learn skills and secure opportunity to do so.

For **Ralph Miliband**, the British system of welfare creates poverty. While 'welfare capitalism' may appear to respond to society's most needy, it in fact exists to support and protect the interests of a ruling elite (Miliband, in Fulcher and Scott (2007) page 585).

Elite groups continually pursue maximum economic, social and political power and control over the majority (subject) population. Subject class wealth, well-being and opportunities are therefore, consciously limited, with income and benefits kept low.

The subject class is in itself structurally unequal in that its most vulnerable members (older adults, lone parents, homeless people) experience additional economic, political and social inequality. Divided in this way, a subject class is not resourced to make a collective and effective challenge to the dominant system.

Activity

You are advised to read up, and take notes on, **cultural** and **structural** interpretations of poverty and inequality *before* attempting the following.

1. For **structural** theorists what should a child born in a deprived area of Scotland expect in terms of *behaviour, experiences* and *life chances* and why is this?

2. For **cultural** theorists, how might people's *behaviour, experiences* and *life chances* be affected by poverty and inequality?

   Revisit 'Sociological Theory – an Introduction' earlier in this chapter, before attempting the following:

3. In what ways do '**cultural**' and '**structural**' views on poverty and inequality relate to *Functionalism* and *Conflict* theory?

Discrimination

This final section will exemplify ways in which social inequality relates to **discrimination**. We start with a table defining key terms and exemplifying each in relation to '**racism**'.

Note: While the term discrimination is not in itself 'negative' (meaning simply to differentiate between), we will focus in this section on the nature, extent and effects of negative discrimination.

Key term	Key term explained	Key term exemplified
Racism	Where prejudicial views and assumptions based on 'race', nationality or ethnic group are evidenced in the attitudes and actions of individuals, groups and institutions. Racist actions are hostile, degrading and violate the dignity of a person or group	**Activity/Further research:** To which 'race' do you belong – and why is the concept of 'race' so problematic for sociologists?
Prejudice	Negative attitudes toward 'others' usually based on lack of knowledge, generalised assumptions and/or fear	'I don't like people who look different, or who come from a different place' **Activity/Further research:** Explain and exemplify the assertion that 'all prejudice is learned'
Stereotyping	Crude and generalised assumptions that 'all' members of a particular social group share similar characteristics, a form of labelling	'Asians live in extended families, look after their own therefore tend not to need Social Care services' 'young black men are into gang violence' 'Scotland is "swamped" by asylum seekers manipulating the system' **Activity/Further research:** Find evidence to support *or* refute the idea that post 9/11 'Islamaphobic' stereotyping exists in Scotland
Individual discrimination	Treating people seen to be 'other' in different, unequal ways	Where a person or group treats another/others differently because of their 'race', nationality or ethnic group. Discrimination takes many forms, including insults and ridicule, exploitation, neglect, exclusion and physical violence – ultimately genocide and 'ethnic cleansing' ('Individual' here refers to discrimination actioned by any number of people) **Activity/Further research:** Find evidence of 'individual discrimination' affecting people who use Social Care services in Scotland
Institutional discrimination	Where discrimination is embedded within the culture and 'normal practice' of an institution	Where discrimination based on race, nationality and/or ethnic group exists *within* the rules and working of society's institutions, i.e. *under-representation* of minority groups in arenas of power and politics, the police and armed forces and *over-representation* in society's lower paid, lower status and most insecure jobs **Activity/Further research:** The Macpherson inquiry of 1999 established the Metropolitan police had evidenced 'institutional racism' in their investigation into the murder of Stephen Lawrence (1993) What forms of institutional discrimination were cited in the Macpherson inquiry?
Direct discrimination	Openly treating an individual or group less favourably. Can be evidenced 'individually' or 'institutionally'	Where an applicant is refused consideration for a job based on their perceived 'race', nationality or ethnic group. Current race relations legislation cites victimisation and harassment too, as unlawful
Indirect discrimination	Usually covert (hidden) – when a rule or condition is applied to all – but not all of society's groups are able to meet it equally	For example, where in a job advertisement, a condition of 'excellent written and spoken English' is stated – yet is not a requirement of the job itself
Marginalisation	When the effects of prejudice, stereotyping and discrimination result in individuals or groups being excluded from accessing 'mainstream' society	Literally means 'to be set aside'; to be and feel separate and 'unheard'. This concept applies to individuals, groups and agencies within society **Activity/Further research:** 1. Describe the role, remit and aims of the Scottish organisation 'BEMIS' 2. Find current evidence of marginalisation affecting ethnic groups in Scotland

Discrimination: key terms explained and exemplified in terms of racism.

From the table on the previous page it becomes clear that **prejudice** and **stereotyping** are interrelated, and form the '*thinking*' and '*believing*' which in turn feed into **discrimination** (the '*doing*'). Discrimination can be experienced in several ways and in combinations of '**individual**', '**institutional**', '**direct**' and '**indirect**'.

Prejudice, stereotyping and discrimination are tied into society's structures, patterns of power and existing inequalities. In order to negatively discriminate, one individual or group has to exploit its economic, political or social '**power**' over another – for example, the 'able' over 'the disabled'.

The effects of discrimination on any individual or group may include **labelling**, **marginalisation** and **exclusion**; all of which impact upon people's capacity to live their own lives.

How prejudicial are the people of Scotland?

Research via the **Scottish Centre for Social Research** (2006) concludes that Scots tend *not* to consider themselves 'prejudicial' in their thinking.

However, 29 per cent of respondents agreed that sometimes prejudice happens for 'good reasons'.

Those with fewer educational qualifications tended to be the most prejudicial (although other 'pockets' existed, i.e. younger people in relation to jobs, older people in relation to homosexuality).

With regard to women, older people and disabled people, prejudice appeared to relate more to attitudes which were 'patronising' rather than 'hostile'.

The places where people lived did not appear significant (i.e. Scotland's most deprived areas did *not* emerge as the 'most prejudicial').

(Extracted, adapted and abridged from Bromley, C., Curtis, J. and Given, L. (2006) Scottish Centre for Social Research – Scottish Executive. Crown Copyright.)

Why do we discriminate?

Often our discrimination arises from processes of 'othering' where, based on *how we see ourselves*, we view others as a separate 'type'. Disabled people are often homogenised (assumed to be 'one group') and are considered 'others' in terms of what they *don't have* or *can't do*. Those who do the 'othering' in this case, define themselves 'non-disabled' or (even less logically) 'able-bodied'.

Sometimes, discrimination arises from perceived or real *competition for resources* and notions of '*entitlement*'. You may have heard stereotypes for example, about 'non-Scottish' immigrants taking 'Scottish' jobs.

Prejudice and stereotypes may be internalised in the course of **socialisation**, for messages about others being '*different*', '*less desirable*' or '*less normal*' abound in our culture.

Activity

Go to http://www.bbc.co.uk/dna/h2g2/A1132480 (or simply look up '**Jane Elliot**'/'a class divided') to study American schoolteacher Jane Elliot's 1960's ground-breaking classroom experiment '*Brown Eyes-Blue Eyes*', then answer the following:

1. By what means did Elliot create **prejudice** and **stereotyping** within the group?
2. What were the effects, for the children involved, of '**labelling**', '**discrimination**' and '**marginalisation**'?
3. What for you, is the most important message of this experiment?

Activity

As part of 'Sexual Health Week 2008', the **Scottish Family Planning Association** promoted the rights of people with a learning disability to have a sex life.

In what ways might prejudice, stereotyping, discrimination, labelling and marginalisation appear in responses to this campaign?

Institutional discrimination

Institutional discrimination is evident where *patterns* of 'inappropriateness' occur in the health care of disabled people, when professionals assume 'symptoms' to be part of a disability, when life is held to be of less value (than 'normal') or when staff simply 'don't know' and leave aspects of the individual's care to parents or friends. It can be seen when school teachers reference heterosexuality only, in the 'relationships' element of a PSE curriculum, when care workers routinely make choices for people who uses services (assuming '*they*' can't, or shouldn't), when college students with particular learning difficulties consistently receive support which is needs-inappropriate, inconsistent or too late, when the criminal justice system responds in different ways to different ethnic groups who commit the same crime, when Scotland has among the lowest rates in the world for rape conviction and when workers in Social Care (which is built on anti-discriminatory practice) make a complaint about homophobia to find their managers 'do not recognise it as an equality issue'.

Multiple discrimination: the discrimination weave

It is an over-simplification to assume that discrimination happens in categories of 'sex', 'age', 'race' and 'disability' because of course, people who are disabled *are* 'black' or 'white', *are* male or female and *are* 'of an age'!

Further research

1. Consult **Mencap's** 'Treat Me Right' (2004) and 'Death by Indifference' (2007) at the Mencap website: www.mencap.org.uk.

   How do the forms of institutional discrimination evidenced in these reviews impact upon the **behaviour**, **experiences** and **life chances** of individuals, their families and service user 'groups'?

2. **Erving Goffman** in his seminal 1968 work *Asylums* describes the impact that living within a 'closed institution' can have on the individual. Where residents are 'closed-off' from the world and are subject to consistent power, control and routine they stand to lose their sense of 'self', their capacity as individuals, to make choices and take responsibility.

   In what ways might Goffman's concept of institutionalisation influence the behaviour, experiences and life chances of individuals?

3. In 'Less Equal than Others', commissioned by **Help the Aged** (Scotland) (2007) one respondent who received Social Care services described her experiences as 'being managed, not cared for'.

   What kinds of prejudice, stereotyping and/or discrimination do you think might contribute to a person who uses services feeling this way?

4. In 'Prescription for Change, Lesbian and Bisexual Women's Health Check 2008', commissioned by **Stonewall**, recurring patterns of 'exclusive' practice in women's health care are apparent: 'Fifty per cent of respondents recorded negative experiences (in relation to their sexuality) in the health sector in the last year, despite the fact that it is now unlawful to discriminate against lesbian and bisexual women'.

   'Healthcare workers continually assume I am heterosexual and ask inappropriate questions about my relationships. I am lectured about safe sex and preventing pregnancy.' (Go the Stonewall website and look up this report now.)

   How might 'normalised' expectations about sexual health affect lesbian and/or bisexual women?

5. The homepage for the website of the '**UK Men's and Father's Rights**' cites 'anti-male' discrimination, as individually and institutionally commonplace in the UK today:

   'Family courts have a powerful default of awarding custody to the mother – in 91 per cent of cases. This is regardless of the mother's conduct, or of her ability to care for her children. A great deal of research has established high correlation between fatherless families and child poverty, family violence, drug abuse, teen pregnancy, school failure and juvenile crime.' (See: www.jrf.org.uk/knowledge/findings/social policy/SP81.asp)

   What are your thoughts on this?

   How might functionalist, conflict and feminist sociologists respond to this statement?

The **Joseph Rowntree Foundation's** 'Disabled Women's Project' (1995) involved three respondent groups – disabled black women, disabled older women and disabled lesbians – and was an attempt to explore experiences and perceptions of **multiple discrimination**. Participants identified factors *beyond* their disability which resulted in additional feelings and experiences of racism, ageism, or homophobia, together with disablism:

'black disabled women voiced feelings of discrimination from within the (essentially white) disability movement, from within their own black cultures (as 'disabled') and from within society as a whole (as black and disabled).'

The Fawcett Society (2006: 8–9) argues that current equality legislation fails to adequately address these 'complexities of multiplicity'. Current Equality Duties too, are limited in their scope and application: 'duties placed on public bodies to eliminate discrimination and promote equality do exist for race, sex, disability – but not age, religion or belief, sexual orientation or transsexual status.'

A single Equality Act to enclose the six 'essential' areas of inequality and discrimination is expected on the statute books in 2009. For further information, see www.equalityhumanrights.com

Abuse and hate crime

According to Help the Aged (Scotland) two-thirds of elder abuse takes place in the home and is perpetrated by someone the older adult 'knows and should be able to trust'. The spectrum of potential abuse can be financial (coercion, exploitation or theft), can involve insults, intimidation, neglect, bullying, aggression and physical violence (including force-feeding and 'rough handling'). (Adapted from www.helptheaged.org.uk)

The consequences of abuse will vary in terms of the emotional and physical health of those affected; the contacts and relationships they have (or do not have), their capacity to and opportunities for, seeking support. Effects can include damage to self-esteem and self-confidence, debilitation via chronic fear and anxiety, depression and 'helplessness' via enforced passivity.

Further research

Go to http://www.helptheaged.org.uk/engb/ Campaigns/ElderAbuse/EnoughisEnough/ default.htm or simply key in 'help the aged' and search from there.

Watch '**Joan's Story**' and download the leaflet '**Stop Elder Abuse**'.

The **Disability Rights Commission** (now incorporated into CEHR) together with **Capability Scotland** commissioned a report: *Hate Crime Against Disabled People in Scotland: A Survey Report (2004)*. 47 per cent of respondents in this social survey recorded experiences of 'hate crime' specific to their disability. Forms of attack included taunts and name-calling, threats, intimidation, spitting, kicking, shoving, theft from person and harassment.

Groups who had experienced the greatest number of attacks were people with mental health problems, learning difficulties and visual impairments. Around 33 per cent of those who had been attacked changed their routines to avoid certain places. In addition to this, 25 per cent recorded they had moved home as a direct consequence of persistent attacks.

Further research

1. The **Scottish Parliament** set up a Hate Crime Working Group in 2003. Your task is to find out (via http://www.scotland.gov. uk/Topics/Justice/criminal/17543/8978) if hate crime exists in Scots law, in relation to *none*, *some* or *all* of the following: age, sex, sexuality, transgender status, religion/belief/ sectarianism, disability.

2. According to research in January 2008 by the **Women and Equality Unit** 'trafficking of women is the third highest black market income earner after drugs and arms'.

   Women are advertised in regional press throughout the country as if they were commodities, with stereotyped 'marketing' per ethnic group (e.g. South Asian women as 'submissive and exotic', South American women as 'hot blooded'). (See: http:www. equalities.gov.uk/publications/Women_Not_ For_Sale.pdf)

   What do you think is being sold here? Why in sociological terms, do you think 'business' is so profitable?

Theories of social interaction and reaction

Look again at 'Symbolic Interactionism' on page 118 in this chapter and revisit the ideas of **Mead** on 'self', **Goffman** on 'roles', **Becker** on labelling and **Link** and **Phelan** on 'modified labelling'.

Edwin Lemert (Lemert (1951) in Sweeney et al (2003), page 276) developed Becker's early work via additional concepts of **primary** and **secondary deviance**. Where 'deviance' relates to behaviour considered outside social norms, 'primary deviance' for Lemert is behaviour which has not (yet?) been labelled. Secondary deviance is behaviour which alters as a *consequence* of labelling.

Case study

A true story

A new sevice user joins your project. For several reasons (these include 'mislaid' files and interrupted care) his history is only partially known. He settles in well, quickly becoming popular with fellow residents and workers.

When files finally arrive, they detail a series of events where several years ago, the man seriously assaulted his own child, was duly prosecuted and 'did time'. When this becomes known, reactions to and relationships with this man start to change. Some staff make their discomfort and disapproval evident, in various ways and to different degrees. 'Extra', non-routine elements of care and support are largely withdrawn. This separation impacts on the man, who begins to appear different in terms of his 'personality' and behaviour. Less relaxed, less sociable, he appears uncertain of his role and place in the unit. He is more isolated from his fellow residents and running notes record his interactions with others as increasingly 'edgy' and 'argumentative'. One day, in response to a worker's curt and unhelpful reply (to his civil question), the man loses his temper and hits out. He assaults the worker.

1. What forms of **prejudice** and **discrimination** can you identify in this scenario?

2. In what way do concepts of 'self', 'roles', 'labelling', 'modified labelling' and Lemert's 'primary' and 'secondary deviance' apply?

Discrimination: the role of Social Care

Jocelyn Mignott is the manager of a residential home:

'I get tired of people calling me "coloured" because they feel it sounds better than black…'

'I get tired of being mistaken for someone else. Take a look at black people – we don't all look the same. I get tired of people who think that to be white is "normal". I get tired of people who pay lip-service to the abhorrence of racism yet fail to confront it in their everyday lives.'
(Mignott, J. in Webb, R. and Tossell, D. (1991))

Activity
Take some time to rework and reword Mignott's statement, this time substituting ideas about **disablism** in place of racism
…and do the same again for **sexism**
… and **ageism.**
What does this exercise show?

In Mignott's experience people routinely fail to recognise, or will play down or deny situations where others appear 'different'. 'Different others' tend to be homogenised and people routinely protest (about discrimination) but do nothing!

Mignott, as a black woman, occupies a position of relatively high social and professional status in that she *manages* the care others *receive*. She is, in addition, able to independently express her thoughts, experiences, reactions and frustrations and has accessed a public forum (*Social Work Today*) to do so. For a majority of people who use services, the picture is very different; inequalities and discrimination are compounded by their status as 'people who use services'.

For workers in Social Care, two of the most important signposts to good practice in terms of promoting equality and anti-discrimination are the promotion of **rights** (more than 'needs') and **empowerment**.

For further reading in relation to equalities legislation and anti-discriminatory practice, see the chapter on Social Care Theory for Practice.

Poverty, inequality and discrimination: preparing for assessment

Remember that your emphasis throughout assessment(s) has to be on the impact or influence of poverty and inequality and/or the nature and extent of discrimination on *behaviour*, *experiences* and *life chances*.

Practice essay

In relation to the people who use services you work with – apply Sociological theory and concepts *and* find current and credible research evidence to argue *for* or *against* the following statements:

> In contemporary Scotland people determine their *own* lifestyles, behaviour and life chances. Everyone can succeed providing they participate in society and take up the resources, opportunities and support available.

> Individual and institutional discrimination remains a fact of life for many who are in receipt of Social Care services.

Conclusion

In this chapter we have considered some key themes, theories and concepts from sociology and applied these to the life situations of individuals and groups in Scotland today. You have been encouraged to develop a *'sociological imagination'* – and a capacity to 'think sociologically' about ways in which family, socialisation, poverty, inequality and discrimination might individually and in combination, influence the lifestyles, behaviour, experiences and life chances of people who use services.

Equality is the right of all of society's members and the Social Care worker is instrumental in supporting individuals and groups to access resources and to receive standards of care which are rightfully theirs – and in challenging situations and practices which limit or discriminate.

Check Your Progress

The following questions will help you reflect on key areas of 'Sociology for Care Practice' and will support you in unit assessment:

1. What does it mean to apply a sociological imagination to the 'private troubles' of client(s) you support?

2. In what ways might common-sense assumptions limit the behaviour, experiences and life chances of clients you support?

3. In what ways might major social institutions influence our behaviour, experiences and life chances?

4. In what ways do structural and cultural perspectives in sociology compare and contrast?

5. Why for sociologists does 'discourse' provide the best route forward in our attempts to understand and respond to 'social problems'?

6. What features of 'family life' are the most influential for an individual's behaviour, experiences and life chances?

7. In what ways are poverty and deprivation understood in Scotland today?

8. What forms of social inequality do you consider have the most limiting effects on the behaviour, experiences and life chances of individuals/groups?

9. In relation to one 'group' of people who use services, how would you describe the nature, extent and effects of discrimination?

10. In what ways might your practice as a Social Care worker be influenced by what you have learned in 'Sociology for Care Practice'?

References: Sociology for care practice

References

Abercrombie, N. et al (1998) *Contemporary British Society*. 2nd edition. Polity Press: Cambridge in association with Blackwell Publishers Ltd: Oxford.

Barrett, M. (1980) *Women's Oppression Today*, Thetford Press Ltd: Norfolk.

Becker, H. (1963) *Outsiders: Studies in Sociology of Deviance*, Free Press: New York.

Berger, P. (1963) *Invitation to Sociology*, Penguin Group: London.

Connell, R. W. (1987) in Fulcher, J. and Scott, J. (2007) *Sociology*. 4th edition. Oxford University Press: Oxford.

Donaldson (1986) in Moonie, N. (ed.) (2005) *Health and Social Care*, Heinemann: Oxford.

Engels, F. (1894) *The Origin of the Family, Capitalism and the State*, Lawrence and Wishart: London.

Fulcher, J. and Scott, J. (2007) *Sociology*. 4th edition. Oxford University Press: Oxford.

Giddens, A. (2001) *Sociology*. 4th edition. Polity Press: Cambridge.

Goffman, E. (1968) *Asylums*, Penguin: Harmondsworth.

Goffman, E. (1969) *Presentation of Self in Everyday Life*, Penguin: Harmondsworth.

Kirby, M. et al. (2000) *Sociology in Perspective: AQA edition*, Heinemann: Oxford.

Laing, R. D., and Esterson, A. (1964) *Sanity, Madness and the Family*, Penguin: Harmondsworth.

Lemert, E. (1951) in Sweeney, T. et al (eds.) (2003) *Sociology and Scotland an Introduction*, Unity Publications: Paisley.

Link and Phelan (1995) in Rogers, A. and Pilgrim, D. (2005) *A Sociology of Mental Health and Illness*. 3rd edition. Open University Press: Maidenhead.

Marsland, D. (1996) *Welfare or Welfare State?* Macmillan: Basingstoke.

Mignott, J. (1991) in Webb, R. and Tossell, D. (1991) *Social Issues for Carers*, Arnold/Hodder: London.

Miller, D. L. (1973) *G. H. Mead: Self, Language and the World* University of Chicago Press: Chicago.

Millet, K. (1970) *Sexual Politics*, Doubleday: New York.

Milliband, R. (2007) in Fulcher, J. and Scott, J. (2007) *Sociology*. 4th edition. Oxford University Press: Oxford.

Mills, C. W. (1967) *The Sociological Imagination*, Oxford University Press: Oxford.

Moonie, N. (ed.) (2005) *Health and Social Care*, Heinemann: Oxford.

Moore, S. (2001) *Sociology Alive*. 3rd edition. Nelson Thornes: Cheltenham.

Morris, L. (1993) *Dangerous Classes: the Underclass and Social Citizenship*, Routledge: London.

Murray (2005) *'The Advantages of Social Apartheid,'* Sunday Times.

Parsons, T. (1951) *The Social System*, Tavistock: London.

Parsons and Bales (1956) in Giddens, A. (2001) *Sociology*. 4th edition. Polity Press: Cambridge.

Prejean, H. (1983) *Dead Man Walking*, Vintage Press: Esser.

Rogers, A. and Pilgrim, D. (2005) *A Sociology of Mental Health and Illness*. 3rd edition. Open University Press: Maidenhead.

Sweeney, T. et al (eds.)(2003) *Sociology and Scotland an Introduction*, Unity Publications: Paisley.

Taylor, A. (2008) Sunday Herald.

Townsend, P. (1979) *Poverty in the United Kingdom*, Penguin: Harmondsworth.

Webb, R. and Tossell, D. (1991) *Social Issues for Carers*, Arnold/Hodder: London.

Zaretsky, E. (1976) *Capitalism, the Family and Personal Life*, Pluto Press: London

Reports

Age Concern Scotland (2005) 'Older People in Scotland'

Energy Watch (2008) 'The Poor Pay More?'

Fawcett Society (April 2006) 'Gender Equality in the 21st Century: Modernising the Legislation'

Help the Aged Scotland, 2007 'Less Equal than Others'

Mencap (2004) 'Treat Me Right'

Mencap (2007) 'Death by Indifference'

Scottish Executive (2006) 'The Future of Unpaid Carers in Scotland', Crown Copyright

Papers

Stephen Hicks (2003): 'The Christian Right and Homophobic Discourse: a Response to "Evidence" that Lesbian and Gay Parenting Damages Children'

Camilla Batmaghelidjh 'My Vision for the 21st Century' (undated and no longer available; reproduced in this instance, with permission from Kids Company, London)

Recommended further reading

For the purposes of this chapter, you will find generic sociology textbooks helpful and relevant. These give description, explanation and commentary *on* the ideas and arguments, of sociology's main theorists and all clearly show chapter and subject headings ('family' etc.).The following are 'core' recommendations only.

HNC appropriate

Sweeney, T. et al (eds.) (2003) *Sociology and Scotland: an Introduction*

Giddens, A. (2001) *Sociology*, 4th edition

Haralambos, M. and Holborn, M. (2008), *Sociology, Themes and Perspectives*, 7th edition

(**Note:** see also in support of this text: www. collinseducation.com/sociologyweb)

Extension reading

This title is more suitable for those who plan to further their interest in academic sociology:

Fulcher, J. and Scott, J. (2007) *Sociology*, 3rd edition

Recommended websites

The following is an introductory list of web pages to support research and assessment in Sociology for Care Practice. Many other agencies and sites are equally relevant:

www.sociologyonline.co.uk (then search subject areas)

www.scotland.gov.uk/Home (then search subject areas)

www.equalityhumanrights.com (CEHR, then link to 'Scotland')

www.jrf.org.uk (Joseph Rowntree Foundation)

www.povertyalliance.org.uk

www.cpag.org/scotland/ (Child Poverty Action Group, Scotland)

www.barnardos.org.uk/scotland.html (Barnardo's)

www.opfs.org.uk (One Parent Families, Scotland)

www.scottishrefugeecouncil.org.uk

www.stonewallscotland.org.uk (lesbian, gay, bisexual, transsexual issues)

www.engender.org.uk (gender-based inequality in Scotland)

www.enable.org.uk

www.capability-scotland.org.uk

www.mencap.org.uk

www.helptheaged.org.uk

www.ageconcern.org.uk

www.news.bbc.co.uk (then search subject areas)

Chapter 5
Social Care: group award graded unit 1

Introduction

The graded unit is a project: a practical activity that relates very closely to you working with an individual in a care setting to plan, carry out and evaluate an activity which promotes the development of the individual. This is, in layman's terms, a piece of work you plan with the individual who you work with which will help to meet his/her needs and which involves drawing up a plan of care. It also involves you and the individual, and where appropriate the care agency you work with, or are on placement with, evaluating this work to assess if the plan was successful and needs were met. This is no mean feat!

You will be asked to identify an appropriate activity/project in discussion with your course tutor and work/placement supervisor and it might include one of the following.

- A **therapeutic activity** which helps your client to relax and/or feel good about themselves. Examples include getting a facial and or massage, a visit to a sauna, visit to the hairdresser and any kind of activity that builds confidence and self-esteem. It can also be an individual's involvement in hydrotherapy or rebound.

- An activity of **daily living** is one that will help the individual in everyday life, e.g. cooking sessions, budgeting, housework, use of transport etc.

- A **recreational** activity could be an outing or day trip somewhere or attending a gym or sports centre, a swimming session (these could also be therapeutic), bowling, badminton etc.

- An **educational** activity is about learning new skills and could also be activities

of daily living e.g. cooking, budgeting, use of pictorial aids to communicate or indeed complete tasks, learning to use the computer etc.

This unit is meant to be challenging and it is probably the unit that causes students more anxious moments than any of the others. However, from experience we would definitely say that, for many of the students who successfully completed it, the graded unit is the one where they felt that they gained the most. Many also reported that they actually enjoyed the experience.

So carry on reading and see what you think! Remember that your college tutor and the placement supervisor are fully aware of what you have to do and are available for support.

The purpose of the graded unit is to provide evidence that you have achieved the following main aims of the HNC Social Care, i.e. to:

- enable candidates to integrate knowledge, theory and practice effectively in a variety of care settings

- enable candidates to develop skills appropriate for working with a range of individuals in care settings

- enable candidates to have a client and carer focus in their practice

- prepare candidates for employment or to develop them in employment in a care setting

- enable candidates to critically evaluate their practice and to be reflective practitioners

- facilitate progression to higher education.

Don't panic; by the time you get to this stage you will have studied most of the following units, although not necessarily completed them, and have some idea of what it all means!

- Psychology for Social Care Practice – will provide you with an understanding of developmental stages of human growth and behaviour, an analysis of the influence on personality from different psychological perspectives and how life experiences affect development and behaviour.

- Sociology for Social Care Practice – will assist you in looking at, and where appropriate, writing about, the influence of the family on individuals' experiences, behaviour and life chances.

- Protection of individuals from possible harm and abuse, which will give you an idea of the framework and policies and procedures designed to protect individuals from possible harm and abuse.

- **Or** your college may choose to do the SVQ unit 'Promote the well-being and protection of children and young people' **or** 'Promote choice, well-being and protection of all individuals'. Either of these units will provide you with the same knowledge as the unit above and all three will also help you to identify through practice the care worker's role in relation to the protection of individuals.

- Social Care theory for practice – this unit allows you the opportunity to show evidence of the Care Planning process and methods and models of care practice. This will be evidenced throughout the graded unit assignment.

- Social policy and its application to Social Service Provision – this helps you to identify the legislation and policies that promote the rights and responsibilities of individuals for whom you care.

- Promote effective communication for and about individuals, promote, monitor and maintain health, safety and security in the working environment and reflect on and develop your practice (all SVQ units). As you will be aware, even if you have not completed the SVQ units, they should allow you to demonstrate your ability to put the theory into practice in a way that promotes the best possible outcome for the individual in need of care.

Undertaking the graded unit will assist you in developing knowledge and putting it into practice in a way that enriches the lives of others as well as enabling you to become an effective, competent worker in the care field.

Gaining a good grade may also assist in you obtaining a place on a degree programme at university should this be an area you wish to pursue.

This chapter has been written with you, the student, in mind. Its main aim is to provide you with support and guidance to help you to plan, develop and evaluate your practical project successfully.

In this chapter you will learn:

The structure of the graded unit
How to define aims and objectives
How to present your work
How to critically evaluate your work

The structure of the graded unit

The graded unit consists of three distinct stages:

- Planning – which involves a plan of action, including an assessment of the needs of the person who uses services

- Developing – which involves putting your plan into action

- Evaluation - which involves an evaluation of the plan, developing stage and the knowledge you have gained undertaking the HNC in Social Care.

Each of these stages will be discussed in greater detail as you move through this chapter.

You should remember that the graded unit is supposed to be an *independent* piece of work. Your tutor should provide guidance and clarification about the project and you may ask questions as you undertake each stage of the unit. Remember that if you require continual guidance and/or clarification your final grade will reflect this. The graded unit is, as can be seen above, undertaken by completing the three separate sections that should integrate to make a free flowing piece of work.

It is also useful to talk about **plagiarism** at this point. Over the last few years, plagiarism has become much more of an issue, mainly due to the Internet and the ease with which students can access and use others' work without acknowledging it. In academic circles plagiarism has always been strictly judged; in some cases, it has meant that people fail their exams or are asked to leave a course. There is no easy way to say it: plagiarism is dishonest as it involves the theft of another person's intellectual property, i.e. their expressed thoughts and ideas. It also shows a lack of respect for the person with whom you are working**.**

Key term

Plagiarism copying the work of another person and using it as your own.

You will be told how many words should be in each section; your centre will give clear guidelines on this. A word of warning may be useful at this stage: you will be penalised if you go more than 10 per cent over or under the stated word count. (There is more on this at the end of the section.)

Before you undertake this piece of work you will have the first of two formal interviews with your tutor to discuss the practical activity that you have selected. Prior to this interview you should have identified the person who uses services with whom you wish to complete the activity and also discussed the proposed activity with your placement supervisor. You should also have received permission/consent from the client or their carer/legal guardian, indicating their agreement to participate in this assessment.

You may have already recognised that the structure of the graded unit is similar to the 'Care Planning Process' where an individual's needs are first assessed; then activities are planned with the aim of meeting those needs

and implemented (developed) with the situation then being reviewed (evaluated). In undertaking this activity, by assessing the needs of your client, identifying aims and objectives, planning an activity to meet these needs, implementing your activity (hopefully to achieve the set objectives) and then reviewing the whole process and your practice, you will be applying the 'Care Planning Process' to your practice.

Your Graded Unit needs to remain a flexible piece of work in that you show that it can be adapted as your client's needs change. It is a practical assignment that will be carried out in the workplace and the activity that is chosen should be relevant to your client's developmental needs. Remember this activity could be therapeutic, educational, recreational or an activity of daily living, and will evidence learning from the mandatory units of the HNC in Social Care.

The graded unit is undertaken in three separate parts, and you have to achieve a pass in each section before moving onto the next section; so you need to be aware that you must write each section in the correct grammatical tense. What does this mean? The Planning stage has to be written in a combination of present and future and a little past tense, i.e.:

- 'I plan to undertake an activity of daily living skills with my client' (Present tense)
- 'I will etc.' (Future tense)
- 'I consulted with my supervisor' (Past tense)

The Developing stage needs to be written in the present and past tense as you provide evidence of how you carried out the activity.

The Evaluation will be a combination of past tense when you evaluate your practice, the present tense when you identify what you have learned from undertaking the HNC in Social Care and the future tense when you identify what improvements or modifications you would make for future planned activities.

Before reading any further, you could try the following exercise, to practise using tense in the correct manner. The first line has been completed for you.

Complete the exercise by inserting words in the correct grammatical tense.

Getting the tense right

Verb	Past	Present	Future
To carry	I carried They carried	I carry	I will carry
To feel		You feel	
To eat			She shall eat
To go			They shall go
To work			
To plan			
	I assessed		
			I will write

Before undertaking this assignment it is important to remember that you are bound by your agency's policy and procedures on **confidentiality** and any reference to your placement/workplace must be anonymous and the individual's name needs to be changed. (A small tip here is to ask the person who uses services what they would like to be called for the purpose of this assessment!)

Remember that you need to obtain permission from the individual with whom you plan to undertake your activity and write about in your graded unit. It may be that you have to speak to your line manager/supervisor about this, as not all clients are able to give their consent and it could be that a family member or the local authority has to be asked for permission for you to write about a specific individual and undertake the activity.

Check this out before making any detailed plans or organising an activity as not all people who use services wish to be written about or involved.

Planning

This stage of the project is worth 30 marks. To gain high marks you must, as already stated, demonstrate a high degree of autonomy.

Once you have gained consent/permission to work with and use information about the person who uses services you will be able to start planning your activity. It may be that you had already identified a specific piece of work that you felt would address some of the unmet needs of the individual with whom you are planning to carry out the activity. Remember that simple activities are easier to implement than complicated pieces of work. Your college tutor will offer guidance on this, as will the placement supervisor.

As you know the graded unit is an independent piece of work where you have to work autonomously. However, you will be given some guidance from your tutor and you are entitled to two formal, recorded interviews with him/her. Prior to the first interview with your tutor, you should have, in consultation with your placement supervisor, selected an individual and identified an activity with them that you believe will meet their needs; you should also have obtained consent.

At this interview you will discuss these points above with the tutor and any other issues pertaining to the plan. If it is not already fixed, you will be given a date to hand in your 'Draft Plan'. After this interview you are able to start developing your draft planning document and work out realistic timescales. This interview will be recorded, as it is only too easy to forget important points made. (See exemplar recording sheet on next page.)

HNC Social Care Graded Unit – Interview Checklist

Student name:

Date of interview:

Student has relevant information and paperwork: YES/ NO
Comments:

Student has completed planning checklist in pack: YES/NO
Comments:

Student has decided on planned project: YES/NO
Comments:

Student has an alternative project if necessary: YES/NO
Comments:

Student has discussed plan with placement supervisor: YES/NO
Comments:

Student has sought permission from relevant people: YES/NO
Comments:

Summary of discussion and agreed submission date for draft of plan:

Tutor signature   Student signature

Interview checklist.

Assessment

So how should you begin the planning stage? This has to be done through the process of **assessment**.

Firstly you need to identify the needs of the person who uses services and demonstrate how you have assessed them using the principles of PIES, i.e. Physical, Intellectual, Emotional and Social categories (see table below). This could be done in a combination of ways, such as talking to your client, observing your client, speaking to Key Workers, if appropriate, consulting with your supervisor and the family/carer, if appropriate, reading daily living plans and/or the Care Plan.

Physical needs	Food, water, shelter, warmth, protection from infection, access to medical services, access to local community, fresh air
Intellectual needs	Opportunities to learn new skills, mental stimulation, problem solving
Emotional needs	Love and affection, unconditional positive regard, praise, encouragement, reassurance, promotion of self-esteem, to feel secure, learning to trust and belonging
Social needs	Opportunities for social interaction, outings, hobbies. Interests, friendships.

Different needs categorised by PIES.

The following activities may start you thinking about the information you already have about your person who uses services. They may also identify what the gaps are in your knowledge and what you need to find out.

Activity

How well do you know your client? Try to answer the following questions:

1. When is your client's birthday and how old is your client?
2. Is the person on medication? If yes, do you know what they are taking?
3. If the answer to (2) is yes, what illness is the medication for?
4. Is the individual on a special diet? If yes, do you know the details?
5. What is your client's favourite meal?
6. What are their likes and dislikes?
7. If you work in a day care setting, do you know where the person lives?
8. If they have moved recently, do you know where they lived before?
9. Do they have a support network in the neighbourhood?
10. Does anyone visit them? If so, who and when?
11. If appropriate, do they have children?
12. Do they have any mobility issues? If yes, what are they?
13. If appropriate, what was/is their occupation or their career?
14. What is their favourite part of the day?
15. Do they have any hobbies?
16. What was the reason for their referral to the placement/workplace/involvement with it?
17. What is the 'goal' that your service is aiming for, with the client?
18. Have you identified their needs using PIES?
19. Make a list of these needs if the answer is 'yes'.
20. If the answer is 'no' do you know how to do this?

In constructing a needs assessment you have to find out what your client needs help with, what their strengths and weaknesses are. This will assist you in focusing on what the client needs to do in future to address his/her needs.

Activity

Try the exercise below to help you focus on needs as a positive outcome.

You will find this much easier if you state your client's needs in positive terms. Below are two lists of behaviours for a fictional client; these behaviours correlate to a need. The needs on the right-hand side are in positive terms; they give you a much better idea of what you need to be addressing. The first four statements have been rewritten in positive terms. You should rewrite the remaining statements on the list so that all those on the left-hand side are restated in more positive terms.

Incorrect: Joe's behaviour in negative terms	Correct: Joe's behaviour in positive terms
He is unfriendly.	He needs to become more friendly and sociable.
He is dirty.	He needs to develop his washing skills.
He is bored and uninterested.	He needs to find a range of stimulating interests.
He cannot cook for himself.	
He makes a mess when drinking from a cup or glass.	
He mumbles.	
He is selfish and won't join in.	
He is scruffy	

The right and wrong way to describe different behaviours.

By doing this exercise you may have been able to identify some needs which can become aims and objectives for the fictional client 'Joe'. If you complete a similar exercise with your client this may also assist you in identifying aims and objectives for your planned activity that may help the individual meet needs.

Remember: you need to evidence how you involved your client in this process.

How to define aims and objectives

Setting an objective, achieving it and receiving praise and recognition for doing so is an empowering experience!

What are objectives?

Objectives help to provide continuity and development throughout what might be a random assortment of activities. Objectives enable connections to be made between activity-based learning and issues or opportunities outside the programme. (Greenway, R. (1993) *Playback A Guide to Reviewing Activities*)

Once you have completed the assessment of needs of the person who uses services, and identified the aims and objectives of the planned activity, you need to start developing your planning document. You should know that:

- 10 marks will be allocated for the assessment of needs and appropriate use of developmental theories and the analysis of the same on the individual service user's behaviour

- 5 marks can be gained through the appropriateness of the identified activity and clear aims and objectives

- 6 marks are allocated for detailing resources and sources of information and the inclusion of legislation and discussion on safe practice

- 4 marks are allocated for identification of methods, models and theories and 5 marks for meeting all deadlines and adhering to timescales and the justification of the approach taken in the plan and developing stages.

So what do you need to include in your draft plan?

- An assessment of needs of the person using services using PIES.

- An analysis of the current developmental needs using relevant psychological and sociological theory with reference to the development of the personality, key life experiences that have affected development and behaviour and the influence of the family. A word of warning here: make sure you provide an analysis and not a description.

- Clearly defined aims and objectives.

- Evidence of the appropriateness of the chosen activity; if you link this to the needs of the individual you should be on the right track.

- Evidence of how the individual came to be requiring care. Don't forget to give reference to legislation.

- A demonstration of how the individual was as fully involved as possible in the planning process.

- Identification of methods and models of practice and how they will be applied in practice. (Do you remember this from Social Care Theory for Practice?)

- A statement on the legislative framework and policies and procedures designed to protect the individual from possible harm and abuse and how they are used in practice.

- Information on legislation and policies that promote the rights and responsibilities of individuals and how this occurs.

- Evidence of resources and materials that are required to carry out the activity. A list will be enough.

- A realistic timescale (your tutor will guide you on the timescales for each of the three parts of the graded unit).

Theory and practice

As you will see if you follow this guide, you are beginning to meet some of the aims of the HNC in Social Care, and the criteria for the graded unit, a huge part of which is to integrate theory and practice to meet the best possible outcome for the individual.

Consider this

Why do we need to integrate theory with practice? As has been recognised for years, to discuss theory without practice is of little use and to practise theory without practice is dangerous. (Thompson N., and Thompson S. (2008) *The Critically Reflective Practitioner*)

Do not be too worried by the use of the word theory. Theories in Social Care are an attempt to explain social relationships. Theories have been developed since it became evident that there were similar patterns of behaviour both in the

life of an individual and in the lives of others experiencing similar situations.

So what can theories explain for us?

- Theories can help us make sense of why someone behaves the way they do, based on previous learned behaviour or their experiences.

- They can identify why an individual's life chances are different because of where they live and their upbringing.

- Theories can also help us to motivate people and enable them to change their behaviour or situation positively.

- Theory can make real sense of the people who you work with and exploring theory can be really rewarding, humbling and exciting for a worker.

The following activities may help you collect all the information that you need to include in your draft plan.

Legislation

First, have you thought about the legislation that you need to work with? Take a moment to consider this. What legislation informs your practice? By adhering to this legislation you promote anti-oppressive practice. If you can think of anti-oppressive practice as a bag of tools, then the legal framework is one of many tools to aid your practice. The following activities might help you in this process.

Activity

We have covered legislation and policies that promote the rights and responsibilities of individuals. You should find out what legislation and which policies in your working environment/placement promote the rights and responsibilities of individuals involved in the service provided.

1. Make a note of what these are.

2. Give examples of practice evidencing how rights and responsibilities are promoted. Try to use examples that are relevant to the activity you are planning.

You should now have identified the legislation that is relevant to the activity that you are planning. Hopefully you have also been able to identify how this legislation integrates with your practice. The next two activities should help you to further integrate theory with practice.

Think of the individual with whom you are planning to undertake the activity and consider their experiences and their needs as they present. Try to identify the psychological and sociological theories and/or perspectives that could explain their development, experiences, behaviour and life chances. You may wish at this point, to revisit these chapters: Psychology for Care Practice and Sociology for Care Practice.

You probably feel ready to start drafting your plan but first a word of warning. This work is discussing the life of another individual, as previously mentioned, so confidentiality has to be paramount throughout this activity.

Perhaps (through the completion of the previous exercise) you have identified perspectives, theories and methods that you feel you understand well and would like to use in your case study. **Note**: not every theory, perspective or method will be relevant to every person who uses services. Do not try to adapt the individual's history or life to 'fit in' with the theory. Your lecturer is likely to notice this and think that something is not right. Remember that they all have experience of working in care.

Also, to adapt details of an individual's life to suit your needs would also show very little respect for that person.

How to present your work

How should you proceed and how should you present the draft plan?

Draft plan

The following is a possible layout although this is not prescriptive; your centre may have devised its own in which case you must adhere to that format.

Introduction: state who you are and where you work or are on placement, explaining briefly your role and a short profile of the client group. (Remember the principles of confidentiality.) For example:

- I am a student on placement.

- I am working with older adults in a day care setting. My role is _____

- I am a student on placement working in a children's unit my role is. My role is _____

_____

- I am employed as a project worker working in the area of alcohol and substance abuse and my role includes _____

- To complete this piece of work I have had to identify a person who uses services, assess his/her needs and plan an activity to address identified need.

- For the purpose of this project/activity I have changed the name of my client to

_____ . This is in line with _____ (policy and legislation) and with the permission of the client.

- The assessment of needs is the first stage in the Care Planning process. The (legislation) gives my client a right to an assessment of needs/a plan of care.

You could at this point introduce what your activity is and what your aims and objectives are.

- Provide some history and background of your client, comparing and evaluating two *contrasting psychological* theories that could explain the behaviour and personality development of your client.

- Use sociological perspectives to describe the structures and roles of family, including the client's family; evaluate one perspective in relation to the impact of the family on the development of your client.

- Show how you assessed your client's needs and link them to the activity, aims and objectives.

- If you haven't already introduced your planned activity you could do so at this point. You need to provide evidence why this is an appropriate activity for your client.

You should explain what methods of intervention you intend using and identify how you plan to do this. For example: I propose to use Task-centred practice and crisis intervention within the project.

Task-centred practice is _____ and will be used throughout because it

_____. Should crisis intervention be used? _____

Other points to consider:
- You should give evidence of how you have planned out this piece of practice.
- Did you need to carry out a risk assessment (see below)? What legislation is involved in this?
- Will you need to collaborate or network with other agencies/professionals or colleagues? Explain the importance of this for good practice.
- What resources do you plan to use?
- Do you have a contingency plan?
- Remember to include a timescale – including deadlines for submitting the different stages of the project.

Note: Risk assessment is essential when working in Social Care. Workers need to continually be aware of risk factors that can arise or exist when working with any person who uses services. Risk assessment means that you take into consideration all situations that might pose a hazard when planning any outing or activity. (These will include time of day, materials, resources, environment, health, transport, weather and so on, and this list is not exhaustive.) Risk assessment should become like second nature, an essential part of good practice. Undertaking a risk assessment does not mean that *incidents and accidents cannot happen but it means that you have done your best* to ensure that they will not. Also, see the section on page 155.

Activity
What legislation informs your practice in relation to risk assessment?

Second tutor interview

Once you have handed in the planning stage it will then be marked and you will be given feedback from your tutor at your second interview. You should be in a position to discuss the assessment of needs at this interview with your tutor. If you successfully pass this stage you can then move on to the next stage – developing, this is where you put your plan into action.

Below is an example of a checklist for a second tutor interview.

HNC Social Care Graded Unit – Second Interview Checklist

Student name:

Date of interview:

Student has submitted draft plan within set timescale: YES/NO
Comments:

Student has completed the assessment of needs of individual: YES/ NO
Comments:

Student has included evidence of materials: YES/NO
Comments:

Student has included evidence of methods: YES/NO
Comments:

Summary of discussion and date for submission of completed project:

Tutor signature   Student signature

An exemplar second interview.

Student testimonials

'The most important thing I have come to realise is that it is essential to plan thoroughly.'

'One of the main strengths of the plan was that it was not rigid.'

'The most difficult thing I found with the planning stage was the time it took; it took a lot longer than I had planned for.'

'My plan was guided by theorists such as Erikson, Bandura and Maslow.'

Developing the project

A total of 35 marks are allocated to the development stage of the project and it should be between 1,200 and 1,700 words. Remember the word count is given to help you to prioritise your notes etc. and you can be only 10 per cent under or over the required word count before being penalised by losing marks.

At this stage you need to demonstrate how you followed your plan and implemented your planned activity with your client, giving an account of the activity that describes how you applied the knowledge and skills you have gained from studying the units of the course. Many of our students claim that this is the most enjoyable part of the project because they are getting to write about what they did, how they did it, where and when. They also offer the following advice.

- Write it up as you go along; do not wait until the last minute as you will lose some of the finer details and may forget the sense of achievement in assisting someone in this way.

- Remember to use reflection as a tool to fully understanding what has occurred. Having written reflective accounts for the SVQ units, they say, helps in completing this stage of the project.

- Keep your plan beside you when writing up this stage of the project as you will gain marks if you show how you followed the plan.

- Do not worry if your plan falls through. You will not necessarily lose marks if you can show how you put the contingency plan in place. Remember your tutors are marking you on the *process* not the product. Marks can be gained if you evaluate thoroughly in that stage of the project the reasons why the plan fell through.

One student says: 'I found it very difficult, doing the plan for this, but I got the rewards at this stage when I could reflect on and write about the good work I did.' (HNC student 2008)

Remember that you have to evidence throughout this stage, and indeed throughout the whole project, the following:

- your role in relation to the protection of the individual with whom you are working

- the beliefs and preferences of the individual with whom you are undertaking the activity

- how you actively promote the independence of the individual

- how you have involved the individual in this activity

- a completed risk assessment.

Note: you need a word for word account of how you developed/carried out the activity with the person who uses services.

Participation of people who use services

Over the years students have had different degrees of difficulty, real or perceived, in encouraging the participation of the person who uses services. In many ways, this participation is an extension of empowerment and **advocacy**.

Encouraging client participation/involvement need not be so difficult. Listening to clients is a means by which the individual can be involved, which is done on a daily basis, as is involving the person who uses services in the Care Planning process, in identifying an activity in which they would like to be involved. Observing the individual when they are engaged in different activities, and assessing likes and dislikes, is also a way of encouraging participation.

It is important to involve the individual in the evaluation, possibly through getting them to complete a questionnaire (see exemplar in review section) which is specifically designed for this purpose and taking into account the ability of the person who uses services. The ability and capability of the individual should not be seen as a barrier to participation.

Note: the extent to which you will be able to do this will vary according to the policy and procedures within your organisation and your role within it. However all HNC Social Care students should be in a position that offers them the opportunity to ensure participation of people who use services.

Key term

Advocacy a process of supporting and enabling people to; express their views and concerns, access information and services, defend and promote their rights **and** responsibilities, explore choices and options. (MIND (2008) *The MIND Guide to Advocacy*, MIND: London)

Risk assessment

A word about risk assessment here, bearing in mind the Department of Health (2007) statement that: 'the possibility of risk is an inevitable consequence of empowered people taking decisions about their own lives'.

Most people are able to balance risk against benefits and will, therefore, take any necessary precautions to minimise the risk. This, however, may not be so easy for many of the people with whom you may find yourself working; so support to achieve this balance may be necessary.

Risk assessments are designed to ensure that risks are minimised. Their purpose is not to limit choice but to raise awareness, in order that decisions can be made with the full knowledge of possible consequences and some knowledge about the measures that need to be taken to reduce these.

Note.

- Remember the relationship between you and the individual with whom you work is paramount to a quality risk assessment.
- Risk has to be seen as a positive as well as a harmful issue.
- It is the main aim of most care organisations to support individuals to be as independent as possible.

Other points to consider

In your plan you stated which methods/ models of care you were going to use and perhaps you indicated when you may use them. You might also have said which sociological and psychological theories and/or perspectives you thought were relevant to your client. If you wish to get high marks in your graded unit you now need to evidence how you have put these into practice.

You need to evidence how you applied the methods of intervention, theories and/ or perspectives; think SVQ here in relation to reflective practice – ensuring you fully explain how you used theories, models and perspectives in practice.

You must show how you used the identified materials and resources. Make sure you include these details at this stage and remember that if you do not use the resources identified in the plan, or indeed use more or different resources, *don't panic* – just keep a note of this and include it in the evaluation stage as a weakness of the original plan.

Do not forget legislation: you may have identified relevant legislation, and included this in the planning stage, but it does not mean you should not include it in the developing stage. This may seem repetitive but including it here shows your tutor that you understand how legislation informs practice and how it gives the client rights and therefore promoted good practice. Do not forget the legislation that relates to risk assessment.

You must demonstrate anti-discriminatory practice and link it to Codes of Practice and care standards within this stage of your graded unit. Did you give your client choice? Did you treat him/her with dignity? Did you ensure the individual's safety at all times and treat the person as a diverse individual? Did the planned activity help to realise their full potential? It is not enough to say 'Yes' to these questions – you need to write here about how you did this. This has to be verified by your placement supervisor as authentic so remember to discuss this with her/him and get a letter from them to support this.

Case study

Peter

Peter has complex learning disabilities and does not communicate verbally. He spent nearly all his childhood and about thirty years of his adulthood in a long-stay hospital for people with learning disabilities. He now lives in the community, in a shared tenancy, and is supported in his daily living skills by staff.

His Key Worker John, feels that Peter is able to understand what people are saying to him and through the assessment of Peter's needs he has observed that Peter got easily frustrated and at times aggressive when he was unable to make his needs known. John had observed that Peter became much calmer if offered a cup of tea and this seemed to settle him. John felt that if Peter could indicate his need for a cup of tea this might enable changes in his behaviour but, as Peter was unable to make his needs known because he had no verbal communication, John had to be innovative in his practice. John thought that if he planned an activity of a 'Daily Living Skill' it would empower Peter and enable him in a step-by-step process of making a cup of tea. This would mean Peter initially observing and copying John's behaviour by getting his cup out of the cupboard and putting his tea bag in it, enabling Peter to indicate that he would like a cup of tea. John would complete all other stages of making a cup of tea initially to ensure Peter's safety.

John had identified that Peter may have learned aggressive behaviour from other residents in the hospital as he was growing up and had simply continued to use this behaviour to gain attention.

John hoped to change this behaviour by giving Peter tools to express his needs and by then modelling his behaviour on John's. Peter's needs could be met and his behaviour changed and he would be empowered to indicate his need for a cup of tea.

1. Can you identify at least one theory and method that could be used to support the activities that are being considered?

2. Explain how these could be applied throughout the activity.

3. What developmental theory could explain why Peter feels the way he does? Give reasons for your answer.

Case study

Courtney (1)

Courtney is a young adult who grew up in a family where she was always criticised and blamed for anything that went wrong. She left home aged 16 and lived rough for a while; she no longer maintains contact with her family. Courtney is now 18 years old and a few months ago moved into a residential unit for homeless persons. It is hoped that Courtney will gain her own tenancy soon.

Courtney has low self-esteem and is quite isolated in the homeless unit where she is living; she finds it difficult to make relationships, believing that no one really likes her. She often comfort eats to combat her loneliness and this has resulted in her becoming overweight. She gets quite depressed when her clothes are tight on her and will eat sweets and ice cream to feel better. Courtney really wants to lose weight and have a healthier lifestyle.

When Courtney was younger she used to go swimming on a regular basis and at one point swam competitively for her school. Courtney has stated to staff in the homeless unit that her parents were never interested in her welfare or life and never supported her in this activity. Her Key Worker in the unit knows from what Courtney has said before that she would like to start swimming again, but she has admitted that she would feel uncomfortable and self-conscious wearing a swimsuit because she knows she is overweight. The student in the unit who has built up a good relationship with Courtney feels that if Courtney could be involved in a simple exercise programme, for example going for a 20 minute walk each evening, this would help her get fitter. She would perhaps start to lose weight and so work towards feeling confident about returning to swimming. It would also mean that Courtney would have one-to-one time with an individual which may boost her self-esteem.

1. Can you identify at least one theory and method that could be used to support the activities that are being considered?

2. Explain how these could be applied throughout the activity.

3. What developmental theory could explain why Courtney feels the way she does? Give

Case study

Courtney (2)

Courtney (see Case study above) had grown up with her mum and younger brother; her dad had left home when she was 3 years old. Courtney's mum always blamed Courtney for the break-up of her marriage, stating that she was a difficult child. Courtney's mum didn't work outside the home as any job that she could have applied for did not pay enough to cover child care for two young children. Money was always tight. The family lived in a terraced home in an area of high priority needs. Very few people in the street were in employment and housing was in a poor state of repair and all council-let.

When Courtney was 11, her mum's boyfriend Jason moved in to live with the family. Courtney never liked Jason and he had no time for her. She has never had a good relationship with her mother and this deteriorated even further once Jason moved into the home. The relationship between Jason and Courtney's mum is 'stormy' to say the least, with the police being called on several occasions.

1. What family structures are identified in the case study?

2. How do you think this has affected Courtney's life chances?

3. Explain how Courtney's family structure may have affected her experience.

Note: See if your SVQ assessor will observe you carrying out the activity with the individual; this is good practice as it shows your ability to wholly integrate theory and practice.

Note: If you provide a detailed account of the activity, which is related to the plan, you may achieve a high mark for this stage of the project. If you do not relate the activity to the plan but give a good account of how you have undertaken the activity in a logical fashion then you should be given a pass mark. If, however, your account of the activity demonstrates little coherence or organisation, and does not relate to the plan, you will most definitely fail to achieve this part of the project.

Student testimonials

'Integrating theories to actual practice has enabled me to provide better support to people who use services.'

'Prior to doing this course my knowledge of psychological and sociological theories was barely existent.'

'I chose Task-centred practice as this allowed me to explore the areas of need with the client and agree the problem areas she considered most important with evaluation and review built in.'

Once the development stage is completed, hopefully within the agreed timescale, and handed in, it will then be assessed by your tutor; if it passes you can move on to the final stage of the graded unit – evaluation.

Evaluation

This stage of the project is worth 30 marks – that is 30 per cent of the total – and should be between 1,000 and 1,500 words. From previous experience we can say that if you want high marks it is unlikely that an evaluation section of less than 1,200 words will achieve it. This does not detract from the fact that it is the quality of the work that is important – not its quantity.

Evaluation is the final part of your graded unit and is actually the stage where you can show real evidence of your learning, identifying the knowledge and skills you have gained throughout your time at college undertaking the HNC in Social Care. You can also identify whether you are good at reflective practice and able to learn from your own experiences and use this information to inform/underpin future practice.

Why evaluate?

The main purpose of review is to increase the value of the work that you do with service users. Reviewing is a process that is used to encourage people to reflect, describe, analyse and encourage them to write down and talk about what they have experienced. It can involve focusing attention on the past, present or future.

Reviewing will help you to learn from and examine the reasons for success or failure of your plan. It will also identify areas where service was deficient and may help you to determine what needs to be done in the future.

Consider this

'I hear – I forget
I see – I remember
I do and review – I learn.'
(Adapted from the words of Confucius, Chinese philosopher 551–479 BC, in Greenway, 1993.)

In this section of the project you are asked to provide an evaluation and review of the activity, which includes:

- an evaluation of the effectiveness of the original plan
- a reflection on your own practice – throughout all stages of the project – that identifies any new learning
- an evaluation of your use of the support systems available to you from all sources, e.g. college support including staff and your placement supervisor and team members.

Look at some of the terminology used here – three words jump out of the page for most students:

- evaluation
- review
- reflection.

What is meant by **evaluation** in the context of the graded unit? It involves not just a description of the activity carried out but an assessment of its usefulness in terms of meeting the aims and objectives and the needs of the person who uses services. To do this, therefore, it is important that you constantly remind yourself of the main aims and objectives of the activity, which need or needs were to be met and so on. To this end, remember that it is a good idea to write the evaluation report with a copy of the plan and development stage in front of you.

Review means again not to merely describe the plan and development stage of the project but to look closely at the strengths and weaknesses – highlighting areas of new learning both for you and the individual with whom you are working. It also involves you in thinking about what you could have done differently, bearing in mind the whole concept of SMART objectives.

Key terms

SMART = Specific, Measurable, Achievable, Realistic, Time-bound

Specific Quantifiable in terms of how many.

Measurable How will you know if you have achieved your goal, where is the evidence?

Achievable Targets should not be too difficult or too far in the future, deal more with the here and now.

Realistic Has to be within the capabilities and fit with what you are looking to achieve.

Time-bound Set dates for completion.

The following activities will assist you in putting these ideas into practice in the process of review.

Activity

Think about a situation in which you were learning something important.

What was helpful and what was unhelpful to your learning?

What could have enhanced your learning?

Can you relate this to the activity you have undertaken with a person who uses services?

Activity

Think about a situation where you tried to help someone in some way.

What did you do?

In dealing with the situation, what did you do that was helpful?

What, with hindsight, could you have done differently?

What have you learned from this that can help you in the future?

Activity

Try to answer the following questions, relating them to this process of reflection.

What has been confirmed or has challenged me?

What have I learned from this project?

What has emerged that I never thought of before?

Is there anything that worries me? Why? Is there anything I can do about it?

Activity

Think over the activity you have undertaken with your client. Try to identify the strengths and weaknesses of your original plan. Did it meet the aims of the activity?

If undertaking a similar activity, what would you change?

Draw up a page-size version of the table below. Now look at the next steps and prioritise at least four action points for yourself regarding things that you could have done differently. These should be SMART. Use these points to reflect on what needs to be included in this evaluation section of your graded unit.

Things I know I did well	Things I have concerns about
Issues arising	Possible next steps

Strengths and weaknesses of the plan and what comes next.

Those students who are able to review the quality of their own work with some **reflection** and who can identify any new learning will gain 15 of the 30 marks available for this section of the project. They should also be able to say how this new learning has had an impact on their practice – not only in carrying out this activity but how it makes them a more confident competent worker (National Care Standards).

Reflection is quite simply a way of learning. It is expected that those who undertake an HNC in Social Care will throughout the course learn how to become reflective practitioners. This will then lead the individual student to demonstrate a capacity for self-knowledge, self-criticism and an understanding that self-awareness and self-development is a lifelong process.

This requires the development of open-mindedness; responsibility and commitment to development, skills in describing situations, processes, cause and effect. It also involves planning for action in relation to your workplace practice and personal development.

Roth (1989), in Maclean, (2006) summarised the basic elements of a reflective process as follows:

- keeping an open mind about what, why and how we do things
- awareness of what, why and how we do things
- asking what, why and how other people do things
- generating choices, options and possibilities
- comparing and contrasting results

- seeking to understand underlying mechanisms and rationales
- viewing our activities and results from various perspectives
- asking 'What if….?'
- seeking feedback and other people's ideas and viewpoints.

There are **5 marks** allocated to the identification of the **strengths** and **weaknesses** of the original plan, and whether or not the plan was successful in meeting the aims of the activity. Note: you will not gain maximum marks by making a statement that reads, for instance, 'The activity met the needs of the individual and I followed the plan'!

It might be helpful at this point to get some feedback about your activity from your client and/or your line manager or SVQ assessor if they witnessed the activity. This could be in the form of a questionnaire or feedback sheet.

For those of you who work with people who have limited communication skills – through age, illness or disability – it might be useful to use feedback sheets that only require tick boxes or marking faces or pointing, such as the example below.

How did you enjoy this activity?

Good   Not so good   Don't know

Would you like to do this activity again?

Yes   No   Not sure

An example of a feedback sheet for people with limited communication skills.

Perhaps you work with people who have no or little verbal communication and also feel that they would be unable to use this type of feedback sheet. If you are trained in 'Talking Mats', the individuals with whom you work could give you feedback through the use of their 'Talking Mats.'

Be as innovative as you can be with regard to questionnaires and feedback sheets. You should always work from the position of 'What can my client do?' rather than concentrating on what they cannot do.

> **Questionnaires**
>
> If you are constructing a questionnaire make sure it is objective, very clear and does not have any leading questions. It would be helpful to test it on a 'critical friend' first.

There are **5 marks** given for the review of the whole project, which should include recommendations for future planned activities (i.e. what you would do differently if you did this again) and which part of the project you would change (i.e. parts of the plan or developing stage or both).

One HNC student says:

'While developing the plan I realised that I hadn't planned to contact the other team members for their views on the activity or any suggested improvements they may have; so I adapted the plan and did this after week one. However, reflecting on this now, after I had identified this omission I should have included reviews every week – as having the support of other team members was invaluable when carrying out this activity.'

There are **5 marks** awarded for identifying the way the project integrates knowledge and understanding of the units from the HNC identified at the beginning of the chapter and your centre's guidance notes, especially where the student identifies skills gained and integration of theory and practice throughout.

Another student says:

'On reflection of the HNC in Social Care, the Social Care Theory for Practice unit enhanced my knowledge of effective communication and the SVQ3 unit Promote Effective Communication for and about Individuals enabled me to put this new learning into practice. Before doing these units I wasn't conscious of the different skills required to communicate effectively or how to use them in practice. I now realise the importance of non-verbal communication and how effective communication enables people who use services to be better supported; e.g. open questions require extended answers and paraphrasing allows clients to hear the worker's interpretation and correct it if it is wrong.'

Writing your evaluation

When writing the evaluation it is sometimes very difficult to think of the right words to use. Often students are left with 'it went really well', 'everyone had a good time', 'I was happy with it' or 'the plan was good'.

These are some words that may be useful when you are writing your evaluation.

Good/poor

Limited/wide ranging

Pleasing/disappointing

Clear/confusing

Effective/ineffective

Successful/unsuccessful

Unbalanced/well balanced

Valid/invalid

Well planned/poorly planned

Appropriate/inappropriate

Presentation

You should check with your college/centre about the standard of presentation expected. You should be told if it should be typed using a word document or if a handwritten project is acceptable.

Remember that if you type up your project on a computer it is much easier and less time-consuming to make changes, should you need to do so. The SQA unit descriptor does not say that your work needs to be word processed but there is little doubt that this makes it easier to read. Also, each page should be numbered.

Ensure that there are no spelling or major grammatical errors. Use the spell and grammar check on the computer and proofread all work before submission. It is in fact a good idea to get someone else to proofread your work; if it

does not make sense to them then it is unlikely to make sense to the person marking your work. Remember, when writing up the project, that in essence you have taken into account the fact that the reader/marker has little knowledge of the subject.

You should avoid over-long sentences. This is a common mistake among students. Sentences that are too long can make written pieces confusing and difficult to understand.

Consider this
Proofreading is very useful. Have you asked anyone else to look at your graded unit? This is very important as often we cannot see our own mistakes until another person points them out to us.

Key term
Appendix a collection of material presented at the end of the project which includes any sources of information helpful to understanding the projects main content.

Appendix

What can be included in the **Appendix**?

A copy of any letters sent out

Copy of initial interviews

Copy of feedback forms/questionnaires

Letter of authentication from supervisor

Interview checklist

(This list is not exhaustive.)

Each item should be numbered and that number is then referred to in the text.

Do not include:

• downloads from the Internet

• photocopies from books, articles etc.

• posters, leaflets etc.

Sometimes students who may be involved in an activity with an individual with a specific learning need or disability have put information from Internet research, leaflets etc. on the condition as an appendix – you should not do this.

References using the Harvard system

If you are going to present your references correctly, using the Harvard system, the examples below show how you should do it:

Cole, M. (2007) *Education, Equality and human Rights,Issues of Gender, Race, Sexuality, Disability and Social Class*. 2nd edition. Routledge: London and New York.

Croxford, L. (1994) 'Equal Opportunities in the Secondary-School Curriculum in Scotland, 1977–91', *British Educational research Journal*, Vol. 20, No.4.

Denston, I.L. and Gray, J.H. (2001) 'Leadership development and reflection; What is the connection?' *The international journal of education management*, Vol. 15.

Rogers, A. (2002) *Teaching Adults*. 3rd Edition, Open University Press: Philadelphia.

Guidance on grading

The graded unit attracts a grade A, B, or C:

- A grade is a piece of work that is described by SQA as 'highly competent'
- C grade is 'competent'
- B grade is somewhere between the other two.

Marks for each grade are as follows:

- A = 70% to 100%
- B = 60% to 69%
- C = 50% to 59%

This is an aggregate of the scores for each stage of the project, taking into account the criteria identified at each stage of the project.

How do you attract high marks?

To attract at least 70 per cent your project has to be a coherent piece of work that flows in a manner that attracts the marker's attention to the following:

- submitted within the agreed timescales
- a project that is of a consistently high quality that clearly shows evidence of all three sections being clearly inter related
- shows clear evidence of the student having worked on their own with little guidance from the lecturer. Very clearly shows evidence of having involved the service user throughout
- evidences a high level of both subject knowledge and practical experience
- very clearly evidences the application of the national care standards
- is very well focused which shows evidence of insight into the main aims of the project and the integrative nature of it
- provides a comprehensive review and evaluation of your learning throughout the course and your ability to apply this to practice consistently throughout the project
- clearly shows evidence of critical evaluation and reflective practice
- includes a comprehensive reference and bibliography guide using an appropriate referencing system. (See previous example of a reference page using Harvard reference system)
- has a coherent structure and is accurate in spelling and grammar
- meets the required word length. Remember plus or minus 10 per cent is acceptable.

On a final note
Student testimonials

'The graded unit required me to pull all the knowledge and skills that I had gained from other units together and apply them in a project.'

'The knowledge I gained from Sociology and Psychology for Care Practice taught me how upbringing and life chances can affect personality, behaviours and needs. Psychology can be used to determine why people behave the way they do and can be used to help change behaviour.'

Check Your Progress

1. Make sure before you hand it in that each stage of your graded unit has covered all the necessary criteria. Look back through this chapter to try to ensure that you have not missed out any relevant points.
2. Have you laid your activity out in a methodical order?
3. Make sure that you keep within the word count for each section.
4. Are you certain that you have not plagiarised anyone else's work? (Remember that if you do this, it shows little recognition or acceptance of your client.)
5. Does your appendix only contain appropriate materials?
6. Have you referenced your sources correctly within your text?
7. Have you constructed your bibliography using Harvard referencing?
8. Have you read over each section of your activity using a spell/grammar check and edited where appropriate?

References

Bradley, G., Parker, J. (2005) *Social Work Practice: Assessment, Planning, Intervention and Review* Learning Matters Ltd: Exeter.

Greenway, R. (1993) *Playback A Guide to Reviewing Activities*, The Duke of Edinburgh Award published in association with Endeavour Scotland: Edinburgh.

Maclean, I., and Maclean, S. (2006) *A Handbook of Theory for Social Care Volume One*, Kirwin Maclean Associates: Rugeley, Staffordshire.

Milner, J., and O'Byrne, P. (2002) *Assessment in Social Work*. 2nd edition. Palgrave Macmillan: Basingstoke.

MIND (2008) *The MIND Guide to Advocacy*, MIND: London.

Murphy, J., and Cameron, L. (2002) *Talking Mats and Learning Disability*, AAC Research Unit: Stirling.

Roth (1989) in Maclean, I., and Maclean, S. (2006) *A Handbook of Theory for Social Care Volume One*, Kirwin Maclean Associates: Rugeley, Staffordshire.

Scott, F., Anderson, A., Johnstone, L., McMillan, M., Paterson, M., and Sayers, S. (2008) *HNC Early Education and Childcare*, Heinemann: Oxford.

Thompson, N. (2000) *Understanding Social Work: Preparing for Practice*, Macmillan Press Ltd: Basingstoke.

Thompson, N., and Thompson, S. (2008) *The Critically Reflective Practitioner*, Palgrave Macmillan: Basingstoke.

Trevithick, P. (2000) *Social Work Skills: A Practice Handbook*, Open University Press: Buckingham.

Chapter 6

HSC 1: Promote effective communication for and about individuals

HSC 2: Promote, monitor and maintain health, safety and security

HSC 3: Reflect on and develop your practice

Introduction

This chapter gives you the opportunity to demonstrate your skills, knowledge and promotion of the care values as part of your practice.

The current HNC Social Care incorporates three competency-based units as part of the mandatory requirements of the award. These units have been taken from the Health and Social Care Scottish Vocational Qualifications framework at level 3. This enables you to be assessed carrying out aspects of the Social Carer's role in placement (or your workplace) in accordance with the standards of competency contained within each unit. Also embedded within the units are the National Occupational Standards, the care value base and the Scottish Social Services Council's Code of Practice for social services workers.

The three units focus on your skills, knowledge learned from the HNC units, and promotion of the care value base in relation to specific areas of practice. Firstly, it concentrates on your ability to establish appropriate methods of communication and developing effectiveness in relation to difficult, sensitive and complex communication and reporting, recording and contribution to secure record keeping (unit 1). Secondly you will demonstrate your knowledge and skills in relation to maintaining the health, safety and security of people who use services, others and the work environment (unit 2). Thirdly, you will learn how to develop your own practice via

reflection and aim towards being a reflective practitioner. This will include identifying ways of developing your practice further via training opportunities and formal and informal supervision and support. Remember, reflective practice is a fundamental requirement of modern Social Care practice (unit 3).

Finally, within this chapter you will learn how your HNC unit assignments are an integral part of the evidence you need for your SVQ portfolio of evidence. After all, Social Care is all about taking a holistic approach.

In this chapter you will learn:

HNC Social Care and its mandatory SVQ units
Evidence requirements and reflective practice
Unit 1: Promote effective communication for and about individuals
Unit 2: Promote, monitor and maintain health, safety and security
Unit 3: Reflect on and develop your practice

HNC Social Care and its mandatory SVQ units

The incorporation of three mandatory SVQ units within the HNC framework reflects the development and growth of diversity within the Social Care sector in Scotland. The establishment of the Scottish Social Services Council following the Regulation of Care (Scotland) Act 2001 has resulted in, among other things, the creation of a national register for all staff working in the Social Services. Currently this is at phase two of the registration process. The Social Services Sector in Scotland is vast, with an increasingly recognised range of care worker roles; so the registration of staff is an ongoing process that will take us into the next decade before it is completed. The HNC Social Care is one of the agreed recognised qualifications for registration for a number of Social Care workers, such as adult residential care workers.

Further research

Visit the website of the Scottish Social Services to see the range of qualifications and details of the registration process: www.sssc.uk.com

Registration is based on each care role with the various client groups having an agreed level of qualification required for the care worker to be eligible to register to continue to practise. Following from this is the expectation that continuous professional development will become a standard requirement for all who are registered.

The SVQ units introduced into the HNC framework require students to be assessed on their competency when in practice, either in an appropriate placement (full-time students) or in their own workplace (day release and part-time students). This enables students to evidence their learning and application of knowledge and skills to their practice which is then assessed accordingly via direct observation and reflective accounts.

This emphasises the fundamental importance of practice learning for Social Care workers. Therefore, as you undertake your HNC, your assignments will incorporate evidence of your learning and application to your practice from across the HN units and the SVQ units as well. This ensures a holistic approach incorporating all aspects of the HNC requirements.

The mandatory units comprise 9 of the 12 credits that must be achieved to complete your HNC Social Care. The remaining credits are units selected from the option sections of the HNC framework which will vary according to your Social Care role, client group and organisational requirements.

The following table highlights the holistic nature of the mandatory units of the award. It provides a broad overview of the learning and application to practice connections across the mandatory HN units and the SVQ units. It is just an indication of integration of the learning that supports your good practice and, as you gather evidence for your HNC via assignments and reflective accounts, *you will identify many more specific links you can use.* In addition to this, the option units you undertake will also provide additional links across to the SVQ units.

HN unit	Examples of SVQ unit connections
Social Care Theory for Practice Learning Outcomes Explain how Social Care values and principles influence practice Understand and apply the Care Planning process Understand methods and models of practice in a Social Care setting Describe and evaluate effective team working in a care setting	All 3 units where Knowledge Points relate to values, Codes of Practice, standards, legislation, policy and procedures, conflicts and/or dilemma and record keeping requirements. Evidence of Practice (performance criteria) could include: <ul><li>reflection on own value base and its impact on your practice – Unit 3</li><li>reflection on how you can develop effective practice – Unit 3</li><li>reflection on your contribution to collaborative working with others – Units 1 and 2</li><li>reflection on your communication styles and methods, collaborative working and your recording of information – Unit 1.</li></ul>
Social Policy and Social Service Provision Learning Outcomes Examine the general processes involved in shaping and implementing social policy and Social Care provision Examine the legislation and policy underpinning Social Care provision Examine key influences on rights and responsibilities and consider the role of quality assurance mechanisms in these processes	All three units where Knowledge Points relate to legislation, organisational policy and procedures, rights and responsibilities and Codes of Practice and standards. Evidence of practice (performance criteria) could include: <ul><li>your implementation of procedures and promotion of a client's rights and responsibilities – Units 1 and 2</li><li>self-reflection on your opportunities and responsibility to further your development and enhance your practice – Unit 3.</li></ul>
Psychology for Social Care Practice Learning Outcomes Demonstrate an understanding of development needs at each stage of the lifecycle Analyse influences on the development of identify and personality from different psychological perspectives Explain how a range of life experiences can affect development and behaviour	There is a particular Knowledge Point connection here with Unit 1, KP 8a) to d) and KP 9 as well as Knowledge Points that relate to factors influencing the individual including the environment – Units 1 and 2. Evidence of practice (performance criteria) could include: <ul><li>reflection on how you applied relevant psychological theories and concepts to enhance your practice/interaction with people who use services – Units 1 and 2.</li></ul>
Sociology for Social Care Practice Learning Outcomes Understand the influence of the family on people's behaviour, experiences and life chances Understanding the causes of discrimination and its effects on people's behaviour, experiences and life chances Describe the cause of poverty and inequality and their effects on people's behaviour, experiences and life chances using sociological theories	All three units where Knowledge Points relate to factors influencing people who use services, discrimination and challenging discrimination and related legislation, policies and procedures and Codes of Practice and the importance of promoting equality and diversity. Evidence of practice (performance criteria) could include: <ul><li>self-reflection on influences that have shaped your personal value base and how this could influence your interactions in practice – Unit 3</li><li>reflection on how you utilise effective communication to combat discrimination and promote equality and diversity – Unit 1.</li></ul>
Social Care: Graded Unit Work with an individual in a Social Care setting to plan, carry out and evaluate an activity which promotes the development of the individual. The project will have three stages to it: planning, developing and evaluating. Students have to apply their knowledge and understanding of other HN units to their graded unit project.	All three units contain Knowledge Points that may relate to the graded unit. Evidence of practice (performance criteria) across the three units may also relate to the graded unit. As the graded unit involves evidence of you planning, implementing and evaluating an appropriate and specific activity you have carried out with an individual there will be many aspects of it where you can cross reference into the three units, depending on the specific activity and interactions involved.

Connections across the HNC Social Care Framework.

Remember the SVQ units incorporate the National Care Standards, SSSC Codes of Practice as well as the care value base and the principles of practice. Because of this they are endorsed by the Scottish Social Services Council and the relevant Sector Skills Council.

Evidence requirements and reflective practice

All the SVQ units follow the same format. Each unit subdivides into *elements* which are the work activities you are expected to carry out in placement or the workplace. The specific work activities where you must provide evidence of your competency are called *performance criteria* (often referred to as PCs) and each element has various performance criteria attached to it. Further to this is the *knowledge evidence*. Each unit has its own list of knowledge evidence (often referred to as knowledge points) of which you have to demonstrate your understanding and how you have integrated this knowledge into your practice. Therefore the evidence of your practice that you provide should incorporate both the performance criteria and your knowledge and understanding that has underpinned your practice. In other words your competency is based on your skills and interactions *and* the knowledge and understanding that underpins your practice.

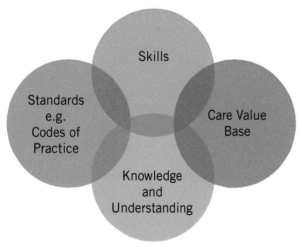

Competency of Practice.

Each unit provides you with clear information about the unit contents and *scope*. The scope

of the unit is clearly highlighted at the start of the unit specifications and you should always read it through before you start to ensure you understand the range of areas or options available to you to provide appropriate evidence of your work practice for that particular unit. You are also provided with the specific evidence requirements for each unit to which you and your assessor must adhere. These are the assessment methods that must be used to provide evidence of your competent practice.

All your evidence is kept within one folder known as your HNC/SVQ portfolio of evidence. In some centres this will be completed on line via an e-portfolio of evidence.

There is an agreed list of assessment methods that can be used by you and your assessor to gather your evidence.

- **Direct observation** of your practice by the assessor. The assessor must observe your practice in relation to the performance criteria and knowledge points for each unit. The assessor will record their observations highlighting which performance criteria and knowledge points were evident and that, in their judgement, you have met those requirements. It is a mandatory requirement that a significant amount of the performance criteria are evidenced via direct observation.

- **Reflective accounts** of your practice are provided by you. You record your actual work practice in sufficient detail to demonstrate your competency in relation to the performance criteria and knowledge points that relate to the particular work activity on which you are reflecting. You have to identify the specific performance criteria and knowledge points you have met within the reflective account and then your assessor will review your reflective account and confirm whether you have met the performance criteria and knowledge points or not. If you have not yet met the performance criteria and knowledge points then your assessor will provide you with advice and guidance on this.

Remember: reflective accounts are about your *actual* work practice, not about what you might have done.

Products are other aspects of your work practice, for example the records you make as part of your job role. There are specific performance criteria that relate to your contribution to recording and record keeping. Products also include your HN assignments. You can identify on your HN assignments any relevant performance criteria and/or knowledge points you have met within the assignment. Each centre will have developed their own tracking document to enable you to do this.

Professional discussions/questions: your assessor may discuss aspects of your practice with you to establish clarification of your skills and knowledge base; this will then be recorded as evidence.

Witness testimony is a statement provided by someone who was present while you were carrying out a work activity that you have utilised as reflective account evidence. It basically supports your reflective account and confirms that your evidence is authentic.

Simulation (artificial creation of work situation) can only be utilised where the work activity is unlikely to occur and only if it is specified in the evidence requirements for that particular unit. For example, Unit 2, element 3 allows for simulation.

These are the different ways in which evidence of your competency in relation to the standards is set out for each of the three units.

However, your main focus is on producing reflective accounts of your work practice – so what is reflection?

Reflective practice

Reflection is when we review a situation and our experience of it and, through this, evaluate our practice. Developing the ability to reflect enables Social Care workers to identify areas of practice where skills and knowledge are effective, as well as highlighting areas where this is less so. This means that development and training opportunities can then be accessed to enhance practice.

In relation to evidencing your competency of practice, reflection is all about describing accurately your practice within the specific work activity you have chosen to focus on. You need to describe all the aspects of your practice including the range of skills, application of knowledge of legislation, Codes of Practice, National Care Standards, organisational policies and procedures and promotion of care values that will provide confirmation of your competency of practice.

Writing a reflective account

A reflective account is therefore all about you and your practice and is essential evidence for HSC SVQ units. It is a conscious process involving you developing self-awareness in relation to your care practice as well as ensuring ongoing learning and development of yourself as a care worker. This is part of the concept of continuous professional development of care workers. This concept is embedded in the Codes of Practice from the SSSC.

Consider this

Take a notebook into placement so that you can keep a reflective diary.

Jot down in it specific situations, your interactions in them, the outcomes and how you have learned from it and so reflected on your practice.

You may be able to use these examples as Reflective Accounts for your HSC SVQ portfolio of evidence.

Remember: what, why and how?

HSC3 Unit 1: Promote effective communication for and about individuals

What is communication?

Communication is the foundation of all human interactions. It is an interaction between individuals which involves information being exchanged.

Approximately 30 per cent of the impact of the communication is based on what is actually said (verbal) and approximately 70 per cent of the impact is non-verbal (body language). Therefore care workers need to ensure that their verbal and non-verbal communication are complementing each other in order for their communication to be effective.

> **Consider this**
>
> How well do you think you communicate with others?

In order to be an effective communicator in your interactions with others you need to understand the three main ways in which you communicate as a care worker:

- verbal
- non-verbal
- through written records.

From this you should then reflect on how effective or ineffective your communication skills are and so identify ways in which you can enhance your communication skills.

> **Activity**
>
> Refer to your Codes of Practice for social service workers and consider how each section relates to your communication skills.
> (Please note that written records are specifically identified in section 6.2.)

You will realise, having carried out the activity above, that your communication skills will underpin your practice in relation to all sections of the Codes of Practice as well as appropriate communication skills being specifically identified in section 2:

'2.2 Communicating in an appropriate, open, accurate and straightforward way' (Codes of Practice (2007), Social Service Workers, Scottish Social Services Council).

Verbal communication

Verbal communication consists of the language being used, the tone and pace of the delivery.

Language conveys meaning to the listener – but only if the listener understands the actual words used. Therefore care workers must consider the most appropriate words to use in different interactions. For example, while it is appropriate to use technical terminology when contributing to a team meeting this may not be appropriate language to use when discussing a situation with a person who uses services. In the second situation, if technical language is used without explanation this could be interpreted as a barrier to open communication. The language used should be altered to benefit the interaction taking place; this can range from complex words and phrases to simple words and phrases. Care workers should always adapt their language to reflect the individual person who uses services, their stage of development, social and cultural background.

Tone and *pace* also convey meaning in relation to the message.

> **Activity**
>
> Try saying the following statement using different tones of voice (such as irritable, friendly, serious) and at a different pace each time (slowly, even pace, quickly):
> 'Morning, how are you today?'
> Now reflect on the impact the tone and pace would have on a person who uses services, and decide whether your communication was effective or not effective.

A care worker's tone of voice should be friendly, and not abrupt or patronising, and the pace should be appropriate for the person who uses services to understand what is being said.

It is worth mentioning that culturally most Scottish people talk at quite a fast pace and it is important to be aware of this, so that the pace of the verbal communication can be adapted.

There are other cultural differences involved as culture is not just about the language used, it is also about the different cultural expectations and norms of behaviour in social settings and how this may impact on communication. For example, in some cultures to question someone in authority is not seen as acceptable, in others gender roles will have an impact on who in the family will contribute to a care review with care staff.

Different cultural backgrounds will also have an impact on how we interpret non-verbal communication.

Non-verbal communication (body language)

Non-verbal communication conveys the individual's feelings during a conversation and can contradict the verbal message being relayed. This then means that the person listening is receiving a mixed message rather than a coherent one.

Non-verbal communication consists of the following areas.

- **Facial expressions** indicate our emotions, for example, smiling (happy), and are easy for anyone to recognise; they can be used by care workers to convey appropriate emotions, such as friendliness or interest.

- **Eye contact** can indicate if the person is listening or not to what is being communicated. It is not about staring, which is inappropriate, but about maintaining regular eye contact during a conversation with a person who uses services which helps to convey that they are being listened to. Equally if eye contact is not maintained during the conversation it can be an indicator that the care worker is bored and not listening which is devaluing for the client.

- **Position and posture** will influence the communication. The individuals involved should all be at the same level so that no one feels they are being looked down on or intimidated. An effective position is to be sitting down comfortably, facing the individual. Leaning forward in a natural,

relaxed manner helps to convey the fact that the care worker is listening and is interested in what is being said.

- **Proximity and personal space** are unique to each individual and must be respected; however they are also culturally determined. The relative physical closeness of two people talking (proximity) and the degree of personal space between them is an indicator of how friendly or intimate the conversation and relationship is. Care workers should always be aware of and respect the personal space of people who use services. To invade it unnecessarily could be seen as being threatening and intimidating.

- **Physical contact** can be a reassuring aspect of communication provided it is acceptable to the individual and the care worker is already aware of this. However, care workers should never assume it is appropriate or beneficial for the client and, if in doubt, should not use physical contact as it can be misinterpreted.

- **Gestures** are usually used to emphasise the message being relayed and can so help with the understanding of the message. Gestures also can carry their own meaning without the need for words, for example, hand waving when leaving someone.

Case study

Hardeep

Hardeep had just started his shift in the residential unit for young people and went to chat to one young person. Hardeep noticed as he approached the individual that he appeared a bit withdrawn; he was sitting on his own, slumped down in the chair, holding his head in his hands. As Hardeep approached he said, 'Hi Peter, How are you today?' in a warm tone of voice and smiled. Peter looked up at the sound of his voice and smiled tentatively back at Hardeep but his eyes dropped away again very quickly. Hardeep decided to sit down with Peter as, from what he had observed of Peter's non-verbal communication, something was bothering him.

What non-verbal signs did Hardeep observe which allowed him to conclude that something was bothering Peter?

Written communication

In addition to verbal and non-verbal communication, care workers have to be competent with all aspects of written communication as well.

Written communication takes a variety of forms and in care practice there can be a number of different records you are responsible for maintaining. Written communication is about ensuring that all relevant information to meet the needs of people who use services is available to those who *need* to know so they can ensure a good standard of care as per the National Care Standards. Written communication should be accurate, factual, fit for its purpose and only available to those who need to know. Confidentiality is an important aspect of the care worker's responsibilities in this area as all people who use services have the right to confidentiality in relation to their personal details and all aspects of the care they receive. Written commutation includes both handwritten records and electronic, i.e. on computer.

Communication differences

As any care worker will know, there are a number of communication differences that may or may not create an initial barrier to communication. Care workers must ensure they are effective in respecting and responding appropriately to communication differences.

Communication difference	Encouraging actions
Different language	• Smile • Have a friendly facial expression • Use gestures • Use pictures • Show warmth and encouragement – repeat their words with a smile to check understanding
Hearing impairment	• Speak clearly, listen carefully, respond to what is said to you • Remove any distractions and other noises • Make sure any aids to hearing are working • Use written communication where appropriate • Use signing where appropriate • Use properly trained interpreter if high level of skill is required
Visual impairment	• Use touch if appropriate to communicate concern, sympathy and interest • Use tone of voice rather than facial expressions to communicate mood and response • Do not rely on non-verbal communication e.g. facial expression or nodding head • Ensure that all visual communication is transferred into something which can be heard, either a tape or somebody reading
Confusion or dementia	• Try to make sense of communication by interpreting non-verbal behaviour • Focus on showing respect and maintaining the dignity of the other person • Do not challenge confused statements with logic • Re-orientate the conversation if you need to • Remain patient • Be very clear and keep conversation short and simple • Use simple written communication or pictures where they seem to help
Physical disability	• Ensure that surroundings are appropriate and accessible • Allow for difficulties with voice production if necessary • Do not patronise • Remember that some body language may not be appropriate
Learning disability	• Judge appropriate level of understanding • Make sure that you respond at the right level • Remain patient and be prepared to keep covering the same ground • Be prepared to wait and listen carefully to responses

Communication differences and encouraging actions (from *S/NVQ Level 3: Health and Social Care (Adults)*, page 19).

Other factors that affect communication include:

- inappropriate environment, for example, too much noise, lack of privacy
- level of well-being of the individual who uses services, for example, distressed, angry, fearful, experiencing pain
- life experiences and stage of development of the individual.

Aids to communication

There are different aids to communication that care workers should ensure are available for people who use services, based on their individual needs, choices and preferences. This may involve the care worker undertaking specific communication training to ensure that they have the skills required to communicate effectively with different individuals.

Some of the main aids to communication include:

- Makaton
- British Sign Language
- visual – pictures/symbol
- Braille
- electronic – computer-generated verbal, written and visual communication
- translator – where the communication differences are language based
- texts
- hearing aids.

Note: To ensure equality and diversity the care worker has to be aware of any communication differences and ensure that people who use services have the opportunity to communicate according to their communication abilities and choices.

Now you need to provide evidence of your effective communication as a care worker, based on your knowledge and understanding, verbal skills and use of communication skills. You need to write reflective accounts of situations in placement where you are meeting the performance criteria in each of the following areas (elements) of this unit as well as having a direct observation of your practice carried out by your assessor.

Element 1 – Identify ways to communicate effectively

This element requires you to provide evidence of your care practice that identifies ways in which you communicate effectively (performance criteria) and your knowledge and understanding of the different aspects of this (knowledge evidence).

You are required to demonstrate that you are competent in establishing communication where there may be communication differences. How do you ensure you have the appropriate information and support to establish and maintain an effective relationship via communication? Also how can you identify and use different styles and methods of communication with people who use services, staff and other key people?

Effective communication is always vital.

In order to be able to identify what effective communication is needed, you have to use your observation skills. Through observation a care worker can identify the ability of the person who uses services to understand and communicate, any factors affecting this and any aids to communication that assist the individual to communicate. Care workers should also ensure that they have all the relevant information about the individual's ability to communicate by reading their case records, asking staff and other professionals and family members about effective communication methods with the person who uses services. Of equal importance is talking openly to the individual about how they prefer to communicate.

Remember that you should also be applying the knowledge and understanding you have gained from the other HN units as well. Life experiences and stages of development have an impact on communication skills and you should refer to the Psychology chapter for further details regarding these factors.

Activity

Now consider an example of the above points from your practice in placement/workplace. Reflect on the situation and your interactions in it and then write a reflective account describing the practice situation, what your interactions were, why you carried them out and how it enabled you to identify appropriate communication methods to communicate more effectively with the person who uses services.

Remember: what, why and how?

Read through the six performance criteria for element one of this unit (HSC3 1) and see how many you can show evidence of in your reflective account. Also read through the knowledge evidence for this unit and see how many you have also shown your understanding of.

Element 2 – Communicate effectively on difficult, complex and sensitive issues

This element requires you to be able to effectively communicate when dealing with situations where the communication may be difficult, detailed and sensitive. This can be a regular aspect of the care worker's interactions with people who use services, their family and other staff/professionals.

There are numerous difficult situations that this can apply to, such as:

- distressing situations
- bereavement and grief
- loss and transition situations
- personal issues and concerns the person who uses services may have
- conflict around rights and choices and related health and safety risks
- confrontational situations.

It is worth remembering that there is an emotional impact in all the above situations that can affect the individual's ability to communicate clearly their needs.

Activity

Think of a situation in which you were involved that included difficult, complex or sensitive issues and reflect on your communication skills.

1. What message was your body language portraying?
2. Were you clear in the words you used?
3. What was your tone of voice?
4. What non-verbal communication was used?
5. Was it an appropriate environment?
6. Would you do anything different if you were in a similar situation again?

The stage of development the individual is at in their life will also have an impact on the interaction in terms of expressing their needs and concerns, understanding of the information being exchanged and degree of participation as well as other factors, for example, physical and/or intellectual disability.

The following chart highlights different life stages and development which we all experience.

	Intellectual/cognitive	Social/emotional	Language	Physical
Infant, birth–1 year	Learns about new things by feeling with hands and mouth objects encountered in immediate environment	Attaches to parent(s), begins to recognise faces and smile; at about 6 months begins to recognise parent(s) and expresses fear of strangers, plays simple interactive games like 'peek-a-boo'	Vocalises, squeals, and imitates sounds, says 'dada' and 'mama'	Lifts head first then chest, rolls over, pulls to sit, crawls and stands alone. Reaches for objects and rakes up small items, grasps rattle
Toddler, 1–2 years	Extends knowledge by learning words for objects in environment	Learns that self and parent(s) are different or separate from each other, imitates and performs tasks, indicates needs or wants without crying	Says some words other than 'dada' and 'mama', follows simple instructions	Walks well, kicks, stoops and jumps in place, throws balls. Unbuttons clothes, builds tower of four cubes, scribbles, uses spoon, picks up very small objects
Pre-school, 2–5 years	Understands concepts such as tired, hungry and other bodily states, recognises colours, becomes aware of numbers and letters	Begins to separate more easily from parent(s), dresses with assistance, washes and dries hands, plays interactive games like tag	Names pictures, follows directions, can make simple sentences of two or three words, vocabulary increases	Runs well, hops, pedals tricycle, balances on one foot. Buttons clothes, builds tower of eight cubes, copies simple figures or letters, for example, O, begins to use scissors
School age, 5–12 years	Develops understanding of numeracy and literacy concepts, learns relationship between objects and feelings, acquires knowledge and understanding	Acts independently but is emotionally close to parent(s), dresses without assistance, joins same-sex play groups and clubs	Defines words, knows and describes what things are made of, vocabulary increases	Skips, balances on one foot for over ten seconds, overestimates physical abilities. Draws person with six parts, copies detailed figures and objects
Adolescent, 12–18 years	Understands abstract concepts like illness and death, develops understanding of complex concepts	Experiences rapidly changing moods and behaviour, interested in peer group almost exclusively, distances from parent(s) emotionally, concerned with body image, experiences falling in and out of love	Uses increased vocabulary, understands more abstract concepts such as grief	May appear awkward and clumsy while learning to deal with rapid increases in size due to growth spurts
Young adult, 18–40 years	Continues to develop the ability to make good decisions and to understand the complexity of human relationships – sometimes called wisdom	Becomes independent from parent(s), develops own lifestyle, selects a career, social and economic changes and social expectations, chooses a partner, learns to live co-operatively with a partner, becomes a parent	Continues to develop vocabulary and knowledge of different styles of language use	Fully developed
Middle age, 40–65 years	Continues to develop a deeper understanding of life – sometimes called wisdom	Builds social and economic status, is fulfilled by work or family, copes with physical changes of ageing, children grow and leave home, deals with ageing parents, copes with the death of parents	Vocabulary may continue to develop	Begins to experience physical signs of ageing
Older adult, 65+ years	Ability may be influenced by health factors; some individuals will continue to develop 'wisdom'	Adjusts to retirement, adjusts to loss of friends and relatives, copes with loss of spouse, adjusts to new role in family, copes with dying	Ability may be influenced by health factors; some individuals may continue to develop language skills	Experiences more significant physical changes associated with ageing

Life stages and development (from *S/NVQ Level 3: Health and Social Care (Adults)* pages 25–27).

In addition to this are the psychological theories of development that can be applied to help a care worker to communicate effectively with individuals, for example, Maslow's hierarchy of needs, Bandura's social learning theory and Carl Rogers' person-centred theory.

Activity

Consider your interaction with an individual you support.

1. At what stage of development is the individual?
2. How has that affected their communication and language skills?
3. Describe how this knowledge and understanding has influenced how you communicated with them to ensure that the interaction was effective.

Remember: what, why and how?

Communication cycle

There are three stages to any interaction – the beginning, middle and end.

- **Beginning**: this is where we 'set the scene' for the interaction; appropriate social greetings are used and the right atmosphere is created (or not created) for progressing onto the next stage.
- **Middle**: this is where the significant exchange of information takes place and so all aspects of your communication skills – verbal and non-verbal – need to be effective.
- **Ending**: this is where the interaction draws to a conclusion and ends. In care work it is important to ensure that the ending is carried out in a positive and valuing manner which demonstrates respect for the people who use services.

What is occurring during the stages of the interaction is a cycle of communication between the two individuals. This cycle involves sending a message, receiving the message, interpreting it and then feeding back to the sender. This cycle is based on both the verbal and non-verbal messages as well as the cognitive interpretation of what is being sent and received.

Active listening

Care workers need to develop active listening skills as part of their practice. This will help to ensure their contribution to interactions in the care setting are as effective as possible, as well as being empathetic and supportive. This is particularly important in difficult and sensitive situations.

Active listening involves hearing what has been said, observing the accompanying non-verbal message to help identify the individual's emotions and, to aid understanding, reflecting back to the individual your understanding of their messages for confirmation. This is known as paraphrasing. Active listening helps to create a supportive relationship and also includes:

- using open questions
- not interrupting
- a relaxed open posture and leaning forward towards the individual to help demonstrate they are genuinely being listened to
- appropriate facial expressions and eye contact to clearly demonstrate interest
- checking understanding throughout the communication cycle
- ensuring privacy.

By using active listening skills a care worker can establish the concerns or issues that an individual may have and is then able to offer appropriate support, advice and information.

Note: Many of the performance criteria within element 2 have aspects of active listening skills contained within them.

Summary

What is involved in communicating effectively on difficult, complex and sensitive issues?

- Understanding the different aspects of communication.
- Adapting your style and method of communication according to each individual's needs and emotional state.
- Ensuring the environment is appropriate for the content of the communication, for example, privacy and confidentiality.

- Understanding the developmental stage of the individual and any other factors that may affect the interaction, and utilising this knowledge to inform your communication.
- Using active listening skills.

The summary above illustrates the performance criteria for this element.

Activity

Consider a recent interaction where you were aware that it involved potentially difficult, complex and/or sensitive information.

Describe how you ensured privacy for the individual and considered the importance of promoting the care values.

Describe what communication skills you were using – verbal, non-verbal, active listening.

Explain why these skills were important and helped the interaction progress.

In conclusion, how did your understanding and use of communication benefit/assist the situation?

Element 3 – Support individuals to communicate

The focus of this element is on your competency in supporting individuals to communicate according to their communication preferences and ability. This may involve a number of factors, including your ability to facilitate communication with the individual and others. It might involve you translating the individual's communication to aid the interaction or developing advocacy skills so that you can accurately represent the individual's choices, needs and point of view to others. It also involves the use of a number of different aids that will help the communication cycle.

Some of the different aids to communication were identified in the beginning of the communication section of this chapter (see page 170). As a care worker you should ensure that you have the information you need about an individual's communication needs and preferences (these should be identified in their Care Plan). Also by talking with the individual you demonstrate respect for their needs as

well as gaining valuable insight into the aids to communication that the individual utilises and finds appropriate.

Your verbal and non-verbal skills and your observations continue to be an important aspect of your effective communication when supporting individuals to communicate as well as following your Codes of Practice in relation to communication and promoting individuals' rights, preferences and informed choices. The level of support required should be based on the individual's needs, preferences and choices; this means that support will vary from individual to individual and situation to situation.

Communication barriers

Sometimes barriers to effective communication can arise. These need to be addressed by the care worker to reduce or, where possible, eliminate their impact on the supportive relationship that is being established and maintained.

These can include:
- inappropriate environment
- emotional status of the individual
- range of disabilities – sensory, physical, learning/cognitive
- cultural differences – language, social behavioural norms, interpretation of meanings.

Activity

Identify two ways in which you can improve communication for two of the potential barriers listed above.

(You can refer back to the communication differences chart at the beginning of the section relating to communication in this chapter.)

The range of communication differences relating to disability has already been covered in the Communication Differences chart earlier in the chapter (see page 172); however, there are other areas still to be considered.

Inappropriate environment

There are some practical steps that a care worker can take to ensure that the environment is appropriate for supportive communication to take place. This includes ensuring it is a private area, it is quiet and there is no one to interrupt. The seating arrangements are important too: how you are positioned in relation to the individual you are supporting, for example, whether you are both seated, on comfortable chairs and there is good lighting to enable observation of facial expressions and body language. By ensuring an appropriate environment the individual can see that you are respecting and valuing what they are communicating. This creates a positive care environment from the start of the interaction.

Emotional status

The emotional status of the individual is significant as distress of any kind will impact on the communication and care workers must adapt to this. It is important to establish whether the individual wishes to talk about their distress at that point in time, whether it is better to sit with them quietly, providing the individual with a comforting presence, or whether the individual wishes to have some privacy and be on their own during their distress so you can return to them after a short interval (unless there is a risk of self-harm).

Another aspect that may be a barrier to communication is if the individual has low self-esteem. They may then lack the self-confidence required to communicate their wishes and choices and so the care worker's support is essential in establishing a positive care environment where the individual feels empowered to express themselves.

Care workers should be careful not to decide *for* the individual or provide an inappropriate level of support that limits or reduces the individual's opportunities and ability to make informed decisions about what the individual wants to do.

Cultural differences

The most obvious difference here is language. People who use services are entitled to have their communication needs and preferences respected (Codes of Practice, Human Rights Act, NHS and Community Care Act, etc.) and your role here would be to request an interpreter to enable effective and supportive communication to take place where different languages are involved.

Equally, you need to be aware of the cultural differences that can occur in relation to the social aspects of communication. For example, you should consider how to address appropriately the person who uses services; a senior family member may communicate on behalf of the individual in initial conversations; physical touch may be deemed unacceptable as part of the communication; and hand gestures can have different cultural meanings – to identify just a few of the cultural differences that can occur.

Finally you need to be aware that different cultural meanings can be attached to the words used which can create differences in understanding.

Activity

Investigate further how words carry different meanings – depending on the cultural interpretation of the word.

Therefore in order to provide appropriate and effective support during interactions with people who use services, a number of factors have to be taken into account; this might include aids to communication to enable effective individualised support. It is important to ensure that any appropriate aids to communication are available and in working order to create a fully supportive communication environment.

Activity

Reflective account opportunity

Review one of the two previous reflective account activities in this section on communication.

1. Is there evidence of your practice in relation to this element?

2. If not, can you expand the reflective account to provide evidence of you supporting the individual to communicate?

3. What did you do to provide appropriate support?

4. Why did you provide that level of support, for example, reduce barriers, create a supportive environment, ensured aids to communication were used?

5. How effective was your practice?

Element 4 – Update and maintain records and reports

This element requires you to show competency in relation to the record keeping required of you within the boundaries of your care role and practice. This includes having the relevant knowledge and understanding of the legal and organisational requirements you must follow when involved in reporting, sharing, recording and safely storing information.

The Data Protection Act 1998 provides the legal framework for gathering, recording and storing information by organisations as part of their duties. There are eight guiding principles to follow. These are that data must:

- be fairly and lawfully processed
- be processed for limited purposes
- be adequate, relevant and not excessive
- be accurate
- not be kept for longer than necessary
- be processed in accordance with the individual's rights
- be secure
- not be transferred to countries without adequate protection.

Records must be kept updated and complete.

This provides the legal framework within which organisations must keep when accessing, recording and storing any individual's information or data. Organisations demonstrate how they are following these legal requirements through their data protection policies and related procedures, and care staff should be following these policies and procedures as part of their care practice.

The importance of data protection, confidentiality and appropriate secure record keeping is further reinforced via the Codes of Practice for Social Service workers and the National Care Standards, as well as via the Care Commission inspection visits.

There are several different types of records that care workers are involved in maintaining. However, whatever the level of detail required, or type of record involved, the information being recorded should always be *factual, accurate, legible, sufficient for its purpose and non-judgemental*.

Activity

Identify four different reasons for recording information about an individual.

There are numerous different reasons for recording information. However the main reasons concern changes in the individual's condition, any decisions or actions you have taken that day in relation to the individual, any difficulties or issues that have arisen and what the resolution was, or any alterations or changes to the service provision for the individual.

Storage and retrieval

Equally, care workers have a responsibility to ensure that they contribute to the safe storage and retrieval of records. Each organisation will have its own safe, secure storage system. If it is a manual (paper-based) recording system then locked, indexed filing cabinets within a locked room, with controlled access only, is a standard way of maintaining security and confidentiality. If it is an electronic system then the individual's electronic files must be password protected and again the password system should be controlled. Further security measures may be in place for electronic files; for example, an electronic system may be set up so you cannot accidentally delete information, files may only have certain areas where you can add information and other sections of the file may be 'read only'.

Whatever the system, the care worker is responsible for following the relevant procedures and ensuring records are updated promptly within a confidential area and stored securely.

Confidentiality

All the above helps to ensure confidentiality of information, giving people who use services confidence in the care organisation and trust in the care staff who are providing support. Confidentiality is a crucial aspect of building an effective relationship with people who use services so it is important that the individual is part of the process of gathering and recording information in relation to themselves. The care worker should ensure the individual is aware of the need to share relevant information with other staff and, where appropriate, other professionals and other care services to provide effective care and support. The individual should be asked for their consent to this exchange of information and remember that information should only be shared with others who need to know. This 'rule' to maintaining confidentiality should always be applied as some people can be interested in knowing but do not *need* to know; so confidentiality must be maintained.

Note: Maintaining and promoting confidentiality relates to a number of points within the different sections of the Codes of Practice for social service workers.

The following table shows how to maintain confidentiality in a variety of different information exchanges.

Type of information	Do	Don't
Telephone calls, incoming	Check the identity of the caller	Give out any information unless you are sure who the caller is
Telephone calls, outgoing	Make sure that you are passing on information to which the caller is entitled	Give out details that the individual has not agreed to disclose
Texting	Use for arranging meetings and appointments	Give any detailed or confidential information
Written information	Check that it goes immediately to the person it is intended for	Leave written information lying around where it can be read by anyone
Receiving faxed material	Check your organisation's procedure for dealing with faxed material. Collect it as soon as possible from any central fax point	Leave it in a fax tray where it could be read by unauthorised people
Sending faxed material	Ensure that it is clearly marked' Confidential' and has the name on it of the person to whom it should be given	Fax confidential material without clearly stating that it is confidential and it is only to be given to a named person If in doubt, do not use a fax to send confidential information
Receiving emailed information	Save any confidential attachments or messages promptly into a password-protected file Acknowledge safe receipt of confidential information	Leave an email open on your screen
Sending emailed information	Ensure that you have the right email address for the person who is receiving the information Clearly mark the email 'Confidential' if it contains personal information Ask for the recipient to acknowledge receipt	Leave an email open on your screen Send confidential information to an address without a named mailbox, for example, info@…

The dos and don'ts of dealing with information (from *S/NVQ Level 3: Health and Social Care (Adults)*, page 67).

Case study

Amy

Amy was writing up an individual's personal file in the office when the phone rang. She answered the phone and was asked for details about another person who uses services. Amy established that the caller was a Social Worker; however she knew she was not in a position to pass on any detailed information over the phone and politely explained this to the caller, offering to get her manager to come to the phone. The caller agreed to speaking with the manager. Amy then left the office with the door open and went to find her manager to explain the care organisation's procedures in relation to confidentiality of information for people who use services.

1. In what ways did Amy maintain confidentiality?

2. In what way did Amy *not* maintain confidentiality?

Occasionally problems can arise with recording and reporting information, such as:

- record/file missing
- electronic password not allowing access to computerised records
- paper-based record filed incorrectly within filing system and so 'lost'
- record/file left in area where anyone could access it.

If there are any difficulties in accessing and updating records then these must be reported immediately, as confidentiality of the individual's personal information may have been breached – which is a serious situation. The manager will investigate and, if the record/file is not found, will then follow organisational procedures in reporting this further within a specified time period.

In summary, what is involved in updating and maintaining records and reports?

- Following legal requirements in relation to data protection.
- Following organisational policy and procedures and Codes of Practice in relation to accessing, recording and securely storing information.
- Maintaining confidentiality of recording, and sharing of information.
- Ensuring the consent of individuals who use services and their contribution to updating records.
- Recording and reporting of all relevant information that benefits the care provision for the individual.
- Ensuring recording of information is factual, accurate, legible, sufficient for its purpose and non-judgemental.
- Follow procedures when difficulties arise in accessing or updating records.

Activity
Reflective account opportunity

Consider the summary above and identify a practice situation which would evidence your competency in relation to you updating and maintaining records and reports. The above points link directly to the performance criteria for this element and, provided your account is in sufficient detail in relation to your understanding, it will also provide evidence for some of the units' knowledge points as well.
Remember: what, why and how?

HSC 3 Unit 2: Promote, monitor and maintain health, safety and security

This unit requires you to provide evidence of your practice (skills, knowledge and understanding) in relation to promoting, monitoring and maintaining health, safety and security in your workplace or placement. You have to demonstrate your knowledge and understanding of health and safety, including relevant legislation and the SSSC Codes of Practice.

Health and safety

Care settings implement health and safety legislation through their health, safety and security policy documents and a range of procedures, including risk assessment, which provide a health and safety framework for staff, people who use services and others. Your responsibility is to ensure that you follow your organisation's policy and procedures as an integral part of your good practice. In addition, your practice should reflect section 3 of the Codes of Practice for social service workers.

'As a social service worker you must promote the independence of people who use services while protecting them as far as possible from danger or harm.'

(Codes of Practice, (2007) Social Service Workers, Scottish Social Services Council.)

However the Social Care worker can experience dilemmas involved in promoting the rights and choices of the individual, while also implementing their responsibilities in relation to the individual's health and safety. Therefore it is important that care workers are clear about who they should refer to, and discuss the dilemma with, in order to identify an appropriate solution acceptable to both the individual and the care team.

Therefore Social Care workers must have an awareness and understanding of their health and safety responsibilities in relation to relevant legislation. The main health and safety legislation included in this section is:

- The Health and Safety at Work Act, 1974
- The Management of Health and Safety at Work Regulations, 1999
- Control of Substances Hazardous to Health Regulations (COSHH), 2002
- Reporting of Injuries, Diseases and Dangerous Occurrences
- Manual Handling Regulations, 1992 (amended 2002)
- Health and Safety First Aid Regulations, 1981.

Risk assessment is another fundamental aspect of promoting the health, safety and security of people who use services and the working environment.

Health and Safety at Work Act, 1974

The Health and Safety at Work Act places responsibilities on employers and employees to work collaboratively and reasonably to solve any health and safety issues or concerns they may have. Consultation over health and safety issues in the workplace should be carried out to achieve agreement on the solution.

The Act is comprehensive and recognises that everyone has the right to be protected from health and safety risks arising from work activities.

The Act created two administrative bodies with powers to investigate and enforce health and safety:

- The Health and Safety Commission – responsible for policymaking and enforcement and answerable to the government of the day
- The Health and Safety Executive – its functions range from enforcement, research, and investigation of serious incidents to liaison with Europe over health and safety standards. Some of its powers are delegated to the Local Authority Environmental Health Department.

Employers' duties

Employers must, as far as is reasonably possible, safeguard the health, safety and welfare of their employees. This particularly relates to:

- safe systems of work
- safe handling, storage, maintenance and transport of (work) articles and substances
- providing necessary information, training and supervision for staff
- providing a safe place of work with safe access
- providing a safe working environment with adequate welfare facilities.

Also every employer with five or more employees must provide a written health and safety policy, detailing general and organisational arrangements for carrying it out, and all employees must have access to it.

Employers must consult with employees on any health and safety issues and health and safety representatives can be appointed to assist. Health and safety representatives have the right to training to be able to carry out their function.

Employees' duties

Employees have their own responsibilities. Employees must:

- take reasonable care of their own health and safety and of others who may be affected by their work practice
- co-operate with their employer as far as is necessary to enable the employer to comply with his/her duties under the Act
- comply with the organisation's health and safety policy and procedures to ensure safe working practices.

The Health and Safety at Work Act has provided the broad framework for health, safety and welfare in all workplaces. It was designed as an enabling piece of legislation, allowing subsequent legislation and regulations to follow on from it as work practices alter or change over time. Hence it is often referred to as an 'umbrella act'.

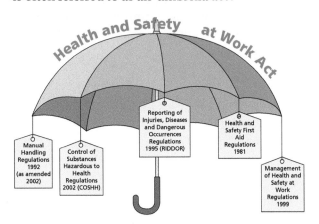

The Health and Safety at Work Act is like an umbrella.

The Management of Health and Safety at Work Regulations, 1999

The original regulations came into force in 1992 and have subsequently been updated as required.

These Regulations and the Fire Precautions (Workplace) Regulations 1997 set out how employers must manage and make arrangements for health and safety in their workplace and make it an explicit requirement for risk assessment to be carried out for all work processes.

Risk assessment

Employers (or designated employees) must carry out suitable and sufficient risk assessment and if there are five or more employees then all significant findings must be recorded. The risk assessment should be reviewed and updated when necessary. There are five basic steps involved in risk assessment.

1. Identify the hazard.
2. Decide who might be harmed and how.
3. Evaluate the risks and decide on precautions (control measures).
4. Record your findings and implement control measures.
5. Review risk assessment and update as necessary.

Other recommendations include the following:

- carry out appropriate health surveillance of employees
- appoint a competent person to help employer fulfil their obligations under health and safety law
- ensure effective emergency procedures are in place
- provide health and safety information, including emergency procedures, risk assessment and control measures for employees, temporary or permanent
- specific provisions are identified for pregnant workers and young people (under the age of 18) who may be at particular risk.

Control of Substances Hazardous to Health (COSHH) Regulations 2005

These regulations cover substances in the workplace that are classified as hazardous to health. Substances include cleaning fluids, detergents, bacteria and body fluids. Basically, any substance that can be an irritant, toxin and/or corrosive is hazardous.

Employers should implement the following steps.

- Identify any hazardous substances and the risks to health.
- Risk assess to identify the precautions needed prior to using the hazardous substance.
- Where possible prevent people from exposure to the hazard but, if this is not practicable, introduce control measures.
- Ensure everyone implements the control measures and the safety procedures are followed.
- If required, monitor exposure of employees to the hazardous substance.
- Health surveillance of employees where necessary or if COSHH makes it a specific requirement.
- Prepare plans and procedures to deal with accidents, incidents and emergencies if required.
- Ensure employees are kept informed and receive appropriate training and supervision.

Employees who work with hazardous substances must follow the precautions/control measures identified when working with the hazardous substance. For example: always use the disposable gloves provided when dealing with body fluids; always follow manufacturer's instructions for using/diluting cleaning fluids; store hazardous substances in their clearly designated safe area and so on.

There should also be clear procedures to follow when disposing of hazardous waste; for example, colour-coded waste bags for different types of hazardous waste.

Activity

What control measures are implemented in your placement/workplace in relation to:

- dealing with bodily fluids
- dealing with cleaning fluids?

What are your placement/organisation's procedures for disposing of hazardous waste?

Every organisation should have a COSHH file which will contain a list of the hazardous substances in use in the workplace. It will also provide details of where they are stored, how they are labelled, their effects and how to deal with an emergency involving the hazardous substance.

Reporting of Injuries, Diseases and Dangerous Occurrences, 1995

Reporting of accidents that result in injuries, certain diseases and specific dangerous occurrences in the workplace is a legal requirement under this Act. This is so that risk factors, causes and intervention can take place. There is a specific RIDDOR form that must be completed and sent to the designated authority, usually the local authority Environmental Health Department or the Health and Safety Executive.

The following are reportable situations:

- death
- dangerous occurrences
- diseases
- accidents resulting in three days or more off work
- major injuries (a list of these should be available in your workplace/placement).

Every workplace has to have a procedure in place for reporting, using the correct form and also ensuring the confidentiality of information as per Data Protection Act, 1998.

Accidents/incidents and accident recording

The Health and Safety First Aid Regulations provide the legal framework for first aid provision in the workplace. Employers should carry out a first aid risk assessment to determine the first aid requirements and then implement their findings.

While RIDDOR identifies specific situations that must be reported to the enforcing authorities, all accidents/incidents at work should be recorded and the records kept for a minimum of three to five years.

The First Aid Regulations specify these requirements. Your responsibility, in the first instance, is to inform your supervisor/line manager and to make sure that the Accident/Incident form is completed accurately, factually and legibly. Many organisations use standardised accident forms, which list the different points that must be covered to ensure that the accident form is completed in sufficient detail. (See also the example of an accident form below.)

Standard requirements of an accident form:

- date, place and time of accident
- person/s involved including their personal details
- circumstances/details of what happened – this may include drawing a diagram of the area if equipment was involved with the accident and identification of any equipment involved
- any injuries sustained by casualty
- any first aid treatment given and by whom
- any further assistance required after accident, for example, casualty taken to hospital/advised to see GP
- name of first aider and names of any witnesses.

As with all record keeping the details are confidential and the completed accident form should be stored in a secure environment, for example, a lockable filing cabinet.

SAVANNAH CARE HOME: ACCIDENT FORM	
Details of person involved	
Name	Polly Davidson (resident)
Address	c/o Savannah Care Home, Greenock, Inverclyde
Occupation	Retired journalist
Details of person reporting accident	
Name	Kara McGregor
Address	c/o Savannah Care Home, Greenock, Inverclyde
Occupation	Support Worker and First Aider
Details of accident situation	
Date	10.04.09
Time	3:30pm
Where accident occurred	In reception area
How accident happened	Ms Davidson arrived back having been taken out for lunch with her family and tripped over her walking stick. She stumbled forward and fell to her knees
If an injury was sustained, please give details and any treatment provided	No obvious injuries apparent although slight redness noted on both knees, Ms Davidson reassured and assisted to her feet and then sat on chair at reception area while I checked for any injuries
Name of witness	Rhuaridh Davidson (nephew)
Please now sign and date this accident form Signature Kara McGregor Date 10.04.09	
For Employer only – complete this box if accident is reportable under RIDDOR,1995	
How was it reported? Date reported Signature	

A completed accident report form.

Manual Handling Regulations, 1992 (as amended 2002)

For full-time students, manual handling awareness sessions should be provided by the college or training organisation they attend to enable you to understand your responsibilities in relation to manual handling. For day-release students, your organisation has the legal responsibility to ensure you have received adequate and sufficient training to carry out any manual handing activities safely.

A summary of the main points:

- manual handling should only take place following risk assessment
- manual handling should only be done when there is no alternative
- you should be trained to use any manual handling equipment supplied in your workplace/placement prior to using it
- you should always use the equipment provided and check it prior to use and if faulty report this immediately
- you must always follow the risk assessment recommendations (control measures).

Further to this you have also to consider the rights and opinions of the individual who uses services and, where possible, actively involve them in the risk assessment. This may create a dilemma or conflict between the individual's wishes and the risk assessment recommendations.

Activity

Reflective account opportunity

If you are attending moving and handling training then you should write a reflective account about it.

Why did you attend?

What did you learn?

How will it enhance your practice?

Give an example of how you applied your training in practice with a person who uses services.

The details from your account will provide evidence for unit 2 and unit 3 (develop and reflect on your practice).

When you are demonstrating evidence of your practice in relation to health, safety and security you also need to show you understand the relevant legislation, and your organisation's policy and procedures as well as implementing your Codes of Practice.

Element 1 – Monitor and maintain the safety and security of the working environment
Element 2 – Promote health and safety in the working environment

In the first two elements of unit 2 you have to show evidence of your practice in relation to how you monitor and maintain the safety and security of the working environment and how you promote health and safety in the working environment.

Firstly, you have a responsibility to contribute to the security and safety of the environment to the benefit of the person who uses services and others. This involves three main areas – the premises, individuals and property.

The premises

This involves following security procedures when people arrive at the service/care home/ project. When answering the door, or if you are responsible for the reception area, always politely check why they are there, who they are here to see and have this information verified before allowing the individual access. All visitor's information should be recorded in the visitor's book or equivalent. This ensures that all staff are aware of any visitors in the environment as well ensuring that everyone can be accounted for during an emergency evacuation, for example, fire evacuation.

If someone arrives unannounced then they should be appropriately challenged. If there is concern about the individual entering the premises, your role is to ensure that a senior staff member/manager is immediately informed so that the situation can be resolved without the unauthorised entry of the individual, so maintaining security and safety of the premises and the individuals within it.

All new arrivals should be recorded.

The safety of people who use services should be promoted while taking account of their rights and choices and ensuring their participation in any relevant risk assessment. This can lead to dilemmas for the Social Care worker when trying to maintain a balance between individual rights and health and safety responsibilities. If the person who uses services has their own home/living area they may have a security system to enable them to restrict and control access to their personal area and belongings; however as a care worker you may have to prompt the individual to always use their security system when someone comes to their door.

Security of property and valuables

All organisations have a policy and procedures relating to the safeguarding of clients' property and valuables, which usually involves making a record of all items when the individual is first admitted.

Further research
Find out what your placement/workplace policy is for:
- safeguarding the people who use the services and their belongings and valuables
- monitoring visitors on arrival
- dealing with unauthorised individuals arriving.

Note: if you have been involved in implementing the above procedures as part of your practice then a reflective account about how you deal with situations will provide evidence for some of the performance criteria in this element.

Finally, for your own security and safety you should always ensure staff know your whereabouts at all times. If you are supporting a person who uses services outside the care premises this may include informing staff where you are going, when you are going and when you should be back; you should also have a mobile phone with you during any times when you are working alone outside the care setting.

Minimising risks before and during work activities

A care worker should always use their observation skills to ensure the area is free from hazards before starting any work activity and, if not, must decide what to do to reduce the risk of accidents due to the hazard. It may be a simple situation where someone has left a chair out in the middle of the room or near the door where someone could trip over or bump into it. The care worker can reduce the risk by ensuring that they move the chair away from that area and place it in a safe place near the wall. As a care worker carrying out your work activities you should be continually monitoring known hazards, observing for any other hazards and taking appropriate action to reduce the risk from any you identify during the activity.

Equally, any risk assessment documentation within an individual's files, or as part of the health and safety policy of the care organisation, should also be checked for information prior to carrying out the activity and then used as the guidelines for carrying out the activity.

Hazards can be classified in the following categories.

- **Environmental hazards** – carpets, floors, corridors, furniture, flexes, cables, etc.
- **Equipment** – beds, lifting equipment (hoists etc.) mobility aids, cleaning fluids, waste disposal containers, electrical and gas appliances, etc.
- **People/individuals** – visitors to the premises, intruders, specific needs of individual person who uses services, for example, dementia, sensory, physical and/or cognitive impairment.

Reducing the risk of contamination and infection is an important aspect of the care worker's role. This includes following the universal precautions such as:

- washing your hands before and after contact with any individual, body fluids, soiled linen or clinical waste
- wearing gloves in all situations where body fluids are present

- dealing with spillage and/or waste according to instructions – appropriate bag/bin and immediate disposal of waste both non-hazardous and hazardous. Remember that COSHH regulations identify cleaning fluids and body fluids as hazardous.

As part of their health and safety induction, care workers should be provided with the relevant information about the safe storage, safe use and maintenance of all equipment that may be used as part of the care and support for a person who uses services. This involves both legal requirements from the legislation already covered and also the organisation's policy and procedures that the care worker must follow to ensure the safe storage, use and maintenance of equipment and materials.

Possible equipment could include:

- wheelchairs
- electric powered bed/chairs
- hoists
- manual mobility aids
- electric bath chair
- shower chairs
- range of kitchen utensils
- electrical and/or gas appliances.

Possible materials could include:

- cleaning fluids
- medicines
- toiletries
- food and drink
- all body fluids.

If a care worker is unsure of the procedures involved they should always seek additional support and advice from their manager to enable them to carry out their role safely.

Therefore, both before and during work activities the care worker must follow safe practice and be a role model in promoting health and safety. This can include supporting others to follow health and safety procedures in relation to the range of activities, including explaining the reasons why it is important to follow health and safety procedures.

Finally, the client's rights, choices and preferences must always be supported and their participation and agreement in risk assessment should always be maintained. The care worker should also support the individual to understand and take responsibility for promoting their own health and safety; however conflict can occur between individual choices and preferences and health and safety. If the people who use services, or others are at risk, then the care worker has a duty to discuss with the individuals the need to raise awareness and report the situation to prevent the risk of harm.

As with all aspects of care practice, relevant reporting and record keeping must take place to monitor and maintain health, safety and security of the individual, premises and working practices. These records can include: risk assessment forms, health and safety audits, Care Plans, request forms for maintenance of equipment, fault identification forms, personal belongings forms etc. The range of forms will, of course, vary across different care organisations.

In summary: what is involved in monitoring, maintaining and promoting health, safety and security in the working environment? It is important to:

- follow safety and security procedures to protect the individual, property and premises from harm
- identify and minimise risks and hazards before starting work activities and seeking additional support as required
- continually monitor for risks and hazards during work activities and follow organisational health and safety procedures to carry out an activity
- ensure equipment and materials are used, stored and disposed of correctly, following health and safety procedures

- take account of the choices and preferences of people who use services while maintaining your own health and safety and that of others
- promote health and safety by using safe procedures for moving and handling and for any other potentially hazardous work activities.
- follow and participate in appropriate risk assessments
- report, record and assist others to report and record relevant health and safety issues
- work within your own role and responsibilities and always act as a role model for others.

Activity

Consider the summary above and identify a practice situation which would evidence your competency in relation to health, safety and security. You will need to provide evidence from more than one practice situation to meet the requirements of these elements.

The summary points link directly to the performance criteria for these elements and provided your account shows sufficient understanding of health, safety and security it will also provide evidence for some of the units' knowledge points as well.

Also review any previous reflective accounts you have completed – is there evidence of your practice in relation to health, safety and security?

If so, you should claim the relevant performance criteria and knowledge from unit 2 as well. This demonstrates a more holistic approach which reflects care practice.

Element 3 – Minimise risks arising from emergencies

This element is about the competency of the care worker in dealing with emergencies and incidents within the boundaries of their role and responsibilities. Emergencies, incidents and accidents can and do occur and therefore care workers need to be aware of the appropriate action that should be taken in such situations.

What is an emergency?

An emergency is an immediate and serious threat of danger and harm to the individual and others. It can be an environmental emergency or a health emergency.

Health emergencies can include sudden illness or collapse, serious falls/injuries and deterioration of the condition of individuals.

Environmental emergencies can include fires, gas leaks/explosions, bomb threats, structural faults in the building and flooding.

Incidents are situations that have the potential (near miss) or actual factors that will cause harm or danger to individuals and/or others. These can include chemical spillage, aggressive situations, missing individuals, missing purse/money, intruders.

Accidents are unforeseen situations that have resulted in injury. The injury can range from minor to major and may have resulted from either environmental factors (worn carpet, obstructions, etc.) or health factors (for example, an individual falling and injuring themselves as a result of a change in their medical condition).

Environmental emergencies

The basic procedures involved in an environmental emergency are identified in each organisation's emergency procedures as required by health and safety legislation. Care workers, as part of their induction, should have been informed of the correct procedures to follow.

An example of this is the basic fire evacuation procedure.

- Raise the alarm via the fire alarm system.

- Designated person ensures fire brigade are informed via a 999 call where appropriate (many internal fire alarm systems are connected to the emergency services' call-out system so it may not need you to phone 999).

- Assist in the evacuation of all individuals appropriately in a calm, reassuring manner and at walking pace, closing all doors behind you.

- Go to the designated fire evacuation point outside the building and report to designated staff member that all are/or are not safely evacuated from the building.

- Do not re-enter the building until officially informed that it is safe to do so.

You should also know where the fire exits, fire blankets and fire extinguishers are positioned within the care organisation.

Activity

Find out the exact emergency evacuation procedures in your place of work or placement.

Check you know where all the fire exits are and that they are easily accessible.

If you are not sure of any aspect of the emergency procedures ask for advice from your supervisor.

Health emergencies and accidents

Unless you have undergone first aid training, and are a qualified first aider, your role in health emergencies and accidents is to assist the more qualified individual who will take control of the situation when they arrive at the scene.

Basic health emergency and accident procedures to follow are:

- identify if any risks/hazards are apparent and if so reduce these risks for own and others' safety

- assess the situation, i.e. what has happened, any obvious signs of injury and ask immediately for assistance and, where appropriate, a more qualified person – first aider, GP, paramedic etc.

- reassure and support the casualty while making the area safe and private to maintain the individual's dignity and privacy

- if required, continue to provide support and assistance when more qualified person arrives

- if any other people who use services were involved, or witnessed the emergency/accident, make sure you also provide them with support and reassurance

- once the casualty has been treated, make sure you report and record accurately in the appropriate health and safety records, client files, accident form or RIDDOR form as required within the boundaries of the Data Protection Act and maintain confidentiality.

It is not only other individuals who have witnessed the emergency/accident who are affected by it, the care worker involved can also be distressed by the situation. Afterwards it is good practice to ensure the care worker, via a supervision session, can be supported and should have the opportunity to reflect on their practice and the impact the situation had on them.

Incidents are many and varied and so there is not going to be one basic procedure to follow; rather, the incident has to be responded to in the appropriate way with calm and clear intervention to resolve it.

Activity

An individual arrives at the door saying that he is here to carry out some maintenance work to the client's flat. You know that no maintenance work is due, however the man is trying to insist that he comes in.

How do you deal with this incident?

The incident in the activity above links back to element 1 of this unit and how the safety and security of people who use services and premises are part of your responsibilities. Any incident should be reported and recorded as part of your responsibilities in the same way as any other aspect of health and safety, such as risk assessments.

In summary: what is involved in minimising risks arising form emergencies?

- Appropriate and immediate action must be taken to deal with any health and environmental emergencies and incidents, including getting appropriate assistance when necessary.

- You can identify and so reduce any risks or hazards that may cause an incident or emergency situation.

- You provide appropriate support and assistance until more qualified staff arrive and make the area as safe and private as possible.

- You provide reassurance and support to others who may be involved in incidents and/or emergencies.

- You ensure you follow the correct safety procedures and assist others to do so as well.

- You report and record incidents and emergencies accurately, legibly and factually in the relevant health and safety documents following the care organisation's procedures and legal requirements.

Activity

Reflective account opportunity

Now consider any recent emergencies, incidents or accidents you were involved in while in placement/work and write a reflective account about your practice during the emergency, incident or accident.

Ensure that you show evidence of your practice in relation to the above summary points to help meet the performance criteria for this element.

Remember: what, why and how?

HSC 3 Unit 3: Reflect on and develop your practice

Element 1 – Reflect on your practice
Element 2 – Take action to enhance your practice

In the introductory section of this chapter the process of reflective practice was highlighted. It is a fundamental aspect of modern care practice. An effective care worker is a reflective practitioner who is open to opportunities for further development of their knowledge and skills; that is why this unit is incorporated within the HNC Social Care framework.

This unit requires you to reflect on and develop your care practice. To achieve this you have to reflect on and evaluate your knowledge, understanding and practice. From this you can then identify the actions you can take to enhance your knowledge, understanding and practice, thus becoming a more effective care worker in meeting the needs of people who use services. The two elements of this unit should not be seen in isolation but holistically.

The SSSC Codes of Practice are clear about your responsibilities in relation to developing and enhancing your practice, in particular section six of the codes:

'As a social service worker, you must be accountable for the quality of your work and take responsibility for maintaining and improving your knowledge and skills.'

(Codes of Practice, (2007) Social Service Workers, Scottish Social Services Council.)

Reflective practice

The start of reflective practice requires the care worker to consider their own personal values, interests and beliefs, recognising the fact that these can affect their behaviour and practice. Our personal values, interests and beliefs have originated from a number of factors which include:

- family (primary socialisation)
- peer group, education, working environment
- life experiences
- cultural background.

All the above, in combination, contribute to the development and establishment of our internal personal beliefs and values which sustain us throughout our lives.

Consider this
How has your family life and upbringing contributed to your personal values and beliefs?

It is important to reflect on personal values and beliefs and how this may affect care practice and behaviour towards people who use services and others in the care environment. Personal values, interests and beliefs can lead to assumptions and prejudice if care workers do not develop self-awareness and reflective skills.

The principles of care require all care workers to develop the ability to promote equality, diversity and social justice and to develop a non-judgemental approach to all aspects of care practice. The SSSC Codes of Practice have the care principles embedded within the different sections, as do the National Care Standards, both of which the care worker is held accountable to. So if a care worker allows their personal values, interests and beliefs to influence their care practice they are not following either their Codes of Practice or Care Standards and are not yet competent in their practice.

Activity
Now take some time to consider the following.
What personal beliefs do you hold?
What are your personal interests?
What are your personal values?
Now consider how these could affect your interactions with a person who uses services who does not have the same beliefs, interests or values as you.

Remember: reflective practice is about thinking about and analysing your day-to-day practice in an open-minded way to identify any changes you can make to improve your practice. It also requires you to listen to others to gain constructive feedback on your practice as part of the reflective process.

Basically it is a three-stage process.

1. Think about your experience of a work situation, your understanding and ideas.

2. Then reflect on what you have learned from this experience.

3. Finally identify how this reflection has identified potentially better practice and how you will apply this.

Reflective practice enables a care worker to identify areas for further development to learn about and then apply this learning to their practice. There are a number of different learning theories that can be applied. Two of these are Kolb's learning cycle and Honey and Mumford's theory of learning styles.

Kolb's learning cycle

Kolb's learning cycle is based on learning through experience. This is known as experiential learning. This theory involves a cyclical progression from one stage to the next.

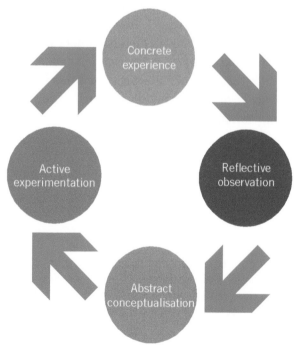

Kolb's learning cycle.

Concrete experience: this is the actual experience and what the individual did within it.

Reflective observation: the individual should then reflect on the experience, both thinking and evaluating it.

Abstract conceptualisation: the individual then applies relevant theories to the experience to aid their reflection. This could also include identifying patterns of behaviour that have occurred. Thus combining reflection with theories and patterns to enable the individual to draw conclusions about their practice and so identify areas to develop.

Active experimentation: based on the conclusions made the individual then alters/adapts their practice the next time they have a similar experience and then the cycle should start again.

Honey and Mumford's learning styles theory

This theory describes four different learning styles an individual uses; although individuals tend to have one preferred style out of the four.

Activists prefer to be involved in the actual experience and like new ideas/experiences and working with others; they may take the lead but are less enthusiastic with passive learning situations or learning on their own.

Reflectors prefer to stand back and observe the experience from the sidelines and think about it from different perspectives; they are analytical and like others to contribute but are less enthusiastic if they have to take the lead in the learning group or are feeling rushed or unprepared for a learning situation.

Theorists prefer to think about and analyse logically the experience. They tend to work with abstract ideas and apply them to complex situations but are less enthusiastic if there is a lack of structure or they have to work with others' emotions in the learning situation.

Pragmatists prefer to get on with the job in hand rather than discussing the potential situation as they have a practical approach and like to try things out; however, they are less enthusiastic if there is not clear guidance on how to do the job or if a lot of the emphasis is on theory rather than the practical aspects of the situation.

Learning can and should be a fundamental part of a modern Social Care worker's practice. It is an active and conscious process and occurs not only in formal training sessions but should occur informally as well. Different informal learning opportunities include observing colleagues practice to enhance one's own practice, being involved in work discussions about what is the most appropriate approach to a situation, asking questions and seeking advice from more experienced colleagues and so on. Learning occurs also through a care worker reading relevant text books, journals and media articles or accessing the Internet or relevant television programmes/documentaries.

Case study

Moving and handling

Amy and Kara were discussing their recent experiences of undertaking their mandatory Moving and Handling two days' training and how they had learned from it. Amy was talking about how she had really enjoyed the practical, hands-on aspects of the training, which had included practising safe moving and handling techniques while working with others in the group. She had found that had really helped her understand what was involved in correct moving and handling and how it would then help her in her job as a support worker. Kara had also found the practical aspects interesting but hadn't enjoyed it as much as Amy had. Kara had preferred the theory sessions where she could sit, listen and think about the theoretical application of moving and handling. She had also found observing others during the practical session more helpful to her understanding of how the training would benefit her in her role as a support worker.

1. Which two different learning styles are being used in this case study?

2. How has it benefited the two support workers to talk about their experiences of learning?

Self-reflection and keeping up to date

Self-reflection is required of care workers. It involves being aware of what personal values, interests and beliefs may affect practice and then taking steps to address this. It also involves recognising what is the preferred learning style and the different ways in which to learn and develop. Social Care workers are accountable for ensuring that their practice is current and up to date and that they have participated in mandatory (legally required) training for their particular job role as per the National Care Standards and Codes of Practice as well as any relevant legistration.

Legislation, Codes etc.	Year	Main responsibilities
Moving and Handling Operation Regulations		
Disability Discrimination Act		
Data Protection Act		
SSSC Code of Practice		

Legislative responsibilities.

Care workers are expected to develop and keep current and up to date in their practice. As new legislation is passed it then impacts on the care organisation, via new or updated policies and procedures, for care staff to understand and implement as part of their practice and may even involve training sessions for all staff to ensure that this takes place.

As mentioned previously care workers can learn about new and changing aspects of Social Care policy and practice via journals, media etc. and should be active in this to demonstrate currency of practice.

Another aspect of being aware of the 'bigger picture' of the Social Care area and its impact on care workers' development is the publication of reports and enquiries into care practice, research and consultation documents relating to care, as well as public inquiries into organisational and individual failures in Social and Health Care practice. This includes in particular the recommendations and conclusions that are drawn from an inquiry as these can subsequently be incorporated into new legislation, for example, failures in protection of children and/ or vulnerable adults, and failures in standards of hygiene.

Further research

Spend some time accessing the Scottish Social Services Council website which will have current and up-to-date publications in relation to the Social Care sector in Scotland. Go to www.sssc.uk.com

While care workers should be continually self-reflecting on their competency, effectiveness and the active support that they provide to people who use services and others, the feedback from others enables a more detailed reflection process to occur. Constructive feedback from others is essential and can be both formal and informal, from within the care organisation and from key people who are outside the care organisation.

Constructive feedback

This is a valuable tool in developing reflective practice as it can assist a care worker in identifying areas for development. However individuals are not always open to or comfortable with constructive criticism from others. It is important to recognise that this type of feedback should be listened to and valued as it provides an insight into your practice from the perspective of others, based on their observations of your practice as it happens. Once a care worker has developed their reflective skills and recognises that reflection is an active, conscious process, then it follows that the care worker will then ask actively for feedback from others – colleagues, manager, people who use services and their families.

While undertaking the HNC Social Care award the care worker can also access feedback from the HNC staff team as well as specific feedback from their assessor in relation to their progress and evidence of practice for the SVQ units they are undertaking.

The main formal feedback within care organisations is via the supervision/appraisal system.

Feedback is an important part of the review process.

Case study

Junaid

Junaid was meeting with his college tutor to review his progress so far with his HNC Social Care award, including his SVQ evidence.

The tutor had arranged for them to meet in the office at Junaid's workplace which he was happy about as he was a bit apprehensive about the meeting. He had discussed this with his manager who had highlighted to him that it was beneficial to have a feedback session with his tutor so that Junaid would be clear about how he was progressing. His manager also reminded Junaid that he should see it as an opportunity for him to raise any queries or concerns he had about any of his assignments and/or college work.

When Junaid's tutor arrived he took her through to the office and they sat down to discuss his progress. Junaid's tutor was aware that Junaid wasn't as relaxed as he normally was and so spent the first few minutes discussing the purpose of the meeting, i.e. a review of his progress so far, and that any feedback from her would be constructive to enable Junaid to further develop his care skills and knowledge. Junaid felt a bit more relaxed after this explanation.

The tutor then asked Junaid how he felt he had been progressing. Junaid thought about this and then responded that he had found the course far more challenging than he had originally expected and he was aware that he had at times, rushed his assignments to ensure he handed them in to meet the deadline. His tutor listened and then confirmed that she agreed with him in his evaluation of this. She suggested to him that this was something he should reflect on to see if he could change his approach, as he was possibly not producing the standard of work that she would have expected from him in his assignments and that perhaps his time management skills rather than his study skills were the area of concern. Junaid was taken aback at this as he had not realised the full impact that rushing his assignments had had on his progress. He recognised that had he spent longer on them it would have provided the level of understanding and knowledge he actually had about his care practice. His tutor allowed him time to reflect on this before asking Junaid what he thought about the way forward for him. Junaid responded by saying that he agreed with her feedback, that he had not thought about it from a time management point of view and actually that was an area that he was not very good at.

Junaid then discussed with his tutor how he could manage his time better in future, balancing his role as a Key Worker, day-release student at college and family demands to try to be more organised in his planning of college work/assignments.

1. Why do you think Junaid was apprehensive about this meeting?
2. Why was it important that his tutor spent time making sure Junaid was comfortable with the meeting going ahead?
3. What benefits were there for Junaid in accepting the constructive feedback?
4. Is there evidence in the case study of Junaid reflecting on his practice as a student?

Supervision/appraisal systems

For supervision sessions to be effective there has to be a mutual understanding of the process and the benefits of it for the individual, the care team, the supervisor and the care organisation. Equally, it has to be organised and carried out in a professional and confidential manner – creating trust and the genuine opportunity for a care worker to raise any concerns they have.

Formal supervision takes place at mutually agreed times in the year; it could be six monthly or annually or more frequently, depending on the care organisation's policy. HNC Social Care students on placement should receive regular supervision throughout their time in placement to support their developing practice.

The supervisor is usually the care manager and all care managers, according to the National Care Standards, must ensure that staff have regular supervision and appraisal and so have access to advice and support. The supervisor's role involves creating a confidential and supportive environment for the supervision, the effective monitoring of the care worker's activities/task and their practice, including any/all specific responsibilities the care worker has in relation to meeting the needs of people who use services and implementation of Codes of Practice and National Care Standards. This role includes:

- the promotion of staff development
- problem solving and establishing conflict resolution
- ensuring legal requirements are adhered to
- ensuring organisational policies and procedures are implemented
- promoting team and collaborative working.

All of the above should be discussed with the care worker to enable them to reflect on their effectiveness. The supervision record is often the starting point for the discussions and should involve opportunities for both to provide written reflective commentary during the supervision session. It also provides evidence of the care worker's continuous professional development (CPD).

Therefore supervision provides the care worker with a forum for reflection on their practice with constructive feedback from the supervisor. This enables the care worker to ensure that, with support, the areas of development that have the potential to enhance their practice are clearly identified and agreed. It also ensures that there is agreement about which aspects of their practice will be prioritised. Then one of the main outcomes or action points from a supervision session is the planning and undertaking of the agreed developmental opportunity within a realistic timescale. This would then be reviewed for its benefits at a subsequent supervision session.

Activity
Preparing for supervision

Think about your care practice.

What do you do well?

What would you like to improve?

Which areas of your practice would you like to prioritise for development?

What developmental/training opportunity do you think would assist you in improving that particular area of your practice?

Are there any other concerns you would want to raise for discussion and to gain advice and support with?

It may be helpful to note down your points to take with you as part of your preparation for your supervision session.

Note: Supervision sessions are also invaluable in creating the opportunity for care workers to discuss and gain support following challenging situations, emergencies and incidents.

Activity

Write a reflective account about your interactions and reflections during the supervision session, including any action points/outcomes that have been agreed. This will cover a number of the performance criteria across the two elements of this unit and some of the knowledge points.

Or

Ask your assessor, provided everyone is in agreement, to sit in on and observe your supervision session and the assessor will then complete a direct observation that will cover a number of the performance criteria and knowledge points.

EVIDENCE SHEET

Candidate		SHEENA MCGREGOR		

Award	HNC Social Care	Unit	1 & 3	
Evidence No.	6	Date	30/04/09	

DO		RA	X	EW		Q		P		WT	

Evidence	PC	KP
I attended my prearranged supervision session today with my supervisor. We met in the unit's meeting room to ensure privacy and confidentiality. My supervisor explained the purpose of the session and we then discussed how I felt I was progressing both in my role as a support worker and also with the HNC Social Care course I am currently doing as a day-release student at my local college. During discussion about my support worker role I reflected how I had felt frustrated initially with one person who uses services as I couldn't communicate well with them as they used minimal verbal communication and mainly communicated by using Makaton. I didn't know any Makaton so I then asked other staff who helped me with this and I had been informally learning Makaton ever since. I had seen the benefits of this in the relationship I was then able to build up with the person who uses services although there were still occasions when I didn't always understand what he was trying to communicate. My supervisor then responded by highlighting that this had shown initiative on my part and she suggested that I should also consider taking up the training opportunity the organisation had available to all staff to attend formal Makaton training. This made me stop and think as I had always known this training was available but I had thought by learning from others it would be sufficient. By listening to my supervisor's feedback I could now recognise that the formal training would benefit me further and so I requested that I be considered for the next formal training session. My supervisor agreed to support me in this and stated that it would benefit both myself and the person who uses services. Because of this discussion I was enabled to reflect on my own value base in relation to communication and that because I communicate verbally I became frustrated that the person who uses services hadn't understood me. I could now recognise that my frustration was based on my assumptions about how people should communicate. My experiences until starting to work in Social Care had not included different forms of communication and so I need to reflect more on how my values and experiences can impact on my interactions with people who use services. I am now more aware of this and need to ensure I consider this when interacting with others, particularly as I am working towards maintaining my practice according to the Codes of Practice.		
Feedback		
Assessor/Candidate/Witness Signature		

Exemplar reflective account following supervision.

Other forms of support, in relation to care practice, are also available to the care worker. These will include colleagues via observation of their practice and discussions to enable problem solving and building confidence in practice, as well as discussions providing advice and suggestions for enhancing skills and practice.

Developmental opportunities

Developmental opportunities are the different ways in which a care worker can increase their knowledge, understanding and skills. These opportunities are many and varied and deciding which one would most benefit the care worker is dependent on what aspect of their practice the care worker wishes to develop, the most effective way of achieving this and the legal and organisational requirements.

Development opportunities include formal training sessions within the care organisation or provided by the local college, local authority or other training providers.

Attending conferences or seminars can also provide a development opportunity needed by the care worker.

Further to this are the developmental opportunities that the care worker can do by themselves, such as reading relevant texts, journals, the media and the Internet to increase knowledge, understanding and awareness.

If you access any training sessions while undertaking this unit you should keep a record of this (such as the one below) to evidence how you are taking developmental opportunities and reflecting on how this will benefit your practice.

Personal development plans

The evidence requirements for this unit recommend that you keep a formal record of your continuous professional development, and a personal development plan (PDP) can be part of this. Therefore the next aspect of reflecting and developing your practice involves considering establishing a personal development plan to aid the development of specific areas of your practice.

A personal development plan is an individual plan of action that enables a care worker to set their own personal development goals and ways to achieve these goals. It is both a self-assessment tool and a structured set of developmental goals to achieve (one of the goals to achieve could be the HNC Social Care). It can be a personal document of the care worker or it can be established with the support of the care worker's supervisor.

The starting point is to carry out a self-assessment of strengths and areas for development. The focus of the PDP then becomes these areas of development as they are converted into the goals that will enhance the care worker's practice.

Personal development plans can include a range of short-term, medium-term and long-term goals. When setting goals it is important that they are SMART. Smart goals are:

- **S**pecific
- **M**easurable
- **A**ctionable
- **R**ealistic
- **T**ime-bound.

A personal development plan should be reviewed at regular interviews to ensure it remains relevant and realistic. Regular reviews also allow for alterations and updating of progress towards the goals.

Getting started involves working through the following three points.

- Self-assessment of current practice – skills, knowledge and understanding. This involves reflecting on your strengths and then areas of development, i.e. areas that are adequate but not strengths.

- What aspects of my practice would I like to further develop? Here you need to think about specific areas; it may be that you have to prioritise which area to develop first, or which area of development may take some time (long-term goals) to achieve.

- What do I need to do to achieve these developments? This is when you start to set your goals, make sure they are SMART goals and also evaluate which are short-, medium- and/or long-term goals.

Event attended	First Aid at Work Course
Training provided by	Davidson Training Partnership
Date and venue	06/09/09 – Park Hall

Content of event

4-day first aid training including exam at the end to become a First Aider at work.

Course content included first aid responsibilities and record keeping, the law and first aid, dealing with emergencies, unconscious casualty and the recovery position, CPR for adults, universal hygiene precautions, bleeding wounds, fractures, strains, sprains and dislocations, diabetes, asthma, burns and scalds, head injuries, stroke, poisoning, asthma, heart conditions.

Why I went (what I hoped to gain)

I had asked to be considered at my 3-monthly supervision session as I wanted to gain the qualification and take responsibility as a First Aider at work. The training department then allocated me a place on the next First Aid at Work course that the local college was running.

What I learned and how I can use it in my work (try to give specific examples)

I have found I am now more confident in health emergencies/incident situations and can provide appropriate support based on the knowledge and skills I gained from the course. I had to reassure a person who uses services just last week after they had slipped and fallen when coming out of the lounge. I was able to follow my first aid training by reassuring the individual, assessing the situation, and checking for any injuries (there were no obvious injuries) and then writing up the accident form as per first aid and health and safety legal requirements.

Signature   Date

Example of the type of record that provides evidence of reflection on continuous professional development.

The following is an example of a PDP that you could use.

NAME	Sheena McGregor, Key Worker
CARE ORGANISATION	Savannah Care Home
DATE OF PLAN	April 2009
DATE OF REVIEW	

Self-assessment	
SKILLS	

Strengths	Areas for development

KNOWLEDGE AND UNDERSTANDING	

Strengths	Areas for development

Time Scale	Start date	End date	Course of Action	Comments
SHORT-TERM GOALS				
MEDIUM-TERM GOALS				
To achieve HNC Social Care	Sep 2009	Dec 2010	Enrol with local college and attend as day-release student. To monitor progress via 3-monthly supervision sessions with manager	
LONG-TERM GOALS				
Registration as key worker with SSSC				

Further comments

Review date	Start date	End date	Progress	Comments
Short-term goals				
Medium-term goals				
Long-term goals				

Further comments

Personal development plan.

Summary

What is involved in you reflecting on and developing your practice?

- You reflect on what you need to be competent, effective and safe in your practice.

- You show understanding of your accountability in relation to Codes of Practice, care standards, legal and organisational requirements.

- You reflect on what is required of you to provide active support to people who use services and others.

- You monitor and evaluate your knowledge, skills, attitudes and behaviour, personal beliefs and their potential effects on your practice.

- You reflect on how well you practise and what could be improved.

- You seek constructive feedback to aid your developing practice.

- You identify areas of development, prioritise these areas and the action you need to take to access developmental opportunities to enhance your practice.

- You utilise supervision and support to aid your reflection and agree the developmental opportunities you wish to undertake.

- You reflect on the developmental opportunities, what you have learned and how it has specifically enhanced aspects of your practice.

- You keep up-to-date records of your professional development in a confidential way.

Activity

Consider any work situation where you are clearly showing evidence of reflection on your practice, the importance of doing this and what aspects of your practice you have enhanced and why.

Write a reflective account on any training sessions you have undertaken – why you went, what you learned and then how you have incorporated that training into your practice.

Have you completed a reflective account about your supervision session?

Check Your Progress

Unit 1

1. What is the purpose of communication?

2. Describe how both verbal and non verbal communication contributes to whether communication is effective or not.

3. What are your responsibilities in writing and storing records?

4. Identify three barriers to communication and then describe how you would deal with each one.

5. Describe how you would effectively communicate a difficult or sensitive issue to service users.

6. Why is it important to know, and share appropriately, information about an individual's communication needs and preferences?

Unit 2

7. What are your health and safety responsibilities in relation to:
   - dealing with hazardous substances
   - security of the premises
   - use of equipment
   - moving and handling?

8. Explain the importance of risk assessment in relation to health and safety.

9. Describe what you should do if there was a health emergency and who you should refer the situation to.

10. What are your legal responsibilities according to the Health and Safety at Work Act 1974?

Unit 3

11. How does reflecting on your practice assist you to develop as a social care worker?

12. "Your own values, preferences and beliefs can affect your practice." Do you agree or disagree with this statement? Give reasons for your answer.

13. Explain how training opportunities are essential for you to ensure you are up to date and competent in your practice.

14. What are the benefits to you of having regular supervision?

References

Morris, C. and Hill, K. (2007) *S/NVQ Health and Social Care Assessor Handbook* Heinemann: Oxford

Nolan, Y., Moonie, N. and Lavers, S. (2006) *S/NVQ Level 3 Health and Social Care (Adults)* Heinemann: Oxford

Scottish Executive (2005), *National Care Standards: various care settings and service users* Scottish Executive: Edinburgh

Scottish Qualifications Authority (2007) *Arrangement Document, HNC Social Care Final version* (Oct.2007), Glasgow

Scottish Social Services Council (2005), *Codes of Practice for Social Services Workers and Employers*, Dundee

Useful websites

www.carecommisssion.com

www.communitycare.co.uk

www.hse.org.uk

www.scotland.gov.uk

www.sqa.org.uk/carescotland

www.sssc.uk.com

Other relevant legislation and regulations in relation to health and safety at work

Health and Safety (Display screen equipment) Regulations (1992)

Personal Protective Equipment (PPE) Regulations (1992)

Health and Safety (First Aid) Regulations (1981)

Employer's Liability (Compulsory Insurance) Regulations (1969)

Electricity at Work Regulations (1989)

Gas Safety (Installation and Use) Regulations (1994)

Additional reading and research

www.hse.gov.uk – Health and Safety Executive

www.healthandsafetytips.co.uk – health and safety tips

Care organisation's health and safety policy documents

Topic 1

Protection including safeguarding and management of risk

Introduction

Social Care workers at all levels in social services organisations have a legal duty of care towards each individual who uses services. People who use services can be and are vulnerable to danger, harm and abuse. Therefore a critical aspect of your care practice is to ensure that the individual you are supporting is protected and to be clear what your responsibilities are in disclosing and recording suspected danger, harm and/or abuse.

This chapter will increase your knowledge and understanding by starting with the topic of risk, risk assessment and management of risk, not only at the level of a Social Care worker's responsibilities, but also within the broader picture of organisational policy and the legislative framework relating to safeguarding and managing risks.

Individuals in need of care have rights, including the right to making informed decisions in relation to how they wish to live their lives. The Social Care worker must respect the rights of people who use services while also ensuring their responsibilities in relation to implementing the organisation's policy and procedures and Codes of Practice in relation to health and safety and protection. The potential dilemmas and/or conflict that a Social Care worker may experience as a result of this will also be explored.

The rights of the individual are embedded in the Human Rights Act, SSSC Codes of Practice, National Care Standards, organisational policies and other important legislation. Care workers should reflect on all of these and incorporate them into their practice including the individual's rights to appropriate and managed risk taking and protection from danger, harm and abuse.

Therefore the second topic within this chapter will consider related concepts, explanations and issues relating to protection of vulnerable adults, young people and children from potential abuse.

In this chapter you will learn:

Risks
Issues involved in protection from abuse
The care worker's responsibilities
Learning from reports and inquiries

Risks

Risk taking within the care context

Risks are part of everyone's day-to-day living. Risks can be calculated, foreseen, unforeseen, minimal or major. Risk taking is part of our right to make informed decisions about how we live our lives and take part in activities of our own choosing.

> **Activity**
>
> Consider the following examples of activities you may choose to do and think about what risks could be involved.
> - Getting the bus to work or college.
> - Celebrating a family birthday by going out for a meal at a restaurant.
> - Crossing the road where you have chosen to cross it, not at a designated pedestrian crossing.
> - Going to the pub for a few drinks with friends.

Now consider two of the examples above in more detail.

Going out for a meal

You may decide that there are minimal risks involved. After all, there are mandatory food hygiene standards involved that the restaurant must adhere to and the local environmental health officers can, and do, inspect food premises regularly. However an unforeseen risk could be an allergic reaction occurring, the consequences of which could range from minor to major. Would this stop you from enjoying a meal out with the family?

Crossing the road where you choose

You may think this is a calculated, foreseeable risk and may also have checked before crossing that the road was safe, so reducing the risk factors. You may have chosen to cross there while knowing it is safer to cross the road at the designated pedestrian crossing. Here you have made an informed decision based on your own perception of the risks involved and have chosen to take the risk. An important point to remember here is the individual's perception

of risks and risk taking and how this can help explain behavioural differences, e.g. between a non-smoker and a smoker.

> **Activity**
>
> Now consider an individual you support in relation to the examples listed above.
>
> What are the risks now? Are they the same as before or different?
>
> If the risks are different, why is this?
>
> What are your responsibilities as a care worker in relation to these risks?

Understanding risks, risk taking and the potential consequences of risk is not as straightforward as it may first appear. Within the care sector it has increasingly become an important focus of care practice.

Risk assessment

A definition of **risk** recognises that the risks involve potentially negative outcomes due to the hazards involved and this could detrimentally affect the individual. Therefore risk assessment is carried out to determine how to reduce the risk by controlling the hazard.

> **Key term**
>
> **Risk** risks involve potentially negative outcomes due to the hazards involved however also can include beneficial outcomes for the individual.

However this definition of risk, although useful in some situations, does not incorporate all the complexities involved. We need to recognise and understand the factors involved in risk and risk taking in order to carry out risk assessment effectively.

Some of the main factors in risk assessment include:
- the individual's right to make informed decisions and choices about their lifestyles
- the individual's perception of risks and risk taking
- social and cultural aspects
- recognition that taking risks can have beneficial outcomes.

Individual's right to make informed decisions and choices about their lifestyles

The care worker's responsibilities in relation to upholding the rights of the individual person who uses services are embedded in the SSSC Codes of Practice, the relevant National Care Standards, the Human Rights Act (1998), as well as being part of the guiding principles in other relevant legislation; for example, the Children (Scotland) Act 1995 and NHS and Community Care Act 1995.

Activity

Refresh your memory – review legislation highlighted within this book and consider how it can impact on effective risk assessment.

Individual perceptions of risks and risk taking develop from a number of influencing factors. The following diagram identifies a number of the influencing factors that shape our **perception**.

Key term

Perception how we see, understand and make sense of the world we live in and so how we interact and behave.

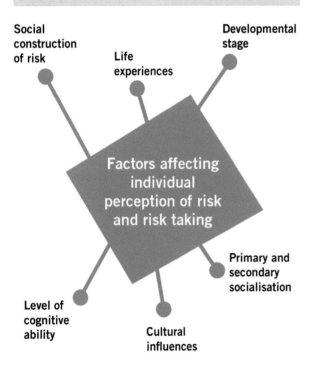

Factors that affect individual perceptions of risks and risk taking.

Social and cultural aspects have to be considered, as within different groups in society there are differences in what is perceived as acceptable and unacceptable risk. For example, for young people there is often a lot of experimenting that often occurs within this group, such as alcohol and binge drinking. Cultural background will also influence our perceptions of risk and risk taking as well.

Activity

Investigate how different cultures perceive risk and risk taking.

Can you identify what is seen as an acceptable risk within one culture yet in another is seen as too risky (unacceptable)?

Is there any difference in relation to whether it is a male or female taking the risk?

Consider this

Care workers need to be aware of and reflect on, the impact which social and cultural influences have on them when involved in assessing risks.

Recognising that taking risks can have beneficial outcomes is as important as taking risks – otherwise why would individuals take risks in the first place? Many people's life experiences have involved taking risks and we have learned and developed from these experiences.

Therefore defining what risks are requires care workers to recognise and understand that risk is a complex and variable concept. It has to include the individual, recognition of the individual's needs, the situation/activity being assessed and the care environment involved, as well as understanding that a definition of risk can be socially constructed.

A working definition could be that risk is the probability that the individual could be harmed in some way by a hazard during the proposed activity. However, the individual does have the right to responsible risk taking as there can be recognised benefits to taking the risk.

The legal framework

The legal framework relating to risk assessment and management must be considered.

All care organisations have a duty to ensure that the legal requirement to identify, assess and reduce risk of danger and/or harm to health and safety arising from work activities is fulfilled. The Health and Safety at Work Act 1974 provides the legal framework of health and safety responsibilities for employers and employees. It also defines the requirements for collaborative practice between employers and employees in relation to health and safety issues. Subsequent legislation and regulations have followed, in particular the Management of Health and Safety at Work Regulations (1999) which lay down the broad requirements for formalised systematic risk assessment procedures, including the documentation of findings and action taken (control measures) and the management of this.

Consider this

Refresh your memory of the health and safety responsibilities of employers and employees and the five-step process of risk assessment described in the HSC SVQ chapter.

Within the last twenty years an ever increasing emphasis on carrying out risk assessment has taken place within the care sector. This is partly due to the changes from institutional-based care to community-based care, which has resulted in a variety of different care environments. More individuals are being supported in their own home but there is also an increased awareness of accountability and increased fear of litigation. There are questions raised about this issue, as it can result in care staff erring on the side of caution and taking a 'safety-first' approach to risk taking and risk assessment. This can then dominate the care provision for the individual rather than a balanced approach of risk assessment being holistically incorporated into the individual's assessment of needs and Care Plan.

Why is this? Many managers and individual staff are clearly influenced by concerns around litigation. Media representation of specific incidents or accidents, and the knowledge that litigation is seen as common practice in other countries, particularly the USA, has increased awareness and concerns. However while there are similarities between the legislation in the USA and Scotland, there are also differences. The Scottish legal system, in relation to health and safety and protection from danger, harm or abuse, is not always understood by care workers in relation to their role and responsibilities. This needs to be addressed so that care workers have the knowledge and understanding required to ensure there is a balanced approach to risk taking and risk assessment so that fears about litigation can be reduced and placed in the correct context.

Fundamentally there is a legal duty of care principle which if breached can result in legal action. This is based on the principle of probable proof of negligence. It is the term *negligence* that is legally recognised.

Organisations have a legal duty to manage **reasonably foreseeable risks**. Breaching these is a criminal offence by the employer and criminal proceedings can be initiated to establish proof of a breach.

Key term

Reasonably foreseeable risks those risks that organisations would be expected to recognise and so be able to predict that the risk could occur within that workplace and through the working practices.

Individuals must also comply with the relevant legislation, organisational policies and procedures relating to health and safety and protection as part of their practice; in addition to these, the SSSC Codes of Practice provide a complementary framework of standards. If litigation relating to negligence is initiated due to loss, injury and/or harm to the individual then this is a civil law matter. Within the civil courts it is the claimant who has to show negligence based on the following three important points.

1. The care worker owed the individual a duty of care – this has to be seen as fair, just and reasonable.

2. The duty of care was breached.

3. The injury, harm, loss was caused by the duty of care – a factor here is identifying if it was reasonable to foresee that injury, harm or loss would occur.

Therefore a care worker who has followed the legal and organisational requirement of their job role has fulfilled their responsibilities and their accountability relating to the health, safety and protection of individuals.

The focus has been on health and safety legislation due to its clear legal requirements for risk assessment, and the length of time it has been in place, but there is also other legislation that relates to risks, rights and protection of people who use services. This range of legislation can also be applicable to the carer's practice depending on the individual who uses services and the specific job role of the carer.

Care Workers have a duty of care to ensure the well-being of an individual.

Topic 1 Protection including safeguarding and management of risk

This range of legislation reflects the different points in time over the last three decades that each Act was introduced and so reflects the social concerns of that time; it is not necessarily a coherent approach to risks, rights and protection. Some of the main acts are listed in the table below.

Activity

Can you identify how risks are reduced by the legislation listed in the table below and what rights are being promoted?

Legislation	Risks/rights
NHS and Community Care Act 1995	
Mental Health (Patients in the community) Act 1995	
The Children (Scotland) Act 1995	
Disability Discrimination Act 1995	
Human Rights Act 1998	
Adults with Incapacity Act 2000	
Regulation of Care Act (Scotland) 2001	
Mental Health (Care and Treatment) (Scotland) Act 2003	

Legislation to promote rights and reduce risk. Can you identify what these rights and risks are?

Risk management

Risk management involves the organisation in ensuring it has a clear policy that specifies its approach to managing risks in relation to its service provision and the person who uses services. It will also reflect the relevant National Care Standards and legislation applicable to its service provision, including the health and safety legislation.

> ### Key term
>
> **Risk management** the process of identification, assessment and so management (via control measures) of risks.

Risk management is about ensuring that all reasonably foreseeable risks (covering people who use services, staff and others) have been assessed and that suitable control measures have been implemented. This clarifies the expectations that individuals and their families can have about the service and their rights and responsibilities in relation to risk taking. The procedures for risk assessment, and the care team's responsibilities, provide the basic foundation for a systematic risk management approach.

Within the management system there should be clear identification of how risks and the control measures are being monitored, reviewed and recorded. It is essential that monitoring takes place regularly to reflect the changing needs of the person who uses services. Risk management should be integrated within the assessment of needs of individuals and ongoing Care Plan reviews.

When compiling the risk management plan for a care service the ideal is to ensure consultation with staff, the individual who uses services and others involved with the service to establish an appropriate risk management plan. It has to include guidance and procedures for both staff and the individual in relation to risks and so protection from danger, harm or abuse as well as acknowledging the rights to informed choice and participation of all.

Case study

Jemma

Jemma lives in a flat where she has one-to-one support for 40 hours per week to enable her to live independently in the community. Jemma has severe cerebral palsy and uses a wheelchair for mobility most of the time as well as other moving and handling aids. Jemma's communication and cognitive skills are also affected by her condition. She discussed with her Key Worker the fact that she would like to go to Spain for a week's holiday in October, to stay in a hotel preferably with a swimming pool. The Key Worker suggested to Jemma that a meeting of the staff who support her, the team leader and Jemma should take place to discuss how to plan for this as there could be a number of risks involved that need to be assessed and then managed.

1. Do you think a meeting would be beneficial to Jemma's expectations in relation to her holiday choice?

2. What risks could you identify that should be discussed at the meeting?

3. How can Jemma and her Key Worker ensure that Jemma's rights and choices are recognised in this meeting?

4. What documentation should the Key Worker ensure is completed in relation to this meeting and risk management?

The process of risk assessment

The underlying principle involved is to assess for reasonably foreseeable risks that could occur due to the activity being undertaken:

Risk = Likelihood of **hazard**

×

Outcome (**consequences**)

> ### Key terms
>
> **Hazard** anything or anyone that has the potential to cause harm (likelihood)
>
> **Consequences** the outcome of an individual interacting with a hazard, e.g. harm. The outcome can range in severity – from low to high.

A 'risk matrix' approach is frequently used which calculates the combination of likelihood and consequences to establish the level of intervention required to reduce the risk. This involves grading the likelihood and consequences outcome in the following way.

Likelihood:

1. = not likely/low
2. = likely/medium
3. = very likely/high

Outcome:

1. = acceptable/low
2. = tolerable/medium
3. = unacceptable/high

This principle is applicable in all risk assessment situations and should be carried out according to the organisational policy and procedures for risk assessment, including using and completing the relevant risk assessment forms. The care worker should have sufficient training and knowledge to carry out this assessment with the participation of the person who uses services and other key staff. In many care organisations a member of the care team has this remit as part of their responsibilities.

The steps involved in the risk assessment process are as follows.

- Identification of the specific work activity requiring risk assessment.
- Identification of the risk involved – what is the hazard and who could be harmed/at risk from it?
- Estimation of the effects of the risk – the likelihood of it occurring and the potential outcome of this.
- Then the evaluation takes place using the risk matrix.
- Findings should be clearly recorded and the actions (control measures) that have been deemed necessary to implement to reduce the likelihood and outcome of an interaction between the hazard and the individual.
- There should be monitoring and regular review of the risk assessment to ensure any changes are taken into consideration.

The risk assessment process follows these basic principles. However in some areas of Social Care work it can be and is a more complex situation, e.g. situations involving abuse, suicide risks, etc.

Consider this

Who is responsible for risk assessment in your placement/workplace?

Is there a designated member of staff?

Discuss the specific policy and procedures for the person who uses services and care service provision in relation to risk assessment to understand its application within the care area you are working in with them.

Risk Assessment Form

Activity	Participants	Hazards	
i.e. specific details including duration/ location and rational for activity	person who uses services, care worker etc.	identification of specific potential hazards	

Hazard	Likelihood X	Outcome (consequences)	= level of risk
1.			
2.			
3.			

Any additional requirements

Monitoring, by whom and when

Review date:

Completed by

Signature

Signature of person who uses services

Date

An example of a risk assessment form.

The Social Care worker's role and responsibilities

Care workers have to understand their role and responsibilities in relation to risk and risk assessment, and potential dilemma situations, within the care organisation they are part of and in their own care practice.

'As a social service worker, you must respect the rights of a person who uses services while seeking to endure that their behaviour does not harm themselves or other people.' (Scottish Social Services Council Codes of Practice for Social service workers, Section 4.)

It can help understanding for care workers to consider having three areas of risk as part of their care practice: the work setting/environment, the client group and then the type of situation.

The care worker has a responsibility in supporting acceptable risk taking via risk assessment procedures. This involves recognition of the three aspects of their care practice necessary to effectively contribute to risk assessment.

1. Awareness of and implementation of relevant legal requirements.

2. Understanding and implementing organisational policy and procedures in relation to risk and risk assessment.

3. Effective interaction at client level in relation to risk and risk assessment. This includes ability to reflect on own practice and utilisation of supervision and support

to improve effectiveness, i.e. accessing advice if unsure or if potential conflict/dilemma arises and also provision of appropriate training to aid professional development.

Dilemmas and conflicts

We will now consider the different types of dilemma and conflicts which can arise. The care value base includes the promotion of choice and independence, which are embedded within the Codes of Practice and National Care Standards as well as relevant organisational policies and procedures and legislation, e.g. Human Rights Act, NHS and Community Care Act and other Acts as well.

Potential dilemmas and/or conflict can arise partly due to the balance that has to be achieved between rights, responsibilities and risks and also, as previously noted, different perceptions of what is acceptable and unacceptable risk. There are different reasons why a conflict or dilemma situation could occur, including the following.

- Right of choice versus concerns about danger and harm – care organisations have a legal duty to assess for, and take action in relation to, reasonably foreseeable risk.

- Lack of shared understanding or agreement as to what is 'reasonable risk' between a person who uses services and their care worker which can result in a safety first approach dominating – which limits the choices of the person who uses services.

- Client perception of what is acceptable risk versus care staff's expert view of level of acceptable risk.

- Individual's choices being in conflict with family member's perception of the risks involved in situation.

- Misuse of power within the relationship between client and care worker – paternalistic, autocratic approach taken by care worker severely limiting an individual's rights and choices.

Care workers have to ensure that there are opportunities for genuine choices and that informed decisions are made as part of the risk assessment process, while also ensuring they are promoting the independence of the person who uses services according to their needs. This involves recognising that choice – it is a complex concept e.g. lifestyle choices including smoking, drinking alcohol, eating healthy/unhealthy foods, using drugs etc.

You might also consider the situation where an individual receiving informal care has potentially been abused yet wishes to remain within the family setting.

Case study

Ken

Ken is 76 years old and lives with his daughter and her family since he had a stroke two years ago. The stroke left him with paralysis on one side of his body and limited verbal communication skills; however his cognitive understanding has been unaffected. The home care worker who supports Ken three mornings a week has raised concerns that recently he appears more unkempt.

The home care manager has visited Ken to assess and discuss the situation with him. Ken is adamant that he wishes to stay within the family home even though he is aware that his care recently has not been of the standard it used to be; but he is still included in all family occasions which he enjoys.

1. What risks are involved with Ken remaining in the family home?

2. Does Ken have the right to this choice?

3. If so, how can the home care worker respect Ken's choice while also taking responsibility for protection from harm?

4. How would a formal risk assessment be of benefit in this situation?

In relation to promoting independence, remember what was covered earlier in this chapter. Our life experiences, growth and development have always included taking risks as part of the process of establishing individual independence. Further to this are the well-documented psychological benefits for the individual's well-being – self-esteem, self-confidence and self-concept.

Therefore, as a care worker, you have to be able to promote the care value base in your practice while at the same time fulfilling your responsibilities in relation to the protection of the person who uses services (and others) from harm and danger. Sometimes the dilemmas and conflicts arise because you have been unable to maintain that balance.

Responsibilities and risk assessment

So what is the care worker's role in carrying out risk assessment?

You need to have a clear understanding of the different factors involved, e.g. perceptions, reasonably foreseeable risks, appropriate actions to reduce risk, participation of person who uses services, legal and organisational requirements, following the principles involved in risk assessment, recording and reviewing the risk assessment and the actions that have resulted form the risk assessment.

Effective interpersonal, personal and communication skills (see the other chapters about these skills) are also essential requirements to ensure understanding of the different perceptions of the situation, as well as ensuring that participation has been open and genuine.

It is important to remember that when risk assessment is carried out effectively it reduces the potential for dilemmas and conflict situation to occur.

In recent years the protection agenda has raised the profile of risk assessment which in turn has potentially increased the 'safety first' approach. This is, in part, due to failures in Health and Social Care practice within and across relevant care organisations. This has been highlighted by the media, raising public concern about the protection of children, young people and vulnerable adults. There has also been new legislation passed during this time which has aimed to provide more legal protection.

The area of protection from harm and abuse is the focus of the rest of this chapter.

Issues involved in protection from abuse

Within this section the issues relating to protection of individuals from harm and **abuse** will be explored. This will enable you to have the knowledge and understanding to recognise and respond appropriately to protection from harm and abuse within the limits and responsibilities of your specific care role.

It builds on the previous section on risks, risk taking and the risk assessment process involved when you are responsible for protecting individuals from harm and abuse while also maintaining the individual's rights.

There are different issues to be explored and the starting point is to be aware of the cultural values and practices that influence how we view protection and abuse. Care workers need to reflect on the impact their own personal and cultural values may have on their care practice, as well as having knowledge of the individual's cultural background and how this may impact on whether the individual sees the situation as potentially harmful and abusive and so in need of intervention.

Definitions of abuse

Definitions of abuse will, therefore, reflect what society deems acceptable/not acceptable treatment of others and this is often embedded in legislation.

In reality there are different types or categories of abuse that have been identified and each category of abuse has a more specific definition to aid understanding. The categories of abuse that will be covered within this chapter are:

- physical abuse
- neglect
- non-organic failure to thrive
- sexual abuse
- emotional abuse
- financial abuse.

Before investigating the categories and the signs that may indicate abuse has taken place, it is important to highlight the fact that this is a complex, sensitive area within care work. Investigations of abuse will involve a number of agencies working collaboratively together within the boundaries of confidentiality and you as a care worker may only have some input into this. However, you have a legal duty to raise awareness of any concerns you may have by reporting and recording the concerns according to your agency's policy and procedures. This responsibility is also embedded within the SSSC Codes of Practice and the National Care Standards applicable to the care organisation you are with.

Secondly there can be more than one explanation of the possible signs of abuse that a care worker may observe and have concerns about. It is imperative that any other explanation or facts have to be ruled out at the start as there can be other reasons for some signs/symptoms which do not require intervention and protection.

There are a number of explanations or factors that could result in the behavioural and/or physical signs you have observed that have given you cause for concern. These can include:

- accidents that have resulted in physical injuries
- medical conditions i.e. brittle bone disease, chronic illnesses etc.
- changes in personal/family circumstances, such as loss, separation, stress, bereavement, resulting in changes in behaviour and/or appearance.

Case study

Angela's situation

Angela, an individual with special needs, has been coming to the day centre for the last year. Staff have noticed that recently she has been very quiet and unwilling to join in the range of activities which she used to enjoy. When members of staff have tried to talk with Angela about it she has been evasive in her answers, so giving further cause for concern. It was also noticed that she seemed reluctant to go home at the end of the day.

- Is there cause for concern?
- Is Angela at risk?

The centre manager decided to contact Angela's Care manager to discuss their concerns further and at this point information was disclosed that Angela's parents had just separated and her father had moved out of the family home. Angela's changes in behaviour were related to her family circumstances and staff were now able to support her through this difficult time of adjustment.

The information which follows outlines the different categories of abuse.

Different categories of abuse
Physical abuse is the deliberate inflicting (or attempting to inflict) of physical harm and/or injury or knowingly not preventing the physical harm and/or injury taking place.   *Signs of Physical abuse can include:*   bruising, lacerations, burns and scalds, punching, broken bones, internal injuries (can often be difficult to detect initially), brain damage.
Non-organic failure to thrive is where a child fails to meet the expected developmental milestones and there are no medical or genetic reasons for this.   *Signs of non-organic failure to thrive can include:*   weight being below the range for that specific age, physical growth/height being below the range for that specific age.
Neglect is not providing sufficiently for the individual's basic physical and/or psychological needs, including basic safety needs. This then results in clear impairment of health and development.   *Signs of neglect can include:*   physical illnesses, unkempt/dirty appearance, lack of warm, safe environment so physical injuries may be apparent, lack of interest in surroundings, isolated, hungry, inappropriate clothing for the surroundings/outdoor environment, weight loss.
Sexual abuse is the deliberate involvement of an individual under the age of consent (16) or being unable to give consent to any activity that results in the sexual needs of the other person being met. This can include situations where there has been no physical/sexual contact such as photos, videos etc.   *Signs of sexual abuse can include:*   physical injuries in the genital area, urinary tract infections, anxiety, depression, self-harm, inappropriate sexual language and behaviour towards adults, inappropriate preoccupation with sexual behaviour, aggressive or antisocial behaviour, sexually abusive behaviour towards other children.
Emotional abuse is the persistent failure to meet the basic emotional needs of the individual. This then results in clear impairment of the individual's emotional development (sense of love, belonging and emotional security) and well-being. Emotional abuse is a factor in all types of abuse.   *Signs of emotional abuse can include:*   individual being withdrawn, presenting a negative view of themselves, being ignored by others and/or being blamed, distressed, anxious, lack of social interactions.

Financial abuse is the deliberate exploitation of individuals' funds including stealing, persuading individual to sign over property/access to bank accounts all of which does not benefit the individual.

Signs of financial abuse can include:

reluctance to talk to others about financial situation/funds, anxiety/fear, not being able to pay for day-to-day costs/bills, unable to explain where money has gone.

It is important to remember that the individual may experience more than one category of abuse, i.e. emotional abuse potentially occurs across all the other categories. Also abuse is a reflection of the breach of trust and abuse of power within the relationship between the individual and the perpetrator of the abuse.

The effect of abuse will vary according to each individual and these can be short and/or long-term in their effects. Care workers need to be aware that these effects vary if they are to be able to effectively support the person who uses services. Below is a range of examples of effects for each category of abuse; however, it is important to be aware that there may be other effects experienced by the individual.

Different effects of abuse
Effects of physical abuse
Bruises, lacerations, burns and scalds, broken bones, brain damage and ultimately fatal physical injuries resulting in death.
In the long term there can be recurring injuries, secondary illnesses and complications, permanent scarring and disfigurement, fear/mistrust, anxiety, brain damage etc.
Effects of non-organic failure to thrive
Poor nutrition and diet have a negative impact on growth and development.
In the long term, developmental delay will occur, regressive behaviour, isolation and lack of trust towards adults or over-dependency on others etc.
Effects of neglect
Physical illnesses occurring, negative effects on self-esteem, isolation and lack of trust towards others/fear of others/authority figures or over-dependency on others.
In the long term, malnutrition can occur with related complications and negative effects on physical health, depression, ability to form and maintain relationships etc.

Effects of sexual abuse
Physical injuries, urinary tract infections, sexually transmitted diseases, pregnancy, inappropriate sexual behaviour, fear/mistrust of adults.
In the long term, promiscuity, fear/mistrust of medical staff/adults/authority figures, eating disorders, self-harm, disruptive behaviour, inability to form and maintain relationships, poor self-esteem, misuse of drugs/alcohol etc.
Effects of emotional abuse
Fear of adults/others, withdrawal, passive behaviour, poor relationships with peers.
In the long term, low self-esteem, withdrawal, depression, inability to form and maintain relationships, withdrawal, hypochondria and potentially suicide etc.
Effects of financial abuse
Mistrust of others, isolation, withdrawal, financial difficulties i.e. unable to pay bills.
In the long term, continued mistrust/fear and low self-esteem as well as loss of possessions and /or home etc.

It is important to remember that there may be more than one type of abuse occurring, so leading to a range of effects in the individual.

Predisposing factors

Now consider the issue of protection from abuse. For a care worker to be proactive in their promotion of the care value base (including protection and their Codes of Practice) they have to be aware of the signs, symptoms and effects of abuse. They also have to consider a range of predisposing factors that can increase the likelihood of abuse occurring. All people who use services are vulnerable to the potential of abuse simply because they are users of a service and therefore in some way dependent on that service and on those who provide it.

This therefore could be considered the first predisposing factor; however it must be stressed here that these factors increase the risk not the certainty that abuse will occur. An effective care worker should be aware of these factors and so be able to support those at risk to help prevent abuse occurring.

Predisposing factors can include:

- family stresses, including unemployment, poverty, inadequate housing and other social factors

- inability of the individual to control their anger
- previous abuse occurring
- substance misuse
- reconstituted family
- stress on informal/family carer
- young carers i.e. lacking experience and skills to manage care situation
- carer with special educational needs
- carers who are socially isolated.

Consider this

Is there a higher risk of certain categories of abuse occurring in relation to each predisposing factor?

For example, the inability of someone to control their anger could result in physical abuse occurring.

Harm, abuse and neglect can occur for a number of reasons and predisposing factors can provide us with some of the potential reasons. However, the picture is more complicated than that as the abusive situation could have been an isolated incident rather than ongoing ill-treatment. The abuse may not have been intentional or deliberate but as a result of the individual being too busy, dealing with too much leading to carelessness and mistakes.

Theoretical perspectives

There are a number of theoretical perspectives that can be applied to assist in explaining why abuse has occurred, so helping the care worker to understand abusive situations and the potential risk involved. We will look at the following theoretical explanations – Situational model, Social Construction theory and Exchange theory. However there are other equally valid theoretical perspectives that can provide insight into why abuse occurs.

Activity

Think about some of the sociological and psychological perspectives that have been covered elsewhere in this book and consider how they would explain why abusive situations occur: Symbolic Interactionism, theories of attachment, i.e. Bowlby and the behaviourist approach and social learning theory.

Social Construction theory is based on the premise that society understands groups and their expected behaviour based on society's beliefs about the group. The social construction theory has been applied particularly to older adults in our society as an explanation of why abuse occurs.

For example, older adults are deemed to be dependent on others and are seen as of less value as a group compared to other groups in our society, such as children. Also consider the social construction of gender roles in relation to explaining domestic abuse in our society.

The Situation Model focused on the external aspects of the situation and how it affects the relationship between the carer and the individual in need of care. Fundamental to this is the fact that the relationship involves dependency of one individual in the caring relationship on the other. This then leads to increasing stress being experienced by the carer which can lead to abuse. Here the abuse has occurred due to the stress and inability of the carer to cope and manage their situation within their caring role in the relationship.

Exchange Theory suggests that social interactions are about the exchange of resources/benefits between the individuals involved in the interaction. In basic terms social interactions are about give and take. Therefore interactions are underpinned by the pursuit of rewards and prevention or reduction of punishments and costs. When social exchanges change and are then seen as not being beneficial, and the costs are perceived to be more than the benefits, then the social exchange ceases; i.e. the relationship is no longer seen as a reciprocal one. However, within families, relationships can change and become far less reciprocal but they do not cease and so abuse can occur.

Case study

The effects of John's accident

John was a successful salesman for a number of years who travelled across Scotland as part of his job. However, he was involved in a serious road traffic accident which left him physically disabled and he now has to use a wheelchair to get around. He was in hospital for four months and has been back at home for the last three months. He also suffered brain damage which has left him with limited short-term memory capabilities.

His wife Margaret is now his main carer, assisting John throughout the day as well as looking after their two young children; she finds that this takes up all her time now. Margaret has also had to adapt to taking charge of the bills etc. which John used to do, but because of his memory loss can no longer manage. Margaret is increasingly worried about whether she can meet the mortgage payments as well as being able to cope with her caring role.

1. What predisposing factors would alert you to the potential risk of abuse occurring in this situation?

2. Which models/theories could help you to understand why abuse could occur in this situation?

3. How would each one explain the abuse occurring?

Institutional abuse

A final and important issue relating to the protection of individuals from harm and abuse is the occurrence of institutionalisation and institutional abuse within the caring services.

Each and every care worker should be promoting the care values via their Codes of Practice and adhering to the National Care Standards relevant to the service they are part of. This all helps to reduce the likelihood of institutionalisation and institutional abuse occurring and maintain appropriate standards of care for the 21st century.

Institutional abuse occurs due to institutionalisation, which is created by the routines, culture and practices of a care organisation that limit the rights, choices and participation of individuals who use services.

Staff can be an integral aspect of institutionalisation occurring and part of this will relate to the culture that develops within an organisation. A blame culture will reduce the opportunity of staff to speak out regarding poor care practice, in addition to this, lack of training and supervision, and adhering to routines and practices that benefit staff rather than the people who use services, will all contribute to a culture where institutional abuse can and does occur.

Consider this

An individual with dementia is routinely given sleeping tablets to prevent her wandering at night in the care home. Her medication has not been reviewed for some time.

Is this poor practice?

Is this an example of institutionalism?

Could this be considered an example of institutional abuse?

Further research

'Remember, I'm still me.' The Care Commission and Mental Welfare Commission joint report on the quality of care for people with dementia living in care homes in Scotland. May 2009.

Read this report in relation to protection from harm and abuse and the promotion of the rights of the individual via the National Care Standards, Codes of Practice and relevant legislation.

The legal and social context of protection from abuse

The legal provision for protection from harm and abuse reflects the social context of that particular point in time. It has been society's response to vulnerable children and young people's experiences of harm and abuse that has created more specific legislation for protection from, and intervention in relation to, harm and abuse. These developments have also been influenced by the recognition of the individual's rights and responsibilities. Further to this has been the incorporation of the **Humans Rights Act 1998** into the Scottish legal system, providing a legal framework of rights for all members of our society.

In the 1980s it was recognised by the professionals involved that changes needed to be made to children's legislation, including the need to review and update 'place of safety orders' which were provided for within the Social Work (Scotland) Act 1968. Added to this was public and media pressure for changes to child welfare and protection following the recommendations of the Clyde Report, which was based on the investigation into the removal of nine children from Orkney. However, it was acknowledged that the Children's Hearing System which had its origins in the Social Work (Scotland) Act 1968 was relatively effective.

The Children's Act 1989 for England and Wales also influenced developments in Scotland in relation to the legal protection and legal rights of children and young people.

The culmination of these and other influencing factors was the Children (Scotland) Act 1995.

The Children (Scotland) Act 1995

This is a major piece of Scottish legislation, however only the sections specifically relevant to protection and intervention are highlighted within this chapter. There are three basic principles promoted throughout most of this Act.

1. The welfare of the child is paramount.

2. No formal order should be made unless it would be better for the child than not making an order. This is known as the no order principle.

3. The child's views must be taken into account when decisions about the child's welfare are made, according to the age and maturity of the child. This includes recognising the child's religious, racial and cultural background.

Debate continues around the child's level of understanding relating to their age/maturity, as it is often interpreted to mean 12 years of age and over; however each child should be encouraged to express their views/opinions.

The Act established three legal orders that can be utilised in situations involving protection and intervention from harm and abuse.

1. Child Assessment Order can be granted by a Sheriff when a local authority applies for it. This is utilised when there is concern that the child is suffering from harm and/ or abuse and that access to the child is being refused. This order enables an assessment of the child to be carried out by the appropriate people; however the child does not have to be removed from their home. This order is seen as less of an intervention than the Child Protection Order.

2. Child Protection Order can be granted by a Sheriff and provides the legal power to remove a child from their home circumstances to a place of safety when there is significant harm or abuse suspected. The order must be regularly reviewed to ensure the child's rights and welfare are being protected.

3. Exclusion orders were introduced to reduce the potential trauma experienced by a child being removed from their home to a place of safety. An exclusion order requires the alleged perpetrator of the harm/abuse to leave the family home or, if they are not resident there, not to visit the child's home. Also the Sheriff has to be satisfied that there is a responsible adult within the home to provide care for the child concerned. Again there is the requirement for regular reviews of the order.

The Act also maintained the **Children Hearing System** which has been an integral part of the Scottish welfare, protection and criminal justice for children and young people since its creation via the Social Work (Scotland) Act 1968. It was proposed in the Kilbrandon Committee's report of 1964 as the appropriate way forward in Scotland, incorporating both child welfare and criminal justice for children and young people within the one-hearing system. The report emphasised the needs and circumstances of the child and this became the guiding philosophy of the Children's Hearing System.

Children Hearings are basically legal tribunals that consider serious situations which are affecting the child's welfare or where the child has offended. The hearing will make decisions about the future needs of the child, including both the care and control aspects of the situations.

It is the Reporter who is the gatekeeper of the system. The Reporter's role is to accept all referrals, to carry out an initial investigation and consider whether there is sufficient grounds for the referral to the Children's Hearing and if the child is in need of compulsory intervention. If the answer is no to these two points then the Reporter will decide that no further action is required. If however the Reporter decides that the answer to either of these two points is yes then he/she will call a Children's Hearing.

The Hearing consists of three panel members who are trained volunteers, plus the Reporter who has an administrative and advisory role; however he/she is not part of the decisions that are taken.

The child concerned and their family members and/or carers will all contribute to and participate in the deliberations and the panel will reach decisions about the child's future welfare. There are three decisions a Children's Hearing may make:

- discharge the case
- continue the Hearing for further information and investigation
- make a supervision order with the child's welfare as central to that decision. The supervision order will specify the details relevant to the particular child and their circumstances. The supervision order must be reviewed at least every 12 months or more regularly as appropriate.

Consider this

Now consider the reasons why there are such specific legal powers and duties in relation to children and young people compared with other people who use services groups. You might consider:

- age/maturity?
- cognitive ability?
- society's view (social construction) of different groups within society?
- concept of vulnerability?

The Child Protection Register is an alert system for children and young people who are deemed to be at risk of significant harm. The register involves a multi-agency approach to identification of those at risk and requires regular monitoring and review of those placed on the register.

Among the other relevant legislation relating to protection from harm and abuse are the following.

Protection of Children (Scotland) Act 2003

This Act established the 'disqualified from working with children' list to prevent unsuitable people from working with children. Currently checks are carried out on any potential employees in the care sector via the Disclosure Scotland service. This means that there are safeguards in place in relation to appropriate/inappropriate people working with vulnerable children and adults and changes are underway to enhance this safeguard.

Protection of Vulnerable Groups (Scotland) Act 2007

This Act will create a continuous vetting and barring system to protect all vulnerable individuals (not just children and young people) in need of care services to support them. Currently it is expected that the Disclosure Scotland service will be incorporated into the new vetting and barring system. Also two lists will be established, one containing relevant information about those unsuitable to work with children (building on the previous legislation) and one for those unsuitable for working with vulnerable adults.

Adult Support and Protection (Scotland) Act 2007

This Act will provide local authorities with new powers to intervene in relation to suspected abuse of adults and will also ensure that local authorities establish statutory adult protection committees to develop strategic interagency working at local level.

This follows on from the 'Protecting children and young people: Child Protection Committees', Scottish Executive guidelines in January 2005, which local authorities implemented to ensure strategic planning and policy in relation to child protection and intervention with a co-ordinated, interagency approach. Each local committee is made up of the range of agencies that could be involved in child protection issues.

Further research

Find out more about the role and responsibilities of your own local Child Protection Committee by accessing your local authority website.

Regulation of Care (Scotland) Act 2001

This established the Scottish Social Services Council (SSSC) which has produced the Codes of Practice for employers and employees to implement as part of the standards expected within the care sector, as well as implementation of the National Care Standards for the different areas of the caring services. The Standards can be broadly divided into three areas – Adults, Children and Young People and Everyone – and incorporate the care value base. They provide details of the rights and standards of care people who use services and their families can expect from the service, including protection from danger, harm and abuse. Each care worker should be familiar with the standards that are specifically applicable to the service they are providing.

(See www.scotland.gov.uk/topics for further information.)

The SSSC also established the Social Service register so that staff at all levels within the care sector will have to be registered to practise and so be held accountable for the standard of care they provide. Currently registration of all staff is well underway and there is a procedure whereby concerns about an individual care worker's practice can be raised and investigated by the SSSC.

Finally the Care Commission was established as the independent, national regulatory and inspection service to monitor, review and investigate the standards of care being provided by care organisations. It has the power to investigate complaints and concerns relating to individuals and service provision and so respond to allegations of neglect and abuse.

Adults with Incapacity (Scotland) Act 2000

This Act was introduced to provide safeguards for the welfare, finances and/or property of any adult incapable of making their own decisions in relation to these areas. An authorised person can be legally appointed to make decisions on the individual's behalf. However there are five guiding principles that the authorised person must follow when making decisions.

- The decision benefits the individual.
- It is the least restrictive option.
- It takes account of the individual's wishes.
- It is taken in consultation with others.
- The individual is encouraged to use existing skills.

The identified authorised person has to be registered with the Office of the Public Guardian. Application for a Guardianship Order (property/financial) is made to the Sheriff's Court as is also the case when applying for an Intervention Order. The Mental Welfare Commission has a role in regulating and supervising the implementation of this Act and the decisions that follow from it.

Mental Health (Care and Treatment) (Scotland) Act, 2003

This Act came into effect in 2005 and provides a set of guiding principles when taking action in relation to individuals with a mental disorder. It also has a series of safeguards which aim to protect the rights of the individual.

All care staff, professionals and services working within the parameters of this Act should ensure that they are implementing the ten principles when taking action in relation to the individual with a mental disorder.

- Action should be non-discriminatory.
- Promote equality.
- Respect for diversity.
- Reciprocity.
- Informal care.
- Participation.
- Respect for carer.
- Least restrictive alternative.
- Benefit to the individual.
- Child welfare should be paramount.

There are a series of safeguards within this Act to protect individual rights which include the following:

1. Named person
2. Advance statements
3. Advocacy
4. Mental Health Tribunal
5. Mental Welfare Commission

Consider this

Now consider how each of the safeguards contributes to protection of an individual from harm and abuse.

If an individual or their family are unhappy with their care then they can refer this to the Mental Welfare Commission. This has the power to investigate individual cases as well as monitor mental health care provision and individuals in need of compulsory measures of care.

Discrimination and marginalisation can result in abuse but equally can be an abusive experience for the individual in itself. It is about individuals being denied their rights, choices and excluded from aspects of our society.

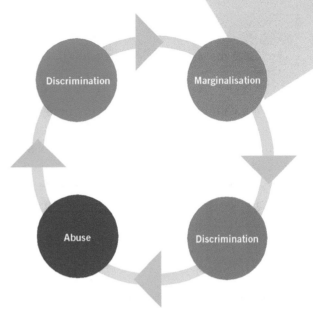

Discrimination, marginalisation and abuse are all interlinked.

Activity

Now identify examples where abuse can lead to discrimination and marginalisation and examples where marginalisation and discrimination lead to abuse.

Care workers have a responsibility to challenge discrimination as part of their anti-discriminatory practice. This, in turn, positively impacts on the care worker's effectiveness in protecting individuals from harm and abuse. Obviously most Scottish legislation is anti-discriminatory and provides a framework for care practice, including the Human Rights Act 1998 and the Disability Discrimination Act 1995 which is covered elsewhere in this book and with which care workers should be familiar.

The care worker's responsibilities

As a care worker you have a crucial role in protecting individuals from harm and abuse. It is a fundamental aspect of your practice which incorporates the care value base. Care workers have a duty to raise awareness of any concerns they have and report any **disclosure** of abuse that has been shared by a person who uses services. This is not an option but a responsibility each care worker must uphold.

It is not common for individuals to openly disclose that they are experiencing abuse. This is why it is so important that you as a care worker know what the signs and behavioural indicators of abuse are and can respond promptly when these circumstances arise. This requires you to raise awareness of your concerns according to your organisation's protection and disclosure policy and procedures.

There are a variety of reasons why children, young people and adults may feel unable to disclose their experiences of abuse. These include:

- fear
- cognitive impairment
- blaming themselves
- level of communication i.e. young child
- no one to trust and so no one to tell
- fear of involvement of authority
- shame
- unable to believe it will make any difference
- fear of losing family and not being believed by family members.

By establishing and maintaining a supportive relationship, based on the promotion of the care standards embedded in the Codes of Practice and relevant National Care Standards, the care worker creates a level of trust in the relationship; this should create the opportunity for disclosure to occur if necessary. Further to this, it provides care workers with the opportunity to raise with the individual any concerns they have in an open and supportive manner.

It is a challenging situation for a care worker when disclosure of abuse occurs; however, the priority must be the safety and well-being of the person who uses services. Disclosure of abuse is one of the main reasons why confidentiality

Reviews on abuse must be carefully handled and properly recorded.

is not an absolute in care practice. In these circumstances, maintaining confidentiality conflicts with the individual's right to protection from harm and abuse; however confidentiality of the information being disclosed must be maintained.

Clear organisational policy and procedures in relation to disclosure, reporting and recording enable care workers to ensure they report appropriately while maintaining confidentiality. In basic terms the rule of informing is who *needs* to know not who *wants* to know.

If in doubt, a care worker should discuss this via supervision to ensure they understand their responsibilities and how to maintain confidentiality in these circumstances.

Case study

Annie

Annie, an HNC student on placement, was very upset as an individual she had been working with over the last two months told her today that they were being sexually abused at home. Annie didn't know what to do but remembered her supervisor saying to her at the start of her placement that if she had any concerns to come and speak with him. Annie went to him and asked if she could speak with him in private. The supervisor and Annie sat in his office and Annie explained what had happened. She explained that she wasn't sure what to do and that it had really shocked and upset her.

The supervisor reassured Annie that she had done the right thing by coming straight to him and then discussed with Annie the reporting and recording procedures involved and the importance of maintaining confidentiality.

He also reassured Annie about her reaction to the situation and arranged for her to have another supervision session with him when she returned to placement the following week.

How did this supervision session benefit Annie in her practice?

Effective interpersonal skills

These are required when responding to an individual who is sharing information about their situation. A person who uses services may disclose sensitive information at any point in time; however it is important that you respond appropriately by actively listening to what is being said and ensure, wherever possible, privacy for them while they are raising their concerns. The use of open questions enables the individual to talk more about their situation as well as allowing you to establish what has been happening.

It is important, however, that leading questions should be avoided. Verbal reassurance should be provided so that the individual knows they have a right to be (and feel) safe and they are not to blame, nor is it their fault and what has happened is not acceptable. Non-verbal communication will also have an impact on the situation and a care worker should be aware of their non-verbal communication and ensure it is appropriately reassuring as well. For example, sitting with the individual and not standing over them, a relaxed body posture and appropriate facial expressions all help to ensure that a supportive, reassuring message is given to the person who uses services.

You should provide a clear explanation of your role in reporting this situation to the person who uses services to ensure their understanding and agreement, where possible, in passing on the information.

Verbal reporting must be followed up by accurate written recording and the care worker must ensure that this takes place. Each organisation will have its own documentation which could be recording in the individual's case notes and completing an Incident, Protection or Disclosure form.

An accurate written record of the situation should include the following points.

- Complete the written record promptly after the incident/disclosure.
- Use the correct documentation provided.
- Ensure the written record is clear, legible and an accurate and detailed description of the situation/disclosure.
- Maintain objectivity; it is not your thoughts or opinion that should be recorded here.
- Ensure confidentiality is maintained in relation to recording, sharing and storing the information.

This record can be used as part of the subsequent investigation and ultimately in a court of law if required.

Activity

Find out what the procedures are in your workplace/placement in relation to the following:

- recording of information relating to disclosure of harm or abuse
- maintaining confidentiality in relation to sharing and storing this information.

Unfortunately the care worker's role may not always be a straightforward one and dilemmas can and do occur in this area for care staff in relation to protection and intervention.

The following three case studies highlight some aspects of this.

Case study
Dilemmas 1

Lizzie is 76 years old and has been living in a care home for the last three years. She was reluctant to participate in activities when she first moved in and since then the care staff leave her sitting in the lounge while most of the other residents participate in the twice weekly activities.

Maryam, a new care worker, has noticed Lizzie sitting on her own and has asked her why. Lizzie responded, 'It's OK. I always sit on my own at these times.'

1. Is this poor practice?
2. Is this an example of institutionalism?
3. Could this be considered an example of institutional abuse?
4. Is there a dilemma here? If so, what is it and how could Maryam deal with it?

Case study
Dilemmas 2

Jack has started his HNC Social Care placement in a residential unit for young people. He was working with another member of staff who was abrupt with one of the young people, refusing the young person's request to join the evening's activities.

When Jack was back in his placement the following week he noticed that the staff member was again unpleasant to the same young person.

1. There is no dilemma here – why not?
2. What response should Jack make to this situation?

Case study
Dilemmas 3

Kara is providing support to Peter who is 29 and has special needs. He lives with his parents at home and Kara has started to support him, three times a week. She has become aware that Peter is unnecessarily dependent and lacking in confidence. She has also observed that his parents are very directive and protective of Peter, making all decisions about his care and choices for him.

1. In what ways is this a dilemma for Kara?
2. How should she respond?

Note: A care worker has a duty to raise awareness of any concerns they may have in relation to the care and support of a person who uses services. This is not an option but a *responsibility* which all care workers have.

Finally, in order for a care worker to be effective in relation to protection from harm and abuse they need to receive sufficient training, support and supervision; this will enable their practice to develop to the level required.

Regular supervision also enables the care worker to express their own views and thoughts in a supportive and confidential environment in which the care worker can also explore the impact the situation has had on them. This will help the care worker to access other sources of support available to them.

Multi-agency collaborative working

Multi-agency collaborative working is the key to ensuring the protection of people who use services from harm and abuse as well as being essential for effective intervention where harm and abuse has occurred.

The single shared assessment of needs enables relevant agencies and professionals to establish with the individual their care requirements, including relevant risk assessment to ensure their well-being and safety.

In relation to responding to allegations of abuse, and investigation of these allegations, a multi-agency approach is required with a real emphasis on collaborative working. Effective collaborative working requires co-ordination and co-operation as well as good communication and clear understanding of the different roles and responsibilities of the professionals and agencies involved. Clear recording and sharing of relevant information and decision making are other factors required for effective collaborative working. All of this is essential for the support and well-being of the individual who is at the centre of the intervention.

There are a number of agencies that can be involved in protection and intervention as can be seen be the diagram below.

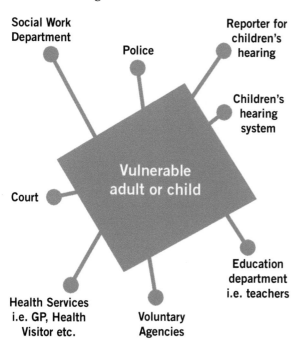

A number of different agencies can be involved in protection and intervention.

Each agency should have its own set of policies and procedures to follow in relation to protection and any investigation required. The role and responsibilities of each agency will vary according to their individual area of legal duty and expertise.

Social work department

This department takes referrals, assesses needs and provides appropriate services. The department will also make referrals of children and young people to the Reporter. It will identify and assess risks and enquire into the circumstances of the child or adult.

Social workers have to monitor and support children at risk and on the child protection register while also providing support to families who have experienced abuse. The social work department will work with the police to carry out joint enquiries and will organise case reviews and child protection conferences. The social work department can also provide and offer support to voluntary and private agencies which may be involved in the care of the individual.

Police

The police work jointly with the social work department as required and will protect the individual who has experienced abuse. The police may request a medical examination as required depending on each case being investigated. They will investigate and gather evidence, interview suspects, identify the offender and prepare cases for criminal prosecutions. This evidence is then passed to the Procurator Fiscal who will decide if there is sufficient evidence to prove an alleged offence and whether it is in the public interest to prosecute. The police will also attend case conferences and reviews.

Education department

The education department, including teachers, classroom assistants and nursery staff, can be involved in identifying abuse, will contribute to the assessment of vulnerable children, attend case reviews and child protection conferences and make referrals of their concerns to social workers, the Children's Hearing via the Reporter or the police. The education department also has a clear role in enabling children to understand how to keep safe.

Health Visitor

The health visitor has a clear role in the prevention of neglect and abuse as well as identifying and assessing children who give cause for concern. The concern may be based on the health visitor's awareness of the factors that increase the risk of abuse occurring within a family unit. Again, referral to social work, police and/or the Reporter should take place. The health visitor's role enables them to have continuous contact with young children to monitor their growth and development and so be able to observe any changes and act quickly. Health visitors also have a vital role in promoting parenting skills as part of their remit.

The statutory, voluntary and private services work together to provide the appropriate support and care which is needed by the individual who has experienced abuse. Obviously this will vary greatly from person to person, however the care worker's supportive role remains constant within this variation.

The range of support available includes counselling, case work, group work, self-help groups and residential provision, including residential care homes, foster care, hospital units etc. Each individual will have their own specific needs that can be met by a mix of these and other services and the individual may require short- or long-term support.

It is important to also consider the family and the impact on the other family members where abuse has taken place within a family. Support services should be available for other family members to enable a family unit to work through the situation and potentially be a functioning family unit.

Case study

Susan

Susan, the youngest member of the family at 9 years old, has been sexually abused by a member of her extended family. This has been investigated and intervention has taken place via the Children's Hearing System and a multi-agency approach to Susan's welfare. It has been agreed that Susan's needs and welfare are best met now by remaining within her immediate family unit. However, her two older brothers and their parents are still struggling with the revelations of what has happened.

What support services do you think would be of benefit to the rest of the family?

Consider this

What role could your organisation have as part of multi-agency working in protection from abuse?

Learning from reports and inquiries

It is a sad and salient fact that there have been serious failures in the provision of care and protection of individuals and people who use services in our society. When serious failures occur then the professional concern, public outcry and media attention usually results in a public inquiry. This leads to a report from the committee set up that investigates what happened, how it happened and what can be done to prevent the risk of it happening again. Very often the recommendations made in these reports are carried forward to shape social policy and new legislation to provide safeguards and reduce the risk of harm, neglect and abuse. The learning from reports and inquiries relating to failures to protect from abuse is therefore very important.

However, it also needs to be remembered that the many successful interventions which have taken place do not reach the public domain for obvious reasons of confidentiality and the right to privacy of the individual concerned.

The majority of inquiries and reports have focused on child abuse and child fatalities although, in more recent years, mental health inquiries have also increased.

The more high-profile inquiries and reports which have had major impact on policy and legislative changes to improve safeguards include the following:

- Maria Colwell Report, September 1974
- Jasmine Beckford – A Child in Trust, November 1985
- The Cleveland Enquiry (Butler Sloss), July 1988
- The Clyde Report (Orkney), October 1992
- Kennedy McFarlene Inquiry, March 2001
- Victoria Climbié Inquiry, January 2003
- Caleb Ness Inquiry, October 2003
- Investigation into Scottish Borders Council, April 2004.

Further research

Investigate the background and the recommendations of one of the reports/inquiries listed below.

The Mental Welfare Commission has produced a number of reports following investigations it has carried out as part of its responsibilities. Visit its website at http://www.mwcscot.org.uk/mwc_home/home.asp and review one of these reports as well.

Inquiries and reports are seen as the acceptable way of society responding and dealing with serious circumstances involving abuse and fatalities. However the focus of these inquiries is around the individual circumstances, and the physical and social environment – as well as structural factors – are not always addressed or considered in the report.

Inquiries and reports can highlight the need for multi-agency collaborative working and the need for national and local policy and procedures in relation to dealing successfully with intervention in harm and abuse situations. The recommendations across a number of inquiries have remained relatively unchanged and the most common recommendations include the need for:

- interagency working
- improved communication between the different agencies involved
- better understanding of other agencies roles and responsibilities
- improved information sharing between agencies
- improved recording of visits
- better staff support, training and supervision.

However, steps have been taken at national and local level to address these recurrent themes both through policy objectives and legislation; for example the creation of local Child Protection Committees and the multi-agency approach involved in this and subsequent recognition of need for Vulnerable Adult Protection Committees as well.

Conclusion

This chapter has highlighted that balancing rights, choices and risks in relation to safety and protection from harm and abuse is a complex area of care practice. The following summarises the main areas covered.

Taking risks is part of the development and life experiences of the individual and should be assessed as part of standard care practice. Relevant legislation provides the framework of policy and procedures to be followed by a care worker; however there can be risk situations which create conflicts between rights and responsibilities.

There is a variety of issues surrounding the area of protection from harm and abuse that a care worker needs to understand to enable effective promotion of the individual's right to protection. Care workers need to develop appropriate interpersonal skills to be able to raise awareness of concerns by following the correct organisational procedures and must respond supportively to disclosure of abuse.

Legislation in relation to protection and intervention in situations of abuse is strongest in the area of children and young people, although there are many Acts that relate to protection of all individuals via the promotion of human rights, principles for practice and embedded care values.

The multi-agency collaborative approach is the way forward in protection and the establishment of committees and changes in national and local policy have increased the effectiveness of prevention from harm and abuse, as well as raising public awareness of what can be done.

Protection and intervention will always be a part of care practice and learning from inquiries and reports can improve the safeguards and standards of practice across all the relevant care staff and agencies to benefit the well-being and protection of the individual.

Check Your Progress

1. Why is risk taking an important aspect of human development and life experiences?
2. Describe your responsibilities in relation to risk assessment and the rights of people who use services.
3. Give a definition of what 'abuse' is and identify the six categories involved.
4. Consider how people who use services can be vulnerable to abuse. Describe two factors that could increase the risk of abuse occurring.
5. Explain how abuse can affect the individual.
6. Describe how you would support someone who may have been abused, including the need for effective interpersonal skills.
7. Discuss your responsibilities in relation to reporting and recording of potential abuse.
8. Evaluate how legislation helps to protect individuals from harm and abuse with reference to at least two Acts.
9. Multi-agency collaborative working is essential for effective protection from and intervention in situations where abuse has potentially taken place. Describe why this is so essential and the different professionals who could be involved.
10. Consider two situations where dilemmas or conflict could arise in relation to the care value base, protection and individual's rights.

References:

Useful websites and references for Protection Chapter

References

Baillie D., Cameron K., Cull L., Roche J. and West J. (2003), *Social Work and the Law in Scotland*, The Open University: Buckingham

Biggs S., Phillipson C. and Kingston P. (1995), *Elder Abuse in Perspective*, The Open University: Buckingham

Lindon J. (2003), *Child Protection: 2nd Edition*, Hodder Arnold: Bristol

MacDonald, G with Winkley, A. (1999), *What Works in Child Protection?*, Barnardo's: Ilford

Mooney G., Sweeney T. and Law A. (2006), *Social Care Health and Welfare in Contemporary Scotland*, Kynoch and Blaney: Glasgow

Scottish Executive (2004), *Hidden Harm: Scottish Executive response to the report of the inquiry by the Advisory Council on the misuse of drugs*, Scottish Executive: Edinburgh.

Scottish Executive (2002), *It's everyone's job to make sure I'm alright*, Scottish Executive: Edinburgh

Scottish Executive (revised 2005) *National Care Standards: Care homes for children and young people*, Scottish Executive: Edinburgh

Scottish Executive (2005), *Protecting children and young people: Child Protection Committees*, Scottish Executive: Edinburgh

Scottish Executive (2004), *Protecting children and young people: Framework for Standards*, Scottish Executive: Edinburgh

Titterton, M. (2005), *Risk and Risk Taking in Health and Social Welfare*, London and Philadelphia: Jessica Kingsley Publishers.

Useful websites

Each local authority has its own website with details of their child and adult protection policies, committees etc.

www.actionforchildren.org.uk

www.ageconcern

www.alhziemersscotland.org.uk

www.barnardos.org.uk

www.carecommisssion.com

www.communitycare.co.uk

www.elderabuse.org.uk

www.hse.org.uk

www.nfer.ac.uk/emie

www.scotland.gov.uk

www.sqa.org.uk/carescotland

www.sssc.uk.com

Topic 2:
Interpersonal skills and understanding

Units covered:
DH3W 34
DH3X 34
DH3Y 35
DH4O 35
DH43 34
DG5D 35

Introduction

This chapter offers guidance and information relating to aspects of communication and interpersonal skills designed to underpin elements within many units of the HNC framework.

Each of the areas covered relate to various aspects of your studies – some relevance may be found when considering parts of your SVQ; some of the HNC optional units may require you to consider communication in various instances; or you may draw upon aspects of this chapter to assist you in your work placement.

It is not possible to relate such areas to specific assignments you may be expected to complete; however good practice requires you to show an awareness of such areas and you may draw upon the information here to inform you of some aspects of some assessments and work life.

In this chapter you will learn:

Types of communication
Dealing with loss and disclosure
Understanding stress and distress

Types of communication

We all communicate and this happens in a number of ways. From birth until death, we express ourselves and, with varying degrees of complexity, engage with others. This section will consider these particular aspects of communication:

- non-verbal communication
- verbal communication
- barriers to communication.

Non-verbal communication

This type of communication relates to all non-language-based interaction. We use a range of skills and processes not only to complement the spoken word, but also to replace the spoken word. For some of our clients, non-verbal communication may be a preferred or necessary main form of interaction. As a worker, you may use a range of non-verbal communication aids; or indeed, you may show more through non-verbal cues than you imagine.

Communication is seen as a general process where we send messages to and receive them from others. This is a surprisingly complex process and is not always successful: for example, intuition may tell you someone is lying, you may be aware that you don't consider someone to be genuine or you may empathise when someone's behaviour leads you to recognise they are stressed. Many of these messages come through non-verbal gestures.

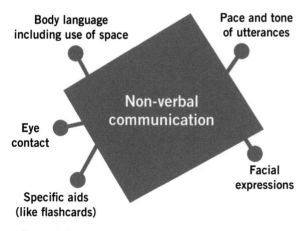

Non-verbal gestures can reveal much.

Facial expression

A facial expression is a huge indicator of mood and sincerity. There is debate about how much social conformity dictates our use of expressions (e.g. smile=happiness) but considering everyday interactions we generally assume certain expressions to mean certain things. The face is often the first point of contact with someone: we may introduce ourselves by looking at a person's face a second before speaking. We may make all sorts of judgements based upon someone's 'looks'. Before even meeting someone, we may see them through a window, and already decide certain things about them by looking at their face.

Activity

Think about your own experiences and people you may have encountered recently. What do their faces and expressions let you know about how they may be feeling? What assumptions may you have made about a person based on their face? Try to make notes of these, following the example below.

Facial expression/look of face	Assumption/impression made
Heavily made-up woman	Vain, self conscious, older
Deep-set wrinkles, skin tone uneven with sunken cheeks	Query – health issues? Sleep deprived? Addiction issues?
Bright eyes, attractive looking, youthful complexion, white even teeth.	Healthy, alluring, confident

While the appearance of someone's face (make-up, hair, skin pallor and such) may be a fleeting facial cue, if you consider the exercise above, the impact of initial impression cannot be underestimated. The saying 'a picture is worth a thousand words' can be apt when considering this form of non-verbal communication.

Some facial expressions seem to be momentary – just movements of eyes. The mouth and forehead can indicate all sorts of emotions and either complement the spoken word or contradict it. Facial expressions may also be intentional or unintentional – when our non-verbal communication matches our verbal communication we can be seen to be congruent. Incongruent communication occurs where there is some misunderstanding or gap between types of communication being used and conveyed.

Consider this

Can you think of a time when your communication was incongruent? Did you say one thing but mean another? Was there a situation where you wanted to appear confident but blushed and felt self-conscious?

The psychologist Fantz, in the 1960s and 1970s, undertook a series of research tasks with infants and concluded that 6-month-old babies seemed to have a fairly complex ability to read and recognise faces and expression. Researchers have also concluded that facial expressions are universal: the expressions for certain emotional states, such as happiness, sadness, surprise, anger, fear and disgust, are the same across cultures.

The power of facial expressions and appearance seems to be something very 'human'. But what happens in situations where the use of facial expressions is limited due to illness or disease, or some other factor?

Consider this

Consider what kinds of illnesses, disabilities, conditions or other influences there may be on a person's facial expressions. Examples may include birth marks, scars or stroke – what else? How might this impact upon an individual's perceptions of relationships and esteem?

In a society that is increasingly dominated by the idea of physical perfection, and when you consider the impact of facial expressions and appearance, the way that someone looks can have a big impact on others' ideas and judgements as well as causing discrimination and bullying.

If you work with someone who has limited non-verbal communication, they may encounter additional barriers in society. They may be misunderstood, ignored or victimised. It is important to examine your own value base and assumptions in all interactions; including those where your initial impression may challenge your value base. The 1998 census estimated that around 400,000 UK residents suffer from a 'scar, blemish or deformity' which severely impedes their quality of life, with public outings being one of the most stressful events identified by people. The UK charity Changing Faces offers a wealth of information and support for people facing challenges because of disfigurement and campaigns for social change.

Pace and tone

We communicate with our voices even when we are not using words; for example, babies are effective communicators and can certainly attract attention without the use of specific language. The expression 'it's not what you say but how you say it' relates to the pace and tone of our utterances.

Activity

Consider the emotions and states listed in the table below. How might each be conveyed through our speech patterns and utterances?

	Voice
Sleepy	
Angry	
Shy	
Sarcastic	
Confident	
Stressed	
Impatient	
Calming	
Frightened	

How does our voice convey these different emotions?

You should be able to recognise that our tone of voice and pace of voice differs under changing circumstances.

There are also a series of utterances which can be used to convey our attentiveness to others – the use of 'ahh', 'ooh' or 'ummm' (particularly in conjunction with facial expressions) can encourage communication. Alternatively, they can convey more negative responses. It is important to use these utterances appropriately and be aware of the subtle, but powerful impact they can have when communicating.

In addition to this it is important to recognise the role of silence in communication. Silence can allow someone space and time to think for a moment before responding, or it can be a powerful tool in asserting authority or attempting to exert power over someone. Failing to allow silence at all may indicate anxiety or stress, or suggest active listening is being neglected. Silence can be both positive and negative.

Body language and posture

Body language refers to all gestures and signs, using your body, incorporated into a communication. This broadly includes the use of recognised signs (like waving or shaking hands), posture and eye contact and how close you stand or sit to others (proximity).

Activity

Imagine it is your first day at college. A room, set out with neatly aligned tables and chairs, is set up. You are one of about twenty people sitting in the room – all chairs (and therefore people) are facing a whiteboard and desk. A person enters the room, walking briskly to the table at the front. They smile warmly towards the class and put a pile of papers down on the table, with a thump! The person turns to the whiteboard and writes up a name. Who do you assume this is?

Now imagine the same person entering the room, quietly closing the door behind them. They do not make direct eye contact with anyone else but move swiftly to the free chair at the side of the room. They place a pile of paper neatly on the desk in front, unpack pens from their case and sit facing forward. Who do you assume this is?

In this scenario you do not have to assume that the person has necessarily dressed differently; simply from the way they have acted and reacted using body language, it is likely that you assume the first example to be the tutor, and the second a fellow student.

In society we have a set of 'signs' which are generally accepted to carry meaning: a wave signifies hello or goodbye, thumbs up may display positivity, a hand held out at length, palm out may mean stop. Also we may use mime gestures inadvertently: if you are in a noisy bar ordering a drink, you may gesture to the bar staff with a wave to indicate you require attention, and mime taking a drink to suggest you are ready to order or point to the drink of your choice. Often, when communicating with children we naturally exaggerate expressions and gestures to add further meaning when language may be limited.

When language skills are limited, gestures and miming can be even more useful.

In Social Care, there may be specific clients who communicate using these methods more readily than by other means.

Consider this

Can you think of a situation where someone you know, or someone who you have worked with, uses gestures to signify a want or need?

Hand gestures, in particular, are frequently used alongside the spoken word to add emphasis or meaning to a communication. Often, we may be unaware of our gestures. Hand gestures during speech emphasise aspects of conversation, and a significant lack of gesture is sometimes associated with deceit, doubt or stress.

Although a lot of body language is not actually universal in its use or meaning, most children are quite easy to 'read' depending on their age and your relationship with them. They may fidget, cover their mouth while talking or fail to look you directly in the eye. In fact, these behaviours, although often masked, are similar for deceitful adults also. It takes us time (albeit a split second) to formulate a lie, rather than immediately tell the truth, and our perception of this detail is amazingly acute. When we lie we also experience, however subtle, a slight rise in stress levels, and our bodies automatically adjust to reduce this stress; again this is something others can often 'read'.

Another area of body language relates to posture. The posture you adopt when communicating can say a good deal about the importance of the communication, the formality or informality around the interaction, and the status of those involved. The posture adopted can be adjusted to assist communication. Postures often indicate the degree of relaxation surrounding an interaction or exchange.

Body language also includes our use of space and zones – often we are forced to be very close to complete strangers, for example on crowded trains, in shops or in public places.

Personal space is like having an invisible bubble around you, and the bubble's size and shape will shift due to a variety of factors. However, close proximity to others can leave some people feeling claustrophobic or uncomfortable. In Social Care, because of the nature of the work involved, we may very much need to 'invade' someone's personal space (even if we don't really know the person, and they don't really know us). Aspects of care work such as personal care, feeding, physical guidance, moving and mobility assistance and medical care can all create very intimate personal space contact. We must be wary and respectful of this.

Factors affecting personal space comfort can include:

- gender
- relationship to others e.g. family member, stranger, professional
- cultural background
- individual personality
- age.

Edward Hall, an American anthropologist, undertook research in the 1960s into personal space and suggested that zones ranged from intimate space of less than 1.5 foot 'bubble', to personal space of about 4 feet with social space extending to around 7 feet.

Some people who use services may use different proximities simply because of their own experiences and feelings, or conditions. If someone is hard of hearing, it may be necessary to position yourself in a way which encourages good eye contact, facial expressions or lip reading. You should be aware of your use of body language to assist communication.

Someone may have physical barriers to overcome in some situations. Using a wheelchair, for example, not only puts the user at a different level, but may also impact upon manoeuvrability. Some physical conditions which limit or inhibit free movement might also impact upon an individual's body language. Conditions like cerebral palsy (a condition which affects movement caused by damage to the brain) often carry symptoms like stiff muscles, spasms or unwanted movements.

Activity

Personal space

Think about yourself in the different situations suggested below and identify if each situation requires close proximity to others on a scale of 1 to 5 (1=very close and 5=not close at all). Then identify which situations leave you feeling awkward and which are not really of concern to you. Again, people differ in their level of contact with others and some of us are more reserved than others – there is no right or wrong.

Scenario	Score 1–5	OK with you?
It is dark outside and you are on the top deck of a bus. The bus is crowded at the back, but you are sitting alone, on the front, window row. The bus stops, you hear someone coming up the stairs and they sit right beside you. They sit between you and the aisle.		
You are out shopping and go into a busy chemist to buy some perfume as a gift. There is a queue at the perfume counter of about five or six people – you join the queue and two or three people filter behind you over the next few minutes – it doesn't take long before you are served.		
As above except: Every single time you move even slightly forward, as people are served, the person right behind you moves too – they move and also inch their bags (on the floor) forward and each time they do this, the bags rest on the back of your ankles.		
You are leaving the supermarket with a full trolley and the automatic exit doors suddenly close on you. Another customer rushes to help, and pulls the doors apart (as they do, the automation kicks in). As they did this, their hand brushed against your shoulder.		
Your best friend has just received some upsetting news. You visit her and give her a big hug – then hold her hand for a few seconds as she dries her tears.		
You are using a public toilet in a café but the lock on the door doesn't work. There is only one toilet, but you'll be quick. Just as you are about to stand up and flush the loo, a stranger barges in, quickly says sorry and leaves the cubicle.		
You are driving along a clear road, keeping to the speed limit, when you notice in your rear view mirror, a car approaching. It seems to be travelling faster than you, but as it gets closer, it slows right down and sits seemingly dangerously close behind you – as if urging you to speed up.		

How do these scenarios make you feel?

When you reflect upon this activity try to be mindful of people who receive care – often their proximity to others can be very much out of their control. If they sought close proximity, like a reassuring hug, it may be deemed as inappropriate by some. Try to think about how their personal space is valued, in comparison to your own. It may also be useful to consider how a baby's personal space is invaded in comparison to an adult's, as they too receive care.

Personal space issues can be heightened by other factors. An example might be that you are familiar with someone and happy to share close proximity with them, until they eat with their mouth open and shower you with crumbs of food. You should also bear in mind the impact of body odour on personal proximity – this may not mean only an unwashed odour, but may also include smoky smells, bad breath or overpowering perfume or aftershave.

Eye contact

A major factor in communication is eye contact: from formidable stares to lack of eye contact altogether, the effect on the overall communication process can be dramatic. Normal eye contact is not usually under the conscious control of the communicator, as becoming aware of eye contact often distorts the natural rhythm or gaze associated with the conversation. There are many influences on eye contact from personality and shyness to gender and status. In general, the more eye contact (even broken eye contact) which takes place between people the greater the level of communication and comfort. The levels of eye contact should, in such circumstances, be reciprocal – that is, one person should not be using eye contact generally more than the other. Although 100 per cent eye contact can seem intimidating and fixed, no eye contact at all may signify lack of interest, power imbalance or deceit.

Consider this

Considering eye contact

Consider, or imagine, a time when you have been in a social situation with a group of three or four companions. Another person is addressing the group but doesn't seem to make any eye contact with you, despite doing so with your acquaintances – how would you or did you feel?

Now consider an extremely stressful event, maybe giving a presentation to an interview panel, or arguing with someone – how did your eye contact change compared with less stressful situations?

Think about a situation where you have become bored with, or distracted from, a lecture or speech. How does your eye contact with the speaker change as your boredom increases? How might the speaker's eye contact encourage your re-engagement?

Others may feel that you are not interested or do not care about what they are saying if you are not aware of eye contact as an indicator of attentiveness. Sometimes, in work situations, you may have limited social time with an individual and this may mean you are completing tasks while chatting. You may be changing bedding as a person sits in a chair before returning to that bed, with your back to them while you hurry through the task.

Consider this

You may be dealing with a group of people in a support capacity; some individuals are louder than others – more demanding of your attention. How can eye contact reassure and include those who are quieter?

Specific aids to assist communication

Good interpersonal skills, a strong value base and self-awareness are some of the strongest skills associated with positive, responsive and accurate communication. However, certain specific tools or skills can further assist people who use services, and others, to overcome barriers to communication. Some of these are more familiar than others.

Something as simple as encouraging an individual to have eye tests and use glasses, can help them to overcome problems. The use of hearing aids may also be an advisable step for some. There are a number of communication aids available, but two of the more specialised ones are Makaton and British Sign Language.

Makaton is a combination of sign, gesture and pictures/images (symbols) which is aimed at assisting communication with those who cannot or do not use speech fully. It is successfully and widely used by those with a cognitive impairment, learning disability, autism or related condition. Unlike more traditional sign language, where facial expressions are considered important, using Makaton requires little face movement. This is an advantage as often people with learning disabilities or cognitive impairments (particularly children) find the rapidly changing human face quite difficult to deal with. First developed in the 1970s, Makaton combines a variety of such tactics to encourage and enhance effective communication. Makaton has developed into an internationally recognised form of communication, used in more than forty countries.

British Sign Language (BSL) was an important influence on the early stages of Makaton development, but it differs from Makaton in its application and skills base. Used mainly by members of the deaf community and their friends, family and associates, British Sign Language uses facial expression, gesture and body language to form an agreed generalised 'script' of communication. This language includes an alphabet and grammar and emphasis, as well as more complex signs.

BSL is the language used by between 50,000 and 70,000 people across the UK. BSL even has regional dialects; a sign used in Scotland may not be the same as one used in England – and it is very distinct from sign language used in other parts of the world, for example, American Sign Language.

Further research

Find out more about Makaton and British Sign Language by visiting their websites:

www.makaton.org

www.british-sign.co.uk

Verbal communication

We have considered some of the non-verbal methods of communication, which can complement what we verbalise or indeed replace entire linguistic-based communication altogether. However, it remains that verbal communication is still a major form of communication; even if it is not the case with your clients, it is likely to remain the main communication method when dealing with your colleagues and other agencies. Verbal communication relates to using language to understand and be understood. We may formally present information in an interview or feedback session, or use skills of persuasion and discussion in a wealth of situations. While many of us use our verbal skills seemingly effectively; there are some pitfalls to communicating in this way. We may:

- talk too much
- talk too quickly
- talk from only our own perspective (rather than that of the listener)
- encounter different dialects or languages which increase misunderstanding
- use jargon or technical terms
- lose our 'thread' and talk off task.

Good verbal communication is usually perceived to be direct, accurate, persuasive, complex and succinct. Instead of saying 'I might do this… a good communicator may say 'I will or won't do this…' By eliminating the element of doubt from communications, the listener will be left with a strong sense of an individual's confidence and meaning. Assertive speaking leaves the impression that the speaker is clear and accurate; for example, we may give a direct answer to a question, but add '… in my opinion' or '… that's only one idea'. Introducing these additional points may be relevant, but an over-reliance upon them can leave listeners sensing the speaker does not value their own contribution. So the words we choose to use can convey a very powerful image to others (even if you are not feeling very assertive, the use of assertive language may give a different impression).

Verbal communication can also mean the written word and, certainly in Social Care, there are numerous notes and reports to be read as well as completed. Writing clearly is important, so that others can read your script as well as writing accurately (stating when something is an opinion rather than a fact). Often, recording information requires a degree of objectivity, and nothing more than is needed should be recorded.

Consider some of the following Care Plan/ communication book extracts. What might you identify as poor or irrelevant or misleading communication?

What could have been written instead without changing the meaning of the message?

What might an Inspector assume about the services based on reading the notes below?

1. The Star Fellowship

Residential Support Service for adults with learning disability

Case notes

Date: 22/08 – I checked on D. in the lounge today he had come from his own flat to the office flat and sat there quietly. He was bored and didn't like the rain, so I gave him a cup of tea. He went back to his flat and has been quiet ever since.

Signed: BN.

Date: 30/08 – Another quiet day for me – I supported W to watch the football as he wanted company and I didn't like to say no so I went here to his house for tea, and the game was rubbish but he seemed to like the result. Has he put a sneaky bet on – I wonder if the backshift will check that?

2. Creation Day Service Medication Check Sheet

Policy: Please sign to agree your administered medication – please note, in all circumstances, a counter signature is required to evidence the correct protocol has been followed and witnessed.

	Date Mon	Date Tues	Date Weds	Date Thurs	Date Fri	Date Sat	Date Sun
Paracetamol 50mg 10am	FMcD	FMcD	DT	DT	DT	MC	MMc
Counter sign	DT	FMcD	MMc	FG			
Franatal Nutrition Drink (250 ml) 21.30pm		H.Mc	H.Mc MC				MC
Counter sign		↓M	↓M	↓M	↓M		

3. Southern Council Advocacy Service

Supervision notes between Ruth McCloy and Solomon McWilliam

Minutes by R. McCloy

Met at 2pm as arranged – Sol a bit late and no agenda brought. Discussed number of referrals, case load, cases closed, training and annual leave requests. Will meet again in 4 weeks – date and time to be set.

What can you learn from these extracts?

Barriers to communication

Many of us generally assume that communication is easy, as it is something we have done all our lives, but significant barriers exist which mean that communication may not be effective as assumed or hoped. Barriers can be broadly categorised under the themes shown in the following spider diagram.

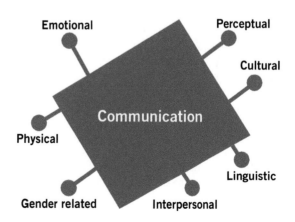

There are many different barriers to effective communication.

Emotional barriers

Emotional barriers may relate to the sender of information (e.g. the speaker) or to the receiver (e.g. the listener). Feeling silly, self-conscious or intimidated may hinder the progress of the communication, or turn it into something is was not meant to be.

Activity

Imagine you are required to introduce yourself to someone: the information to be shared does not change, but how might you react emotionally to the situation or circumstances under which you must communicate? How might this alter the communication process for you? What else might be on your mind? How comfortable would you feel?

Look at the different scenarios below and consider how you might feel.

Different scenarios

Busy, noisy and unfamiliar: you are on a blind date, and the person of your dreams waves hello and comes over to meet you. You are in a restaurant, which has a large dinner party sitting next to your table. They are really enjoying themselves but are obviously having a few drinks too many. They see your blind date approach, assume they know what is going on and start to heckle 'Go on mate'; even worse, they burst into singing 'Love is in the Air' as your date sits down.

Powerful positions: you start your new job today and have been given a 'buddy' to show you around. You meet the staff at reception, the cleaning staff, some of the residents of the homeless unit and finally the Area Manager calls you in to her office to meet you. You enter the office alone.

Emergency situation: you are working as an assistant on a phone line which deals with cold-calls from members of the community who are feeling desperately depressed or alone. It is 3am and you are in a small office with three other workers – it has been a quiet night. Your phone rings and a distraught man, clearly crying, says 'who's this?'.

Disclosure: you are the manager of a small residential unit offering emergency shelter to victims of domestic violence. It is late at night when the front door rattles; outside you see a car speed off, and on the doorstep is a woman carrying a small baby. She is clearly distressed and soaking wet from the rain.

Interview: You are awaiting an interview for an important job and your name gets called to go through to the interview room. You are dressed smartly, have a presentation prepared in your briefcase and enter the room with a confident knock on the door. You walk in, to see three men sitting across from you, separated by a large boardroom table. They all look up, none smile and one beckons you to sit down.

These very general examples should help you to understand that what we have to say is only part of the communication barrier; what can be more alarming to us emotionally is the context we find ourselves in when having to communicate. Our own emotional state, be it anxious, stressed or concerned, will drastically alter our responses and how we perceive the others around us. Our own emotional well-being, our own experiences, life circumstances and personality all impact upon how we feel able to express ourselves. This is the area we will consider next.

Perceptual barriers

How we think about ourselves in relation to others, how we feel on a certain day or how we imagine we should be, all impact upon how we perceive a situation. Freud's defence mechanisms, for example, clearly explore the relationship between our communication versus our perceptions of situations. Even unknowingly, we can use communication to infer or deflect perceived threats. If we have a pessimistic day, we may feel that out perceptions are altered. The glass seems half empty rather than half full, for example.

Often, the people using services who we encounter have poor self-esteem, have been marginalised in some way or have identified communication problems. Their perceptions of communication are likely to be significantly different from another's simply because their lives have been very different.

If you receive Social Care services it is probable that you will receive them, or have received them, over an extended period of time. Your perceptions of self, perceptions of power and perceptions of social acceptability, will all be moulded by that fact.

Case study

Millie

In 1947, at the age of seven, Millie was placed in a psychiatric unit for offensive behaviour. She was described as 'defiant' by her parents, was poor to respond to school teaching and was thought of as 'insolent'. A happy young girl, she loved being outdoors and playing was her favourite pastime. She enjoyed 'rough and tumble' games with the boys and was often in trouble for stealing apples from a neighbour's orchard. She was 'spirited' and 'fanciful' and her parents, who had six other children, were struggling to cope. Millie spent the next 60 years in the same psychiatric hospital: she never married, never had children, or worked in paid employment. She did not have friends outside the hospital, never went out on dates, or kept in touch with her family. She couldn't drive a car, and hadn't 'seen the world'; she could barely write and her education had never been advanced. The furthest Millie had been was to the local town for shopping trips twice a month, and all of her interactions had been with fellow psychiatric patients or staff members.

Now, nearing 70 years of age and still fiercely independent despite it all, Millie secured a supported tenancy in her hometown, with a 24-hour support package.

Her support team were a mixture of men and women, all excited to be part of a brand new service; most were very recently recruited to support Millie and two other 'discharged patients' in the small shared house. Her Key Worker was identified as Catherine, a 22-year-old worker, with previous experience in care.

1. Imagine what Millie's perceptions of the world may be like, in comparison to your own.

2. How might this affect general communications and interactions?

3. Use the following table to assimilate your thoughts and responses, considering the examples as prompts for further thought and discussion.

Millie's perceptions	How might communication be affected
Having spent a virtual lifetime in hospital, with limited opportunities, and knowing a little of the personality she once displayed, how might Millie see herself?	Does she feel like a 70-year-old woman with a lifetime of experience? Will she relate to Catherine as a peer (identifying with her youth) or as a patient, or as an elder?
Millie may be offered opportunities she could only once have dreamed of – extremely enthusiastic staff may be overly keen to make up for Millie's years in an institution.	Enthusiastic, fast-paced communication, offering lots of choices may make Millie feel overwhelmed and defensive, or even hostile.
Millie has usually stayed in a bigger group situation, in a large building with large peaceful grounds. Moving to a residential property with two others is a more intimate environment. Moving to town, her personal space may be more private, but certainly more intense and crowded in certain ways. Her ability to wander will be inhibited and she may find it hard to find peace away from traffic, other houses and other people.	

The example of Millie shows how perceptions can affect communication.

Our perception of any situation is just that – a perception. How we think someone should or could react towards us, or what another person could or does expect of us, can directly impact upon our communication and relationship with them.

Physical barriers

Earlier in the chapter we briefly mentioned some of the physical barriers which may hinder communication, such as particular conditions, illnesses or aids. Physical barriers can often also include very practical issues. For example, is there enough room to communicate well? Are there too many people around? Are rooms too small or too large, too hot or cold? Are telephones plentiful, or computer systems repetitive and slow? All of these issues, and more, can impact upon the work you do and the success or otherwise, of communication.

Given the often sensitive nature of care work, it is important to uphold the values of dignity and respect, and to maintain confidentiality when dealing with situations and information.

Others may see confidentiality as a barrier to effective working: a concerned mother may want to know about her adult daughter; a neighbour concerned about child welfare in the house next door might want to know if social workers know about them; an anonymous caller may ask if a certain person is resident in a unit. The freedom and accessibility of information may be a barrier which requires to be upheld. In some circumstances, however, inter-agency working may become a barrier if communication is slow, partial, or unnecessarily withheld, or inaccurate. Indeed, some of the major inquiries into social service failure (consider Victoria Climbié or Baby P to name only two) identify poor communication as a major flaw in protection cases.

According to the law on data protection, files, records and information cannot be too easy to access, as this would lessen the security of the information. The barrier of locking cabinets, protecting computer files and keeping paperwork in the office are necessary–time must be allowed for this good practice within the working day.

Often, the physical surroundings Social Care workers operate in are outside their control: much work is done in people's homes, for example, or in very busy and demanding group situations where staff may be 'on hand' throughout their shift. It is important then, to reflect upon both the necessary and the unnecessary barriers to communication which are unique to Social Care and particular workplaces.

Cultural barriers

Often, when we mention 'culture' the first and only examples of differences which people think of may be race and ethnicity. Of course, this is an important area affecting communication; we must be mindful of traditions and customs which could make others feel uncomfortable or disrespected in some way. However, culture can relate to other issues like background, gender and even class – these issues can combine with issues of race and ethnicity, and other factors to build complex barriers.

Cultural differences may also mean language barriers. In most local authority areas interpreters for anticipated languages (like Polish, Chinese or Indian languages) should be available; in addition, leaflets, forms and other written communication can often be translated into languages as needed, and are often readily available.

Although it is not expected that you should become familiar with a range of customs pertaining to particular cultures, good communication shows a degree of sensitivity to others and a degree of reflection on the part of a communicator. Often discomfort or awkwardness during a communication is less about someone's awareness of culture, and more about issues of personal comfort, which may happen to incorporate aspects of culture. Using personal touch, for example, may be inappropriate not only culturally, but also with relation to gender differences, age and power/status. Facial expressions may not seem to match a worker's expectations (use of eye contact, smiles or gestures) but awareness of this may inform the worker of any underlying issues, as well as any preferences for communication this suggests. Earlier in this chapter we learned that research has suggested universal expressions for several emotional states; however, the openness with which someone shows these facial expressions may be culturally sensitive.

Activity

Consider the following examples of social interactions and consider what impact cultural differences may have or what cultural issues may be 'at play'. How could some of the barriers you identify be lessened? (Whether these are language differences, gender differences or difference in perceptions of class and status.)

Going to the doctor

Hamid is 30 years of age and has been forced to go to the doctor after suffering from painful indigestion; he hates going to the doctor and hopes the doctor doesn't decide to do any tests today. When in the doctor's office, Hamid finds himself faced with an unknown young woman – she explains that she is a locum doctor for the day. Uninspired, Hamid really wishes he hadn't bothered to come and is shocked when, after he describes his symptoms, the doctor tells him to stop eating spicy food. She didn't ask about his diet at all or about any other aspects of his health.

Teen angst

You are working a backshift in a children's residential service; your client group range from 12 to 15 years old and are a mixture of boys and girls. One of the residents is late home, beyond her agreed curfew time. You wait for the night shift staff to come on, so you can then go and look for her. Before the next shift arrives, she appears at the door; her clothes are torn, and she smells of alcohol. She seems to be under the influence of alcohol and you fear that she may have been attacked – but she seems to be in fits of laughter and won't calm down or stop singing and dancing as you let her in.

Conclusion

This section of reading has introduced a variety of ideas and concepts relating to interpersonal skills around verbal and non-verbal communication. You should be in a better position to be aware of the complex methods used when communicating, in a range of situations and be able to reflect upon your own skills, and how this impacts on others. You may also be able to identify communication needs you wish to explore in both your professional and personal life.

Dealing with loss and disclosure

This section of the chapter on interpersonal skills focuses in on the emotional and challenging area of loss and disclosure. Again, it does not necessarily relate to specific assessments (although it does closely tie in with optional units and some SVQ elements) but it should give you a basic understanding of some of the skills and ideas relating to such areas, which will inform your practice and may even provoke further enquiry.

Dealing with loss

Loss is a difficult area to deal with; it implies emotional situations and will be something that most, if not all of us, experience during our lifetime. Loss and grief are linked – grief is an emotional response to an actual or anticipated loss or detachment from something of value. Loss triggers grief; but what may be a relatively trivial loss for one person may signify something much more intense and urgent in another. The most devastating loss can be the death of someone close; however, loss may also relate to changes in life circumstances including the loss of a job, the loss of status, temporary loss or deteriorating health, loss of possessions or loss of skills. In its broadest sense, loss is often about change; whether this is anticipated or unexpected and we all deal differently with different situations.

Theories and models of loss

There are various theories and models of loss; some of which we will consider in this section.

One of the most influential writers in the area of loss was Elisabeth Kübler-Ross, who wrote *On Death and Dying* over forty years ago. Her work remains influential today. While Kübler-Ross based much of her work on grief and dying, her insight and model of grief can be useful in a broader context. She describes grief as a process covering five stages, and devised these in the context of someone progressing through terminal illness. The five stages are:

- denial
- anger
- bargaining
- depression
- acceptance.

In the first stage of denial, she claims that many individuals cannot grasp their new reality; they believe 'this isn't real' or 'this cannot be happening' and often this temporary phase can be disorientating for individuals. A failure to accept a terminal diagnosis may leave the person looking for solutions and trying a variety of therapies in a bid to beat their illness. When denial cannot continue, and the reality of a loss sets in, anger may be experienced; misplaced anger can affect others and there may be a need to blame others for what has happened and find fault.

The bargaining stage involves the individual becoming aware of their own mortality and the reality of death as part of life's process. It is here that even non-religious individuals may converse with a 'higher power'; asking for more time or to be allowed to live to see certain events: 'please let me live to see my children go to school', for example. Stage four involves the individual experiencing depression; they may seem to disengage from the world around them, distance themselves from loved ones or things and be difficult to engage with. It is not appropriate to cheer people up in this stage, but more useful to allow the next stage to evolve from this state. Acceptance is the final stage, where the individual comes to terms with the inevitability of their mortality and adjusts accordingly.

Later these stages were recognised as being useful for a variety of grief and loss situations.

Look at the following case studies. Each relates to a different type of loss. Can you apply any of the stages outlined by Kübler-Ross to them?

Case study

The terminal illness

You are working with a young woman called Dianne. She has been diagnosed with late stage, terminal cancer and has undergone extensive medical therapies to prolong her life. There is now nothing more that can be done, and she and her family have decided to face the future with minimum medical intervention. As she has a 6-year-old son, with autism, she has support from the local social work department. Dianne is a single parent, so there is also involvement with other family members to look at her son's future needs. It is not expected that Dianne will survive longer than two or three months at most and her loved ones are aware of this.

Dianne was home from hospital for some weeks, but became very unwell and has recently moved to a specialist hospice in her home town. She is very weak, is heavily medicated, but relies upon daily visits from her sister and her son to break the monotony (as she calls it).

Before moving to the hospice, Dianne had her house decorated as she felt it needed a clean. She used to say that she wanted to enjoy next summer in the garden, so spent quite a lot of her savings on landscaping it. She also invested in a newer car to take her son out for his birthday next autumn – she had planned a trip to a seaside resort.

When Dianne moved to the hospice, her sister discovered she had been using the Internet to contact psychics and spiritualists and had run up some debts on credit cards using these websites. Records suggest she was in contact with various phone and chat lines almost daily; all related to some aspect of spiritualism.

Today Dianne's sister and son arrived, as usual, at teatime to visit. Dianne is awake but doesn't even make eye contact with the visitors; after they stay for about twenty minutes she screams at her sister and yells 'Go away... get out! You have always got it easy.' Obviously, this outburst is very hurtful to both her sister and her son and they leave in tears. Not long after they go, Dianne is ashamed and saddened by her own behaviour and she sleeps poorly that night.

Case study

Working life

Martin has been an accountant in a leading local retailer for almost his entire working life; he is now in his late 50s and his family have grown up. His wife works part-time in teaching and he has been looking forward to retirement and seeing the world. He had been quite ambitious when he was younger, but felt loyal to the company after it supported him years ago when his first son was born. Complications during the birth had meant his wife was unwell after the labour, and his employers allowed him compassionate leave. He always got on well with the 'girls' in the office and in many ways the job has suited his steady personality. However, at the end of the working week, he was called to the manager's office and given redundancy papers. He is no longer required to work or serve notice and will receive payment in lieu of his duties. This has totally shocked him. That night, after the meeting with his boss, he went home but didn't say anything about it to his wife – that was three weeks ago, and now he feels he can hardly approach the subject.

Martin still follows his long-established morning routine, wearing a suit and packing a briefcase with papers from his desk at home. He walks the same route to work, but instead of going in, he just keeps on walking. He has become very distracted and feels empty inside; and feels there must be some mistake. He tried to phone work, but was told no one could speak to him, and he has heard through the 'grapevine' that many of his fellow workers were also laid off. Martin feels very old and rather silly; but also very bitter when he thinks about the years of long hours and loyalty he has shown the company. What kind of future will he have now? What will he tell his wife? Such questions leave him feeling exhausted and anxious and he has started drinking in pubs at lunchtime; it kills time and gets him out among people.

Case study

Memories

Robert is 57 years of age and has been rather forgetful lately. A retired musician, he has had a very successful career in radio and has brought up, together with his adored wife, two daughters who are now married and live away. He is not sure how long he has felt this sensation of fear and loneliness, but it seems to be getting worse and is very hard to describe. He recognises that he forgets words more often than he used to but thinks it might just be age. However, the other day something frightening happened to him. He went in the car to the local garage – a trip he has done many, many times – and his wife phoned him to ask where he was, but he didn't know; he had got lost and didn't recognise his surroundings. His wife asked him about different landmarks and he made his way back home safely, but both he and his wife were shaken and frightened by the incident. He has been to the hospital for tests a few times, but cannot really understand what they are for. Yesterday, his wife went out to lunch with her friends and he found a booklet under the bed – it was called 'Prepare for Alzheimer's – a real guide'. He simply broke down in tears. Could this be the reason for his feelings? Surely he cannot be ill – he is still so young and has so much to look forward to!

There are other theories relating to loss and grief, in addition to the work of Elisabeth Kübler-Ross and another approach to loss can be understood in terms of the work of Worden. Worden (1991) identified four tasks of grieving; he recognised that grieving facilitated change and growth in an individual, claiming that grief is a process and not a state of mind. The four stages are identified as:

- accepting the reality of the loss
- working through the pain and grief
- adjusting to the new environment (without the person lost)
- emotionally adapting and moving on.

You may notice an apparent similarity between the work of Kübler-Ross and Worden, but Worden was focused more on the loss of a person and he went on to recognise that grieving can become 'complicated mourning'. This is where an individual gets 'stuck' at a stage and reacts negatively to the mourning process so as to cause some concern. Factors which might increase the risk of complicated mourning include:

- the history of the mourner (have there been significant repeated losses over a period of time?)
- how the lost person died – was it particularly vicious or unusual and was social support available?
- or whether the personality of the bereaved person may influence transition from one stage to another.

To consider the nature of loss, you may find it useful to think about Bowlby's Attachment Theory (page 82) which recognises that humans form attachments and that the breaking of these attachments can affect, potentially in the longer term, our safety and security needs and, in some instances our behaviours and personalities. From the time we are born we learn attachment and rely upon these early relationships to serve as building blocks for future encounters; loss and grief, and the processes of recovery, also have a bearing on an individual's development and personality, even in the short term.

Loss and grief affect us all.

Further research has also identified different general reactions to more difficult types of loss; suicide survivors, for example, have been identified as having relatively untypical grief responses (in comparison to other situations); parents who lose a child suddenly are particularly recognised as experiencing intense loss reactions (Lang and Gottlieb, 1993) and some research has suggested that adolescents have limited capacity to express their emotional response to loss and display behaviour rather than explain feelings (Kandt, 1994). What may be usual for one person is not the same for another, and although models of mourning or processes of grief attempt to fix our expectations of stages, they do not suggest that each stage will be experienced equally or similarly by different individuals.

Using models or theories which relate to loss and grief may help you to see the process in identifiable chunks; it may also help you to rationalise the process to remove, or control, your own anxiety from such situations. However, interpersonal skills at such times become extremely important – unresolved or 'mis-managed' grief can have serious consequences and self-awareness on the part of a worker, together with a high degree of sensitivity are needed.

Consider this

Reflect upon your own life and consider things you may have lost. Some examples may be clear to you, but think more broadly and identify a range of losses and grieving you may have experienced. What were some of the emotions you experienced?

Dealing with disclosure

Disclosure usually relates to someone divulging information to you, which is of a personal or sensitive nature. The issue of disclosing information runs alongside confidentiality agreements and is a complex and sensitive issue.

More common instances of disclosure surround abuse and protection issues; in particular abuse situations involving youngsters or other particularly vulnerable individuals. In terms of sexual abuse, these types of disclosures are thought to be amongst the most delayed and difficult for younger people. Elliot and Briere (1994) found that 75 per cent of children did not disclose within a year of the first abuse incident, and 18 per cent waited more than five years to disclose.

As is the case with some of the areas discussed in the previous section on grief and loss, a disclosure can be seen as more of a process than an event. Disclosure may not involve the complete retelling of a story and it may not only be communicated verbally. Behaviours may alert you to suspect an individual is experiencing something worrying or unwanted and physical signs may highlight further concerns. Disclosure may be seen to be accidental or purposeful.

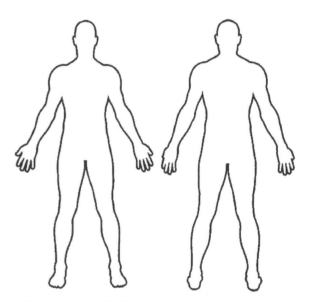

A body map is useful for recording physical signs of abuse.

A body map may often be used to record any injuries or marks of physical signs of abuse. Often, depending upon the age, ability and lifestyle of an individual, certain injuries or marks are entirely appropriate. In many instances, triggers of suspicion are aroused when physical signs complement emotional signs of abuse; coupled with verbal disclosure, the information gathered can significantly indicate abuse.

Evaluative responses

However, disclosure is not just about abuse but is concerned with the relaying of difficult, complex and sensitive information. An individual may disclose very personal details about their life history or circumstances to a worker, despite not knowing them well. The reasons for this may be varied but, as care workers, often our involvement with individuals is at a time of crisis, when communication is key. Caplan (1989) believes that crisis makes us more susceptible to other's suggestions and communications; with this in mind, it is important to fully utilise interpersonal skills so as not to damage relationships or hinder the client. Carl Rogers (1961) in his book *On Becoming a Person* identifies the exchange of emotional issues to be significant in testing interpersonal skills. He hypothesises that people make evaluative assumptions about another's statements or communications, based on their own position. He asserts that we '… form an evaluation (to any emotional statement) … from our own point of view'.

Example: the lesson

After leaving a lecture one student turns to another and says 'That was really boring, I didn't enjoy that at all!' The response from the other student is most likely going to involve either approval or disapproval of the initial statement: 'I know, I didn't like it much either.' Or: 'What do you mean?! I found it interesting… and I'm going to read more about it.'

The team meeting

'So staff' says the shift supervisor, 'I think it would be a really good idea to change the Key Worker system and can I ask you to think about ways to do that?'

'I don't think so…' says Gordon, a member of the team. 'I am really settled supporting David and he has come on really well.'

The supervision session

Staff member, hopeful of promotion, suggests, 'Can I be considered then for forthcoming counselling training? I think it will help me to understand my client more fully and I have always wanted to do that kind of work.'

But the supervisor responds, 'I don't think so! I doubt it has anything to do with your work at all; what are you doing with your time?'

Considering these basic examples, how do you think the same messages might be conveyed avoiding evaluative statements? How might avoiding evaluative statements lead to more trusted, comfortable and respectful dialogue?

Open and closed questions

It is important to be aware of the type of responses you use, just as you need to have awareness of the use of open and closed questions. To distinguish between open and closed questions, consider some examples. Closed questions tend to elicit (or require) a very limited response; perhaps even just a 'yes' or 'no' answer. There is little room to add opinion or contextualise the information given.

A form asking for factual details would be an example of the use of closed questions: name, address, date of birth and such, require factual answers. Attempting to elicit more complex responses, using closed questioning, is not particularly effective. Emotional questions like 'Are you happy?' or 'Is there something wrong?' are closed in the sense that they require little effort to answer – in either example a simple 'yes' or 'no' response essentially ends the thread of conversation. Closed questions are very good at clearly identifying information needed and, when time is short, they have a role to play – either in verbal or written communication.

Open questions are generally more inviting. The response is likely to be more time-consuming and more complex – perhaps even involving reflection and thought from participants. On an application form, you may be asked to write about 'What interests do you have outside work?', and this is very much more open than other sets of application questions (as suggested above.) Often open questions begin with what, why, describe or how and require responses that are more likely to include personal information. If you are seeking effective communication, or building a relationship with another person, then open questions may be rather more satisfying than closed ones.

Activity

Question types

Look at the list of questions below and try to identify which are open questions and which are closed questions.

1. How are you feeling today?
2. Did you sleep well?
3. Are you hungry?
4. What are your favourite foods?
5. Did you enjoy your shopping trip?
6. How was the shopping trip – can you show me what you got?
7. Tell me about your work experience; what were the highlights for you?
8. Did you enjoy your job?

Being aware of different types of questions allows you to enter into discussions equipped to communicate appropriately. However, questioning is only part of the process. Another part of the process is listening; and this requires awareness of how to listen and how to best translate the 'messages' another person sends.

Active and reflective listening

Listening is not always the same as hearing!

Active listening, as the name suggests, is beyond the often passive listening we engage in. To actively listen, we must be aware of a variety of signals given off by others. Body language, tone of voice, gestures and posture, to name but a few, can all complement or contradict the spoken word.

One of the more effective ways of engaging and encouraging responses from another person is to use reflective listening. This requires the listener to reflect back their understanding of the context of previous communication at appropriate points. This is a way of 'checking back' that the message has been understood correctly. The reflection should not be parrot-like repetition, but an encouraging and brief check. Some phrases you might use to reflect back and engage another person could include:

- 'So, let me get this right… you are unhappy with the service because…'

- 'In other words, you felt really angry…'

- 'What you are saying is that you really want to cook tonight…'

Not only does this process assist communication, it also helps to calm any emotional situations by effectively slowing the exchange and allowing the listener to share control of the process. As a rapport-building tool, reflective listening is a powerful aid to encouraging and valuing another person's dialogue and opinion. This is, when considering Social Care values, one of the most dignified and respectful attitudes workers can display: namely that they are interested and concerned about what a person who uses services has to say. Reflective listening encourages emotional understanding between communicators. Feelings of empathy (rather than false concern or disinterest), understanding viewpoints (not always feeling forced to agree, but always respecting) and building a rapport all encourage further emotional trust. In building this trust, a client will have their security needs better met, and hopefully feel comfortable sharing information and disclosure with the reflective listener.

Understanding stress and distress

Stress and distress are separate things; they are often linked but not necessarily intrinsically so. Stress can be viewed as a biological term, which describes a response to a real or perceived threat, either emotionally or physically.

Distress implies suffering or discomfort as a result of stress. Distress can be seen as a consequence of failure to manage stress appropriately. If stress is felt in response to an imagined threat, distress can cause symptoms which are as real as symptoms caused by actual threats.

Continuing to use a biological analogy in the first instance, the body may experience stress when running – our level of distress will rely upon factors associated with the stressor (source of stress – running). Such factors will include our age, weight, fitness, the running conditions, the clothes we are wearing, the terrain we are traversing and so on.

Although the example above uses a physical activity to illustrate the difference between stress and distress, the same exercise could be repeated involving a range of situations.

This section of the chapter aims to help you to understand the impact and triggers for stress and to recognise how distress and stress can be managed or confronted – with a view to minimising the negative impact they have. Being aware of stress in yourself will enable you to reflect and analyse your own coping strategies; this in turn will enhance the communications you have with others and help stress to be contained.

Stress

Stress is a word which is often used, and stress is a condition often experienced; just as distress is often felt. Stress is not always bad: a life without stress would be very tame, may not be stimulating and is unlikely to present you with opportunities to learn and grow. Obstacles which are overcome often become learning opportunities; however, too much stress and distress can become unhealthy and unpleasant.

Hans Selye was a pioneer in the study of stress. He worked in the 1930s and beyond, often using animals to test his hypothesis. One of the more well-known contributions made by Selye was his General Adaptation Syndrome (GAS) or Stress Syndrome. Through researching patients recovering from injury and disease, as well as carrying out animal experiments, Selye recognised a pattern to symptoms which seemed to be consistent despite varying illnesses. He recognised that this may be due to a common feature experienced by patients, namely the commonality of being unwell. Selye attributed certain symptoms to being the body's response to illness in itself – namely, the body's response to the stress of being ill. This collection of problems and symptoms he called General Adaptation Syndrome. Selye was able to study the responses to illness which people encountered, and identify universal stages encountered by all stressed individuals, as shown in the table below.

Stage	Response to stress
Stage one	Alarm reaction or 'fight or flight' response. This stage encompasses a wide range of physical reactions to a stressor – pupils dilate, heart rate increase, breathing increases, blood flow changes causing skin tone changes, adrenalin is released and so on. This is a very excited phase and the body cannot sustain this level of hormonal or system activity indefinitely.
Stage two	Because of the physical limitations of the 'fight or flight' response, the body builds up resistance to the stress felt. This can often mask the extent to which the body is forced to cope with stress in an ongoing way – an individual might not feel adrenalin-fuelled and 'ready to go' but they may feel flushed or have heart palpitations or have trouble unwinding. In themselves, such symptoms may be inconsistent or transient however.
Stage three	If the stress is ongoing, the body becomes exhausted with it and physical consequences occur. Some noted consequences of this stage can be serious and include: – gastro-intestinal ulcers – high blood pressure – headaches and digestive problems. With complications including: – impaired immunity to infection (frequent coughs and colds) – heart damage and even heart attacks – exhaustion.

Selye's three-stage stress model.

The GAS model helps us to understand the relationship between stress and illness and research suggests there is indeed a link between stress and illness, supporting Selye's three-stage model. While Selye did include animal studies in his research, humans have the added capacity of complex thought – that is, they are able to think about the things that stress them. This may assist individuals to rationalise and combat stress, but in some cases it can also increase our perceptions of stress; this creates stressful thoughts, which then lead to stress reactions.

Acute and chronic stress

Stress is usually associated with a negative event or perception. If someone says 'I feel stressed' we generally sympathise, but, as mentioned earlier, stress is also a motivator and an inevitable condition in certain situations. Acute stress is a rapid, short-lived response to a situation and our bodies experience hormonal changes which make us more alert. Acute periods of stress are generally seen to be relatively harmless to an otherwise healthy individual. An example of this might be seeing a wasp fly towards you when you hate wasps – your heart rate might increase, you may breathe more heavily and your palms might feel clammy; but this is short-lived. Humans have the capacity to adapt to stress, and this forms the basis of many treatments aimed at combating phobias (irrational fears). An example of this may be if you hated spiders and sought help to overcome this irrational fear (irrational because *most* spiders, especially in Scotland, are not harmful or dangerous). A therapist might expose you to spiders (pictures, spiders in a bottle, spiders in a tank and then loose, roaming spiders) repeatedly until your stress reaction becomes so weak, you cease to fear them.

Chronic stress, on the other hand, is seen to be more physically (and psychologically) damaging. Chronic stress is longer-term stress over a period of time, and can often involve feelings that the stressor is pervading all aspects of your life. You may spend days or weeks worrying about forthcoming exams, for example, and your body will respond differently to this type of stress (GAS model for example).

Transactional analysis

Selye's model is not the only way researchers have tried to explain stress. Although this model proposed universal stress reactions and generalised about the consequences of such situations, it does not fully explore more complex aspects of human emotions and physiological responses. Another example of a stress model goes by the name of transactional model. This model looks at the interaction of two things: perceived demands and perceived ability to cope with those demands. The interplay of these two factors gives rise to various stress levels in individuals.

Environment and demands ➡ ➡ **Perceived ability to cope = Outcome**

The transactional model considers perceived demands and the ability to cope with these demands.

Activity

Consider the statements in the following table about potentially stressful situations and consider which situations you would find stressful. Rate them on the scale suggested. Ask some other people to consider the list also – is it the same as your list? Why do you think there are differences in answers? How many of the situations are actually threatening in reality?

Statement	Min. stress					Max. stress
	0	1	2	3	4	5
You see a spider run across the floor, heading for your bare feet.						
You are in an unfamiliar city and have to drive through the centre of town, through lots of one-way systems and through complicated roundabouts.						
You have an important meeting to attend and leave the house twenty minutes later than planned – you cannot be late, but the traffic is terrible.						
You are arguing with your young children, it is late and past their bedtimes but they keep getting up and coming downstairs ignoring your requests for them to stay in bed. You have your assignment to complete for tomorrow and cannot get peace to study.						
You come home from a busy day at work and your partner hasn't done any housework or started cooking the evening meal – again!						
You expected your flatmate home an hour ago. They haven't yet appeared and haven't been in touch – this is very unusual.						
You are alone at home and it is dark outside; you close the living room curtains to see a solitary, shaded figure standing in front of your house – apparently staring in.						
You buy some new shoes and pay with a £50 note. You are given change for a £20 note but the shop assistant refuses to believe you. The shop is crowded and you feel you are not being listened to.						
You go for a doctor's appointment and you have to take off your clothes for an examination.						
You are walking near your home when you hear a car brake suddenly and see that a dog has been hit by the car – it is limping away from the scene, clearly injured and the car drives off.						

How stressful would you find these situations?

Lazarus and Folkman (1984) developed transactional analysis as a model involving two appraisals of an event or situation.

1. Primary appraisal is your belief that an event is stressful. Is it threatening?
2. Secondary appraisal involves an individual's perceived ability to cope with the threat.

In completing the exercise above, you should try to be clear about approaching the task thinking about the primary and secondary appraisals – and then working out if, overall, you perceive an event to be threatening at all.

Environment

Common stressors for most people relate to the environment they find themselves in – noise, heat and overcrowding all have the potential to create stress for individuals and affect behaviour.

Animal studies, involving rats, have shown that an expanding population living in increasingly densely populated conditions precipitates an increase in antisocial behaviour. A study in the 1960s by Calhoun showed that rats, in such circumstances, increased violent behaviour – killing, sexually assaulting and eating each other. More recent reports have suggested an increase in crime in densely populated human communities and Evans (2006) studied children's development in overcrowded situations (like residential care) and concluded that 10–12-year-olds significantly withdraw from social situations if overcrowding is a factor.

We seem to live in a noisy world – televisions, mobile phones, computers, cars, planes, traffic all impact upon the immediate environment we occupy. Noise can often become stressful in social, but particularly work, situations. But a sudden unexpected noise is alarming to us;

consider our environment 400 years ago – no electricity, no cars or planes, smaller settlements and so on. A sudden noise would have been quite startling to most and trigger a stress response.

Thinking about Selye's model, we have adapted to our environment so that most noises now fail to trigger stress reactions – we know that a boom of music from a car is not the same as a roar of a predator. We hear shouting in crowds and do not assume a threat is present.

Some research is also discovering the impact of sounds that we cannot hear – frequencies which fill our atmosphere but are inaudible in normal conditions, such as the buzz of pylons and electricity conduits. Certainly, most of us require a degree of peace to think and become uncomfortable if we cannot concentrate in a certain environment.

Other sources of stress

Other common sources of stress include personal relationships, lack of close friends, life events like marriage, divorce and bereavement, excessive workload and individual personalities (are you a 'born worrier'?). Some situations we can control, some we cannot; some we may find exciting and stimulating, others we might find intolerable and stressful. The important aspect of stress to remember is that it can be decreased through a range of stress management techniques.

Meditation can help to reduce stress levels.

Stress management – reducing distress

When things seem out of control – your family are demanding, bills need to be paid and you don't have enough money, deadlines loom for work-related tasks, you are not listened to, there is never enough time – your stress levels may rise. The first step, in trying to take control of your stress, is to realise you are in control of your life. By empowering yourself, you can take positive steps to a happier and healthier lifestyle.

Taking control of your life can be represented in analysing and recognising various aspects of your situation and responses to the world:

- physiologically (health, relaxation and diet)
- cognitively (understanding thought processes and coping strategies)
- socially (seeking support and social time)
- emotionally (recognising defence mechanisms and emotional maturity).

Our responses to stressful situations, ironically, also tend to be negative habits – we may eat more or less and neglect our diet. We may smoke more. We may drink more alcohol. We may use more drugs, for example if headaches are caused by stress, we may increase pain relief medication. Our immune system may be impaired, leaving us physically at a low ebb. We may be restless and our sleep may suffer, increasing our tiredness and we may use more tea or coffee or caffeine products. Often, by using such methods to 'cope' we tackle the symptoms of stress in the short term. We do not tackle the actual source of stress, and physiologically (physically) we suffer – quite often doing ourselves more harm than good.

Considering the transactional model of stress discussed earlier, the key to effective stress reduction lies in our perceptions. If we can alter or manage our perceptions of stress and our perceptions of how we deal with a situation (I *can* do it, rather than I *cannot* do it) then we can intrinsically alter the pattern of our distress.

Relaxation and exercise

Using relaxation techniques forces our bodies to enter a physically relaxed state. Stress increases certain physical reactions – muscles tense, the respiratory system works harder, blood pressure goes up. By taking part in controlled breathing, yoga or meditation, we immediately reduce theses physical symptoms and lower our heart rate, reduce our blood pressure, relax our muscles. Considering Selye's model, this may break the damage of ongoing stress which our bodies can experience in response to ongoing negative external influences.

Exercise is also seen to be an important part of our holistic health. Not only does it require us to take a break from routine tasks (a walk takes us away from noisy televisions and crowded houses or open books), it also increases our muscle tone and flexibility, improves muscle tension and posture problems and increases our cardiovascular health.

Cognitive tools

Cognitively we can take time to reflect upon our priorities in life and to consider the actual position we are in. Is it time to start to say 'no' to some requests? What's the worst that can happen? Will I still be worried about this next year? These thought tools can help us to contextualise our current situation and gain a more realistic perspective. Even thinking back to a time we were worried about something in the past may help us to realise that the world didn't end – or we got through it all despite feeling worried.

Using a stress journal as a tool to specifically identify our stress triggers may help us to understand the particular patterns or symptoms which indicate that stress is building. Taking action sooner rather than later may empower you to feel in control of life and stress. Professional counsellors can help with specific problems, but spending a little time reflecting by yourself can be a quicker, and less expensive, option.

In the busy world in which we live, where roles and expectations dictate many of our actions, taking social time-out is a therapeutic stress reliever (as long as a lot of alcohol is not involved!). Friends are often of great help in stressful situations; being able to share your troubles and talk (even over the phone) with someone you trust can minimise feelings of isolation and desperation. This informal counselling allows us to express ourselves, gain another's insight and opinion and may also be an opportunity to share practical advice.

Tache et al (1979) found that cancer was more common within socially isolated groups like divorcees and widows. Research into personality and ill health has also found that personality types who cannot express themselves openly, who 'bottle it up' and do not share their emotions are more likely to have cancer. A study into heart disease (Meyer Friedman and Ray Rosenman, 1974) followed a number of men over an eight-year period and found that 257 men developed coronary heart disease during this time. When they undertook personality tests, 70 per cent were found to have a Type A personality (characterised by ambition, competitiveness, hard work, impatience and quick temper). Reaching out to others, it would seem, and being sociable is good for our health!

Being emotionally aware of ourselves may also encourage a sense of control – emotional maturity allows us to tackle issues with a strong sense of personal identity and confidence. An emotionally mature person takes responsibility for their own life and well-being. Things cease to be the fault of others; ownership is taken by the individual. Symptoms of emotional *immaturity* can include the following.

- Explosive behaviour and temper outbursts – you receive results for an assessment which are below your expectation and immediately storm out of the room or burst into tears. You fail to read the feedback fully or engage with the tutor – your immediate emotional response, over which you seem to have no control, utterly dictates your behaviour.
- Egocentricity or self-centredness – an emotionally immature person may seek seemingly constant attention in relation only to their needs. Associated with low self-esteem, egocentric individuals are not simply 'selfish' people but see most situations only from their perspective. They may seek reassurance and acceptance in a demanding fashion – constantly taking, rather than giving. The self-centred person requires gratification and positive feedback: 'Do I look good in this?' or 'Did they like me do you think?' Or they may show negative self-image awaiting a contrary response from others, 'I look so fat today' anticipating others to challenge this negative statement.
- Gratification drives – an emotionally immature individual may seek immediate emotional gratification. This may show itself in requiring an immediate response to a question, or through expecting to be heard above others. It may reveal itself in an unwillingness to accept faults in themselves and a tendency to blame other people for their insecurities due to 'lack of care' or ability: 'If I had been shown how to do this properly, I wouldn't be in this mess.'

Emotional maturity is not an end-point but a maturation process. It is not necessarily related to physical age or experience. In many ways, we are as mature as we allow ourselves to be.

Defence mechanisms

Something which we may not be aware of immediately is our emotional response to threats in terms of defence mechanisms. Freud's personality theory considered the ways in which we may alter our perception of reality to protect ourselves from the most painful aspects of our being. Defence mechanisms certainly help us to cope with stressful events, but they do not necessarily allow us to mature and they can become habitual ways of coping with reality. Sigmund Freud, and later his daughter Anna, identified several defence mechanisms including:

- **displacement** – unconsciously moving your emotional responses from one situation to another – moving the emotional response away from the person causing it, to an innocent third party; an example might be that you are feeling angry because your partner has been rude to you but assuming your friend has been unfriendly and expressing your anger towards him instead
- **denial** – simply refusing to acknowledge the reality of a situation – one example might be related to our earlier discussion on Kübler-Ross' four tasks of grieving, where a dying person may genuinely believe they will recover
- **projection** – similar to displacement, this involves moving your unacceptable feelings on to someone else. You may wake up in a

very grumpy mood, go downstairs and snap at your partner 'What's up with you then?' without provocation.

Often, according to psychoanalytical theories, the key to recognising many of the common defence mechanisms is to undergo particular treatments like hypnotherapy, dream analysis or extended counselling to unlock the unconscious.

By combining even some of these suggested methods to tackle stress – a walk every day, a chat to a friend over coffee once a week, writing a diary to study events of the day – stress could be tackled. By learning or trying healthier ways to deal with stress, you improve your own well-being, but are also likely to respond to situations more positively – so making you more effective in professional and social situations.

Conclusion

This chapter has considered a range of interpersonal and related matters. As earlier stated, it does not necessarily 'fit' within the larger academic HNC framework as some 'subjects' do; but it acts as a guide to practice, communication and well-being with issues which will underpin many of your interactions and knowledge. Elements of values, psychology and counselling are explored practically here – to underpin your academic knowledge and SVQ experience in a meaningful way. By being aware of some of the issues discussed in this chapter, you should be able to reflect and practise more effectively and research areas you feel are more relevant to you, as you see fit. This means you should feel more able to present yourself confidently as a holistic practitioner and recognise some of the complexities of interpersonal interactions in the context of teams in workplaces, classroom situations and client interactions.

Check Your Progress

1. What types of communication do we use?
2. What factors can affect our use of personal space?
3. What are some of the barriers to effective communication?
4. In what ways might verbal communication be misleading?
5. What is meant by the term disclosure and how might disclosure occur?
6. What are some of the theoretical models available to help us understand the nature and process of grief?
7. What is positive and what is negative about stress?
8. What positive steps can be taken to manage and reduce stress?

References

Burnard, P. (1999), *Practical Counselling and Helping*, Routledge, London

Caplan, G. (1989), *Population-Orientated Psychiatry*, Human Sciences Press: New York

Cardwell, M., Flanagan, C. and Williamson, M. (2007), *Higher Psychology* Nelson Thornes Publishing: Cheltenham

Coulshed, V. (1998), *Social Work Practice*, Macmillan press, Basingstoke

Elliott, D.M. and Briere, J., (1994) "Forensic sexual abuse and evaluations for older children: Disclosure and symptomatology" in *Behavioural Science and the Law* vol. 12 (261-277)

Friedman, M. and Rosenman, R. (1974), *Type A Behaviour and Your Heart*, Knopf: New York

Kandt, V.E. (1994), "Adolescent Bereavement: Turning a fragile time into acceptance and peace" in *School Counselor*, vol. 41 (p. 205-211)

Lang, A. and Gottlieb, L. (1993), "Parental grief reactions and mental intimacy following infant death" in *Death Studies* vol. 17 (233-255)

Lazarus, R. and Folkman, S. (1984), *Stress, Appraisal and Coping*, Springer Publishing Company: New York

Palmer, S. and Cooper, C. (2007), *How to Deal with Stress*, Kogan Page: London

Rogers, C. (1961), *The Therapists View of Psychotherapy*, Constable: London

Trevithick, P. (2000), *Social Work Skills: A practice handbook*, Open University Press: Buckingham

Worden, J.W. (1991), *Grief Counselling and Grief Therapy: A handbook for the mental health practitioner 2nd edition*, Springer Publishing: New York

Websites

www.adhd.com.au/grief.htm
www.bodylanguageexpert.co.uk/
www.stress.org.uk

Topic 3

Profiles of people who use services and themed directory

Units covered:
DH44 34
DH3R 35
DH42 34
DH3V 34
DH41 34

Introduction

The purpose of this chapter is to enable you to work sensitively and effectively to provide support to some of the most vulnerable individuals and groups within society. Fundamentally it will give you a general understanding of the rights of individuals and vulnerable groups, as well as dealing with issues of equality and diversity. It will offer an explanation for some of the behaviours displayed by vulnerable people who use services. It also provides information on the role of the worker in understanding and supporting people to reach their full potential and access the goods and services that will allow them to do this – just the same as you and I.

One of the main difficulties in working with people is that there is no specific instruction booklet that fits all; no one has written a manual with the answers to all the difficulties and problems you may face when working with individuals with such diverse needs. Social Care workers have to rely on their skills, qualities, and knowledge gained from experience, to help them overcome the anxieties associated with working in Social Care. To do this the effective worker will continue to strive to become a reflective practitioner. Of course there are standards to which you must work and all care organisations must provide training for all staff. This chapter will increase your knowledge and understanding of profiles of people who use services to aid your journey through the whole HNC course or some units for professional development.

In this chapter you will learn:

Working in partnership with people who have a learning disability
Working with autism
Understanding dementia
Mental health issues in a care setting
Working with problematic substance abuse
Youth and community justice
Supporting children and families

Working in partnership with people who have a learning disability

If you work in care with people with a learning disability, whether as a paid worker, student on placement, in a voluntary capacity or in a carer role, such as supporting a family member, you may wish to undertake the unit 'Working in Partnership with People who have a Learning Disability'. So what is a learning disability and how is this defined? The Scottish Executive Document (2000) *The Same As You* suggests the following definition about learning disability and it reflects the current understanding in Scotland of people who have additional support needs due to a learning disability that they have.

People with learning disabilities have a significant lifelong, condition that started before adulthood, that affected their development and which means that they need help to:

- understand information
- learn skills and
- cope independently.

So who are these people whose development has been affected and why do they need support? It is estimated that twenty out of every 1,000 people in Scotland have a mild or moderate learning disability, while three or four people in every 1,000 have profound or multiple disability (*The Same as You*). In order to understand better the current circumstances of people with a learning disability it is necessary to look briefly at the history of learning disability. This can help us start to understand the position of some individuals in the present day and how the legacy of care may have impacted on their lives. Not everyone who you may work with will have spent time in an **institution** but some people did and it is important that you can start to understand what some of their upbringing was like and how this may have an effect on their current lives.

Key term

Institution an establishment for care or education.

A short history of learning disability

In recent times there has been much legislation to improve the lives of people with a learning disability, including the following:

- Adult Support and Protection Scotland Act 2007
- Mental Health Care and Treatment (Scotland) Act 2003
- Regulation of Care Scotland Act 2001
- Adults with Incapacity (Scotland) Act 2000
- Human Rights Act 1998
- Disability Discrimination Act 1995 and its amendments in 2003
- Children (Scotland) Act 1995
- NHS and Community Care Act 1990

and to some extent:

- The Race Relations Act 1976
- The Sex Discrimination Act 1975
- The Social Work Scotland Act 1968.

But in earlier times, people with a learning disability had few rights if any and were often marginalised and oppressed within society. They were originally 'classified' as 'imbeciles, moral defectives, feeble-minded persons and idiots' (Mental Deficiency Act 1913). They were often institutionalised in large colonies from a very young age where it was believed they would be 'protected' and looked after; but often this was for the 'protection' of society – an 'out of sight out of mind' attitude. The Eugenic movement was also quite prominent within Britain and the western world at this time and this also impacted on and influenced the lives of individuals within these large institutions. The Eugenic Education Society founded in 1907 campaigned for better protection of society from the genetic influence of people who had a learning disability. The Eugenic movement argued that only the fittest nations made up of healthy and fit individuals should complete the world. They argued that people who had a disability or impairment, or mental health problem or some other perceived social failing, should not have children since their children would be the same and society would be swamped.

Institutionalisation

Legislation such as the Mental Health Act 1959, the Chronically Sick and Disabled Person's Act 1970, the Education (Mentally Handicapped Children) Scotland Act 1974 and the Education (Scotland) Act (1980 and amended in 1981) paved the way for caring for oppressed groups within society and began to promote rights. However, although laws mean change it does not happen overnight. **Institutionalisation** and organisational structures that were mechanistic – if not in theory but certainly in practice – impacted on the lives of the individuals who lived within the institutions and took time to change.

The living conditions within some of these institutions or 'colonies' left much to be desired. 'Patients' shared communal clothing and had few if any personal possessions. They slept in what were known as Nightingale wards that offered little privacy and the bathrooms often had rows of open toilet cubicles, with two baths to the same room being commonplace. These conditions were not just current in the 1930s but continued until far more recently than that

– possibly within the current lifespan of some people only now aged in their 30s and 40s. These Nightingale wards often accommodated up to twenty people and this was where they lived their whole life, although there was a communal day room. Staff to patient ratio was not high. Routines were important and patients quickly learned to follow the rules.

If you have undertaken or are doing the Psychology for Social Care unit, you might have started to understand why some of the people who you support behave the way they do. Considering the idea of institutionalisation will reinforce this thinking. Perhaps your client eats their food very quickly and drinks their tea really hot and takes it with milk and sugar? This would be part of their behaviour and the routine that may have been learned while they lived in an institution. If you did not eat your food or drink your tea quickly enough someone else would. Remember there was a low staff-to-patient ratio and nearly always there was a tea trolley with large teapots – with the tea already 'milked and sugared'. Choice did not exist.

Note: If you cannot visualise what an institution is like, or how it might impact on a person's life, watch the film 'The Magdalene Sisters' based on a book on the Magdalene laundries, produced by Peter Mullen. This will give you some idea of what life could have been like for people who use services. The Magdalene laundries did exist!

What happens if people become institutionalised? They do not expect privacy, do not get choice, are not treated as individuals where their dignity is promoted and are not allowed to take risk. A condition called 'learned helplessness' develops.

This is a psychological condition in which a human being has learned to believe that he/she is helpless in a particular situation. They have come to believe that they have no control over their situation and that whatever they do is futile. As a result, the person will stay passive in the face of an unpleasant, harmful or damaging situation, even when they do actually have the power to change their circumstances. 'Learned

Institutionalisation has damaging effects.

helplessness theory' is the view that behaviour results from an individual's perceived lack of control over the events in their life, which may result from prior exposure to (actually or apparently) uncontrollable negative events.

Perhaps you can see that some of the behaviour of people who use services may be based on 'learned helplessness'. But could they do more for themselves if you give them the opportunity? Are they rigid in their patterns of behaviour? Behaviourists believe that all behaviour is learned. So if behaviour is learned then it can be unlearned.

In about thirty years time the legacy and effects of institutionalisation will hopefully be eradicated, as the generation of people who have been empowered by the NHS and Community Act 1990 and Regulation of Care Act 2001 grows up and benefits from **normalisation**.

'Some features of institutionalisation are still present in the 21st century. People who use services fit in with the routine, service and staffing rotas of the organisation. Choice for people who use services is still limited both in terms of what is available and what is provided. There is still no real commitment to person-centred care. Basic needs are met but the quality of care can still be poor. Services are organised for the benefit of staff not the person who uses services.'
(Adapted from Maclean and Maclean (2006) *A Handbook of Theory for Social Care,* page 135)

Advocacy and empowerment

Advocacy has its origins in the legal field. Here advocacy is the term applied to the work lawyers do in court and elsewhere in representing their clients. Advocacy in Social Care can involve speaking, writing and acting on behalf of others. It can also be through people themselves and is about people finding/developing ways to speak for themselves in order to protect their rights and to advance their own interests. It involves training and group support to help people learn skills and gain emotional strength to advocate for themselves. It is about improving the status of people who use services and not just about improving services.

In lay terms **empowerment** means giving power back, where it rightly belongs, to people who use services. Remember that some individuals who have been institutionalised, or have learned 'learned helplessness' through over-protection, or lack of involvement in planning or decision making in their own lives for whatever reason, often believe 'the worker' to be all powerful. They often believe that the worker knows what is best for them and due to this will never voice their own views. To give power back to a person who uses services (a human right) is not only humbling but also good practice and involves **social inclusion** and advocacy.

Person-centred planning

One of the ways to ensure that people who use services do not become marginalised, but have the same opportunities and access to services within the community as everyone else, is through the use of **Person-centred planning**.

Person-centred planning is about an application of values into practice. It aims to expand the power that people have to choose life conditions and experiences that make sense for them. Person-centred planning begins when people decide to listen carefully and in ways that can strengthen the voices of clients who have been or are at risk of being silenced. Planning alone does not change people's lives but it provides a forum for creative problem solving. However, this will only happen if people work together in a sustained and careful way. Person-centred planning can only come from respect for the dignity and completeness of the person who uses services.

Rights

Rights can include moral rights, equal rights and human rights. Everyone is entitled to all these rights but not everyone has had access to them in the past, or even now has full access to them today. Although legislation has been put in place to try to ensure that everyone has the same rights and access to services and resources, this does not always happen. Institutional care and its effects have left a shocking legacy, not only on those unfortunate individuals who were confined to care in the large institutions but also to a generation of the 'general population' who have grown up in ignorance and fear about people with learning disability.

Working with autism

If you work in a care setting with people who have **autism** you may wish to undertake this unit as part of a professional development programme or, if you are undertaking the HNC in Social Care, your centre may well have included this unit as one of the option units.

Within this section of the chapter you will gain information and knowledge that will assist you in identifying and, going some way towards understanding:

- the nature of autism
- the triad of impairments
- an awareness of intervention strategies.

Definitions and causes

So what is autism? The National Autistic Society describe it as a lifelong developmental disability that affects the way a person communicates and relates to others. It is also described as one of the conditions on a spectrum i.e. the Autistic Spectrum Disorder (ASD) which also includes Asperger's syndrome. People with autism have difficulties with everyday interaction. It is called a spectrum because, while all people with autism share areas of difficulty, their specific condition will affect them in very different ways.

Over the last twenty to thirty years there have been many theories on the complexity and nature of people with an Autistic Spectrum Disorder; some individuals are able to live an 'ordinary' seemingly 'everyday' life while others will require 24-hour support for the whole of their lives. It is important to note at this point that not everyone with an ASD has a learning disability. Some may have a mild to severe learning disability and others none at all, although they may have dyslexia. Children with autism often lack imaginative play and can rarely create a play situation using objects around them. They will often play the same game the same way over and over again and watch the same DVD over and over again.

The cause of autism is unknown; however research suggests that genetics may be involved. There is also some evidence to suggest that the condition may be linked to environmental factors, such as pollution, poisoning or infection during pregnancy. The MMR injection was considered a link although the National Autistic Society has stated that there is no scientific evidence to support this claim. There is, according to the Society, some evidence to suggest that there is no single cause and what has been evidenced is that it is not caused by emotional deprivation or by the way a person is brought up – nor is it the fault of the individual. What is also clear is that a child with autism will become an adult with autism. At present therefore there is no cure; however there are a range of interventions which people may find helpful.

The National Autistic Society reports that there are over half a million people in the UK with autism, which accounts for one in a hundred people.

All people with an Autistic Spectrum Disorder have difficulties in three key areas, known as the triad of impairments.

Triad of impairments

These key areas are:
- difficulty with social communication
- difficulty with social interaction
- difficulty with social imagination and creativity.

Activity

Individually or in groups research each of the above key areas of difficulty and then compare your answers with the text below.

Social communication

For people with an ASD, body language can appear as foreign as if someone was speaking a foreign language – they have the ability to hear but not read the signs that people communicate with their body. They therefore find it very difficult to read facial expression or understand what is being expressed through use of tone of voice or sarcasm or wit. Many have a very literal meaning of language so always say exactly what they mean; others may not speak at all or have very limited speech although it is thought that they do understand what is being said if this is without inflection or relying too heavily on tone and non-verbal language.

However, it is apparent that everyone with an ASD uses the language they have in limited and unusual ways, e.g. the content is often repeated over and over again, and even adults who are more able have a tendency to monologue about their own interests and preferences at length. Less able individuals do not actually converse with others. They may ask or answer questions, state facts or make their views known but they cannot involve themselves in social everyday chat.

Social interaction

Once again we have to be clear in emphasising that the abnormalities of social behaviour which occur in people with ASD are quite varied. Wing (1996) explains it like this.

> ### Wing's four types of autism-related social behaviour
> - The aloof group – who behave as though other people do not exist.
> - The passive group – who are not completely cut off from others. They accept social approaches from others but do not initiate interaction.
> - The active but odd group – make active approaches to other people but do so in a peculiar fashion to make demands of others or to go on and on about their own concerns.
> - The overly formal, stilted group – who are highly able older adolescents or adults who are excessively polite and formal and cope well by sticking rigidly to the rules of social interaction.

Remember socialising does not come easily to many of us and we have to learn how to do it. People with autism have difficulty in recognising and understanding emotions and feelings expressed by others and in expressing their own; this can make it more difficult for them to fit in. They may appear insensitive to others, to appear to behave strangely or inappropriately and insensitively. Because of this, people with an ASD find it difficult to form friendships; some may want to interact with others and form friendships but are unsure of how to go about it as they do not understand the unwritten rules of social interaction. Many prefer to be on their own.

Social imagination and creativity

Social imagination allows us to understand and predict other people's behaviour, make sense of abstract ideas and to imagine situations outside our normal daily routine.

> ### Activity
> Close your eyes for three minutes and imagine that you are on a desert island.
>
> Open your eyes and write down or draw a picture of yourself on that island.
>
> What are you doing? What colour is the sky?
>
> Look round the room and make something useful or playful out of the items that come to hand. (This can be done in the classroom or at home.)

Both of these activities should help you to show empathy to those in your care who have an ASD and are unable to do what you just did and get enjoyment out of it.

Difficulties with social imagination and creativity can make it difficult for individuals to understand and interpret other people's feelings, thoughts and actions, to predict what may or could happen next in a situation or cope in new or unfamiliar situations. For many, a strict routine is very important to them. They also have no understanding of the concept of danger and cannot prepare for change because they do not understand the need for it nor plan for the future as they cannot imagine what that is.

This is not to say that those with ASD lack imagination; there are many who are accomplished artists and musicians. Mozart and Beethoven are thought to have had an ASD as did Vincent Van Gogh, L.S. Lowry and Andy Warhol.

Parents may find that their child:
- resists physical contact
- avoids or makes poor eye contact
- is detached in their own little world
- prefers to be alone – plays on the periphery of it all
- is difficult to befriend
- lacks basic social skills
- has little or no interest in other people
- is unaware of danger.

Intervention strategies

It has been estimated that only 15 per cent of sufferers from ASD are able to leave home and function totally independently. Therefore the majority of autistic adults need care.

The triad of impairments are used to diagnose ASD and all elements have to be present; this being the case it is important in your work with individuals that this triad of impairments are addressed in the development of a Care Plan. In doing so, all care values must be evidenced as well as notice taken of the National Care Standards and all legislation relevant to the individual with whom you are working. One of the most important things in working with people with ASD is that there is a diagnosis and that a Care Plan is formulated using Person-centred planning as mentioned before.

Given the complex nature of ASD, intervention strategies may include:

- de-escalation
- medication
- distraction and diversion
- using boardmaker, picture exchange communication systems (PECS), symbols
- reflexology, massage
- aromatherapy, sensory room.

Understanding dementia

You may wish to study this unit if you care for someone who has **dementia**, in a paid or voluntary capacity or as a family member. Every person with dementia is different and the illness can bring many problems, but not everyone will be affected in the same way. As you read through this section of this chapter, hopefully it will give you a greater understanding about dementia and how to deal with the effects of the illness on an individual.

There are 700,000 people living with dementia in the UK today – a number that is forecast to double within a generation. In addition to this, 25 million people or 42 per cent of the UK population are affected by dementia through knowing a close friend or family member with the condition and 60–67,000 of these people live in Scotland. This number is expected to rise to between 102,000 and 114,000 by 2031.

One of the most important things about working with someone who is suffering from confusion or memory loss is to get a proper diagnosis initially, as many conditions and illnesses can cause forgetfulness. Not everyone who has memory loss has dementia. Grief, stress, over/under medication, thyroid, diabetes, infection of any sort, constipation, high/low blood pressure, heart disease, dehydration, lack of food, some cancers – these are just a few of the conditions/illnesses that can cause confusion or memory loss. Often the condition goes undiagnosed for several years when the symptoms are mild and it can be hard to make a firm diagnosis in the early stages.

Types of dementia

Alzheimer's disease

Alzheimer's disease is the most common of the dementias and is diagnosed by excluding all other causes. Confirmation of the diagnosis is possible only after death at a post mortem examination by identifying the plaques and tangles in the brain that characterise this disease. The disease was first diagnosed in 1906 by Dr Alois Alzheimer in Germany. It is a progressive illness where the symptoms gradually get worse. There is no known cure, although certain medications have been identified that inhibit the progress of the illness – particularly if it is diagnosed in the mild or moderate stage. No single factor has been identified as the cause.

Is there a genetic link? The World Health Organization has undertaken research which indicates that a history of dementia in a first-degree relative (parent, sibling) increases chances of developing the illness by between two and five times. But as it is a relatively rare illness in people under 80 years old, your chances of developing dementia would not be until you were very old. There are a few families where Alzheimer's is inherited as a dominant gene, so the chances of their members developing it are one in two. But the number of these families can be counted on the fingers of one hand within the western world.

An exception to this tenuous genetic link is in the incidence of Alzheimer's developing in individuals who have Down's syndrome. Nearly all people with Down's syndrome develop, by the time they reach their thirties, the amyloid plaques and neurofibrillary tangles, typical of the brain changes in Alzheimer's. At the same time they develop an Alzheimer's type dementia (Smith, T. (2004), page 8).

Vascular dementia

The second most common type of dementia is vascular dementia including multi-infarct dementia. In these types of dementia the blood supply to the brain is damaged in some way. Causes can include: high blood pressure, heart problems, high cholesterol and diabetes, lack of physical activity, smoking, increased intake of alcohol. There is a narrowing of the arteries, slowing down or blocking blood supply to vital areas of the brain. In multi-infarct dementia tiny strokes cut off the blood supply to small areas of the brain and the brain cell dies. These strokes can be so small that no one notices them at the time. The individual may deteriorate quite suddenly and then suffer no further deterioration until the next 'stroke'. So the illness progresses in a 'step like' fashion.

Dementia with Lewy bodies

Dementia with Lewy bodies is the third most common cause of dementia. It is similar to Alzheimer's disease in that it is caused by the death of nerve cells in the brain. Lewy bodies is the name given to the abnormal collection of protein in the nerve cells of the brain. Some of the individuals diagnosed with Lewy bodies disease also develop the signs and symptoms of Parkinson disease. This, like Alzheimer's, is a progressive disease and although difficult to diagnose it causes spatial disorientation.

Frontal lobe dementia

A rarer type of dementia is frontal lobe dementia, including Pick's disease, which damages the frontal lobe and/or the temporal parts of the brain. These areas are responsible for behaviour, emotional responses and language skills. The individual may be more likely to do things at the wrong time or in the wrong place, have difficulty in finding the right words or behave inappropriately. In the early stages memory is still intact but the personality and behaviour of the person changes. About one in five cases of frontal lobe dementia is inherited and it often starts at a younger age than Alzheimer's.

Although Alzheimer's disease is more common in people aged over eighty there have been some occasions when individuals in their twenties have developed the disease. However, there are other dementias more associated with this age group. A small number of people with the HIV virus that causes AIDS develop dementia as a result of a direct effect of the virus on the brain, or infections or tumours that develop after the weakening of the immune system that is caused by AIDS. **Creutzfeldt Jakob Disease (CJD)** the form of dementia that has been linked to infected beef is extremely rare, occurring in about one in a million people in the UK. This link to eating infected beef has only been made in the form of CJD that affects young people – no such link has been found in the most usual form of CJD, which occurs in late middle age, progresses rapidly and causes death within about a year. CJD is associated with abnormal forms of protein within an individual.

Huntington's disease is a rare dementia that occurs in parallel with problems controlling body movements and usually begins in the thirties and forties. An individual can have this illness for a long time, in some cases twenty-five years.

Management

For all of the above dementias there is no cure but, as previously mentioned, there are some drugs and medications that can slow down the progression of some of the illnesses. There is no room in this chapter for the debate on what some may say is the 'postcode lottery' of medical treatment.

The following types of dementia are the only ones where progression can be halted. In some cases this means an individual changing their lifestyle.

- Head injuries can cause dementia until the pressure on the brain is removed.
- Dementia caused by alcohol abuse (often known as Korsakoff's syndrome) is statistically increasing. It is caused by a lack of vitamin B1 which is needed for the brain. Unlike other dementias there is potential for partial or full recovery if people change their lifestyles and stop drinking.

If you check the medical literature you will find that there are several more diagnosed types of dementia all linked to brain degeneration; but the management of these illnesses remains the same as the management of every form of dementia.

Person-centred care

As you have been reading through this chapter you will have already come across references to Person-centred planning and Person-centred care; this way of working is not unique to only one client group but should be used with each client group with whom you work. Person-centred planning and Person-centred care is good practice that promotes the rights of individuals as laid down by The Regulation of Care Act 2001 and the National Care Standards (check back to the chapters on Social Policy for Care Practice or Social Care Theory for Practice).

'Person-centred care' involves putting the individual at the centre of the work. This concept of care has been developed since the 1970s when the 'Medical Model of Care' was introduced.

The social model of care

The starting point of the medical model was the 'ideal body' in looks, physique and health. Remember what you have already read about the Eugenics movement. From a medical model point of view any individual with an impairment, disability or mental health issue was a deviation from the 'normal' and needed to be changed or treated. The worker was seen as the 'expert' and the person with the disability or impairment or mental health issue was the 'problem' and needed to be 'cured or corrected'. Can you link this to Sociology for Social Care Practice, i.e. Functionalism? The 'Medical Model of Care' created a form of labelling as it saw the condition first and not the individual.

The Social Model of Care strived to change this perception of disability/illness. What was 'normal' was questioned and the concept of 'Diversity' was embraced: a person is impaired by society and not the other way about. This model of care believes that each of us is a unique human being and that it is the environment which disables an individual. The effect of the environment on an individual is compounded by a person's illness, condition or disability being viewed negatively by society. The social model works to counter the negative stigma associated with the labels applied to people. The social model of care is based on the ethos that it is essential not to reduce someone's identity to a label.

Legislation

The Adults with Incapacity Act 2000 is concerned to strive for a balance between an individual's rights and the protection required for that person if necessary. Where possible it should take account of the present and past wishes of the individual – so far as they can be ascertained by any means of communication. Sometimes other pieces of legislation, such as the Data Protection Act 1998 and The Regulation of Care Act 2001, can take precedence – especially in relation to 'safety' aspects – particularly where there is no 'Power of Attorney' or Guardianship in place. Power of Attorney can be set up by an individual when they are still able to manage their own affairs, on the basis that they can still manage for themselves but, if something untoward should happen to them, or there is a vast degeneration in their condition then Power of Attorney, if in place, can be activated within a short timescale should the need arise.

Communication

Communication is central to a truly Person-centred approach to the care of individuals with dementia. Most people who have just had a diagnosis will still have intact communication skills. However, good communication skills by the carer are essential at this point, particularly the skill of listening.

People who have dementia, particularly in the mild and moderate stages, have good days and bad days. That is why the skill of listening attentively and having attending behaviour is so important. Individuals in the later stages of dementia also have good days and bad days, or maybe they might have good mornings or afternoons. Good listening skills and observational skills are so important in being aware of the changes in an individual. Patience is paramount when working with an individual with dementia, as is paraphrasing to ensure you follow the instructions of your client. When the individual's capacity for instruction is constrained because of their illness, it would be hoped that through Person-centred planning and care the needs of the individual have been previously identified and incorporated into their Person-centred plan.

Memory aids and pictorial aids are useful tools as the disease progresses, as can be a 'Life Story Book' if already developed. Although an individual may lose the ability to communicate verbally, other forms of communication can be used involving the senses. Familiar smells, music – including singing – and touch are all important in the care of someone with dementia. Person-centred planning should continue to the end of life and should be more than just meeting their basic needs.

Environment and design

Many people working with individuals with dementia will have given little thought to the design of buildings such as day centres, care homes or sheltered housing. It is not part of our training to understand the effect of the built environment on an individual, but the environment can drastically help or hinder the individual with dementia. If a building has steps and stairs then the person with poor mobility is disadvantaged. The same applies to cognitive impairment. Unfamiliar buildings cause confusion and disability. If individuals can find their way around a building they will be less disadvantaged.

Identical carpets and colour schemes are confusing, particularly for someone with dementia. How often when you park your car in a large multi-storey car park do you look for landmarks that will remind you where your car is when you return? Homes should be laid out with visual landmarks that make it easy for people to find their way about.

There is now a general consensus on dementia design and many authors have made lists of principles which can be applied to buildings and features which are more applicable but cannot cover everything. An amended example from

Judd et al (1998) is as follows.

> **Design should:**
> - compensate for impairments
> - maximise independence
> - enhance self-esteem and confidence
> - demonstrate care for staff
> - be orientating and understandable
> - reinforce personal identity
> - welcome relatives and the local community
> - allow the control of stimuli.

There is also a list of good design features.

> **Good design features for people with dementia will include:**
> - small size
> - familiar, domestic and homely in style
> - plenty of scope for ordinary activities (unit kitchens, washing lines, garden sheds)
> - unobtrusive concern for safety
> - different rooms for different functions
> - age-appropriate furniture and fittings
> - safe outside space
> - single room big enough for lots of personal belongings
> - good signage and multiple cues where possible (e.g. sight, smell and sound)
> - use of objects rather than colour for orientation
> - enhancement of visual access
> - controlled stimuli, especially noise.

This may seem very straightforward but is not always easy to put into practice. Carers should be aware that the physical environment may need to be modified as an individual's dementia progresses.

Gardens are really important and can be used for a range of activities. There is increasing evidence that physical exercise improves cognitive function. They can also be peaceful places.

Use of technology

In this technological age there are opportunities to improve the quality of life for an individual with dementia and promote their safety and dignity. For example there can be reminder devices that ask people to check for keys or to lock their doors, pagers linked to computers, alarms on phones to remind an individual to take tablets. It is also possible to make personal DVDs about an individual's life and there is technology to adapt videos and cinematic film onto DVDs.

Smoke alarms, carbon monoxide detectors, sensor pads, motion detectors and alarms on doors and key safes have been in operation for years, but there are now also devices that turn off cookers if they have been left on. Induction cookers have under-used potential, for example, they don't turn on if a pot is empty. There are also temperature-controlled buildings, that adjust the heating as the weather changes, and compensatory devices that unplug baths if the water reaches a certain level.

Although the ethics behind Global Positioning Systems and surveillance are open to debate (and the feeling of 'Big Brother watching you'), for the carers of an individual with dementia these devices can be of great comfort as they know that if the person gets lost and strays outside they can still be located.

Because of the type of illness that dementia is, and the way in which it progresses and affects the life of the individual, it is essential that their rights are maintained wherever possible. Carers have to find the balance of maintaining an individual's rights as laid out in the National Care Standards and at the same time promoting their safety.

Mental health issues in a care setting

This unit is designed to enable candidates to develop their knowledge and understanding of mental health issues. It is intended for students working with or on placement with individuals with mental health issues in any care setting.

This section of the chapter is designed to introduce students to the current thinking about people who are experiencing mental health issues.

What is a 'mental health issue'?

It can vary with the individual and with the type of 'issue' experienced. One way of looking at it is expressed by Friedli:

'Mental health influences how we think and feel about ourselves and others, as well as how we interpret events.

It affects our capacity to learn, to communicate and to form, sustain and end relationships. It also influences our ability to cope with change, transition and life events, such as having a baby, moving house, or experiencing bereavement.'

(Friedli, L. 2004)

Another approach might be to simply state that mental health is affected by some 'issues' (like unwelcome thoughts or difficult feelings) in the same way that physical health is affected by a chest infection or a broken leg.

People with mental health issues might have a significant, lifelong condition that started before adulthood, that affected their development and which means that they might need long-term care; or they might experience a complete dislocation from the reality of their lives which only lasts for a short period of time.

Conditions where people lose touch with the reality of their own lives are termed *psychosis*. Conditions which come into this category are *schizophrenia* and *bi-polar disorder* (sometimes called manic depression).

On the other hand the individual might experience a *neurosis* which might involve some episodes, or longer periods of their lives,

of psychological discomfort such as anxiety or depression. This may leave them knowing that there are feelings and/or thoughts which disrupt their lives and prevent them from living the kind of life that they want – feelings which they can feel powerless to change.

Scottish government statistics would suggest that at any time one in four of the adult population will be experiencing some form of mental health problem.

There are a variety of ways of looking at mental health issues:

- the medical model understands that there is a biological foundation to the symptom
- the moral model is perceived as a behavioural modification approach to mental health problems
- current Social Care theory identifies the individual as the disadvantaged person who uses services and central to all interventions and support.

Legislation

People who experience severe mental health issues, which prevent them from making decisions about their lives, are governed by legislation which protects their rights and choices. This legislation includes:

- The Mental Health Care and Treatment (Scotland) Act 2003
- The Regulation of Care Scotland Act 2001
- The Adults with Incapacity Scotland Act 2000
- Human Rights Act 1998
- Disability Discrimination Act 1995 and its amendments in 2003
- NHS and Community Care Act 1990
- The Race Relations Act 1976
- Sex Discrimination Act 1975
- Social Work Scotland Act 1968.

These days, it is rare for people to be admitted to hospital for mental illness. Indeed when we look at the statistics, of one in four of the population experiencing mental health problems, then we see that this means that there will be 250 out of every 1000 adults in this category. Out of those 250 only about **six** will be admitted to hospital (based on figures from Goldberg and Huxley, 1992).

People experiencing a **neurosis** have many of those feelings.

However, the difference for people in this condition is that the feelings are more intense, last longer and have a much more profound effect on the individual's capacity to live life the way that they would want to. The feelings can have a mild effect on things like work or college performance; alternatively, relationships and the ability to deal with everyday things like paying bills or buying groceries might be impaired. Or it might be that the person suffering from these feelings can be so debilitated that they are unable to work or form personal relationships or deal with essential daily tasks like personal hygiene.

Key policies and strategies

There are certain key policies and strategies that currently influence mental health care. These include the following:

- The National Programme for Improving Mental Health and Well-being
- The 'Choose Life' strategy
- Scottish Health at Work (SHAW) programme
- Doing Well by People with Depression (CCI, programme)
- Breathing Space
- National Resource Centre for Ethnic Minority Health
- The 'see me, not the illness' campaign
- The Scottish Centre for Healthy Working Lives
- Mental Health in the Workplace Training Programme (MHiW)
- Scotland's Mental Health First Aid.

Care and support

There is both professional and voluntary care and support for those with mental health problems.

There are many different professionals who can help the individual with mental health problems and these include: General Practitioners, psychiatrists, clinical psychologists, nurses in psychiatric hospitals, community psychiatric nurses (CPNs), occupational therapists, social workers, psychotherapists, counsellors and befrienders.

Many of the workers/professionals who you have identified will work within one or more of the organisations listed below:

- The National Health Service
- The National Schizophrenia Fellowship
- MIND
- Huntington's Society
- Richmond Fellowship
- Mental Health Associations
- Local housing associations
- Advocacy services.

Case study

Grace

Grace was recently diagnosed with obsessive-compulsive disorder (OCD), and she has experienced obsessive thoughts and the need to perform ritualistic behaviours for as long as she can remember. Before being diagnosed with OCD, she was bewildered by her own behaviour: 'knew it was irrational,' she explains, 'and I thought I was crazy.'

When Grace begins to obsess about a given thought, it dominates her mind to the exclusion of all other thoughts. For example, if her husband doesn't feel like talking Grace will expend enormous mental effort considering the possible cause and remedy. And she will have great difficulty in coping with the day-to-day activities that she would normally do.

An obsessive thought may also intrude without an obvious trigger, at such times, the thought usually centres around one of several painful events in her early life, or the guilt that she feels when she thinks about how her behaviour is affecting her family, which she will then replay continually. She will be doing fine, perhaps getting on with chores around the house or talking to her husband or a friend, and then, suddenly, thoughts come into her mind and she can't get rid of them. To cope with these obsessive thoughts, Grace sometimes performs ritualistic behaviours, such as excessive cleaning or vacuuming, which offers some degree of relief.

Grace finds that her symptoms become more pronounced when she is under stress or having a busy day. Grace explains that her compulsive behaviours are motivated by a 'little voice' that puts doubt in her mind, driving her to perform and repeat some act a fixed number of times.

For example, she may need to check that she has locked the front door three, six, or nine times. Furthermore, giving in to one compulsion may trigger a series of additional compulsions – checking that the windows are locked, that the iron is unplugged, that the cat has food – rituals which themselves must be repeated a fixed number of times.

Grace's husband has a heart condition and she knows that her obsessive behaviours can generate feelings of anger and frustration in him. This makes her feel even more guilty and stressed and in turn increases the likelihood of obsessive thinking dominating her day, which increases the stress on her husband and family and so the cycle continues.

It is not unusual for a series of compulsive rituals to occupy more than an hour and a half of her time. And if this happens before going to bed or during the night her behaviour has a detrimental effect on her family. She doesn't get any rest and neither do they. 'Sometimes,' she explains, 'it can be very hard just to get out of a room, or get to bed and stay there.'

Grace meets regularly with a psychiatrist, and she is now taking medication which she thinks helps but she finds herself sometimes obsessing about side effects and feels the need to constantly check her own pulse and temperature.

All of this has left her exhausted and feeling that her family is falling apart and that it's her fault. She doesn't know what to do about it and has contemplated suicide in the past, although these thoughts have subsided since being prescribed the medication by the psychiatrist.

Which workers might be best to help Grace?

Activity

Which organisations are currently working in your area?

What services do they offer mentally ill people?

Working with problematic substance abuse

This section is designed to help you to understand the legal and societal issues relating to problematic substance use, and to understand the role of the Social Care worker in helping individuals to manage and control it. We will look at the use of a wide range of legal and illegal substances, in all social groupings.

It will introduce you to the following:

- the influence of the worker's personal values on responses to problematic substance use
- the effect of stereotyping and labelling on individuals affected by problematic substance use
- individual and societal factors, for example the effect and significance of factors such as child abuse, domestic violence, deprivation, dysfunctional family life, neighbourhood youth culture, trauma and mental health issues upon the development of patterns of problematic substance use, contributing to problematic substance use.

Activity

What are your own attitudes to substance use?

Do you drink alcohol?

How much? Are you aware of the unit system of measuring alcohol intake?

Make a diary of your own weekly intake of alcohol. Or if you don't use it yourself ask someone who does to help you with this activity.

Perhaps a measure of the sensitivity of this topic can be seen in the suspicion that this request will generate!

Consider this

Do you smoke tobacco?

Have you attempted to give it up?

Have you ever used prescription medication to deal with emotional difficulties?

What advice have you had from your doctor about how long this should continue?

Treatment strategies

There are different treatment strategies to assist those individuals experiencing problematic drug use, whether these are legal substances or prescription medications or illegal substances. The so-called 'Medical Model' is still used in some areas of the NHS.

There are also interventions such as self-help groups like Alcoholics Anonymous and Narcotics Anonymous. Interventions that are outgrowths of this include the so-called 'Minnesota Model' which relies on a highly structured residential treatment regime.

Then there are interventions based on the cognitive behavioural model which suggests that if an individual can change and take control of how he or she thinks this will allow the individual to regain the control that they think and feel that they have lost to the substance.

There are a number of interventions that grow out of this approach. For example:

- **motivational interviewing** which is a client-centred, directive method for enhancing intrinsic motivation to change by exploring and resolving ambivalence
- **cue exposure** where the individual identifies 'triggers' to substance use and then learns new responses to these stimuli
- **harm reduction strategies**.

There are other strategies. This list is not exhaustive.

Legislation

There are also different legislative strategies to combat problematic substance abuse. Key legislation includes:

- The Misuse of Drugs Act 1971
- Health and Medicines Act 1988
- Social Work (Scotland) Act 1968
- Children (Scotland) Act 1995
- Criminal Justice Act 2003.

Other agencies

Helping agencies

Examples of helping agencies are:

- drug action teams
- family and carer support groups
- counselling agencies.

Activity

Which agencies operate in your area?
What services do they offer?

Case study

Frances

Frances is a 45-year-old woman who lives alone. She has a sister who lives quite far away and whom she rarely sees or speaks to. She works as a staff nurse in a nursing home where she is well thought of as a caring person.

Frances has been taking the same dose of tranquillisers for the past sixteen years, ever since her mother died of a heart attack. Her GP, who prescribed them on a repeat prescription, recently retired and her new doctor feels that she should be considering stopping the tranquillisers and looking at ways of living without the medication.

This has caused Frances great anxiety and she is very angry that her doctor is picking on her (as she sees it) like this. Her doctor has refused to prescribe any medication unless she attends for counselling.

1. Which of the approaches mentioned above might be useful in working productively with Frances?

2. What legislation might apply?

3. Which of the helping agencies might be best placed to help Frances?

Case study

Tom

Tom is a 33-year-old man who has been required to attend for counselling as a result of an agreement that his lawyer made with the court.

He has been charged with shoplifting and has admitted to having a drug problem, as a possible way out of a custodial sentence. He is currently living with his girlfriend of five years and her two children from previous relationships.

Tom mainly uses heroin, but smokes cannabis every day and will take other drugs if they are available. He especially likes ecstasy at the weekend.

Tom has tried to get onto a methadone programme in the past but was assessed as unsuitable, which leads him to continually complain about how useless the drug services are in this area.

1. Which approach might be best when working with Tom?

2. What legislation might apply?

3. Which of the helping agencies might be best placed to help Tom?

Activity

Using the classification system laid down in the current drug legislation, identify which class of drugs Frances and Tom in the case studies above are reported to be using. Describe any penalties that may be applied for using these substances.

Information agencies

These information agencies and various Scottish and UK government agencies monitor and provide information about the impact of substance use on our society.

Scottish Drugs Forum

Drugscope
Centre of expertise for England and Wales.

Lifeline
Online catalogue of Lifeline publications.

Know the Score
A network of drug-related organisations that provides information and advice on drug issues.

Release

Provides a range of specialist services to drugs users, family friends and professionals concerning drugs and the law.

Daily Dose

website featuring links to key news stories and research on drug and alcohol from around the world.

Activity

Try to find out more about the impact that problematic substance use has on the way that society functions.

For example, what impact does it have on:

- family life
- policing costs
- mental and physical health in our communities?

What links have been made between drug and alcohol use and working life?

Youth and community justice

'More than one in four of all teenagers in the UK have committed a criminal offence in the last 12 months according to a draft official report on youth justice seen by *The Guardian*.'
(*Issues* 37 page 13)

Why do young people offend?

If you work with young people who have offended or who are at risk of offending it is useful to read 'The Report of the Advisory Group on Youth Crime (Scottish Executive publication 2000), before you even start work on this unit, in order to gain a greater insight into why some young people offend. Later in this chapter you may identify issues that arise for families. These same issues may be factors that contribute to reasons why this deviant behaviour occurs. (Deviance is more fully discussed in both the chapters on Sociology for Care Practice and Psychology for Care Practice.)

Key term

Deviance – behaviour that is outside the norms of what is acceptable behaviour within society.

However, the following activity may help you to become more aware that one individual's perception of '**deviance**' can be totally different from that of another.

Activity

Identify three behaviours that you have done which could be viewed as being deviant. An example might be talking loudly in a library.

Do you consider that these behaviours break the law?

Is there any behaviour that you undertake that you know is illegal? (For example, getting someone to do a 'job on the side' and not declaring it for tax purposes.)

If you cannot think of any illegal behaviour, consider the following.

- Where do you place driving at 33 miles an hour in a built-up area with a speed limit of 30 mph?
- Do you use your work phone for personal use?
- Have you ever taken a pen from work home?
- Did you drink alcohol in a pub before you were eighteen?

A personal note

I sat in a class in a school one day and was asked if I had ever 'battered' someone. I replied no but that I 'might' have slapped one of my sisters when I was about 10 years old. The student replied that she didn't mean just to slap, she meant 'pummel' another person. The body language which she displayed meant that I didn't need to look up the word 'pummel' in a dictionary. Have I ever done this to anyone? No – not even to my sisters when I was a child. However, this pupil thought it was OK to get into a real fight with someone and 'pummel' them; she also thought it was acceptable to discuss this with me. I have heard comments from individuals in other situations that weddings are great as 'there is always a big fight and punch up during the day'.

The point of this personal note is that workers need to be aware that what is acceptable from one person's viewpoint may not be acceptable from another's. Sometimes what an individual thinks is acceptable behaviour is actually illegal. 'Pummelling or battering' someone should never be acceptable and in most cases is illegal and a chargeable offence.

Deviant behaviour

Sometimes we have to work with individuals who have never been socialised into treating someone with respect and dignity and have been socialised into a very different way of behaving. This way of behaving has not only been reinforced by their primary socialisation but also through the process of secondary socialisation. For some young people there could be a 'kudos' of following in the footsteps of a significant other. This significant other may have impressed on the young person that deviant behaviour is acceptable and rewarding.

Look through your notes on significant others (from the unit 'Psychology for Care Practice') to understand how this occurs. If you are undertaking this unit as a 'stand alone', it would be worth visiting your local library or doing some research on the Internet for information. Then you may be able to understand how you could use this theory to change behaviour. You might already know that behaviourists believe that we are all born 'blank slates' and that any behaviour which we learn can be unlearned. As care workers we need to learn strategies to help young people to grow and develop and learn to behave in ways that are acceptable to society; and, of course, also to become aware of what is unacceptable behaviour.

The biggest problem with identifying what is deviant behaviour is, as previously stated, that not everyone's perception of what is deviant behaviour is the same. However there are norms laid down by society and a legal system that people require to live by and be accountable for their behaviour. So what happens when young people are continually involved in antisocial behaviour?

Children's Hearing System

Before 1970 all children and young people who had offended were dealt with by Juvenile Courts. This changed dramatically in 1971 when the **Children's Hearing System (Children's Panel)** came into operation. This system came about as a result of the Kilbrandon Committee Report, published in 1964, and was established by the Social Work Scotland Act 1968. The Kilbrandon Report was based on work by Lord Kilbrandon who believed that, whether children had offended or been offended against, it was essential that the best interest of that young person must be paramount when making decisions about a child or young person's future; and the Hearing System was more able to ensure this than the Juvenile Courts had been. The Children's Hearing System is now regulated by the Children Scotland Act 1995 but the 'ethos' remains the same, particularly where the child has committed an offence. The Children's Hearing System is to prevent young people from being exposed to the criminal justice system in the hope that they will be given a chance to reform before their behaviour has more serious consequences.

> ## Key term
>
> **Children's Hearing (Children's Panel)** a meeting specially set up for young people or children who are experiencing problems. It is Scotland's Juvenile Justice and Welfare System.

The Children's Panel consists of a group of specially selected and trained volunteers. They need no formal qualifications as the training they undergo is intensive. The panel members come from a wide range of different backgrounds. They are appointed by the Scottish Executive Ministers on the recommendations of the Children's Panel Advisory Committee.

In Scotland children under the age of 16 who may need care and protection, or who have committed an offence, can be referred to the Children's Panel on the following grounds:

- beyond control of any relevant person
- falling into bad association

- failing to attend school
- having committed an offence
- being exposed to moral danger
- suffering through lack of parental care
- being a victim of physical or sexual abuse.

The first four of the above grounds are relevant to the young people being discussed in this chapter. However it is extremely likely that some of these young people have already attended a Children's Hearing on the last two grounds. Remember there are many contributing factors in relation to deviance.

Youth Courts system

Both the Children's Hearing system and the 'Youth Courts system' should always have the needs of the person who uses services as paramount. From the beginning, the Children's Hearing system has acknowledged that every child has a right to a fair hearing – whether they had been offended against or had offended. The Hearing always regards the child's needs as paramount, in line with the Children (Scotland) Act 1995, and this also adheres to the European Convention (of which we are members) on Human Rights Article 6 (Thomson (2004), page 290).

In Scotland, children under the age of 16 or those who are already in the 'Care System' aged between 16 and 18 years, who are charged with less serious offences, may appear before a Children's Panel.

'Children will only appear in the Sheriff Court and the High Court of Justiciary if they are accused of murder, assault which endangers life or driving offences that are punishable by disqualification.'
(Crossan and Wylie, (2004), page 61)

In 2004 the Antisocial Behaviour (Scotland) Act 2004 was introduced. It is fair to say that not everyone welcomed this Act. Some saw it as undermining the Children's Hearing System with decisions for some children being made by courts and not the Children's Panel.

> **Key term**
> **ASBO** a civil order against behaviour that causes 'alarm, harassment or distress'. It can be used for anyone aged 12 or above.

An Antisocial Behaviour Order or **ASBO** is an order issued by court prohibiting a person from committing specific antisocial acts, or from entering a certain area. An ASBO is effective for a minimum of two years and if it is broken it results in a criminal offence. The local council will normally apply to the court for an ASBO and these orders are used to try and control all kinds of antisocial behaviour.

The Scottish Executive's Youth Justice Agenda had already established in June 2003 a pilot Youth Court within one Sheriff Court. This had followed on from fast-track Children's Hearings being introduced in February 2003 for persistent young offenders in three pilot schemes within Scotland. The rationale within fast-track hearings was to see the child as a young person first and as an offender second, maintaining the principles of the Children's Hearing System and the Kilbrandon Report. The following year a second pilot Youth Court was established in another Sheriff Court.

> **Key term**
> **Youth Court Objectives** reducing the frequency and seriousness of offending by 16 and 17-year-olds, and in some cases 15-year-olds, through targeted and prompt disposals with judicial supervision and continuing social work involvement.

When they were both established, many of the procedures, agencies and personnel were similar in the two pilot courts. So, in the operation of the Youth Court, there were not surprisingly some similarities. However what has emerged is that there are clear differences in the types of young people who are prosecuted in each Youth Court and correspondingly the types of disposal imposed. One court deals with less persistent offenders than the other and there are concerns that it may have been more appropriate for some young people who were first offenders to have been dealt with by the Children's Hearing System. Perhaps you are already working with one of these young people or it may be that you are in an area where Youth Courts have not been established.

Irrespective of whether a young person attends a Children's Hearing, or is involved in the 'Youth Courts system', both these systems should always have the needs of the young person as paramount.

> **Key term**
>
> **Restorative Justice** Restorative Justice supports victims, offenders and communities in seeking to repair the harm caused by crime, with mediation a favoured approach (Donnellan (2004), page 37).

Restorative justice

Restorative justice is a process whereby victims, offenders and communities are collectively involved in resolving how to deal with the effect of an offence and its implications for the future. It is seen as a valuable means of addressing offending by young people – enabling them to understand and making them aware of the harm they have caused by their offending. Restorative justice is a response to offending that respects the dignity and equality of each person involved. It is primarily designed to deal with an individual offence, although there is evidence to suggest that it can have an effect on reducing re-offending. It usually involves a meeting or conference, where the offender sits down with the victim, family members and also perhaps people from the community or related in some way to the crime. The purpose of the meeting is to discuss the offending behaviour and come up with ways for the young person to repay the victim or community for their crime. This repayment could be an apology in the form of a letter or some kind of voluntary work.

Restorative justice is expected to form an integral part of work with young people who have offended. So it is extremely likely that if you work with young people within the Justice System you will become involved with restorative work.

Supporting children and families

This section of the chapter is to help you as a care worker to understand developmental and societal issues that are relevant to parenting and child development. In doing this you will be able to help families to meet the developmental needs of their children. It is therefore intended for students who are working (or who intend to work) in family support work in their role as social work assistant or home carer and those working with children and young people in the community or residential setting.

In this section of the chapter you will draw information from the following units within the HNC Social Care and the designated chapters within this book. These units are Sociology for Care Practice, Psychology for Care Practice, Social Policy, and Social Care Theory for Practice as well as Topic 1 on protecting individuals from possible abuse and harm.

In this section we will look at:

- the meaning of family
- types of families in Scotland today
- parenting styles
- issues that may arise for children and families
- support for families.

> **Key facts**
> - 1 in 5 people in Scotland are under 16
> - 6 babies are born in Scotland every hour
> - Families with children make up 54 per cent of all those living in poverty
> - (Figures from www.nch.org.uk)

Family

To gain an understanding of what we mean by family complete the following activity.

Do either of the definitions given below bear a resemblance to your own?

Do you see any significant differences between the two definitions?

Types of families

To get an idea of a profile of a person who uses services we should look at the types of families in which children and young people live in Scotland today. They may include the following.

Extended family – this is a large family group which includes grandparents, parents, brothers, sisters, aunts, uncles and cousins all living in very close proximity to each other.

Nuclear family – this type of family usually consists of parents and their children living independently from any extended family members. The parents may or may not be married to each other.

One-parent family – in this type of family the child or children are brought up by one parent who is usually the mother but may sometimes be the father.

Reconstituted family – a family, in which there is a child or children from one partner, but not both, living together in the one home. This type of family is often referred to as a **step family**.

Same sex families – when a same sex couple live together with children they have adopted, or with children that they may have had from a heterosexual relationship in the past**.**

Nuclear family.

Also, some children may live in a **foster family** while others may be **looked-after** children and accommodated by the local authority in a children's unit or residential school.

Parenting styles

The type of family in which a child lives may have a bearing on their own parental ability and style of parenting.

We could consider here the role/functions of a parent. Perhaps we could identify that it is the parent's duty to ensure that the child is well fed, is warm and has a roof over their head. They also have to ensure that the child attends school and that their health needs are addressed. Parents have a responsibility to teach their children the skills that they require for independence in later life. Sociologists state that our values, norms and moral code are passed on through our parents and/or significant other, so once again we look towards parents to teach their children what is right and wrong, the customs and manners and the code of conduct expected by a child or young person in Scotland today.

Developmental psychologists have, since the early 1920s at least, been interested in how parents influence the development of their children. Through research Baumrind (1968, 1991) identified three styles of parenting.

Further research

Use the Internet to find a quiz such as 'what type of parent am I?'. (Handy hint: use a search engine of your choice, type in parenting styles, then quiz and what type of parent am I?)
Review your style with the information below!

Authoritarian

An authoritarian style is displayed by parents who always try to be in control and exert that control on their children; they set strict rules in an effort to keep order but do so with little expression of warmth or affection. In effect they tell children and young people what to do – with no room for discussion or for the child to make choices. They are very strict with their children and tend to be very critical of the child who does not obey or meet the required standard. Authoritarian parents do not explain why they want the child to do something – it is expected that they will do it because they were told to.

Research indicated that children from strictly authoritarian households do not learn to think for themselves. They tend to do reasonably well in school and are less likely to be involved in criminal behaviour, but they have poor social skills, low self-esteem and high levels of depression.

Permissive

The permissive parent exercises minimal control and tolerates far more immature behaviour than any of the other styles. Children are allowed to set their own schedules and activities, e.g. what time they go to bed, what clothes they wear and so on – even when the child is not perhaps ready to take this kind of control. They are generally speaking more responsive than they are demanding; they give up most control to the child and they do not wish to be tied down to routine.

Children who have permissive parents are more likely in later years to be lacking in self-assertiveness, may be non-achievement-orientated and may have difficulty forming and sustaining lasting friendships.

Authoritative

Often referred to as democratic, authoritative parents are said to help children learn for themselves and to think about the consequences of their behaviour. They tend to operate on the belief that both the child and the parent have rights and needs. Parents provide clear expectations for their children and give them an explanation as to why they expect their children to behave in a certain way and they do this in a warm, nurturing style.

Parents with an authoritative style give their children choices based on their ability and will actively seek to reward good behaviour in favour of looking for negatives.

It is thought that children who experience this style of parenting will become self-reliant, content, socially responsible, self-controlled and co-operative.

Issues for children and families

Activity

Working individually, or in a group, try to think of and list as many issues as possible that may arise for children and families.

You may have come up with some or all of the following types of issues:

- poverty
- health issues of children
- health issues of parents
- employment patterns e.g. women in employment, shift work, fathers as carers, family friendly working hours/flexibility
- availability of childcare
- cost of childcare
- children's rights
- legislation
- housing issues
- parenting styles
- environmental issues
- divorce
- loss/bereavement
- income
- marital status of parents
- type of family
- community support mechanisms
- alcohol/drug use
- ethnic origin
- access to services.

Some of these issues will have their roots in sociological factors – refer to the chapter on Sociology for Social Care Practice.

Support for families

Key term

Family Support any activity or facility provided either by statutory or by community groups or individuals aimed at providing advice and support to parents to help them bring up their children. (Audit commission (1994), page 39)

Family support is about a whole society approach and not just professionals 'doing things'. It involves others working in partnership with parents and children, providing the correct support and advice necessary to meet the needs of the individual family. It is hoped that the correct type of support, delivered at the right time, will help to alleviate the stress caused by the issues facing many families today (see above). The right support will also boost self-confidence and self-esteem, enabling the parents to increase their capacity to nurture and protect their children in a warm, supportive environment.

Activity

Take a few moments to note down the type of support available to families and /or that which you think should be available. Perhaps you could begin this exercise by noting down the support that you might have in parenting, e.g. other family support such as husband/partner, parents or sibling support, after-school care etc.

As you saw from earlier in this section there are many different types of families just as there are many different issues that can affect families. Obviously there should be varying types and degrees of support available for different families and this should come from the statutory as well as the private and voluntary sector. Individuals should have a choice in the support they need and all support agencies and individuals should give credence to the National Care Standards.

Historically there has been reluctance on behalf of communities to intervene in the privacy of family life, or to tell parents how to bring up their children. It was not until the setting up of the welfare state in 1948 that health and education became universal services for children and their families. (In order to get an idea of what life was like for children and families before 1948, you could visit the 'Annie McLeod experience' in Lanark.)

From the late 1990s there has been a more concerted effort by the government to respond to a change of position – from children being the sole responsibility of their parents to one where the state and our society have an interest in securing the future stability of society. Large sums of money have therefore been invested in improving the quality of provision for education and health of our children, for example establishing pre-school care for every child aged three years of age. (Refer to the document 'Every Child Matters', 2003.) The introduction of the Children Scotland Act 1995 saw, for the first time, the shift in understanding that children have rights. These rights are not 'handed out' by their parents but their own rights as a child, including the right to live a life free from harm and abuse (refer to Topic 1 on protection of individuals from harm and abuse).

Types of support

Some of the different types of support available to children and families include:

- advocacy services
- Barnardo's projects (look at Barnardo's website for a full list and explanation)
- support at home service available through the local social work department
- before and after school care/clubs
- childcare information services
- community alternative
- befriending projects
- friendship and support services to a child or young person with a disability
- joint education and social work initiatives (check your local authority website for further information)
- sitter services
- occupational therapy services
- shared care and shared care plus
- short breaks for children and young people with disabilities
- 'Who cares?' Scotland
- supporting people; promoting independence
- services for young offenders (see previous section in this chapter)
- substances misuse general services (refer to substance misuse section of this chapter).

Check Your Progress

1. What legislation informs your practice in the following situations?
   - In working with People who have a Learning Disability
   - People with Autism
   - People with Dementia
   - Mental Health Issues
   - People involved in problematic substance abuse
   - Youth and community Justice
   - Supporting Children and Families
2. What is Learned Helplessness?
3. What is the Autistic Spectrum and triad of impairment?
4. Can you identify the range of dementias?
5. What is a Mental Health Issue?
6. What is the Medical Model of care?
7. What is the Social Model of care?
8. What do you understand by stereotyping and labelling?
9. Can you identify social issues associated with problematic substance abuse?
10. What do you understand by the term deviance?
11. What is restorative justice?
12. Can you name different types of families in Britain today?
13. Do you now know different parenting styles and their possible effects on children?
14. What supports are available to children and families in your area?
15. What is the Children's Hearing System?
16. Have you read the government publications identified in this chapter?

References and bibliography

Learning disability

Braye, S. and Preston-Shoot, M. (2000) *Empowering Practice in Social Care,* Open University: Buckingham.

Coulshed, V. and Orme, J. (1998) *Social Work Practice: an Introduction.* 3rd edition. Palgrave: London.

Gates, B., Edwards, H. M. (2007) *Learning Disabilities: Towards Inclusion.* 5th edition. Churchill Livingstone Elsevier: Oxford.

Maclean, I. and Maclean, S. (2006) *A Handbook of Theory for Social Care Volume One,* Maclean Kirwin Associates: Staffordshire.

Miller, J. (2005) *Care Practice for S/NVQ3,* Hodder Education: London.

Mooney, G., Sweeney, T. and Law, A. (eds.) (2006) *Social Care, Health and Welfare in Contemporary Scotland,* Kynoch and Blaney: Paisley.

O'Brien, J. and Lyle O'Brien, C. (2007) *A Little Book about Person-centred Planning,* Inclusion Press: Toronto Ontario.

Parker, J. and Bradley, G. (2005) *Social Work Practice Assessment, Planning, Intervention and Review,* Learning Matters: Exeter.

Scottish Executive (2000) *The Same as You? A review of services for people with learning disability,* Scottish Executive: Edinburgh.

Seligman, M. E. P. (1975) *Helplessness: on depression, development and death,* W. H. Freeman: New York.

Autism

Wing, L. (1996) *The Autistic Spectrum,* Constable: London.

Dementia

Judd, S., Marshall, M. and Phippen, P. (1998) *Design for Dementia*, Hawker Publications Limited: London.

Marshall, M. and Tibbs, M. (2006) *Social Work and People with Dementia: Partnerships Practice and Persistence*, The Policy Press: Bristol.

NHS (2008) *Coping with Dementia: A Practical Handbook for Carers*, Health Scotland: Edinburgh.

Smith, T. (2004) *Living with Alzheimer's Disease*, Sheldon Press: London.

Mental health issues

Friedli, L. (2004) 'Title of article,' *Editorial Journal of Mental Health Promotion*, Vol. 3, No. 1, pp. 2–6.

Goldberg and Huxley (1992) *Common Mental Disorders*, Library of Congress.

'Mental health improvement: evidence-based messages to promote mental wellbeing,' (2007) paper presented to Scottish Government.

Youth and community justice

Citizenship Foundation (2007) *Young Citizens Passport Scotland*. 2nd edition. Hodder Gibson: Paisley.

Crossan, S. J. and Wylie, A. B. (2004) *Introductory Scots Law: Theory and Practice*, Hodder Gibson: Paisley.

Donnellan, C. (ed.) (2004) *Issues 83: Dealing with Crime*, Independence Educational Publishers: Cambridge.

Firth, L. (ed.) (2007) *Issues 137: Crime and Anti-Social Behaviour*, Independence Educational Publishers: Cambridge. (Note: now out of print and replace by Volume 137.)

Maclean, I., Maclean, S., and Shiner, M. (2006) *Social Care and the Law in Scotland*. 6th edition. Kirwin Maclean Associates: Rugeley, Staffordshire.

Mair, J. (2009-2010) *Avizandum Statutes on Scots Family Law*. 7th edition. Avizandum Publishing Ltd: Edinburgh.

Manson-Smith, D. (2008) *The Legal System of Scotland*. 4th edition. The Stationery Office: Edinburgh.

Murdoch, G. P. (1949) *Social Structure*, Macmillan: New York.

Storey, T., Turner, C. (2005) *Unlocking EU Law*, Hodder Arnold: London.

Thomson, J. (2004) *Family Law in Scotland*. 4th edition. Lexus Nexis-UK: Edinburgh.

'Youth Justice and the Children's Hearing System,' *ADSW Criminal Justice Conference*, Alan D. Miller Principle Reporter SCRA.

Useful websites

www.scotland.gov.uk/publications Evaluation of Airdrie and Hamilton Youth Court Pilots

https://login.westlaw.co.uk/app/document?&src=rl&srguid=ia

Edinburgh Law Review 2005 The Antisocial Behaviour (Scotland) Act 2004 Alison Clelland

www.northlan.gov.uk/caring+for+you/children+and+families/children+panels+Young Offenders Children's Hearings

www.scotland.gov.uk/youth/crimereview/docs (Scottish Executive Report of Advisory Group on Youth Crime)

www.nch.org.uk NCH Action for Children

www.scotland.gov.uk/News /Releases2009/03 Restorative Justice

www.scotland.gov.uk/publications 2005/07 Restorative Justice Services in the Children's Hearings System

www.scotland.gov.uk/publications 2008/06 Preventing Offending by Young People: A framework for action

Legislation Grid

Relevant legislation and organisational policy and procedures

Introduction

Laws, in their simplest form, can be defined as society's behavioural rules on how people can live orderly, safe and peaceful lives. The process of making these formal rules is usually through primary legislation – the passing of laws by Act of Parliament. These Acts, or Statutes, come into force when a majority of Members of both Houses of Parliament vote them in.

The original idea for a law can come from one of several sources. These sources include the government, advisory agencies (such as the Commissions for Equal Opportunities or Human Rights), pressure groups and charities supporting a particular cause or interest (like Age Concern) or individual Members of Parliament (MPs) who promote certain issues (such as the quality of care in nursing homes or whether young people should be prosecuted for carrying knives).

Ideas for new laws are first aired in an open-ended discussion document known as a Green Paper. If it is decided to take them further, the discussion produces a set of proposals which is published in a White Paper, as a Bill. The Bill is discussed, voted on, amended and consolidated during three separate debates in Parliament, and then passed to the House of Lords for final approval. When everyone agrees that it says what is needed, it goes to the Queen for Royal Assent. At this stage it passes from a Bill to an Act, and becomes law.

Within Europe the European Union adopts legislation in the form of Directives and Regulations. These Directives and Regulations must then be adopted by European member states within their own domestic legislation.

In Scotland health (and Social Care) is the responsibility of the Scottish Parliament so legislation and policy differ from England, Northern Ireland and Wales. These variations are shown in blue below.

Legislation, policy or procedure	Website	Relevant content	EU directive implemented by the Act
Data Protection Act (1998) Access to Medical Records 1988	www.dh.gov.uk	The protection of the individual personal data with regard to processing and safe storage: • storing confidential information • protection of paper-based information • protection of information stored on computer • accurate and appropriate record keeping.	95/46/EC
Freedom of Information Act (2000) Freedom of Information (Scotland) Act 2002	www.dh.gov.uk	Introduced to promote a culture of openness within public bodies. Allows anyone the right of access to a wide range of information held by a public authority. Access to information is subject to certain limited exemptions, such as information about an individual. It is under this Act that individuals can access their health records. In Scotland this Act established the Office of Scottish Information Commissioner who is responsible for ensuring public authorities maximise access to information.	95/46/EC
Health and Safety at Work Act (1974)	www.hse.gov.uk	• Ensuring the environment is safe and free from hazards. • Assessing risks before carrying out tasks. • Checking equipment for faults before use. • Use of appropriate personal protective clothing. • Handling hazardous/contaminated waste correctly. • Disposal of sharp implements appropriately. • Shared responsibilities – employers and employees.	89/391/EEC
Manual Handling Regulations (1992)	www.hse.gov.uk	• Preparing the environment before moving or handling anything. • Checking equipment is safe before use. • Safe moving and handling of patients. • Safe moving of equipment/loads.	90/269/EEC
Control of Substances Hazardous to Health (2002) (COSHH)	www.hse.gov.uk	• Storing cleansing materials correctly. • Labelling of hazardous substances correctly. • Appropriate handling of bodily fluids such as blood and urine. • Appropriate handling of flammable liquids/gases. • Appropriate handling of toxic/corrosive substances/liquids.	67/548/EEC
Reporting of Injuries, Diseases and Dangerous Occurrences Regulations (1995) RIDDOR	www.hse.gov.uk	• Reporting accidents and injuries objectively and accurately. • Reporting diseases to the appropriate bodies. • Reporting dangerous occurrences to the appropriate bodies. • Completion of relevant paperwork.	89/391/EEC

Legislation, policy or procedure	Website	Relevant content	EU directive implemented by the Act
Lifting Operations and Lifting Equipment Regulations (1998)	www.hse.gov.uk	The Lifting Operations and Lifting Equipment Regulations aim to reduce risks to people's health and safety from lifting equipment provided for use at work by ensuring it is: • strong and stable enough for the particular use and marked to indicate safe working loads • positioned and installed to minimise any risks • used safely, that is, the work is planned, organised and performed by competent people • subject to ongoing thorough examination and, where appropriate, inspection by competent people.	89/655/EEC amended 95/63/EC
Environmental Protection Act (1990, section 34) and the Environmental Protection (Duty of Care) Regulations (1991)	www.dh.gov.uk	Section 34 of the Environmental Protection Act (1990) imposes a duty of care on persons concerned with control of waste. It places a duty on anyone who in any way has a responsibility for control of waste to ensure that it is managed properly and recovered or disposed of safely.	2006/12/EC
Human Rights Act (1998)	www.dh.gov.uk	The European Convention on Human Rights was passed by the Council of Europe in 1950 in response to the Universal Declaration of Human Rights, which was drawn up by the United Nations (UN) in 1948. The Human Rights Act is the UK's response to this European law. It includes: • involvement of the individual and informed consent • individual treatment and respect • appropriate response to patient need • ensuring individuals exercise their rights and can make choices • ensuring individuals' privacy and dignity.	The European Convention on Human Rights (1950)
Mental Capacity Act (2005) Mental Health (Care and Treatment Act) Scotland 2003	www.dh.gov.uk www.bma.org. uk	Provides a legal framework for making decisions on behalf of individuals who lack the mental capacity to make decisions. This includes: • the capacity to consent to/refuse treatment • promoting the best interests/advocacy of the individual • supporting individuals appropriately in the decision-making process. Under the Act it is a criminal offence to ill treat any person who lacks capacity, with the punishment of possible imprisonment. Similar requirements to England.	English and Welsh legislation Scottish legislation

Legislation, policy or procedure	Website	Relevant content	EU directive implemented by the Act
Care Standards Act (2000) and the Protection of Vulnerable Adults (POVA) Scheme	www.dh.gov.uk	The Care Standards Act established a major regulatory framework for Social Care, to ensure high standards of care and improvement in the protection of vulnerable people by the use of the POVA scheme. This scheme provides an effective, workable measure to safeguard vulnerable adults from people who are unsuitable to work with them. From 26 July 2004, individuals should be referred to, and included on, the POVA list if they have abused, neglected or otherwise harmed vulnerable adults in their care or placed vulnerable adults in their care at risk of harm. By making statutory checks against the list (with the Criminal Records Bureau, CRB), providers of care must not offer such individuals employment in care positions.	UK legislation
Regulation of Care (Scotland) Act 2001		In Scotland the Care Commission regulates and inspects all care services in Scotland. It uses National Care Standards to ensure that patients receive the same standard of care wherever they live in Scotland. The *Codes of Practice for Social Service Workers and Employers* sets out the standards that all Social Care workers in Scotland must meet. Social service workers and those working in Social Care will be registered with the Scottish Social Services Council.	
Disability Discrimination Act (2005)	www.dh.gov.uk	It is unlawful for a provider of services to discriminate against a disabled person, in terms of employment or in the provision of services. Employers must make reasonable adjustments to the physical environment to accommodate those with disabilities, either employees or disabled users of the service.	Treaty of Amsterdam (1997)
Community Care and Health (Scotland) Act 2002		On 1 July 2002 free nursing and personal care for elderly people was introduced in Scotland. Older people who qualify receive payments of £145 per week depending on their needs.	

Glossary

Abuse – causing physical, emotional and/or psychological harm to the individual and so involving a failure to protect the individual from harm and/or neglect

Achievable – targets that are not too difficult or to far in the future, but deal with the here and now

Advocacy – a process of supporting and enabling people to express their views and concerns, access information and services, defend and promote their rights and responsibilities and explore choices

Affiliation – to be alongside someone or something – agreement or to be in close agreement

Appendix – a collection of material presented at the end of the project which includes any sources of information helpful to understanding the projects main content

ASBO – a civil order behaviour that causes 'alarm, harassment or distress'. It can be used for anyone aged 12 or above

Assessment – this is a participatory process. It involves establishing trust and understanding is to be obtained. The most effective way of achieving understanding may be to enable people to describe their own situation in their preferred language and at their own pace. Assessment should be a process of working alongside people.

Autism – comes from the Greek word autos meaning 'self', which is perhaps at the very core of the condition

Behaviour – put simply, what people do

Children's Hearing (Children's Panel) – a meeting specially set up for young people or children who are experiencing problems. It is Scotland's Juvenile Justice and Welfare System

Confidentiality – the appropriateness of sharing information when everything is taken into consideration

Consequences – the outcome of an individual interacting with a hazard, e.g. harm. The outcome can range in severity – from low to high

Culture – a recognised and shared way of doing things or belief systems common among a group or society

Dementia – is an illness of the brain that causes deterioration of cognitive and intellectual functions. It presents as a gradual decline in mental ability, memory and concentration, problem solving and thinking. It becomes more common as people age but 80 per cent of people over eighty remain mentally alert

Deviance – behaviour that is outside the norms of what is acceptable behaviour within society

Dilemma – this is where there is uncertainty or conflict between alternatives or choices

Disclosure – the sharing of information with others

Empowerment – involves the exercise of one's rights as a citizen

Ethics – moral principles or a recognition of right and wrong

Eugenics – relating to or tending towards production of fine offspring

Experiences – what people see, learn, are taught and so on

Family support – any activity or facility provided either by statutory or by community groups or individuals aimed at providing advice and support to parents to help them bring up their children

Hazard – anything or anyone that has the potential to cause harm (likelihood)

Holistic – to take an holistic approach to working with people in a way that emphasises the importance of the whole and the interdependence of its parts. Sometimes reference is given to the whole being mind, body and emotions

Institution – an establishment for care or education

Institutionalisation – becoming dependent upon the routines and narrow confines of an institution, resulting in such characteristics as apathy, lack of initiative and inability to make personal plans

Intervention – to get involved; to interfere with events or processes

Knowledge – awareness and understanding of concepts and facts

Ku Klux Klan – American organisation proposing white supremacy

Learned helplessness – in early 1956, Martin E.P. Seligman and his colleagues, while studying the relationship between fear and learning, accidentally discovered an unexpected phenomenon while doing experiments on dogs using Pavlovian theory (classical conditioning). He dubbed it "Learned helplessness"

Life chances – literally chances in life – opportunities and resources people can – or cannot – access. A complex array of factors determine, for example, how long we will live, how 'educated', 'qualified' and 'employable (etc.) we will become

Measurable – how will you know if you have achieved your goal, where is the evidence?

Methods – a way of doing something, especially systematic

Normalisation – a principle based on the notion that all individuals should have access to common life experiences regardless of disability

Objective – taking a viewpoint that is not biased, i.e. is not influenced by emotions or personal prejudices

Oppression – to keep down or make suffer – to oppress is to exert power over others negatively

Perception – how we can see, understand and make sense of the world we live in and so how we interact and behave

Person-centred planning – this is a process of continual listening and learning, based on what is important to an individual as they present and what they need/want for the future. The planning is centred on the person

Plagiarism – copying the work of another person and using it as your own

Prejudice – beliefs held about individuals or groups based on an assumption and stereotype – pre-judging someone or a situation without personal insight or knowledge

Principle – a rule of conduct or expected practice

Process – routine way of dealing with something

Realistic – targets have to be written within the capabilities and fit with what you are looking to achieve

Reasonably foreseeable risks – those risks that organisations would be expected to recognise and so be able to predict that the risk could occur within that workplace and through the working practices.

Restorative justice – restorative justice supports victims, offenders and communities in seeking the repair the harm caused by crime, with mediation a favoured approach

Risk – risks involve potentially negative outcomes due to the hazards involved. However also can include beneficial outcomes for the individual

Risk management – the process of identification, assessment and so management (via control measures) of risks

Self-esteem – feeling of pride or competence in yourself (or lack of) – how a person feels about themselves

Skills – capacity to do something – demonstrated ability to do something

SMART – Specific; Measurable; Achievable; Realistic; Timescale

Social inclusion – a term preferred by the Scottish executive to social exclusion and referring to the perceived need to have certain groups of individuals re-engage with wider society

Social justice – the distribution of advantages and disadvantages in society

Specific – quantifiable in terms of how many

Timescale – setting dates for completion of roles

Values – the worth we place upon someone or something

Youth Court Objectives – reducing the frequency and seriousness of offending by 16 and 17 years olds, and in some cases 15 year olds, through targeted and prompt disposals with judicial supervision and continuing social work involvement

INDEX

C